T0259834

Using and Understanding Java Data Objects

DAVID EZZIO

Using and Understanding Java Data Objects
Copyright ©2003 by David Ezzio

ISBN (pbk): 1-59059-043-0

Technical Reviewers: Regis Le Brettevillois, John Mitchell, Abe White

Editorial Directors: Dan Appleman, Gary Cornell, Martin Streicher, Karen Watterson, John Zukowski

Assistant Publisher: Grace Wong

Project Manager: Tracy Brown Collins

Copy Editor: Ami Knox

Production Editor: Julianna Scott Fein

Composition: Susan Glinert

Indexer: Valerie Robbins

Proofreader: Elizabeth Berry

Cover Designer: Kurt Krames

Production Manager: Kari Brooks

Manufacturing Manager: Tom Debolski

Distributed to the book trade in the United States by Springer-Verlag New York, Inc., 175 Fifth Avenue, New York, NY, 10010 and outside the United States by Springer-Verlag GmbH & Co. KG, Tiergartenstr. 17, 69112 Heidelberg, Germany.

In the United States: phone 1-800-SPRINGER, email orders@springer-ny.com, or visit http://www.springer-ny.com. Outside the United States: fax +49 6221 345229, email orders@springer.de, or visit http://www.springer.de.

For information on translations, please contact Apress directly at 2560 Ninth Street, Suite 219, Berkeley, CA 94710. Phone 510-549-5930, fax 510-549-5939, email info@apress.com, or visit http://www.apress.com.

The source code for this book is available to readers at http://www.apress.com in the Downloads section.

This book is dedicated to my wife, Theresa,
and our daughters, Pearly and Sarah.

A man is a fish who swims in the sea of a woman's love.

Contents at a Glance

Contents

About the Author

David Ezzio wrote his first application, which analyzed French elections, for a college professor in the sixties. After a detour through philosophy and other pursuits, he has worked with software teams building desktop applications, character recognition software, and Internet-related software. He has worked exclusively with Java since 1997 and is a Sun Certified Java Developer. Dave founded his consulting practice, Yankee Software, in 1988 and helped found MaineJUG in 2001. He is a member of the JDO 1.0 maintenance group.

Dave holds a bachelor's degree in mathematical logic from Yale University and a master's degree in philosophy from the University of Chicago. In his free time, Dave hikes, rides his bicycle, reads history, and sails his Laser Tippity. An occasional cook, he currently takes pride in his popovers. He lives in Maine. His e-mail address is dezzio@ysoft.com.

About the
Technical Reviewers

Regis Le Brettevillois has cofounded LIBeLIS (Paris, France), one of the JDO vendors, where he is acting as CTO. Before founding LIBeLIS, he was senior consultant for Versant, an ODBMS vendor. He has been in charge of Java/Database architecture for customers like Banque Nationale de Paris and France Telecom. Before this, he was consultant and R&D engineer for LM Informatique (Paris), OTI (Ottawa, Canada), and Andersen Informatique (Paris). Regis has been involved in various Java and Smalltalk projects in which object distribution and persistence technologies were strategic. Regis has a postgraduate diploma in computer science from the University of Nantes.

John Mitchell is the founder of Non.net—a Technological Business Risk Management™ consulting practice. Along with developing and rescuing distributed enterprise systems, John advises investors and executives on technology and high-tech companies. Over the past 15 years, John has been the CTO of ElasticMedia, HealthLogic.com, jGuru, and the MageLang Institute. He cowrote *Making Sense of Java: A Guide for Managers and the Rest of Us* and created the "Q&A" and "Tips & Tricks" columns at JavaWorld. John is writing books on distributed systems, software development, and technological risk management.

Abe White is a senior software architect at SolarMetric (http://www.solarmetric.com) and is the original author of Kodo JDO (http://www.solarmetric.com/Software/Kodo_JDO/). He became interested in JDO while working in research and development at TechTrader, where he specialized in object/relational mapping, object/XML mapping, and Java Enterprise technologies. Abe also has extensive experience with Java byte code manipulation, and is the creator of the open source Serp Bytecode Toolkit (http://serp.sourceforge.net). Abe was a founder of The Basement, a nonprofit entity based at Dartmouth College, his alma mater. The Basement creates Web-based solutions for academia. Abe is a member of the JDO Expert Group.

Acknowledgments

A LOT OF PEOPLE had a hand in making this book. I thank all the folks at Apress who pulled everything together. Particular thanks to Ami Knox, the copy editor; Tracy Brown Collins and Sofia Marchant, the tag-team project managers; John Zukowski, the Java editor and Visio wizard; and Gary Cornell, the publisher.

I thank Craig Russell, the JDO specification lead, and the other members of the JDO maintenance group for answering my questions and responding to my suggestions.

I thank my technical reviewers, Abe White, Regis Le Brettevillois, and John D. Mitchell. They labored long and hard, and their many comments made this book better than it would otherwise have been.

For an author, a book is more than a business proposition. It is a labor of love and passion. I thank all those who encouraged me in my work. In particular, I thank my children, Pearly and Sarah, who frequently gave me impromptu encouragement. Their love of books inspired me. I thank my father, James Ezzio, and his wife, Mary, for their kind words and generous deeds. Finally, I thank my wife, Theresa. Her confidence in my abilities made the book possible.

Introduction

JAVA DATA OBJECTS (JDO) specifies a transparent persistence service for Java objects. The specification describes a general framework for storing and retrieving the persistent state of Java objects. The JSR-12 expert group defined JDO using the Java Community Process. JDO includes a specification, a reference implementation, and a technology compatibility kit (TCK). All three can be downloaded from the Java Community Process Web site (http://www.jcp.org/jsr/detail/12.jsp). A number of vendors have created implementations of JDO and provide versions of their products that you can download from the Web. URLs to some of these vendors are found near the end of this introduction.

Java programmers use tools to make their projects successful. Most applications and server-side components involve moving data between objects in memory and persistent storage. JDO promises to change the way that Java programmers store and retrieve object state. JDO simplifies the application's code, increases the application's portability, and helps to separate concerns in the application's design. Compared to existing alternatives, JDO makes persistence easier to understand, easier to model, and easier to code.

Who Should Read This Book

This book is intended for Java programmers and application architects. It assumes that you know how to program in Java, and it assumes that you want to use JDO and understand how it works. This book emphasizes what you need to know to use JDO effectively.

By no means do you need to understand everything in this book to use JDO effectively. JDO encapsulates many of the details of data storage, and for that reason, it is easy to use. Paradoxically, because much of what is familiar about storing and fetching data is hidden from view, JDO can be confusing. This book attempts to give you more than enough information to understand the details of JDO and its behavior. Depending on your background, temperament, and current needs, you may find there are parts of this book that you can skim or skip.

JDO has the simplicity of a violin. It is easy to pick up, and it almost instantly produces sounds. But if your purpose is to produce music, knowledge and skill are required. The purpose of this book is to help you acquire the knowledge and skill needed to use JDO successfully.

What Is JDO?

JDO specifies a persistence service for those objects whose state outlives the lifetime of a single invocation of a Java Virtual Machine (JVM). Nearly every program saves the state of some objects and either restores this state on a subsequent invocation or shares it with another concurrently running program. The state preserved is both the state within objects and the relationships between objects.

JDO is a persistence service because it connects Java objects in memory to the long-term storage of their state. By using a service that is concerned only with persistence, applications can isolate the work of moving state between memory and a datastore to one area of code. Without a persistence service, the code to interface with the datastore is spread throughout the application. By using JDO, the application programmer can make persistence a modular component. As a result, the maintainability of the application improves. It is easier to find bugs, fix them, avoid introducing new bugs, and upgrade the capabilities of the application.

Although most applications need to persist some objects, not all objects require persistence. Many objects in a program are simply transient, which means their state is created as needed and discarded when the program stops executing, if not before. Some objects are transient but use persistent objects or the information in them. For example, an object that sums the sales figures from a collection of persistent invoices may itself be transient.

JDO Specifies a Uniform Persistence Service

JDO specifies an Application Programming Interface (API) to a library of services that the application program can use for persistence. JDO also specifies the persistent services that are provided transparently to all persistent objects. JDO ships with a reference implementation of this API that may be suitable for prototype development. Numerous vendors have created new products or adapted existing products to support the JDO specification. These products will compete against each other in terms of robustness, performance, supported datastores, support for optional JDO features, ease of configuration, flexibility, and so forth.

JDO encapsulates and simplifies the programming issues that are unique to persistent objects. It provides a service to find, update, and delete existing persistent objects and to store new persistent objects. It encapsulates the mapping of object state in memory to persistent state in the datastore. It ensures that multiple changes made to persistent objects in memory are stored in an all-or-nothing fashion in the datastore. Lastly, it allows multiple concurrently executing applications and threads to share access to the persistent state.

JDO offers a uniform set of persistence services that do not vary with the datastore used or the deployment environment chosen. JDO implementations can be built for a variety of datastore architectures, such as files, object databases, relational databases, and generalized transaction processing services. Because JDO encapsulates the datastore, it allows the application to use the same set of services regardless of the datastore selected. The uniformity of JDO allows the application to remain blissfully ignorant of the differences in query languages, data models, and access interfaces between the various datastores. When it comes to deployment architectures, application code that uses JDO may be deployed in stand-alone applications, client/server applications, servlets, and Enterprise JavaBeans (EJBs). For the most part, the same set of JDO services is available in all of these environments.

A Large Part of JDO's Persistence Service Is Transparent

When using JDO, the application programmer does not write persistence-related code in the application data classes—these are the classes that define the objects that have persistent state. Instead, the programmer creates the application data classes as if persistence were not an issue. He declares the fields that contain the object's state and writes the methods to access and modify the state of the object in memory.

JDO requires an enhancement step for all application data classes. The JDO vendor supplies a tool, called the *enhancer,* that the programmer uses to add the persistence-related code to application data classes. As a result of enhancement, JDO can manage the application data objects as persistent objects. Because enhancement usually occurs after compilation, persistence-related code is usually not visible in the source code of the application data classes.

Transparent persistence is powerful because it requires no coding by the application programmer and because it imposes few design and coding constraints. When an application uses JDO, persistence code is effectively absent in the source code of application data classes. Yet, at runtime, the data objects are alive. They can be fetched from the datastore by queries or identity. If one persistent object references another, the reference is instantiated transparently when used. When a transaction is active, the data object's persistent state is transactionally consistent with the datastore, and modifications made to it will be reflected in the datastore when the transaction is committed.

The Advantages of JDO

The programmer's toolbox contains many tools that can be used to store and retrieve an object's state. Java serialization saves an object graph and restores it across space and time. An object's state can be written to XML text streams or stored in custom file formats. Object-oriented database management systems (ODBMS) and object-to-relational (O/R) mapping software can be used to store the object's state in a database. JDBC provides a universal API to relational databases and is currently the principle way to store persistent state. Many of these alternatives offer the advantages of being widely available, widely used, and well understood. What advantages does JDO hold over them?

JDO Compared to Serialization, XML, and Custom File Formats

Serialization is simple to use, and the serialization mechanisms are largely transparent to the application's code. It is the persistence mechanism of choice in a large number of cases. Where there is one-to-one communication between peers or between a client and service, serialization is often an excellent choice for copying objects from one JVM to another. It is also a reasonable choice for an application that needs to store or read infrequently a small amount of persistent state. For example, a text editor or Web browser might serialize the configuration object for its user. Nevertheless, serialization has several deficiencies when used for general-purpose persistence. Serialization loads into memory the entire graph of objects at once, and therefore it is slow and memory consuming when the purpose is to view a small part of a large object graph. Serialization has no transactional mechanisms and therefore it does not support concurrent updates to the serialized objects. It also lacks a query mechanism. Finally, serialization must store the entire graph of objects if any object in the graph has changed.

Although XML and custom file formats have their strengths, they suffer from many of the same disadvantages as serialization and have other disadvantages of their own. Unlike serialization, XML and custom file formats require a fair amount of code to move the persistent state in and out of the object. In addition, the application becomes responsible for managing object references. If A refers to B and C refers to B, how does the shared use of B become represented in the file format? The application must make the decision and implement it.

In contrast to serialization, XML, and custom file formats, JDO provides a transactional service that permits and regulates concurrent access to the same underlying persistent state. JDO loads the object graph lazily. As the application uses the references to persistent objects, JDO loads the objects into memory. JDO stores the persistent state for only the objects that have changed within the transaction. It has a query mechanism, and it manages object references. For these reasons, JDO offers significant advantages in many cases.

JDO Compared to ODBMS and O/R Mapping

Because JDO sprang from concepts pioneered in the development of object-oriented database management systems, JDO retains similarities to object databases. However, the interface to each vendor's ODBMS is distinct from the interface offered by the next vendor. Although the Object Data Management Group (ODMG) specified a standard interface, the standard has not been widely adopted by vendors or application developers. JDO provides a single service that can access all object databases for which a JDO implementation is built.

Several object-to-relational mapping products already provide a persistence service for Java applications. Unfortunately, each of these products uses a product-specific interface to access the functionality of the persistence service. JDO offers the hope that all O/R mapping vendors will come to support a common interface.

JDO Compared to EJBs with CMP

In EJB containers, container-managed persistence (CMP) maps entity EJBs to their persistent state. JDO may displace, but it does not replace, CMP. For application developers who are looking for more flexibility than the current CMP provides, JDO offers a simpler way to write EJBs that use bean-managed persistence. For vendors who are looking for a more flexible way to implement CMP in their EJB containers, JDO offers a way to plug in a variety of datastore architectures to their CMP mechanisms.

JDO Compared to JDBC

Relational database management systems are the workhorses of data storage, and JDBC is the primary interface Java programs use to access them. Although successful, JDBC requires a fair amount of glue code to manage persistence. Sometimes application programmers write an entire persistence service, but more often, the glue code is written on a class-by-class basis.

Application programmers will find that JDO offers several advantages over JDBC. To begin with, storing and retrieving object state requires much less code. JDO encapsulates entirely the object construction and deconstruction steps found everywhere in the code that uses JDBC. Because the application programmer no longer writes the code to move persistent state in and out of objects, less code is written. Because JDO transparently provides lazy loading, change tracking, and storage of modified state, the application data classes remain largely ignorant of persistence mechanisms. As a result, these classes are not complicated by a need to explicitly interact with a persistence service.

As another advantage, JDO reduces the amount of skill needed to map an object model to a relational model. Depending on the tools provided by the JDO implementation, the object model of the persistent objects and the relational model can come together in one of three ways. Either the object model can be constructed with the tools deriving the relational model, or the relational model can be constructed with the tools deriving the object model. In some cases, the tools allow programmers to work iteratively from both models to a meeting in the middle. In the typical development effort using JDO, either the relational model or the object model is the driving consideration, and the other is derived by tools.

JDO offers one more significant advantage over JDBC. Only the object model needs to be considered when constructing queries. For the application programmer using JDO, there is no relational model. Likewise, during query coding, column and table names in the database are not used. To determine whether a query can be constructed for some set of objects, it is only necessary to examine whether the objects, fields, and relationships needed are present in the object model. If so, then the query can be constructed from this information. As a result, the application programmer does not need to understand SQL. The JDO implementations for relational databases map JDO queries to SQL transparently.

Some will question whether it is truly an advantage to remove the application programmer from the construction of SQL. It is commonplace to tune some SQL statements in an application in order to achieve higher performance. In addition, stored procedures are often used for the same purpose. By removing SQL from the application programmer's domain, doesn't JDO take a step backwards in terms of performance? The answer has two parts. First, it is quite reasonable for a JDO implementation to provide these features, even though they are not specified by JDO. Current JDO implementations are already addressing these features, and it can be expected that future versions will concentrate more and more on enhancing performance. Second, application programmers are by nature jacks-of-all-trades. They do what needs to be done to get the application running. Often they are not expert SQL coders. This lack of expertise is part of the reason why the SQL statements in applications need to be tuned in the first place. It is quite possible that the typical application would benefit from using persistence software whose specific concern is to make efficient use of the relational database.

Compared to JDBC, JDO provides the application programmer with a high-level persistence service. JDO encapsulates all the details of how persistence is accomplished. The application programmer must decide only a small number of high-level issues. He must decide what classes of objects and which particular objects of those classes need to be persisted. Within those classes, he must decide which fields need to be persistent. Finally, he must decide where to draw the transactional boundaries. These are high-level issues of persistence that JDO does not encapsulate. By exposing the irreducible issues of persistence and encapsulating everything else, JDO gives the application programmer a powerful conceptual and executable framework that allows him to build more robust applications in a shorter period of time.

JDO Has the Potential to Become Ubiquitous

Because of the advantages that JDO offers in encapsulation, uniformity, transparency, and portability, the creators of this standard hope that it will become ubiquitous, in the same way that JavaServer Pages, Java servlets, Enterprise JavaBeans, and JDBC have become ubiquitous for the Java platform. By using JDO instead of the existing alternatives, application developers have greater flexibility to choose the datastore appropriate for the application, more choice among competing implementations, greater flexibility to choose the deployment environment, greater power to build a robust design, and speedier development. If, as the creators hope, JDO becomes ubiquitous, then all application developers will become more productive and valuable as they acquire the skills to use another powerful tool in the Java toolbox.

A Short History of JDO

Much of the world's transactional data resides in relational databases. Relational databases model the world using tables of rows and columns. The SQL language is used to manipulate and interrogate the relational model. On the other hand, object-oriented programming languages like Java model the world with graphs of objects. The objects are manipulated in memory by modifying the values of member variables.

Java programs often use relational databases as the datastore, but difficulties and inefficiencies are common. One difficulty is that a fair amount of code must be written to move data from objects to the relational database and back. This code is often repetitious and tied to the relational model. As a result, cut-and-paste errors are introduced. Significant difficulties arise because the application programmer is faced with two models of persistent state, one in the relational model created in the database, and the other in the object model of the application. The programmer must decide whether to implement a full mapping between these two models or only a partial mapping. The first choice is a lot of work, only some of which may be used, while the second choice leads to a patchwork of model synchronization and mapping code that develops as the program design evolves. Whatever he decides, the application programmer must maintain the two models and the code to map between them. The whole business is particularly vexing because application programmers can see that there must be some general-purpose solution that would replace the code they are writing, debugging, and maintaining. Inefficiencies and errors creep in all over the map, but particularly because the typical object-oriented programmer is not proficient in SQL and relational data modeling.

Object databases were created to make it easier and more efficient to manipulate persistent data with object-oriented languages. In the early 1990s, the vendors of object-oriented database management systems were hoping to grow their market by adopting a common interface to object databases. From this desire, the Object Data Management Group was formed. In spite of three revisions of the ODMG specification, it was clear by the late 1990s that object databases were not loosening the grip of relational databases on the world's transactional data.

Although the success of object databases was a disappointment to some, engineers could still see the value of a general-purpose persistence service to handle the mapping between object models and relational databases. Consequently, during the 1990s, object-to-relational mapping tools were created. These O/R mapping tools provided a way for the application programmer to use a packaged general-purpose persistence service, rather than writing his own. Although programming teams have enjoyed good success using these tools, their use is not widespread, and their interfaces remain individual and proprietary.

By the time the Java Specification Request for JDO was adopted by the Java Community Process in June of 1999, the original vision concerning the best way to move data from a datastore to an object-oriented program had narrowed on one end and widened on the other. In terms of object-oriented languages, the vision was narrowed to Java alone. In terms of reaching the datastore, the vision was widened to include relational databases, object databases, and indeed any type of transactional datastore. The basic notion is that Java programmers should have one transactional persistence API, for which the market provides different implementations for different datastores.

As JDO evolved in the expert group, the Enterprise JavaBean specification was adopted by vendors and the development community as the primary model for building and deploying distributed objects on the Java platform. The response in the evolution of JDO was to find the ways that JDO could be used in EJB component development. EJB developers will find that they can use JDO to substitute for the use of JDBC. This substitution might occur in session beans that use JDBC, or it might occur in entity beans where the developer is using JDBC to implement bean-managed persistence.

More than two-and-a-half years after the JDO Java Service Request was submitted, the Java Community Process released JDO 1.0 in March 2002.

JDO 1.0.1

In 2003, the JDO maintenance lead released JDO 1.0.1. The 1.0.1 release offers minor improvements over the 1.0 release. It clarifies some obscurities, resolves some ambiguities and discrepancies, and offers several minor enhancements. When discussing an issue where the 1.0.1 specification differs from the 1.0 specification, this book describes the improvements offered by the 1.0.1 version. When the issue is sufficiently important, this book also draws attention to the differences between the 1.0.1 version and the 1.0 version.

Who Is Implementing JDO 1.0?

There has been worldwide interest in the JDO standard. A number of vendors are selling implementations that target relational databases. These implementations generally work with any relational database for which there is a JDBC 2.0 driver. The open source example code that accompanies this book features the products of three vendors that target relational databases. The three vendors are SolarMetric (http://www.solarmetric.com) with the Kodo implementation, LIBeLIS (http://www.libelis.com) with the Lido implementation, and Signsoft (http://www.signsoft.com) with the IntelliBO implementation. They were selected because they had early versions of JDO, they updated their versions regularly, and they had free trial versions and good support.

JDO implementations are also starting to appear on the ODBMS side. Poet (http://www.poet.com) is providing a JDO interface to its FastObjects database. Poet and other vendors are supporting the JDOCentral Web site (http://www.JDOCentral.com). This site has a lot of information on JDO and available implementations

As part of the specification process, Sun Microsystems is providing a reference implementation of JDO using a b-tree file datastore. Sun also hosts the informal expert group's Web page at http://access1.sun.com/jdo.

Open source implementations of JDO are starting to appear. ObJectRelationalBridge at Apache's Jakarta project (http://jakarta.apache.org/ojb) is an ODMG 3.0-compliant object database that is in the process of implementing a JDO interface. In addition, TriActive JDO and XORM can be found at http://sourceforge.net.

Fear, Uncertainty, and Doubt (FUD)

JDO appears to be a disruptive innovation that threatens the established turf of some software products and the dynamics of the markets in which they compete. A standard response from vendors who find their established products competing against new products with radically different value propositions is to cast the upstart in an unfavorable light. Any confusion (or FUD) delays the customer migration to the new alternative. To its credit, JDO has elicited FUD from some vendors of established products. In these circumstances, FUD is normal, and the best thing to do is ignore it.

A Note on the UML Diagrams Used in This Book

In this book, Universal Modeling Language (UML) class diagrams are used to introduce the various classes and interfaces of JDO that are important to the application programmer. The standard UML class diagram consists of three boxes.

Class Name
Attributes
Operations

The top box contains the class name. The middle box contains the attributes of the class. These are the static or member variables of the class. The bottom box contains the operations of the class. When an interface is diagrammed, the top box typically contains the string "<<Interface>>" to identify that the diagram's subject is an interface.

In this book, the standard UML class diagram has been modified to provide more information. Instead of three boxes, the UML class diagrams used in this book have four boxes.

extends *implements*
Class Name
Operations
Properties

The top box contains, as before, the class name. The box has been expanded to include a line for the name of the class that the diagrammed class extends (if other than Object) and a second line for the interfaces that the class implements. For the

JDO classes and interfaces presented in this book, there are no attributes of interest. For that reason, the box is present but looks more like a double line.

The third box contains, as before, the operations of the class. In this book, the only operations examined are public. An annotation is used to indicate when the operation is overloaded. When the operation is followed by the plus sign ("+"), there are more parameter signatures than the one shown. This annotation is used to keep the UML class diagrams as brief as possible.

At the bottom of the UML diagram, a fourth box is introduced where JavaBean-conforming properties are listed. JavaBean properties are methods that generally come in get/set pairs and are backed by a private attribute in the implementation. The getter method returns a reference or primitive of a particular type and the setter method uses one parameter of that return type. So, for example, the method pair

```
public int getCount()
public void setCount(int num)
```

defines the JavaBean property *Count* for the class. Boolean properties can be a little bit different, because the "get" method may be an "is" method instead. For example, the method pair

```
public boolean isFast()
public void setFast(boolean flag)
```

defines the Boolean property *Fast*.

Because JavaBean properties are well understood, it is briefer and clearer to have one entry in the UML properties box rather than two entries in the operations box. For example, four operations are required in the operations box to indicate the two properties *Count* and *Fast*:

```
getCount: int
setCount(num: int): void
isFast: boolean
setFast(flag: boolean): void
```

On the other hand, to represent the same information in the properties box requires only two entries:

```
Count: int
Fast: boolean
```

If the property name is the same as the type that the property returns, then the return type is omitted. For example, the entry "Synchronization" in the property box indicates that there are two methods in the class:

```
public Synchronization getSynchronization();
public void setSynchronization(Synchronization sync);
```

Not all JavaBean properties are read/write. Some are write-only, and some are read-only. In these cases, the corresponding getter method or setter method is not provided in the class. In this book, to indicate a read-only property, the UML property entry is followed by a minus sign, as in the following property entry: "Initialized: boolean –". A write-only property is indicated by a plus sign at the end of the property entry.

How This Book Is Organized

This book assumes that you will download the JDO distribution from the Java Community Process Web site (http://www.jcp.org/jsr/detail/12.jsp). In that distribution, you will find the JDO reference implementation, the JDO Javadoc, and the JDO specification. The JDO specification targets primarily those who write JDO implementations. In contrast, this book aims to provide application developers with the information that they need to use JDO.

This book is divided into two parts. The first part, and the bulk of the book, is intended to supplement the Javadoc by discussing the concepts and nuances of JDO from the application programmer's point of view. This part of the book is conceptual rather than hands-on. It will guide your understanding of JDO.

The second part of the book is primarily hands-on and examines the open source programs called the *JDO Learning Tools*. The JDO Learning Tools are programs that use JDO. There are two groups of programs in the JDO Learning Tools. The first group are atypical programs that explore the behavior of JDO. By using them, you can gain a deeper understanding of how JDO implementations behave.

The second group of programs in the JDO Learning Tools are simple but typical applications. They are intended to be exemplars for application architectures. Three architectures are considered in detail.

- Swing client/server applications

- Web applications that use JavaServer Pages and Java servlets

- Enterprise applications that use a JDO inside of Enterprise JavaBeans

The second part of the book discusses the application design issues and code patterns for each architecture. The discussion draws upon the concepts covered in the first part of the book.

The source code for the JDO Learning Tools is available from the publisher's Web site (http://www.apress.com) as well as from SourceForge.net (http://sourceforge.net/projects/jdo-tools). This book uses the 1.0 version of the JDO Learning Tools.

To run the tools and examples, you will need to download either the reference implementation of JDO or a trial version of a commercial implementation of JDO. Chapters 8 through 11 provide instructions for setting up your testing environment. The JDO Learning Tools provide build files for Kodo, Lido, IntelliBO, and the reference implementation. The JDO Learning Tools will evolve over time. You are encouraged to contribute improvements to make future releases of the JDO Learning Tools better for all of us.

Basic Concepts in JDO

JAVA DATA OBJECTS (JDO) defines six interfaces, one helper class, and an inheritance tree of exception classes that application programmers use. For most of these interfaces and classes, the Unified Modeling Language (UML) diagrams presented here will be quite small. Although small, JDO is conceptually interconnected. As a result, application programmers need to understand the implications of its options and operations.

JDO shifts the perspective that application programmers have of an object's persistent state and how to handle it. Application programmers are used to working with datastore interfaces like JDBC where the task is to move state between memory objects and the database. In contrast, JDO provides a persistence service that hides the datastore service. JDO also hides much of the code that activates persistence. Some basic operations of persistence are still exposed. These include beginning transactions, committing transactions, inserting new objects, and deleting preexisting objects. When using JDO, application programs are designed and coded to interact with a persistence service for objects rather than a datastore service for object state.

JDO is small, and the general idea of how it works is simple. JDO uses the toolkit pattern. For the most part, the specification defines interfaces, while the JDO implementations provide classes that implement these interfaces. Figure 1-1 shows the application's view of JDO. This figure shows five (of the six) interfaces that JDO defines for applications: PersistenceManagerFactory, PersistenceManager, Query, Transaction, and InstanceCallbacks. It also shows the PersistenceCapable interface, which is one of the interfaces that JDO defines for the implementation's use rather than the application's use.

Application programmers create *application data classes* to model the persistent state and persistent relationships of the entities in the business domain. Application data classes are ordinary Java classes that contain some amount of state and may or may not contain a good deal of behavior. *Application data objects* are instances of application data classes.

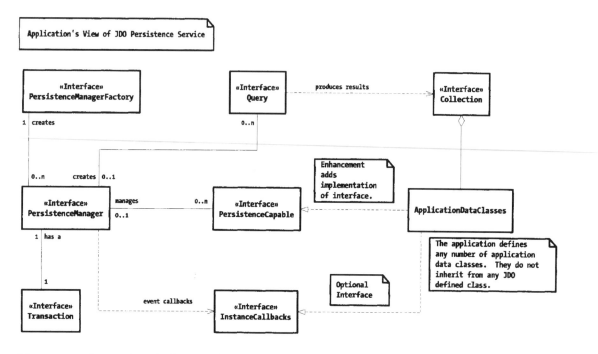

Figure 1-1. The application's view of JDO

Before application data objects can interact with JDO, they must implement the PersistenceCapable interface. The process of making an application data class implement the PersistenceCapable interface is called *enhancement*. JDO implementations provide a tool, usually called the *enhancer*, to enhance application data classes. The tool might create or modify source code files, or it might create or modify compiled class files. However it works, the enhancer has the responsibility to add the code that implements the PersistenceCapable interface. JDO manages the objects of enhanced application data classes through the PersistenceCapable interface.

Most JDO implementations opt to perform byte-code enhancement of the compiled class files. The byte-code enhancers accept as input the compiled class files created by compiling the source files for unenhanced application data classes. They produce as output modified class files whose classes, because of the modifications, implement the PersistenceCapable interface. Byte-code enhancement adds an extra step to the build process.

The enhancer does more than simply add the code that implements the PersistenceCapable interface. It also adds code that enables the objects of application data classes to use the JDO persistence service. It may even add code to classes that are not application data classes if these classes have access to the persistent fields of application data classes. Chapter 5 describes enhancement and the effects it has on application data classes and other application classes.

JDO divides the application's persistence code into two separate areas of concern. In the first area, the application controls the basic operations of persistence. To do this, the application gets a persistence manager factory and from that obtains a persistence manager. The application uses the persistence manager to perform life cycle tasks such as inserting and deleting persistent objects. From the persistence manager, the application obtains query objects to perform queries and the transaction object to control transactions. The `PersistenceManagerFactory` interface is described in Chapter 6, and the `PersistenceManager` interface is described in Chapter 3. Queries are covered in Chapter 2, and transactions are covered in Chapter 4.

In the second area of concern, the application defines application data classes. Their primary purpose is to hold persistent state and to model persistent relationships, but they may also define any behavior that is required. The application's designers and programmers can, for the most part, design and code the application data classes just as if persistence were not an issue. In particular, these classes do not derive from any JDO-defined class. The enhancer integrates the application data classes with JDO by inserting all the code required for them to implement the `PersistenceCapable` interface and to otherwise interact with the JDO persistence service.

The Persistence Services of JDO

JDO provides the full range of persistence services. Persistence services are sometimes called CRUD for Create, Retrieve, Update, and Delete. In JDO, the Create, Retrieve, and Delete services are explicit; that is to say, JDO provides methods to add, find, or delete specific objects. On the other hand, the Update service is transparent; that is to say, JDO does not offer an update method that the application calls for those objects whose persistent state has been modified. Instead, the Update service occurs implicitly as a result of committing the transaction. In fact, whenever it is reasonable to do so, JDO creates and retrieves persistent objects transparently as well.

Transactions

Transactions are not on the list of CRUD services, but they are an integral part of JDO. JDO provides transactional semantics and the explicit methods to begin and complete transactions. Applications that use JDO can modify the persistent state in the datastore only within a transaction. The modifications, including additions and deletions, are committed to the datastore only when the JDO transaction commits.

When a service supports transactional behavior, the client that uses the service can group its interactions with the service into units of work called *transactions*. The transactional service guarantees that the client, when it is ready to end a transaction, has two options. The client can ask the service to *commit* the work, and if the service is able to do this, then the results of all of the interactions are accepted and stored. On the other hand, the client can ask the service to *roll back* the work, and in this case, the service discards any modifications made within the transaction. Either way, the client gets all or nothing. Either everything is committed or nothing is committed. The service may not be able to commit, in which case, the client has no choice but to roll back. The service can always roll back, and if it doesn't receive a request to commit or roll back from the client, it will eventually roll back the transaction on its own. The all-or-nothing behavior of transactions is called *atomicity*.

Atomicity is just one of the four required properties of a transactional service. The transactional service must also guarantee that the work of a transaction, once committed, cannot be lost. This property is called *durability*. Transactional services are responsible for preventing multiple clients from interacting with each other in unpredictable ways. This property is called *isolation*. Transactional services are responsible for ensuring that the state, when stored, satisfies the defined rules for *consistency*. For example, if one of the rules is that the date of birth cannot be null, then the transactional service is responsible for refusing to commit any state that violates the rule. Taken together, these four properties of a transactional service, atomicity, consistency, isolation, and durability, are called the *ACID properties* of transactions.

In JDO, transactions are an explicit service available through the Transaction interface. JDO's transactions support the ACID properties. One Transaction object is associated with each persistence manager, and therefore each persistence manager supports one active transaction at a time. The Transaction interface provides methods to begin, commit, and roll back transactions. The Transaction interface is covered in Chapter 4.

Creating Persistent Objects

The application creates new objects of the application data classes whenever it likes by invoking the Java new operator. These newly created objects do not correspond to any state in the datastore, and for that reason they are called *JDO-transient* objects. Because JDO is not aware of the existence of JDO-transient objects, they are also called *unmanaged* objects. The application can make unmanaged application data objects *persistent* by calling the persistence manager's makePersistent method. Thereafter, the application relies on JDO to insert the state of the newly made persistent object into the datastore when the transaction commits.

Objects can also be made persistent implicitly by assigning an unmanaged object to the persistent field of a persistent object. When the transaction commits, JDO follows the reference in the persistent field to the unmanaged object and makes it persistent as well. This action is a JDO feature called *persistence by reachability*, and it serves as an example of transparent persistence.

Retrieving Persistent Objects

JDO provides several ways to retrieve persistent objects:

- The application can retrieve persistent objects individually by JDO identity.

- It can iterate all the persistent objects of an application data class using an extent.

- It can iterate a collection of objects that satisfy a query.

To retrieve persistent objects by any of these methods requires one or more explicit calls to JDO. Chapter 2 describes extents and queries.

In addition, JDO will retrieve objects transparently when the application's code uses the references to persistent objects that are contained within other persistent objects. Unlike serialization, which loads the entire graph of interconnected objects into memory at once, JDO loads the objects as the references to them are used. This feature of JDO is called *transparent navigation*.

As an example of transparent navigation, consider an application that has two application data classes, Person and Dog. As Listing 1-1 shows, the Person class has a member field that refers to a Dog object, and getter-setter methods to set and return the Dog reference.

Listing 1-1. A Person *and His or Her* Dog

```
public class Person
    {
    private Dog myDog;
    // ... other member fields omitted for brevity

    public Dog getDog()
        {
        return myDog;
        }

    public void setDog(Dog newDog)
        {
        myDog = newDog;
        }

    // ... other methods omitted for brevity
    }
```

When the application needs the reference to the dog that the person owns, it executes the following code:

```
// somehow we have a reference to a persistent person
Dog dog = person.getDog();
// ... do something with the dog
```

This example shows transparent persistence at work. Because the application data classes were enhanced, when the myDog reference is used as the return value in the getDog method shown in Listing 1-1, JDO either finds in memory or creates in memory the persistent Dog object that the person owns. The application programmer does not write code to make this happen. JDO provides this service transparently for persistent application data objects.

Updating Persistent Objects

The application does not explicitly request that JDO update information in the datastore. Instead, the application modifies the persistent object in memory either by setting a member field's value or by calling a setter method. When the persistent object's state changes, the code that the enhancer added to the application data class notifies JDO of the change. As a result, the object becomes transactional and JDO takes responsibility for ensuring that the change is flushed to the datastore when the transaction commits.

Using the example of the Person and Dog classes again, the code in Listing 1-2 starts a transaction, makes a change to a persistent Person object, and commits the transaction.

Listing 1-2. Storing Modifications Upon Transaction Commit

```
// somehow, we have a reference to the persistence manager
pm.currentTransaction().begin();
// somehow we have a reference to a persistent person
// and to a persistent, but unowned, dog
person.setDog(poundDog);
pm.currentTransaction().commit();
```

The important code in Listing 1-1 and Listing 1-2 is the code that is not there. The setDog method, like the getDog method, is not special. It simply assigns the parameter to the myDog field. As a result of transparent persistence, JDO tracks the change and knows that the Person object and its myDog field have changed. If the object wasn't transactional before the change was applied, it becomes transactional. When the transaction commits, JDO writes the change to the datastore. From the point of view of the application, the code that modifies a Person object is not entangled with the code that controls the transaction's boundaries.

Deleting Persistent Objects

When the time comes to remove a persistent object's state from the datastore, the application calls the persistence manager's deletePersistent method. After deletePersistent is called, the state of the deleted object is removed from the datastore when the transaction commits.

JDO does not provide a general mechanism to implicitly delete objects. Using the example of persons and dogs once again, it is not the case that deleting the dog's owner will cause the dog to be deleted transparently. However, some JDO implementations may provide for cascading deletes in a manner that is implementation dependent. In addition, the application can implement cascading deletes by using the InstanceCallbacks interface, as described in Chapter 7.

Although JDO provides the API to insert, delete, and find objects with persistent state, much of the simplicity and power of JDO comes from the persistence services that are provided transparently to the application. Persistence by reachability, transparent navigation, and implicit updating of the datastore upon transaction commit are three important examples of transparent persistence. Transparent persistence arises because many interactions between persistent objects and JDO are hidden from the application. The code that supports the interaction is inserted into the application data classes in the enhancement step.

Managed and Unmanaged Objects

In order to provide persistent services for the application's data objects, JDO must manage the objects. Within a Java Virtual Machine (JVM), JDO manages some objects and does not manage other objects. If JDO manages an object, it manages its persistent state, or its transactional state, or both. JDO is able to manage the objects of certain classes, while it cannot manage the objects of other classes. Those classes whose objects JDO can manage are called the *persistence-capable* classes.

The persistence-capable classes include all the application data classes. These are the classes that the application defines for the primary purpose of holding persistent state. These classes are enhanced, usually during the build process.

In addition, JDO identifies system classes from the java.* packages that implementations must in some cases, or may in other cases, support as persistence-capable classes. Every JDO implementation must or may support the following system classes:

- Arrays (optional)

- ArrayList (optional)

- BigDecimal

- BigInteger

- Boolean

- Byte

- Character

- Date

- Double

- Float

- HashMap (optional)

- HashSet

- Hashtable (optional)

- Integer

- LinkedList (optional)

- Locale

- Long

- Short

- String

- TreeMap (optional)

- TreeSet (optional)

- Vector (optional)

These classes are called the *supported system classes*.

The member fields of an application data class are divided into three groups: persistent fields, transactional fields, and unmanaged fields. The persistent fields and the transactional fields, taken together, are called the *managed fields*. JDO can manage persistent fields both persistently and transactionally, while it can manage transactional fields only transactionally. JDO ignores the unmanaged fields. The application programmer can specify in the JDO metadata, which is an XML file, whether a member field is persistent, transactional, or unmanaged. If the JDO metadata does not specify how the field is to be managed, the enhancer tool applies defaults that determine the management for the field. Chapter 5 explains the structure and default values of the JDO metadata.

When JDO manages an object persistently, it manages the synchronization of the object's persistent fields with the state stored in the datastore. The properties of the Transaction interface define when the synchronization occurs. After synchronization, the values of the object's persistent fields match the values found in the datastore. At the same time, JDO inserts new information into the datastore and deletes old information from the datastore to match the persistent objects added and deleted within the transaction.

When JDO manages an object transactionally, it manages both the persistent and transactional fields at and within transactional boundaries. Upon successful commit, the current values of the transactional fields are retained in memory, and the current values of the persistent fields are synchronized with the datastore. As determined by the *RetainValues* property in the Transaction interface, JDO may retain in memory the current values of the persistent fields after commit, or it may clear them to their Java default values. Upon rollback, the persistent state in the datastore remains unaffected by the changes made in the transaction. As determined by the *RestoreValues* property in the Transaction interface, the values of persistent fields and transactional fields may be restored to the values that the object had prior to being modified within the transaction. Chapter 4 describes the Transaction interface and its properties.

JDO may not manage a data object, or it may manage it transactionally, persistently, or both. JDO's management of the object also varies depending on whether the data object is a first class object or an embedded object.

First Class Objects and Application Data Objects

A *first class object* (FCO) is the primary kind of persistent object, and by default, all application data objects are first class objects. First class objects have many distinguishing features. A first class object has its own JDO identity. JDO identities will be described in detail in the section "The Three Types of JDO Identity" later in this chapter, but for now, it is sufficient to know that a JDO identity refers to one and only one object's state in the datastore. The datastore saves the state of a first class object independently of any other object. JDO saves in the datastore the relationships in memory between FCOs, and it re-creates the same relationships in memory when the objects are retrieved.

FCOs can be retrieved by queries and by JDO identity. FCOs usually have extents. An *extent* is an iterable grouping of all the objects in the datastore that are assignment compatible with an application data class. Chapter 4 explores the Extent interface.

FCOs track their *dirty* fields, that is to say, the managed fields that have changed within the current transaction. As a result of tracking, JDO can limit the datastore synchronization to the objects and even the field values that have changed.

The persistent fields of FCOs can be navigated within queries. Using the JDO query language, the programmer structures the query filter as a Boolean expression that tests persistent fields for particular values.

Second Class Objects and Embedded Objects

Although the concept of a second class object (SCO) is an old concept in discussions of object-oriented persistence, many Java programmers may be unfamiliar with the term. A String object is a good example of a second class object.

In the following code that briefly defines the class Dog, the weight of the dog is represented by a member field of type float, and the name of the dog is represented by a member field of type String. The objects of the Dog class are first class objects and the objects of the String class are second class objects.

```
public class Dog
    {
    private float weight;
    private String name;

    // ... constructors, getter-setter methods
    // and business methods are omitted for brevity
    }
```

In memory, the name field refers to a String object that contains the dog's name. In memory, the String object's lifetime may be independent of the Dog object's lifetime. In addition, several dogs may share the same name by sharing the same String object.

The relationship between the dog and its name is quite different in the datastore. In most datastores, the dog's persistent state contains his weight in one field and his name in another. If the dog's state is removed from the datastore, his name and weight are removed with it. If information about three dogs named "Lilly" is stored in the datastore, then the name "Lilly" appears three times in the datastore as the value of the name field of three different dogs.

The architecture of the datastore determines what classes of objects are stored as second class objects. Most datastores store the objects of the supported system classes as second class objects.

Embedded objects are nearly the same thing as second class objects, except that you are looking at them from the JDO perspective rather than the datastore perspective. JDO determines which objects are embedded independently of the datastore architecture. All of the objects of the supported system classes are embedded objects. JDO manages embedded objects as dependent objects of the application data object that refers to them. As a result, when the application data object is deleted, the persistent state corresponding to the embedded objects is deleted as well.

The JDO specification discusses the possibility of designating some application data objects as embedded within other first class application data objects. In essence, this is intended to be a way for the application to define a second class object. Although the concept is in the specification, it is not well defined by either the 1.0 or 1.0.1 specification. Any behavior documented by a particular JDO implementation may be implementation dependent.

Leaving aside the possibility of embedding an application data object, the only difference between second class objects and embedded objects comes down to the case of those datastore architectures that store the objects of some supported system classes as first class objects rather than as second class objects. For some types of object databases, this situation arises for the collection classes. In this case, the JDO implementation must take special steps to enforce the JDO requirement for the dependency of embedded objects. Likewise, if you disregard the possibility of embedding an application data object, then all application data objects are first class objects.

Embedded objects never have a JDO identity, and they cannot be fetched independently of the application data object that refers to them. Queries return first class application data objects, not embedded objects, in their results. Embedded objects are never members of a JDO extent.

An embedded object participates in a transaction only when the first class application data object that refers to it has joined the transaction. All persistence services for an embedded object are implicit and result from actions that occur on the application data object that refers to it. Embedded objects are always inserted into the datastore, deleted from the datastore, or retrieved from the datastore as a result of the corresponding action on a first class application data object. JDO treats the relationship between a first class application data object and the embedded object that it refers to as a containment relationship. When the application deletes an application data object, the embedded objects that it refers to are also deleted.

JDO offers excellent support for the supported system classes in its query language. Query filters can use the persistent fields whose types are the supported system classes. Chapter 2 describes JDO's query language.

Although it is possible for the application to chain embedded objects, as for example when a HashSet contains a set of Date objects, JDO does not mandate support for chaining embedded objects.

In summary, persistence-capable classes divide into two types, the application data classes and the various system classes that the JDO implementation supports. JDO always manages the objects of the supported system classes as embedded objects. In the JDO metadata, they must be marked either explicitly or by default as embedded. Chapter 5 discusses the JDO metadata.

Replacement and Sharing of Embedded Objects

From time to time, JDO changes the Java object that represents the embedded object's persistent state. Therefore the application should expect that the object identity of the embedded object may change. After completing a transaction or making an object persistent, affected application data objects may refer to different but equivalent embedded objects. When comparing embedded objects, the application should use Java object equivalence (the equals method) rather than Java object identity (the == operator).

JDO does not support sharing embedded objects among first class application data objects. Although the application may assign an embedded object to the persistent field of multiple application data objects, JDO's actions almost never create shared embedded objects. When JDO creates or replaces the embedded objects that an application data object refers to, each application data object will usually refer to its own embedded object. For example, when embedded objects are shared, as shown in Figure 1-2, JDO does not generally store the relationship in the datastore.

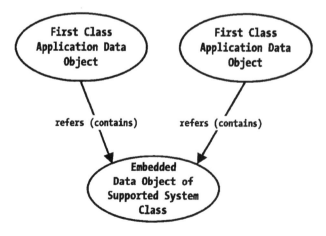

Figure 1-2. Transient relationship in memory created by the application

Instead, when JDO later retrieves the state of the two application data objects and the embedded objects that they contain, it typically creates the relationships shown in Figure 1-3. As you can see, instead of one shared embedded object, JDO creates two unshared embedded objects. As a result, applications should never rely on application data objects sharing one embedded object.

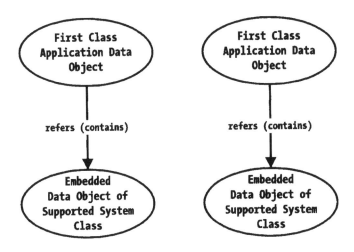

Figure 1-3. The relationship re-created in memory by JDO

As mentioned earlier, some datastores will store the objects of some supported system classes as first class objects. For these datastores, if the application data objects share embedded objects of this type, it is possible that the JDO implementation may not undo the sharing. In this case, when the application data classes share one embedded object as shown in Figure 1-2, JDO may re-create in memory the same relationship when the objects are later retrieved. The application cannot rely on the general rule that shared embedded objects are not shared in the datastore and that JDO will not re-create a shared relationship in memory upon later retrieval.

As a general rule, sharing embedded objects is harmless only when the supported system class is immutable and the application uses Java equivalence to compare two embedded objects. The application should always avoid sharing mutable embedded objects. It is possible that a future version of JDO may prohibit the sharing of mutable embedded objects.

Change Tracking in Supported System Classes

Embedded objects have the responsibility to notify the first class application data object that refers to them when they have changed and to track their own changes, but JDO permits supported system classes to duck this responsibility in some cases. When the supported system class is an immutable type, such as Integer or String, then there is no way for the objects of that type to change. Consequently, there is no need for the immutable system classes to support change notification or tracking.

When the supported system class is a mutable type such as a Date or HashSet, then one of two situations arise. In the first case, the application creates the mutable object and assigns it to the persistent field. Because of the assignment, JDO receives all the notification that it needs that the field's value has changed. In this case, the objects of supported mutable system types do not notify their containing application data objects when they change.

There is one case where the embedded object of a mutable supported system class must notify its containing application data class of any changes made to it. After JDO creates the mutable embedded object to hold the persistent state that it reads from the datastore, any change to the embedded object must cause a notification to the containing application data object. The application data object needs this notification because JDO manages transactions through application data objects. How will this notification occur? Certainly, the Java collection classes, like HashSet, do not contain the logic to notify. Instead, when JDO created the object to hold the state, it did not create an instance of the supported system class, but rather an instance of a derived class of the system class. The JDO implementation supplies these derived classes to implement change notification, change tracking, and other features.

JDO's use of classes derived from the supported mutable system classes is transparent to the application. Their use has no impact on the application's logic. Applications are free to use the instances of the supported system classes whenever they like.

Arrays

Support for arrays is an optional feature of the JDO implementation. Arrays are embedded objects in JDO and are usually stored as second class objects in the datastore. JDO imposes several limitations on arrays that it does not impose on the other supported system classes. JDO does not support the use of arrays in its query language. Although implementations may support change notification, JDO does not require that implementations support change notification for arrays. Consequently, any portable application that uses arrays must take responsibility for informing the referring application data object when the array is modified. (The makeDirty method in the JDOHelper class, described in Chapter 7, handles this task.) When arrays are supported, the implementation decides what type of array elements it supports. It may support arrays of primitives, arrays of application data objects, arrays of other supported system data objects, arrays of arrays, or any combination thereof.

Unmanaged Data Objects

At runtime, for various reasons, JDO may not manage all the objects of persistence-capable classes. Unmanaged objects of persistence-capable classes come into existence in a variety of ways.

- They may be newly created by the application.

- An application data object can stop referring to an embedded object, making the embedded object unmanaged.

- JDO allows the application to explicitly make any managed application data object unmanaged by calling the persistence manager's makeTransient method.

- The application will obtain only unmanaged objects through serialization. When a managed data object is serialized, the deserialized data object is unmanaged.

- A clone of a managed data object will be unmanaged.

While data objects may be managed or unmanaged, JDO never manages the objects of classes that are not persistence capable.

An unmanaged object is called a *transient* object in the JDO specification. Unfortunately, the specification uses the term *transient* in two different but related ways. On the one hand, a transient object is an object that JDO is not managing at all, and on the other hand, it is a data object that JDO manages transactionally but not persistently. The confusion is compounded by the Java keyword transient, which has nothing to do with JDO.

To reduce confusion, this book follows three conventions:

- A transient data object is an object of a persistence-capable class that JDO is not managing persistently. JDO may, but usually does not, manage a transient data object transactionally.

- An unmanaged object may or may not be a data object, but in either case, JDO is not managing it persistently nor transactionally.

- The specification uses the term *transient* to name one of the ten management states that a data object may be in. The next section of this chapter describes management states. In this book, the term *transient* is never used in this sense. Instead, the term *JDO-transient* is used to name the management state that the specification calls *transient*. In this book, the term *unmanaged object* is a synonym for *JDO-transient object*.

Finally, Java serialization is orthogonal to JDO's management of data objects. You may define application data classes that implement, or do not implement, the Serializable interface. You may define persistent, transactional, and unmanaged fields that are, or are not, transient fields. Chapter 5 describes JDO's interaction with Java's serialization mechanisms in detail.

An important design principle followed by JDO is that unmanaged objects behave in exactly the same way as the object would behave if JDO were not present at all. There are only a few places where the unmanaged objects of an enhanced class differ in behavior from the objects of the unenhanced class. Chapter 5 covers the impacts of enhancement.

Defining Core Terminology

Here are some fundamental definitions for this chapter and the remainder of the book:

- *Application data class:* A class defined by the application programmer primarily to hold data that will be stored in the datastore.

- *Application data object:* An instance of an application data class.

- PersistenceCapable *class:* Synonym for an application data class. This term stresses the fact that application data classes after enhancement implement JDO's PersistenceCapable interface.

- *Persistence-capable class:* Either a PersistenceCapable class or one of the classes from the Java standard packages that the JDO implementation supports.

- *Data object:* An instance of a persistence-capable class. A data object may be unmanaged, managed, transient, persistent, transactional, transient and transactional, persistent and nontransactional, or persistent and transactional. It may be stored as a first class object or as a second class object. The JDO specification uses the term *JDO instance* instead of *data object*.

- *Persistent object:* A data object when JDO is managing it persistently.

- *Transactional object:* A data object when JDO is managing it transactionally.

- *Managed object:* A persistent, transactional, or persistent and transactional data object.

- *Transient object:* Any object that JDO is not managing persistently. The JDO specification also uses the term as a synonym for an unmanaged object.

- *JDO-transient:* The management state that indicates that JDO is not managing the object at all. The specification calls this the *transient state.*

- *Unmanaged object:* Any object that JDO is not managing either transactionally or persistently. The term *unmanaged object* is a synonym for *JDO-transient* object.

- *First class object:* A data object that is stored independently in the datastore with a JDO identity. In JDO, application data objects are usually first class objects.

- *Second class object:* A data object that is stored in the datastore as part of a first class object. In JDO, objects of the supported system classes, such as String, Date, Long, and HashSet, are usually second class objects.

- *Identity value:* The value of an attribute, or a list of attributes, that uniquely identifies one persistent state in the datastore.

- *JDO identity:* An object that contains the identity value and can be used to obtain the corresponding application data object.

- *Identity string:* The string obtained from the toString method of a JDO identity object. This can be used to obtain an equivalent JDO identity object.

The Ten Management States of Data Objects

JDO defines ten management states for application data objects. The management state of an application data object determines the implicit actions that JDO takes on the object and the explicit actions that JDO allows on the object. Table 1-1 shows these ten states grouped by the two management dimensions.

Table 1-1. JDO Managed Life Cycle States

Management Dimension	Transactional	Nontransactional
Persistent	Persistent-clean Persistent-new Persistent-dirty Persistent-deleted Persistent-new-deleted	Persistent-nontransactional Hollow
Transient	Transient-clean Transient-dirty	Transient (JDO-transient)

Data objects of the supported system classes do not directly have management state. They have management state indirectly as a result of their relationship to application data objects. If the persistent field of a persistent application data object refers to an embedded object, then the embedded object is persistent; otherwise, it is not. The embedded object's transactional state is likewise acquired indirectly. If a persistent or transactional field of a transactional application data object refers to an embedded object, then the embedded object is transactional; otherwise, it is not.

Three of the states in Table 1-1 occur only when the JDO implementation supports optional features. The transient-clean and transient-dirty states occur only when the implementation supports the `javax.jdo.option.TransientTransactional` option. The persistent-nontransactional state occurs only when the implementation supports any of the five transactional options of JDO, such as *NontransactionalRead* or *RetainValues*. The remaining seven management states occur in all JDO implementations.

 NOTE The `supportedOptions` method in the `PersistenceManagerFactory` interface returns a string for each optional feature of JDO that the implementation supports. Chapter 6 describes this interface and the various option strings.

As Table 1-1 shows, when JDO manages the object both transactionally and persistently, the object is in one of five management states:

- It is persistent-clean when its persistent fields hold the values that are, or will be verified to be, consistent with the datastore in the current transaction.

- It is persistent-dirty when at least one transactional or persistent field has been modified during the current transaction.

- It is persistent-new when the transient object has been added to the current transaction for insertion into the datastore as a result of a call to the persistence manager's `makePersistent` method. An object can also be persistent-new because it can be reached by persistent fields from an object that was made persistent. This feature is called *persistence by reachability.*

- It is persistent-deleted when the object existed in the datastore but has been marked for deletion within the current transaction as a result of a call to the persistence manager's `deletePersistent` method.

- It is persistent-new-deleted when the object is both added for insertion and later marked for deletion within the current transaction.

When an application data object is not persistent, its management state is one of the three transient states:

- It is JDO-transient when it is neither persistent nor transactional. In this case, JDO is not managing the object, so this state is also called the *unmanaged state.*

- It is transient-clean when the JDO implementation supports the `javax.jdo.option.TransientTransactional` option and the JDO-transient object is passed to the persistence manager's `makeTransactional` method. An object can be in the transient-clean state even when a transaction is not active.

- A transient-clean object becomes transient-dirty when any of its transactional or persistent fields are changed within a transaction. After the transaction commits or rolls back, the transient-dirty object becomes transient-clean again.

When an application data object is persistent but not transactional, its management state is one of the two persistent and nontransactional states:

- It is hollow when the values of its persistent fields have not been read from the datastore. An application data object might be returned in the hollow state after any retrieval operation. After a transaction is committed or rolled back, a transactional and persistent application data object will become hollow when the transaction is not configured to retain values.

- It is persistent-nontransactional when some or all of its persistent fields have values that were synchronized with the datastore either outside of a transaction or in a previous transaction. Because the state is not transactional, the values of the persistent fields may no longer match the values in the datastore.

The Attributes of Management States

As you read this book, you will find that the following adjectives are continually applied to application data objects:

- Persistent

- Transient

- Clean

- Dirty

- New

- Deleted

Table 1-2 defines, by JDO management states, when these adjectives can be properly applied to objects. Note that the term *transient* applies when the object is not persistent, and the term *clean* applies when the object is transactional but not dirty.

Table 1-2. Attributes of the JDO Management States

State	Persistent	Transactional	Dirty	New	Deleted
JDO-transient					
Transient-clean		x			
Transient-dirty		x	x		
Hollow	x				
Persistent-nontransactional	x				
Persistent-clean	x	x			
Persistent-dirty	x	x	x		
Persistent-new	x	x	x	x	
Persistent-deleted	x	x	x		x
Persistent-new-deleted	x	x	x	x	x

Table 1-2 shows no distinguishing mark between an object in the hollow state and an object in the persistent-nontransactional state. An object is hollow when it does not hold any of its persistent state, and it is persistent-nontransactional when it holds at least some of its persistent state.

As Table 1-2 shows, an object cannot be new or deleted unless it is persistent. When a transaction is not active, the only objects that can be transactional are the objects in the transient-clean state.

Identity and the Uniqueness Requirement

When JDO manages a persistent object, it periodically synchronizes the state of the object with the state in the datastore. How does JDO match up objects in memory with the state in the datastore? Is it possible for two objects in memory to refer to the same state in the datastore? By understanding JDO identity and the uniqueness requirement, you can answer these questions.

In Java, two references to objects may refer to the same object or distinct objects in memory. Likewise in JDO, two distinct persistent objects in memory may refer to the same or distinct datastore objects. The term "datastore object" is really shorthand for the longer phrase "the object's persistent state in the datastore." Persistent state in the datastore usually does not look or act anything like a Java object, but it is convenient to use the shorthand in place of the more precise term.

In the Java language, the == operator determines whether two references refer to the same object in memory or distinct objects in memory. On the other hand, to determine whether two persistent objects in memory refer to the same or distinct datastore objects requires the use of the *JDO identity*. JDO identity is implemented in a separate object, called the *identity object*, that JDO associates with the persistent object. The association between a persistent object and its JDO identity object is show in Figure 1-4. All persistent application data objects have a JDO identity. Application data objects that are not persistent, which includes those that are JDO-transient, transient-clean, and transient-dirty, do not have a JDO identity. The objects of supported system classes never have a JDO identity.

By definition in JDO, two persistent application data objects in memory refer to the same datastore object if their JDO identity objects satisfy the equals method. In the JDO identity object's equals method, the values of one or more fields are compared. The values of these fields are collectively called the *identity value*. In Figure 1-4, the identity value is shown as contained within the JDO identity object. Because the two JDO identity objects in Figure 1-4 satisfy the equals method, their identity values are the same, and for that reason, the application data objects represent the same persistent state in the datastore. By definition, there is no such thing as two distinct persistent states in the datastore with the same identity value.

JDO does not hand off to the application a reference to the JDO identity object that JDO uses internally. Instead, when the application asks for a JDO identity object, it receives a copy of the internal identity object. For that reason, the application never has the opportunity to alter how JDO links the persistent object to its persistent state in the datastore.

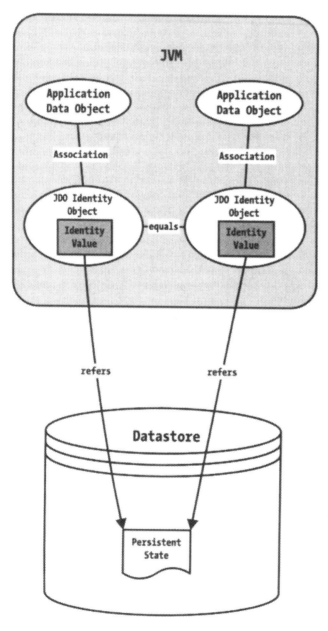

Figure 1-4. Two application data objects referring to the same persistent state

The Three Types of JDO Identity

There are three flavors of JDO identity, and the JDO metadata associates each application data class with one of these flavors. The first two flavors, *datastore identity* and *application identity,* are called the *durable* JDO identities. As the name implies, the durable identity value is stored in the datastore. As would be expected, the datastore ensures that all durable identity values are unique. The third flavor of JDO identity is *nondurable identity.* As its name implies, its value is not stored in the datastore. Indeed, the purpose of nondurable identity is to avoid the overhead of storing unique identity values in the datastore.

All of the application data classes that are related by inheritance to another application data class must use the same flavor of JDO identity as the least-derived application data class in its inheritance hierarchy. For example, if Truck and Car are application data classes that inherit from the Vehicle application data class, then the flavor of JDO identity used for Vehicle must also be used by Truck and Car. On the other hand, if Truck and Car inherit from Object instead, then they could use different flavors of JDO identity, because applications do not enhance the Object class.

Every JDO implementation must support one of the two durable identity types. It may, at its option, support either or both of the other two identity types. Chapter 6 demonstrates how to determine the options that a particular implementation supports.

Datastore Identity

When datastore identity is used, the JDO implementation takes complete responsibility for managing the object identities for the application data class. The identity class is defined by the implementation, and the JDO implementation selects a mechanism for generating the identity values. As a result, the application programmer will find it convenient to use the datastore identity in many cases.

Enhancement does not add any additional instance fields to the application data class to hold the datastore identity. Because the identity value is not stored in the application data object, the datastore identity value is opaque to the application data class. The application has no access to its type or value, except by reflection on the identity object. JDO does not permit the application to change the value of a datastore identity. Different implementations are very likely to have different datastore identity classes and use different algorithms for calculating the identity value. For that reason, it is not meaningful to compare the equality of datastore identity objects that come from different implementations.

The JDO implementation may impose additional restrictions on when it is meaningful to compare the equality of datastore identities. For example, if the datastore reassigns identity values during reorganization, it is not meaningful to compare a datastore identity obtained before the reorganization with a datastore identity obtained after the reorganization.

Although JDO gives implementations a free hand in the details of implementing the datastore identity class, any datastore identity class must meet the following seven requirements:

- It must be public.

- It must implement Serializable.

- It must have a public no-argument (no-arg) constructor.

- All of its instance fields must be serializable and public.

- It must have a constructor that accepts one string.

- Its toString method must return a string that can be passed to its string constructor, as well as to the persistence manager's newObjectIdInstance method, to obtain a new identity object that is equal to the original object from which the string was obtained.

- Its equals method must return true if and only if the two datastore identity objects contain the same identity value, and its hashCode method must return the same integer value for different identity objects when they contain the same identity value.

Two of the requirements on the list are especially interesting. First, the datastore identity object is serializable. Hence, it can be stored and passed to other JVMs. Second, the toString method returns a string that can be used to re-create the identity object. In this book, this string value is called the *identity string*. An identity string is very useful when dealing with HTML clients, because you can round-trip the string to them. This gives you the opportunity to avoid holding state on the server for each client. Datastore identity, like application identity, is a magic cookie. The application can pass it to the persistence manager's getObjectById method to obtain the corresponding persistent object.

It is tempting to view the identity string as a surrogate for the identity object, but this is not strictly the case. While it is true that equality of identity strings necessarily implies the equality of the identity objects that can be obtained with them, it is not true that equality of the identity objects implies the equality of the identity strings that they produce. The reason for the asymmetry is this: the string constructor in the datastore identity class can parse the string. Therefore, the toString method can safely construct a string that contains extraneous information. The constructor would ignore the extra information when creating the identity object.

As a result, identity strings returned from equivalent identity objects (or even two strings from the same object at different times) could turn out not to satisfy the equals method of the String class. Although the specification allows this nonisomorphic behavior by its silence, most implementations are, in fact, providing isomorphic mappings between identity objects and their identity strings.

Application Identity

The responsibility for defining and managing application identity is shared between the application and the JDO implementation. The identity value of application identity is composed of the value of one or more primary key fields declared in the application data class. The primary key fields are persistent fields in the application data class whose values, taken together, are unique for each object in the class of objects.

The responsibility for managing the uniqueness of the identity value is shared between the JDO implementation and the application. The datastore fails any transaction that attempts to store an object whose primary key is already being used by another object of the same class. The application retains responsibility for creating unique application identities. Some implementations allow the application to alter the key's fields containing the application identity value after the object becomes persistent.

When the application makes persistent an unmanaged application data object that uses application identity, JDO constructs the application identity object using the values of the primary key fields in the data object.

NOTE   The implementation supports changing the application identity after the object becomes persistent if the implementation returns the "javax.jdo.option.ChangeApplicationIdentity" string from the supportedOptions method in the PersistenceManagerFactory interface. Chapter 6 describes this interface and its operations.

The JDO metadata identifies which application data classes use application identity, which fields in the application data class are key fields, and which class is used for the application identity. In some cases, the JDO implementation will provide a tool to generate the application identity class. In other cases, the programmer must define the class. Either way, the identity class used by JDO at runtime may be a subclass of the defined application identity class.

The application identity class must meet the first six requirements of the datastore identity class. JDO also requires that application identity classes meet three additional requirements:

- The instance fields in the identity class must include the key fields in the application data class, and their names and types must be the same.

- The equals and hashCode methods must use all of the fields that correspond to the key fields in the application data class.

- If the class is an inner class, it must be static.

Application identity provides two advantages over datastore identity. One, application identity classes are portable across JDO implementations. Because of portability, comparisons between the application identity objects are always meaningful, even across JDO implementations. Porting an application that uses application identity to a subsequent JDO implementation is easier because the application can continue to use the same identity values. It is usually not possible to continue using the same datastore identity values after changing JDO implementations. The second advantage of application identity arises because the application may know the key values before it has the persistent object. Because it is trivial for the application to construct an application identity object when it has the key values, application identity is very useful for retrieving individual persistent objects when their key values are known.

Regardless of the type of identity, JDO constructs the identity objects as needed. In the case of application identity, the application is responsible for ensuring that any new application data objects added to the datastore have unique primary keys. If a new object has keys that duplicate the keys of an existing persistent object, the transaction's commit will fail by throwing a JDO exception. The specification is not clear about the type of JDO exception to expect.

Example of Application Identity

Creating an application identity class that meets all nine requirements is straightforward. For example, consider the Heffalump class in Listing 1-3.

Listing 1-3. The Heffalump *Class and Its Application Identity Class*

```
public class Heffalump
    {
    private String name;    // primary key
    private String color;   // persistent fields
    private int    snozzle_length;
```

```java
static public class HeffalumpOID implements java.io.Serializable
   {
   public String name;

   public HeffalumpOID()
      {
      }

   public HeffalumpOID(String name)
      {
      if (name == null || name.length() <= 0)
         throw new IllegalArgumentException(
               "The name may not be null or empty");

      this.name = name;
      }

   public boolean equals(Object other)
      {
      // if two references to the same object, they must be equal
      if (other == this)
         return true;

      // if the name field is not defined, then they can't be equal
      if (name == null)
         return false;

      // Note the use of the instanceof operator below.
      // This use allows an object of a subclass of HeffalumpOID
      // to compare equal.
      // The instanceof test also catches the case where other is null.
      if (!(other instanceof HeffalumpOID))
         return false;

      HeffalumpOID hoid = (HeffalumpOID) other;

      return name.equals(hoid.name);
      }

   public int hashCode()
      {
      return name.hashCode();
      }
```

```
    public String toString()
       {
       return name;
       }
    }

public Heffalump(String name, String color, int snozzleLength)
   {
   if (name == null || name.trim().length() <= 0)
      throw new IllegalArgumentException(
            "The heffalump's name cannot be null or empty");

   this.name = name.trim();
   this.color = color;
   snozzle_length = snozzleLength;
   }

//... additional behavior for the Heffalump class
}
```

The Heffalump class in Listing 1-3 uses name as its one key field. Multiple key fields might have been used, but the Heffalump is a simple class. HeffalumpOID, the heffalump's application identity class, meets all nine requirements. In its equals method, the HeffalumpOID class checks that the key field is not null. The check is required because of the availability of a public no-arg constructor. The equals method uses instanceof to check for class compatibility. Since the JDO implementation may extend the application identity class, polymorphic equality is needed to ensure that an instance created by the application and an instance created by JDO are equal when their identity values are the same.

Recommended Types for Key Fields

The JDO specification recommends that the key fields be drawn from the following types:

- Primitives

- String

- Date

- Byte

- Short

- Integer

- Long

- Float

- Double

- BigDecimal

- BigInteger

The JDO implementation may choose to support additional types of key fields.

Using Application Identity for Related Compound Keys

Although the list of recommended types for key fields is long, JDO cannot handle, in an ideal fashion, related compound keys. The difficulty is best illustrated by an example.

To model a company's personnel structure, there may be a Division object and a Team object. Each Division has a name that is unique within the company. The name is the division's primary key. Each Team has a name that is unique within the Division. The primary key for the team is the division name together with the team name. Each Division has a collection of the Teams within it, and each Team has a reference to the Division to which it belongs.

What is the best way to define the application identity class for Team? The tempting choice is to declare a compound key for Team, as shown in the following code:

```
Division division;  // reference to this team's division
                    // and  first part of primary key
String   name;      // this team's name
                    // and second part of primary key
```

Given the key fields for Team, the rules for application identity require the following field declarations in the team's identity class:

```
public Division division;
public String name;
```

But Division is not a simple type; instead, it is another application data class. It may not implement the Serializable interface. Even when it does, applications usually do not want a business object contained within an identity object. The Division class does not come from the recommended field types for application keys, and for the reasons mentioned, its use is suspect. Ideally, JDO would map the Division field in the Team class to the division's key field in the team's identity class, but JDO 1.0 does not support this mapping.

The better choice for the team's application identity class is to declare the division's key field divisionName in the Team object, as shown in the following code:

```
String divisionName;   // name of this team's division
                       // and  first part of primary key
String name;           // this team's name
                       // and second part of primary key
Division division;     // reference to this team's division
                       // but not a primary key
```

By using the divisionName and name fields as the key fields for the Team class, the team's identity class can conform to all of the required and recommended constraints for application identity.

Declaring both a divisionName and a reference to a Division introduces duplication of information in the Team class. The duplication requires some synchronization code. For example, the divisionName should be set when the Team.setDivision method is called. If the application allows a Division to change its name (this is allowing it to change its primary key), then the setter method will have to ensure that the new name is propagated to all of the division's teams. The need for synchronization code for redundant information is clearly not ideal. A future revision of JDO may improve how JDO handles related compound keys.

Using Application Identity in Related Data Classes

JDO imposes complex constraints on the use of application identity for application data classes that are related by inheritance. Implementations may not break any of these rules, but they may have rules of their own that are more restrictive. Application developers that want a thorough understanding of how to use application identity in inheritance trees of application data classes really need to understand three things. What are the most restrictive rules for defining application identity in inheritance trees? If you follow these rules, then your use of application identity will work everywhere. What are the most liberal rules for defining application identity in inheritance trees? If you require behavior that breaks any of these rules, then you will not find a JDO implementation that supports your strategy. Finally, what are the rules that limit the JDO implementation that you have selected for your application? The implementation's rules may fall at either extreme or in the middle.

Chapter 5 explains the most liberal rules that JDO allows. This section describes the most restrictive rules that work everywhere. There are only two rules that you need to follow for portability.

First, application data classes that are not derived, directly or indirectly, from the same application data class should use distinct application identity classes. If you follow this rule, you will not associate in the JDO metadata the same application identity class with different application data classes.

Second, the application should associate the least-derived application data class, whether abstract or concrete, with a concrete application identity class. When you follow this rule, the application data classes that derive from the least-derived application data class cannot declare additional key fields. Instead, all of the key fields are declared in the least-derived application data class.

NOTE   The `objectid-class` attribute of the JDO metadata's `class` tag associates an application data class with an application identity class.

If these two rules are too restrictive for your application, then you may want to understand the more liberal and complex constraints explained in Chapter 5, or you may want to explore the limitations of your selected JDO implementation.

Nondurable Identity

Providing for nondurable identity is an optional feature of the JDO implementation. As the name suggests, the identity value of nondurable identity is not saved in the datastore with the persistent state. The reason for using this type of JDO identity is to achieve the highest efficiency when inserting records into the datastore. It is suitable for things like log entries that are primarily write-once.

Because nondurable identity is not stored in the datastore, there is no guarantee that the same identity value will be used to refer to the same persistent object state on multiple occasions. Data objects with nondurable identity can participate in only one transaction. If a query that fetches a data object with a nondurable identity is run twice, the second data object returned is different from the first, even though they both represent the same datastore state. A nondurable identity can be used only within the persistence manager that issued it and only within the transaction in which it was obtained.

The JDO implementation defines the nondurable identity class. The JDO specification imposes a few requirements on the nondurable identity class:

- It must be public.

- It must have a public no-arg constructor.

- All of its instance fields must be serializable and public.

Although applications may use nondurable JDO identities for special cases, as a rule, applications use the two types of durable identities for their application data classes.

NOTE   The type of JDO identity used for an application data class is specified in the JDO metadata and is fixed at class enhancement time. Chapter 5 describes the JDO metadata.

The Uniqueness Requirement

Given either the persistent object or its identity object, JDO can provide the application with the other. By comparing their identity objects with the equals method, the application can determine whether two persistent objects refer to the same persistent state in the datastore. Just as two references refer to the same object in memory when they satisfy the == operator, two application data objects in memory refer to the same state in the datastore when their identity objects satisfy the equals method. Likewise, two distinct objects in memory refer to different states in the datastore when the comparison of their identity objects is valid, but comparing them with their equals method returns false.

The type of JDO identity determines when the identity object's equals method performs a meaningful comparison. For either datastore or application identity, the equality test is valid across queries, transactions, and persistence managers. For application identity, the equality test is also valid across JDO implementations. For distinct nondurable identity objects, the equality test is valid only when it returns true.

Knowing how to tell when two data objects refer to the same persistent state is good, but knowing when there may be, or when there may not be, a multiplicity of data objects that all refer to the same persistent state is better. In short, does JDO limit the potential for multiplicity?

Although the equality test between identity objects is robust, JDO provides a simpler test that handles the typical case. This simpler test exists because JDO imposes the uniqueness requirement on JDO implementations. To understand the uniqueness requirement, consider the following conditions:

- Let **A** and **B** be two (possibly distinct) persistent objects in the memory of the same application data class.

- Let the application data class use a durable identity, either datastore or application.

- Let **A** and **B** be managed by the same persistence manager.

- Let **A'** and **B'** be the two (possibly distinct) persistent states in the datastore that **A** and **B** refer to respectively.

Under these conditions, the uniqueness requirement is the rule that if **A'** and **B'** are the same persistent state, then **A** and **B** must be the same object in memory. In other words, every persistence manager creates no more than one persistent object for any persistent state.

The uniqueness requirement applies regardless of how the references to persistent objects were obtained, as long as the application uses the same persistence manager to obtain them. The application may obtain the references from a query, by fetching an object by identity, by making a transient object persistent, or by navigating the persistent fields of other persistent objects.

NOTE   The uniqueness requirement does not prevent garbage collection of persistent objects. The implementation does not hold a strong reference to persistent objects that are hollow or persistent-nontransactional. When the application does not hold a strong reference to these objects, they may be garbage collected. After garbage collection, if the application again retrieves the same datastore objects, JDO will create new persistent objects with an equivalent durable identity. The creation of duplicates after garbage collection has no effect on application logic, since the application cannot have at the same time references to both the garbage-collected object and the duplicate object.

In the typical case, application code handles the persistent objects of one persistence manager at a time. In this case, a test for the object identity (==) of the possibly distinct application data objects is sufficient to determine whether the possibly distinct application data objects refer to the same or different persistent states in the datastore.

The Uniqueness Requirement Simplifies Application Code

The uniqueness requirement simplifies the application logic that manipulates persistent objects. Within the confines of one persistence manager, the term "same object" means both the same object in the datastore and the same object in memory. The uniqueness requirement ensures that either both conditions are satisfied or neither condition is satisfied.

The uniqueness requirement is notable for the issues that the application code avoids because this requirement is enforced. If there were multiple application data objects within the same persistence manager that referred to the same datastore object, then who is responsible for ensuring that they have the same representation? In the event of inconsistent changes in duplicate objects, which object updates the datastore? The uniqueness requirement prevents these issues from arising when durable identities are used. Each persistence manager can manage at most one object with a durable identity for any persistent state. When two distinct application data objects represent the same state in the datastore, but the objects are managed by distinct persistence managers, then the inconsistencies between the two representations are handled by the transactional semantics, which Chapter 4 details.

The uniqueness requirement is Ockham's razor in JDO. William of Ockham was a fourteenth-century philosopher who remains famous for saying in an ontological debate that objects should not be created needlessly. His rule became known as Ockham's razor. In JDO, a persistence manager maintains the simplest representation in memory of persistent state because it never creates more than one persistent object to represent the same persistent state.

Satisfaction of the uniqueness requirement is what allows the application to rely on JDO to simply and consistently represent persistent relationships in memory. Remember the earlier example of two persons owning the same dog. If two persons a and b are fetched within the same persistence manager, and they own the same dog, then the truth of the expression a.myDog == b.myDog is the simple and consistent way that JDO represents in memory the relationship in the datastore.

No Uniqueness Requirement for Nondurable Identity

If nondurable identity is used, then multiple application data objects may represent the same state in the datastore and be managed by the same persistence manager. As a result, it is possible for two persistent objects, using nondurable identity and managed by the same persistence manager, to have inconsistent changes for the same persistent state. The JDO implementation is responsible for throwing an exception if it is asked to commit any transaction where this situation arises. (Although the specification is not clear, the thrown exception is likely to be a

`JDOUserException.`) It is the application's responsibility to prevent this error condition from occurring to avoid failures during commit.

Linking a Transient Object to Persistent State

So far the discussion has centered around application data objects in memory and how they refer to persistent state in the datastore. The JDO identity is the link from the persistent application data object to its persistent state. On the other hand, transient application data objects do not have a JDO identity, and therefore JDO does not recognize any linkage from them to persistent state. In some situations, as when application data objects are passed by value, the application may find it necessary to remember the JDO identity even after JDO has discarded it.

Application data objects are not always persistent. As described earlier, there are many ways that application data objects become transient. However it happens, upon becoming transient, the application data object loses its JDO identity.

Although the transient application data object loses its identity, the notion that it still represents a particular persistent state in the datastore can remain. This can be seen by considering an example where the business service uses serialization to communicate with the client. Suppose the application builds a remote service to examine and modify customer information using JDO. This service finds `Customer` objects and allows the client to modify the customer's information. As mentioned earlier, serialization delivers only unmanaged objects to the recipient. As a result, the remote client views, modifies, and returns to the service unmanaged `Customer` objects. When the service is called to modify a customer, it receives a JDO-transient `Customer` object from the client. There can be no doubt about the application's intent: the returned `Customer` object represents the same customer in the datastore as the original `Customer` object that the service fetched and sent via serialization to the client. Hence, the notion that the returned `Customer` object represents a particular persistent state in the datastore has not disappeared, but its association with its JDO identity has disappeared.

The fact that an application data object can lose its JDO identity may seem counterintuitive, or at least unhelpful. There are times when the application's intent clearly justifies saying that a transient application data object refers to a persistent state in the datastore, even when JDO does not provide the JDO identity object to support this assertion. A future version of JDO will likely address this issue. Until then, JDO provides features that the application can use to create or remember the JDO identity associated with a transient application data object.

Application identity makes it easy to produce the identity object that goes with a transient application data object. Since the primary key fields are in the application data object, it is usually trivial to ensure that they always contain valid values. JDO will require that the key fields are loaded when the object is loaded from the datastore or inserted into the datastore. The application can do its part by requiring that the key fields be supplied to construct the object. As a result, the identity value should be present in the primary key fields of every application data object that has application identity. Using the values of the key fields, the application can construct the application identity object whenever it likes.

When the application data class uses datastore identity, the situation is more complex. In this case, the application data object must capture its identity object, or the corresponding identity string, while the object is still persistent. JDO provides two ways to obtain the identity object, the persistence manager's `getObjectId` method and the `getObjectId` method in the `JDOHelper` class. After obtaining the datastore identity object, it should be stored in an unmanaged and serializable instance field of the application data object. Once stored, any copies made of the object will have a reference to its identity object. The callback methods defined in the `InstanceCallbacks` interface, which is described in Chapter 7, can be used as triggers to capture the identity object or its corresponding identity string. Chapter 7 presents an example of this usage.

Summary

This chapter introduces JDO's persistence service and defines much of the vocabulary needed to discuss it. As often happens when a paradigm changes, new terms are required to describe the new concepts and their interrelationships. This chapter uses, so far as possible, old and familiar concepts to define the new terms.

JDO is a paradigm shift for application programmers who are used to working with a datastore service. JDO encapsulates and removes from the application all of the work involved in interacting with a datastore service. In place of the datastore service for information, JDO provides a persistence service for objects. This service ensures that some aspects of persistence are taken care of transparently without requiring the application to make explicit requests.

Although JDO hides some persistence services, it also exposes the aspects of persistence that the application must control. Queries and transactions are among the most important of JDO's explicit services. The next chapter describes how to construct and execute a query using JDO.

CHAPTER 2

Queries

THE ABILITY TO retrieve objects by queries is an essential feature of a persistence service, and for that reason, this book begins with JDO's query service. Queries are used to find persistent data objects that meet a set of conditions. A JDO query can search for the relevant objects either in the datastore or in a collection of persistent objects in memory.

Queries are one way that an application can retrieve references to persistent objects, but there are a variety of other ways. An application can retrieve an application data object using an identity object. An application can also iterate through all persistent objects of an application data class using the Extent interface, which is discussed in the next section. An application may obtain a reference to a persistent object by navigating the persistent fields of other data objects. Once obtained, references to persistent objects remain valid as long as the persistence manager that produced them remains open. As a result, a persistent application data object can be fetched in one transaction and modified in a later transaction.

Although there are many ways for the application to obtain a reference to a persistent object in memory, the typical application will make heavy use of JDO's query service. This chapter describes the Query interface in JDO. It begins with the Extent interface because extents are often used to construct queries. It describes the configuration of JDO queries, including setting the query filter and declaring variables and parameters. It compares JDO's queries to SQL queries. This chapter concludes by examining how the development process benefits by using the JDO query service.

The Extent Interface

The Extent interface specifies a group whose membership is managed by JDO and the datastore. Unless explicitly turned off in the JDO metadata, all application data classes are associated with an extent. An extent holds information and resources related to the class of objects in the datastore. Extents are used primarily to specify the objects in the datastore to examine when executing a query, but extents can also iterate the entire class of persistent application data objects. When a query uses an extent, the JDO implementation usually translates the query into the datastore's query language and sends it to the datastore service. The persistence manager is the factory that creates Extent objects.

An extent acts like a read-only collection but does not implement the Java `Collection` interface. Like a `Collection`, it can be iterated, but it does not have a `size` method, and it has no mutating methods. There are two ways to determine if a particular object is a member of an extent. The extent can be iterated, or a query can be executed that uses the extent. The application cannot add objects to, nor can it delete objects from, an extent directly. Instead, the application accomplishes these tasks indirectly by calling the persistence manager's `makePersistent` and `deletePersistent` methods.

Extents and the Persistence Manager's IgnoreCache Property

Extents are always up-to-date with regard to the effects of committed transactions. If a committed transaction added an object to the extent by the `makePersistent` method or removed it from the extent by the `deletePersistent` method, a new iteration of the extent will always include the addition and exclude the deletion. These committed transactions might be previous transactions for the current persistence manager from which the extent was obtained, or they may be transactions committed by other persistence managers. It depends on the implementation whether an open iterator on an extent reflects the committed transactions that have occurred since the iterator was opened.

On the other hand, it is possible that an extent will not include the additions or exclude the deletions made within the current, uncommitted transaction. Whether the effects of calling `makePersistent` or `deletePersistent` are visible to a new iterator depends on the setting of the *IgnoreCache* flag in the persistence manager that produced the extent at the time that the iterator is obtained. If the flag is set to false, then the extent's iterator will include the additions and exclude the deletions made within the current transaction. In other words, when the *IgnoreCache* flag is false, uncommitted changes in the current transaction are treated the same as committed changes in previous or other transactions. If the flag is set to true, then the iterator may exclude the changes made within the current transaction. In this case, the setting is a hint which the implementation may, or may not, follow.

The Factory Method That Produces Extent Objects

Although Chapter 3 describes the `PersistenceManager` interface, this is the appropriate place to look at its factory method that produces `Extent` objects.

```
public Extent getExtent(Class adClass, boolean getSubclasses)
```

This method is the only way to obtain an Extent object. The adClass parameter is the Class object for any application data class. The getSubclasses flag determines whether the extent includes objects in the subclasses, if any, of the adClass. As long as the persistence manager remains open, an Extent object can be used and reused.

An application data class does not have an extent if the JDO metadata turns off this feature for the class. In this case, getExtent throws a JDOUserException. Chapter 5 describes the JDO metadata.

Starting with JDO 1.0.1, an application can obtain an extent regardless of the value of the transaction's *Active* property or its *NontransactionalRead* property. Chapter 4 discusses the Transaction interface.

Figure 2-1 shows the UML class diagram of the Extent interface. Six methods define the four operations and two read-only properties shown in Figure 2-1.

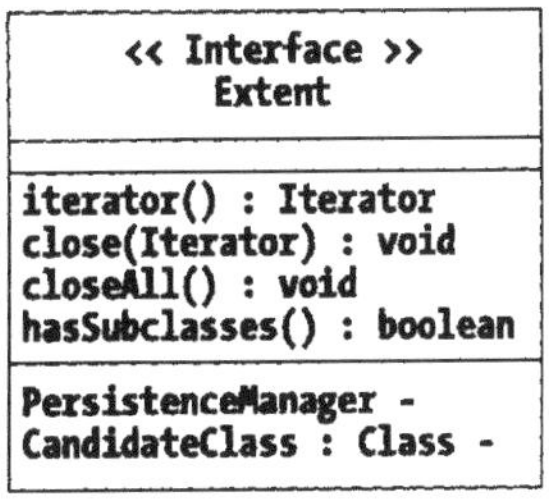

```
┌─────────────────────────────────┐
│        << Interface >>          │
│            Extent               │
├─────────────────────────────────┤
│ iterator() : Iterator           │
│ close(Iterator) : void          │
│ closeAll() : void               │
│ hasSubclasses() : boolean       │
├─────────────────────────────────┤
│ PersistenceManager -            │
│ CandidateClass : Class -        │
└─────────────────────────────────┘
```

Figure 2-1. The class diagram of the Extent *interface*

The Read-Only CandidateClass Property

The Extent interface provides a getter method that returns the read-only *CandidateClass* property.

```
public Class getCandidateClass()
```

This method returns the Class object for the application data class used to obtained the extent. Every persistent object returned by iterating the extent is assignment compatible with the *CandidateClass*.

The Read-Only PersistenceManager Property

The Extent interface provides a getter method that returns the read-only *PersistenceManager* property.

```
public PersistenceManager getPersistenceManager()
```

This method returns the persistence manager that produced the extent.

Determining Whether the Extent Includes Subclasses

The Extent interface provides one method to determine whether the extent includes objects of subclasses of the *CandidateClass*.

```
public boolean hasSubclasses()
```

The value returned by the hasSubclasses method is the value of the flag passed to the getExtent method. When true, iterators return objects in the *CandidateClass* and all of its subclasses, if any. When false, iterators do not return objects in the subclasses of the *CandidateClass*.

Obtaining an Iterator over the Extent

The Extent interface provides a factory method that returns iterators.

```
public java.util.Iterator iterator()
```

The iterators obtained from the extent iterate the objects of the extent. Iterators obtained from an extent do not support the mutating methods in the Iterator interface. Calling a mutating method in the iterator results in an java.lang.UnsupportedOperationException. To obtain an iterator, either the transaction's *NontransactionalRead* property must be true or the transaction must be active. If these conditions are not met, then this method throws a JDOUserException. Chapter 4 describes the Transaction interface.

Closing Extent Iterators

The Extent interface provides two methods to close an iterator.

```
public void close(java.util.Iterator iter)
public void closeAll()
```

The close method closes an iterator. Because the iterators are likely tied to resource usage in the datastore, they should be closed when no longer needed. After an iterator is closed, its hasNext method returns false and its next method throws a java.util.NoSuchElementException. Closing an iterator has no effect on new or other existing iterators for the extent.

The closeAll method closes all open iterators on the extent.

The Design of JDO's Query Service

JDO's query service has two parts, the Query interface and the query language (JDOQL). The syntax and semantics of JDOQL are similar to the syntax and semantics of Java, except that JDOQL has a smaller syntax that is less type constrained than Java. The JDO implementation can perform the query in memory, or it can translate the query into the native query language and interface of the datastore. JDO permits the implementation to support additional query languages. While support for additional query languages is optional, support for JDOQL is required.

JDO supports queries on extents of persistent objects in the datastore. It also supports queries on collections of persistent objects in memory. The JDO implementation may use the datastore's native query language and interface, or it may use its own query logic. Most implementations have both capabilities. The implementation is expected to support large results sets. JDO does not favor the capabilities of any particular datastore, but most JDO implementations optimize query execution for the datastore that they target. The JDO query service allows queries to be compiled for better performance.

JDO and its query capabilities are firmly rooted in the object model of the data classes. JDOQL provides the ability to compare field values and navigate references and collections. With these capabilities, powerful queries can be constructed in JDOQL. These queries are simple for Java programmers to create and understand because they are based on the application data classes and on a query language that is similar to Java.

A complete query language for the data classes would include every query that could be executed by manipulating the classes. Although powerful, JDOQL is not a complete query language. One limitation is the inability to navigate arrays contained within the application data class. A more important limitation is the inability to invoke the methods of the application data class. Because methods cannot be invoked, JDOQL cannot refer to an application data class as an implementation of an interface. The inability to call methods arises because most datastores save only the object's state and not its behavior.

The Query Interface

The Query interface is used to construct and execute queries. Figure 2-2 shows the class diagram of the Query interface. 20 methods define the 11 operations and 5 properties shown in Figure 2-2.

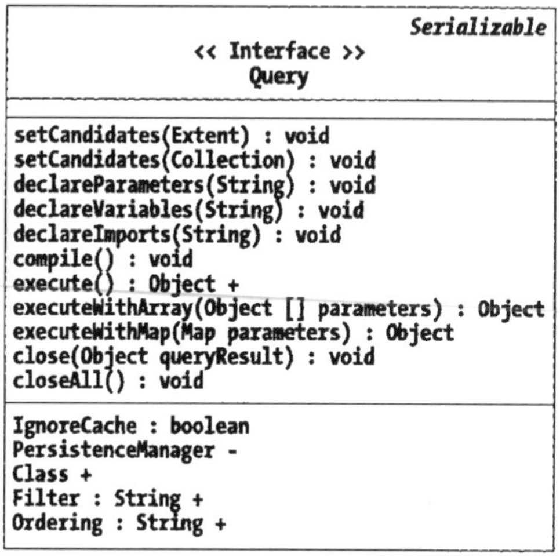

```
                                           Serializable
                       << Interface >>
                          Query

  setCandidates(Extent) : void
  setCandidates(Collection) : void
  declareParameters(String) : void
  declareVariables(String) : void
  declareImports(String) : void
  compile() : void
  execute() : Object +
  executeWithArray(Object [] parameters) : Object
  executeWithMap(Map parameters) : Object
  close(Object queryResult) : void
  closeAll() : void

  IgnoreCache : boolean
  PersistenceManager -
  Class +
  Filter : String +
  Ordering : String +
```

Figure 2-2. The class diagram of the Query *interface*

Queries are serializable and can be stored. A deserialized query is no longer related to its original persistence manager. For that reason, the only use for a deserialized query is to obtain a new query with all the same settings from any open persistence manager. The newly obtained query is related to the persistence manager that produced it. It is not compiled, and its candidates are not set. Otherwise, its settings are the same as the original query.

After configuration, a query can be executed any number of times in the same transaction or in different transactions. Each time the query executes, it selects objects from the candidates based on the query filter, the candidate class, and the parameter values. The query returns the selected objects in the results collection. The results collection is empty when no candidates satisfy the query.

Setting the Query's Candidates

The Query interface provides two methods to set the query's candidates.

```
public void setCandidates(Extent extent)
public void setCandidates(java.util.Collection collection)
```

When queries are executed, they select objects from a range of candidates. These methods specify the range as either an extent or a collection. If a collection is used, it must contain persistent objects that are managed by the same persistence manager that produced the query. If an extent is used, it must come from the same persistence manager that created the query. Using an extent to set the query's candidates is a hint to the JDO implementation to send the query to the datastore service. Using a collection, on the other hand, usually causes the JDO implementation to execute the query against objects in memory.

Setting the Query's Candidate Class

The Query interface provides a setter method for its write-only *Class* property. This property is also called the query's *candidate class*.

```
public void setClass(Class candidateClass)
```

Queries select objects from the candidates that are assignment compatible with the query's candidate class. The candidate class is always an application data class. When the query's candidate class is set, but the query's candidates are not set, the query uses by default the extent associated with the query's candidate class. In other words, if you want to run a query against an extent, you have the option of setting only the *Class* property and ignoring the *Candidates* property.

Generally, when queries run against extents, the candidate class of the query is the same as the candidate class of the extent. The ability to independently set the query's candidate class becomes important when the query runs against a collection of candidate objects, as the collection may contain objects of different classes.

Setting the Query's Filter

The Query interface provides a setter method for its write-only *Filter* property.

```
public void setFilter(String filter)
```

The query selects matching candidates on the basis of a query string, which is stored in the write-only *Filter* property. Later sections of this chapter, starting with "The Syntax of the JDO Query Filter," describe the syntax and semantics of the JDO Query Language (JDOQL) used in the query filter.

Declaring the Query's Parameters

The Query interface provides a method to declare the parameters that can be passed when invoking the query.

```
public void declareParameters(String paramString)
```

The query filter may, or may not, use query parameters. By declaring parameters, the application can determine at runtime the values to be used in the query filter. The application declares parameters by passing a string to the query's declareParameters method. The syntax of this string is the same as the parameter declaration clause in a Java method. For example, the following string declares two parameters of types Foo and Bar:

```
"Foo foo, Bar bar"
```

The following string declares one integer and two Date parameters:

```
"int count, Date yesterday, Date today"
```

All of the parameters must be declared in one parameter string, and the names must be distinct. Field names in the candidate class, parameter names, and variable names share the same name space. If a parameter name is the same as the name of a field in the candidate class, the field name is hidden. The field name may still be accessed in the query filter by using the this.fieldname syntax.

JDO allows the application to declare parameters of primitive types, but the parameters passed to the query's execute methods must be objects of the corresponding wrapper types. When the declared parameter is a primitive, the wrapper object passed to the execute method cannot be null. JDO implementations may require that parameters be primitives or persistent-capable types. They may also require that all application data objects be managed. In all cases, if the object passed as a parameter value is managed, it must be managed by the persistence manager that produced the Query object. Using transient application data objects and objects of classes that are not persistence-capable for parameter values is not portable across JDO implementations.

Declaring the Query's Variables

The Query interface provides a method to declare the variables that can be used in the query filter.

```
public void declareVariables(String varString)
```

By using variables, the application can construct more complex query filters. Later sections of this chapter, starting with "Query Variables," describe the syntax and semantics of the variable string and the use of variables in the query filter.

Declaring the Query's Imports

The Query interface provides a method to declare the types that must be imported into the query's name space.

```
public void declareImports(String importString)
```

In some cases, the declared parameters and variables, or the query filter, require the importing of type names. The declareImports method sets the string that handles this need. The type of the candidate class, all the types in the package containing the candidate class, and all the types in the java.lang package are automatically imported. Otherwise, the class or interface type must be imported unless it is fully qualified when used in the filter, parameter, or variable strings.

The imports string has the same syntax as the Java import statement. For example, the following import string identifies another place where the query can look to find classes used in variables and parameters:

```
"import example.persistent.*;"
```

Wildcards are permitted but not required in the import string. The import string may contain multiple import statements separated by semicolons. All import statements must be contained in one string.

Ordering the Results

The Query interface provides a setter method for its write-only *Ordering* property.

```
public void setOrdering(String orderingString)
```

The order of iteration for the objects returned in the results collection is specified by an ordering string that is stored in the write-only *Ordering* property. The "Ordering Results" section later in this chapter describes the ordering string in detail.

Running the Query

The Query interface provides six methods to run the query. Most of these methods take parameters that are used when evaluating the query filter.

```
public Object execute()
public Object execute(Object param1)
public Object execute(Object param1, Object param2)
public Object execute(Object param1, Object param2, Object param3)
public Object executeWithArray(Object [] params)
public Object executeWithMap(Map params)
```

Each of the five methods that execute a query returns the selected objects in a Collection called the *results collection.* The results collection is returned as an Object and must be cast to Collection. The objects included in the results collection are assignment compatible with the query's candidate class. The results collection cannot be modified. Any attempt to modify the returned collection results in a java.lang.UnsupportedOperationException.

The results collection may be very large, but it can always be iterated. The returned collection may be used in another query. The results collection returns a value for the size method. This value may be the size of the collection, or it may be Integer.MAX_VALUE when the JDO implementation does not know the size.

The parameters of the execute methods are matched left to right with the parameter names declared in the parameter string. The executeWithArray method accepts an array of values. The parameter at index zero is matched with the leftmost parameter in the parameter string. The executeWithMap method accepts a Map object that contains the parameters. The keys in the map are matched by name to the names in the parameter string, and the value associated with the key is used as the parameter's value.

The query must pass values for all declared parameters in each execution of the query. The query does not remember the parameter values used in an earlier execution of the query.

For the execute methods to succeed, the persistence manager that produced the query must be open and either the transaction must be active or the transaction's *NontransactionalRead* property must be true. Otherwise, the execute methods throw a JDOUserException. Chapter 3 describes the PersistenceManager interface, and Chapter 4 describes the Transaction interface and its properties.

Closing the Query's Results

The Query interface provides two methods to close the results collections obtained from running queries.

```
public void close(Object resultsCollection)
public void closeAll()
```

The results collection is an instance of a collection class supplied by the JDO implementation. It may use resources in the datastore. When the results collection is no longer needed, it should be closed. The close method closes one results collection produced by the query. The closeAll method closes all open results collections produced by the query.

When a results collection is obtained by executing a query in a transaction, the specification does not define how the results collection behaves when it is left open after the transaction ends. Any behavior that you observe is likely to be implementation dependent. For portability, the application should close any results collections that it obtained within the transaction either before or immediately after completing the transaction.

After the results collection is closed, it can no longer be used or iterated. Existing iterators on the results collection return false from the hasNext method and throw the NoSuchElementException from the next method. The application can continue to use the persistent objects that it found in the results collection prior to closing it.

Compiling a Query

The Query interface provides a method to compile a query prior to using it.

```
public void compile()
```

Although any query can be compiled, because queries that use parameters are often reused, it makes sense to compile them. The implementation can optimize compiled queries for higher performance. In the case of a relational datastore, the compiled query is likely to use a prepared statement for faster performance. Compiling a query may detect problems with the query's configuration prior to execution.

The IgnoreCache Property

The Query interface provides getter and setter methods for its *IgnoreCache* property.

```
public void setIgnoreCache(boolean flag)
public boolean getIgnoreCache()
```

The read-write *IgnoreCache* property in the Query interface determines whether the query uses the data objects that are persistent-new, persistent-deleted, and persistent-dirty in determining the results of executing a query against an extent. The initial value of the *IgnoreCache* property is inherited from the persistence manager that produced the Query object. The section "Using or Ignoring the Cache in a Query" later in this chapter examines this property in detail.

The Read-Only PersistenceManager Property

The Query interface provides a getter method for its read-only *PersistenceManager* property.

```
public PersistenceManager getPersistenceManager()
```

This method returns a reference to the persistence manager that produced the query.

Factory Methods That Produce Query Objects

The newQuery methods in the PersistenceManager interface are the factory methods that produce Query objects. Although the PersistenceManager interface is described in Chapter 3, this is the appropriate place to describe its newQuery methods.

```
public Query newQuery(Class candidateClass)
public Query newQuery(Extent candidates)
public Query newQuery(Class candidateClass, Collection candidates)
public Query newQuery(Class candidateClass, String filter)
public Query newQuery(Extent candidates, String filter)
public Query newQuery(Class candidateClass, Collection candidates, String filter)
```

When the query executes, it must know or be able to determine three things: its query filter, its candidates, and its candidate class. Each of these factory methods is a convenience method that produces a query ready to use, as long as the filter does not use parameters or variables. If the filter is not defined when the query executes, the filter evaluates to true for every candidate instance. If the candidate class is not defined when the query executes, but an extent provides the candidates, then the query's candidate class defaults to the extent's candidate class. Likewise, if the candidates are not defined when the query executes, but the candidate class is defined, then the candidates default to the extent that is associated with the candidate class.

After obtaining a Query object, the application can perform any additional configuration required by using the operations and properties of the Query interface.

```
public Query newQuery()
```

This factory method produces a Query object that needs configuration before it can be used. You may find that your code is more self-documenting when you use this method and the Query configuration methods than when you use the convenience factory methods.

```
public Query newQuery(Object query)
```

This method returns a new Query object associated with the persistence manager. Its primary use is to create viable Query objects from deserialized Query objects. The returned Query object does not have its candidates set, and it is not compiled. Otherwise, it has the same settings as the Query object supplied to the method. The deserialized Query object and the persistence manager must come from the same JDO implementation.

```
public Query newQuery(String altQueryLanguage, Object altQueryObject)
```

JDO implementations must support JDO's Query Language, but they may also support another query language. With this method, the application can construct a Query object that uses a vendor-supported query language and a vendor-defined object.

The Syntax of the JDO Query Filter

The selection logic of the JDO query is expressed in the filter string, which uses terms, operators, and query methods to create a Boolean expression. For every object in the extent or collection of candidates, if the Boolean expression of the filter string evaluates to true for that object and the object is an instance of the query's candidate class, the object is included in the results collection. If the filter string is not specified, or if it is specified as the empty string, it defaults to true. In this case, every candidate that is an instance of the candidate class satisfies the query filter.

The Terms of JDOQL

The most frequently used term of a query filter is the name of a persistent field in the query's candidate class, which is always an application data class. In the simple case, the field name is compared to another term. The examples that follow use the field names defined in the classes Foo and Bar, shown in Listing 2-1.

Listing 2-1. The Persistent Fields of the Foo *and* Bar *Classes*

```
public class Foo
    {
    private String    name;
    private int       number;
    private Bar       specialBar;
    private HashSet   myChildren; // collection of Foo elements
    private HashSet   allMyBars;  // collection of Bar elements
    ...
    }

public class Bar
    {
    private int   size;
    ...
    }
```

 NOTE You might want to bookmark Listing 2-1, as the Foo and Bar classes are used for many examples in this chapter.

If Foo is the candidate class, then the names of the fields in Foo can be used directly in the query filter. The following query filter selects all the Foo objects where its number is 5 and its name is "Mars":

```
"number == 5 && name == \"Mars\""
```

Note that the query filter is a string and is, therefore, quoted. Any strings contained within it must be quoted as well, and for that reason, their quotation marks must be escaped. The query filter can use field names that are private as well as any other level of accessibility.

Although the filter looks very similar to a Java expression, the use of the equality (==) operator to compare name to "Mars" is not a Java idiom. In Java, the expression

```
name == "Mars"
```

can be false even when name contains the string value "Mars". In Java, the equality operator compares JVM identity, but when comparing strings, it is usually the string values, not the JVM identities, that should be compared. The following expression shows the Java idiom that compares string values:

```
name.equals("Mars")
```

The use of the equality operator in the query filter works because JDOQL has different semantics than the Java language. In JDOQL the equality operators (==, !=) compare the values of embedded objects and the JDO identities of application data objects. (You may recall from Chapter 1 that embedded objects do not have a JDO identity.)

The keywords this and null can also be terms in the filter expression. The keyword this refers to the candidate that is being evaluated. Using Foo as the candidate class, the following query filter selects all the Foo objects whose specialBar field is not null:

```
"specialBar != null"
```

Reference fields can be navigated within the query filter by using the field access (.) operator, as in the following example that finds all Foo objects with a special Bar object whose size is 2:

```
"specialBar.size == 2"
```

In a query filter, if a reference is null, then any subexpression using the reference evaluates to false. For that reason, the check for the null value in the following example is unnecessary:

```
"specialBar != null && specialBar.size == 2"
```

In general, the root terms of a JDO query filter expression or subexpression must be one of the following:

- One of the four keyword literals: null, this, true, or false

- A literal numeric, character, or string value (for example, 42, 3.14, 'c', or "John Smith")

- The name of a persistent field in the candidate class, or of a persistent field reached from these by one or more field access (.) operators (for example, specialBar or specialBar.size)

- A declared variable or parameter or a persistent field reachable from these by one or more field access operators

Parameters and variables are covered in the sections that follow. Literal string values are contained within double quotes that must be escaped within the query filter string, as the preceding examples show. Literal numeric values may be integer or floating point.

The final static members of a class would be a wonderful addition to the list of terms for JDOQL. Although the 1.0 specification allows this feature, it does not require it.

The Operators of JDOQL

The terms of JDOQL can be used to build Boolean expressions using the operators shown in Table 2-1. Most of the operators of the Java language are listed in Table 2-1.

Table 2-1. JDOQL Operators

Operator	Description
==	Equal
!=	Not equal
>	Greater than
<	Less than
>=	Greater than or equal
<=	Less than or equal
&	Boolean AND
&&	Conditional Boolean AND
|	Boolean OR
||	Conditional Boolean OR
!	Boolean NOT
~	Integral bitwise complement
+	Addition or string concatenation
-	Subtraction or unary sign inversion
*	Multiply by
/	Divide by
( )	Explicitly delimit subexpression
(type)	Cast to type
	Field access

The XOR (^) operator is not on the list. Although JDO 1.0 is inconsistent on this point, JDO 1.0.1 does not include the XOR operator.

The semantics of the operators are similar to, but not identical to, their counterparts in the Java language. The equality operators (==, !=) test JDO identity for application data classes and perform the semantic equivalent of the equals method for the supported system classes. The equality operators never test JVM identity. String concatenation (+) occurs only between strings and does not support the *string + primitive* construct of the Java language. Strings can be compared with the ordering operators (<, <=, >, >=). JDO leaves it to the implementation and the datastore to determine whether this is a lexicographic or locale-specific comparison. Whether the string comparisons are case sensitive also depends on the implementation.

The equality operators and the ordering operators accept both numeric primitives and the Number types (Byte, Integer, Float, Double, Long, Short, BigDecimal, BigInteger). For the Number types, the operators use the wrapped value within the object. The equality operators and the logical operators (!, |, ||, &, &&) do the same for boolean and Boolean. The equality and ordering operators perform time-value comparisons between objects of the java.util.Date class. The math operators (+, -, *, /, ~) accept both numeric primitives and the Number types. Arithmetic terms are promoted to compatible types for operations.

As was mentioned earlier, when specialBar is null, the expression

```
specialBar.size == 2
```

throws a NullPointerException in Java, but for the same condition in JDOQL, the expression evaluates to false. In general, when a NullPointerException arises during filter evaluation against a candidate, the innermost expression containing the field operator evaluates to false. The overall filter expression may still evaluate to true, and as a result, the candidate may still be included in the results collection. In this way, JDOQL shields the query execution from the hazards of individual candidates that may have a null reference in the fields that the JDOQL filter navigates.

Beginning with JDO 1.0.1, JDOQL also shields the query evaluation when a ClassCastException arises from using the cast operator. For each candidate where the exception is thrown, the innermost subexpression that gives rise to the exception evaluates to false. The overall filter expression may still evaluate to true, and as a result, the candidate may still be included in the results collection. In essence, the shielded cast operator acts as an instanceof operator in JDOQL, because it evaluates to false if the candidate is not of the right type.

The conditional Boolean operators (&&, ||) ensure that the right term is evaluated only if that evaluation makes a difference in the expression's value, but this feature is not tested by the JDO certification test suite. Because operators with side effects are not present in JDOQL, the conditional Boolean operators are an optimization with no semantic consequences.

Some Java operators are missing in JDOQL. The instanceof operator, the increment and decrement operators, and all of the assignment operators are not part of JDOQL. None of the operators included in JDOQL have side effects. Most of the bitwise operators are excluded, and the new operator is not supported. The array access operator ([ ]) is also missing.

JDO implementations may add other operators to JDOQL. Using these extensions limits the portability of your application between different JDO implementations.

The Query Methods of JDOQL

JDOQL defines four query methods for use within the query filter. Two of the query methods operate on strings, and two operate on collections. Table 2-2 lists the four query methods.

Table 2-2. JDO Query Methods

Query Method	Description
startsWith(String)	Tests if the string begins with the passed string, no wildcards
endsWith(String)	Tests if the string ends with the passed string, no wildcards
contains(Object)	Tests if the collection contains the object
isEmpty()	Tests if the collection is empty

The startsWith query method tests whether a string begins with a particular substring. For example, the following query filter on the candidate class Foo finds the foos whose names begin with "Jo":

```
"name.startsWith(\"Jo\")"
```

The endsWith query method tests whether a string ends with a particular substring. The startsWith method is found in the Java String class, but when startsWith is used in a JDOQL query filter, what it signifies depends on whether the query runs against objects in memory or against an extent in the datastore. If the query runs in memory, then the String class's startsWith method is called. If the query runs in the datastore, then the startsWith method is translated into the semantic equivalent in the datastore's query language. When the startsWith and endsWith methods execute in the datastore, JDO does not define whether they are case sensitive or case insensitive.

If a collection reference is null or if the collection is empty, the isEmpty method evaluates to true and the contains method evaluates to false. The contains query method has a special meaning when used with a variable. The section entitled "The Special Syntax and Semantics of the contains Method" that comes later in this chapter describes the contains query method.

In JDOQL there is no general support for methods, but implementations may support additional nonmutating query methods in JDOQL. By using an implementation-supplied extension, you limit the portability of your application.

A *General Difficulty with Interface Types*

Java interfaces are used to model the common behavior of unrelated classes. Since Java does not support multiple inheritance, an interface handles the need to put a common type on classes that do not share a common implementation. Generally, application data classes are fine-grained objects with only the behavior necessary to access and maintain the integrity of their data fields. As a result, many application data classes are simple classes that do not use application-defined interface types for persistent fields. On the other hand, for those classes that use such fields, be aware that JDOQL imposes limitations.

Although application data classes have persistent fields, interfaces never have persistent fields. The only members of interfaces are methods and static fields. As Chapter 5 explains, static fields are never persistent. To query on a field that is an application-defined interface type, the query filter must cast the field to one of the application data classes that implements the interface. If several application data classes implement the interface, a separate filter clause might be required for each implementing class. Clearly this approach is not modular since the query filter must be changed each time a new class implements the interface.

For these reasons, the use of application-defined interface types in the design of application data classes imposes one of two costs on the application's design. Either the fields of application-defined interface types cannot be used in queries, or the query filter is dependent on the list of application data classes that implement the interface.

Query Variables

Variables are used to refer to the range of objects within an extent. When the query filter uses a variable, it evaluates to true only when there is at least one object in the extent of the variable such that all the subexpressions that use the variable evaluate to true. For example, the following query filter uses the variable someBar:

```
"allMyBars.contains(someBar) && someBar.size == 3"
```

The filter selects a Foo object only when there is at least one Bar object that meets two criteria: the Bar object is a member of the foo's allMyBars collection, and its size is 3. Variables are typically used to navigate collection fields within the query.

In the preceding example, the only Bar objects that need to be considered are the objects that are members of the allMyBars collection field. When the range is limited to the members of a collection field, the variable is a constrained variable. Otherwise, the variable is an unconstrained variable that ranges over the entire extent of the variable's application data class. The distinction is important because JDO implementations are required to support constrained variables, but they are not required to support unconstrained variables.

The application declares variables in the string passed to the declareVariables method. The variable someBar is declared in the following string:

```
"Bar someBar;"
```

The syntax of the variable string is the same as the syntax for local variable declarations in Java with two exceptions: only one variable can be declared for each type declaration, and the trailing semicolon is optional. For example, if the query filter required a Foo variable and a Bar variable, either of the following two variable declaration strings work equally well:

```
"Foo foo; Bar bar;"
"Foo foo; Bar bar"
```

Notice the missing semicolon in the second string.

If two Foo variables are required, then the following declaration string works:

```
"Foo x; Foo y;"
```

On the other hand, the following string would not be accepted, because each variable needs to be matched with its type:

```
"Foo x, y;"
```

All variables for a query must be declared in one variable string. The variable strings do not accumulate.

In most cases, the type of a variable will be an application data class. In any event, a variable type must be a persistence-capable type.

The names of variables must be distinct, and they cannot duplicate parameter names. If a variable name is the same as a field name in the candidate class, it hides the field name, which can still be accessed using the this.fieldname syntax.

Multiple variables may be used in a query. During filter evaluation, there is no requirement that different objects be used for different variables of the same type.

For example, to find all Foo objects that have at least two children, use the following variable declaration:

```
"Foo childA; Foo childB;"
```

and this query filter:

```
"myChildren.contains(childA) && (myChildren.contains(childB) && childA != childB)"
```

Without the inequality expression, the same child could satisfy both the first contains expression and the second contains expression.

Some JDO implementations support unconstrained variables. In this case, the unconstrained variable ranges over the corresponding Extent of its application data class. If the class does not have a corresponding Extent, then the subexpression using the variable always evaluates to false. For example, when the JDO implementation supports unconstrained variables, you can find all the Foo objects that have the same name by declaring the variable

```
"Foo y;"
```

and using this query filter:

```
"name == y.name && this != y"
```

The Special Syntax and Semantics of the contains Method

Informally, a variable is constrained if it is limited to the objects contained in a persistent collection field. Formally, the definition is based on the syntax of the query filter. A variable is constrained if each OR expression that uses the variable also uses a contains query method to limit the variable's range to the members of a collection field. The contains expression must be the left term of an AND expression where the variable is used in the right term. The following query filter, used earlier:

```
"allMyBars.contains(someBar) && someBar.size == 3"
```

satisfies the requirements, but the following filter, which commutes the && operator, does not:

```
"someBar.size == 3 && allMyBars.contains(someBar)"
```

Implementations that require constrained variables accept only the first form of the query.

Other query filters may appear to satisfy the conditions but, in fact, do not. For example, the following filter appears to satisfy the condition:

```
"books.contains(someBook) && someBook.categories.contains(someCat) &&
    someCat.name == \"Travel\""
```

In fact, the conditions for a constrained variable are not met, since the AND operator associates to the left. As a result, the expression

```
 books.contains(someBook) && someBook.categories.contains(someCat)
```

is the left term for the last expression.

```
someCat.name == "Travel"
```

Because the left term is an AND expression instead of the required `contains` expression, JDO implementations that require constrained variables do not accept this query filter.

On the other hand, when parentheses are added as shown in the following example, JDO accepts the query filter because the requirements for a constrained variable are met:

```
"books.contains(someBook) &&
    (someBook.categories.contains(someCat) && someCat.name == \"Travel\")"
```

The Semantics of Constrained Variables

Semantically, a constrained variable is an existence expression. Consider again the example that follows:

```
"allMyBars.contains(someBar) && someBar.size == 3"
```

This JDOQL expression means, "There exists a `someBar` that is a member of `allMyBars` such that `someBar.size` equals 3."

For a practical example of the semantics in action, consider the two `Foo` and four `Bar` objects presented in Table 2-3. The preceding query filter selects every `Foo` object that has at least one `Bar` object of size 3 in its `allMyBars` collection. For the objects in Table 2-3, `foo1` is selected because of `bar2`, and `foo2` is selected because of `bar3`.

Table 2-3. The State of Two Foo and Four Bar Objects

Object	allMyBars	Size
foo1	bar1, bar2	
foo2	bar3, bar4	
bar1		2
bar2		3
bar3		3
bar4		4

The preceding JDOQL expression can be negated as shown in the following expression:

```
"!(allMyBars.contains(someBar) && someBar.size == 3)"
```

In JDO 1.0, there was some confusion on the semantics of this negated query expression. JDO 1.0.1 resolved this confusion. Starting with JDO 1.0.1, this negated expression means, "There does not exist a someBar that is a member of allMyBars such that someBar.size equals 3."

Without delving into the propositional calculus that underlies this logic, you can see intuitively that the following for-each statement is semantically equivalent to the negated existence statement, "For each someBar that is a member of allMyBars, someBar.size is not equal to 3."

Regardless of which semantic statement you prefer, the meaning of the negated query expression is the same. When the query expression is evaluated, foo1 is rejected because of bar2, and foo2 is rejected because of bar3. The query results in this case are empty.

DeMorgan Rules Do Not Apply to Constrained Variables

In Boolean logic, DeMorgan rules allow semantically neutral transformations of some negated Boolean expressions. For example, if A and B are Boolean expressions, then the expressions

!(A && B)

!A || !B

are semantically equivalent, that is to say, either both are true or both are false. The same is the case for the following pair:

!(A || B)

!A && !B

In the case of JDOQL, the expressions that use constrained variables cannot be transformed in either a syntactically or semantically neutral way by the DeMorgan rules. Using DeMorgan's rules, the negated query expression

```
"!(allMyBars.contains(someBar) && someBar.size == 3)"
```

transforms to the following query expression:

```
"!allMyBars.contains(someBar) || !(someBar.size == 3)"
```

The transformed query expression no longer contains a constrained variable, since the syntactic rules discussed earlier for a constrained variable have been broken. As a result, those JDO implementations that do not support unconstrained variables reject this query filter based on its syntax.

For those implementations that support unconstrained variables, the semantics of the transformed filter have also changed. The left side of the OR is true when there is a Bar object anywhere in the extent of Bar objects that is not a member of this Foo object's allMyBars collection. The right side of the OR is true, when there is a Bar object anywhere in the extent of Bar objects whose size is not 3. In the case of the objects in Table 2-3, foo1 is selected because of bar1, bar3, or bar4, and foo2 is selected because of bar1, bar2, or bar4. As you can see, the transformed query filter does not select the Foo objects that the untransformed filter selected.

Because DeMorgan rules fail for JDOQL expressions that use constrained variables, you must take care when constructing complex, and particularly negated, expressions that navigate collections. Fortunately for application developers, complex JDOQL filters are the exception rather than the rule.

Ordering Results

The results are returned in a collection whose order of iteration can be controlled by setting the query's write-only *Ordering* string property. The ordering string consists of one or more ordering clauses separated by commas. Each ordering clause consists of a field expression followed by one of the two keywords ascending or descending. The field expression may be a simple field name of the candidate class, or it may be a compound field name using one or more field access operators. The fields must be persistent, and their types can be any of the following:

- Primitives except `boolean`

- Wrapper types except `Boolean`

- `BigDecimal`

- `BigInteger`

- `String`

- `Date`

Like the other strings that determine the query's behavior, there is only one ordering string for each query.

The ordering clauses are evaluated from left to right. If the clause to the left does not determine the relative ordering of two objects in the results, then the next clause to the right is evaluated, and so on, until either the ordering is determined or all the clauses have been evaluated. A field expression evaluates to null if any of the component field names evaluate to null. When a field expression evaluates to null, it depends on the implementation whether the object containing the null reference comes before or after objects that have values for the field.

Let's look at several examples that illustrate the syntax of the ordering string. Listing 2-2 shows the persistent fields of the `Song` and `Label` application data classes. When `Song` is the candidate class, any of the following strings can be the ordering string:

- "title ascending"

- "label.name descending"

- "label.hometown ascending, title ascending"

In the first case, the results would be in ascending order by the title string, in the second case in descending order by the name of the label, and in the third case, in ascending order by the label's hometown and, within that, in ascending order by the song's title.

Listing 2-2. The Persistent Fields of the Song *and* Label *Classes*

```
public class Song
    {
    private String title;
    private Label  label;
    ...
    }

public class Label
    {
    private String name;
    private String hometown;
    ...
    }
```

Using or Ignoring the Cache in a Query

Each persistence manager controls a cache of persistent application data objects in memory. When a transaction is active, the persistent objects can become transactional. JDO assumes responsibility for the consistency of transactional and persistent objects with the corresponding state in the datastore. If these objects are modified, JDO assumes responsibility for synchronizing their changed state with the datastore before the transaction commits.

When the query ignores the cache, the persistent and transactional objects in the cache are not considered when determining the query results. On the other hand, when the query uses the cache, the modified state in the cache may determine the query results. This modified state includes the state of persistent-dirty, persistent-new, and persistent-deleted objects in the cache.

Consider the Truck objects described in Table 2-4. Before the transaction begins, there are three trucks, T1, T2, and T3, that are all painted red. After the transaction begins, the three trucks are retrieved and loaded into the cache. During the transaction, the T1 truck is deleted. A new T4 truck with the color blue is made persistent, and the color of the T3 truck is changed to blue. (For simplicity, the Truck class represents the truck's color in a String field named, appropriately, color.)

Table 2-4. The Cached State of Red and Blue Trucks Prior to Query Execution

Identity	Color	Management State
T1	Red	Persistent-deleted
T2	Red	Persistent-clean or persistent-nontransactional
T3	Blue	Persistent-dirty (color changed)
T4	Blue	Persistent-new

When the application uses the two query filters

```
"color == \"red\""
"color == \"blue\""
```

which trucks are found? For the first query, if the cache *is not ignored*, then only T2 is found. T1 and T2 are not found because T1 has been deleted and T3's color has changed to blue. On the other hand, if the cache *is ignored*, then T1, T2, and T3 are found, because the changes in memory do not affect the query results. The second query has a similar story. If the cache is not ignored, then T3 and T4 are found; otherwise, no blue trucks are found.

The query inherits the value of its *IgnoreCache* property from the persistence manager that produced it. When the query's *IgnoreCache* property is false, it determines the query's behavior, but when it is true, it is only a hint. When the query ignores the cache, the specification does not make it clear whether JDO is guaranteeing to ignore all the changes or only so many of them as is convenient. On the other hand, if the query is directed to not ignore the cache, then the query must consider all the changes in the cache that could affect the query's results.

The setting of the *IgnoreCache* flag affects query results only when three conditions are met. First, the transaction for the query's persistence manager must be active. When the transaction is not active, there are no persistent-new, persistent-deleted, or persistent-dirty objects in the cache. Second, the query must run in the datastore. If the query runs in memory, then the uniqueness requirement ensures that cached objects are used. Third, some persistent objects must have been added, deleted, or modified in the transaction. Setting the *IgnoreCache* flag to true or false never alters the query results unless these three conditions are met.

Applications use the *IgnoreCache* flag to trade off accuracy in the query results for better performance. To understand how the *IgnoreCache* flag may affect performance, it is helpful to consider some implementation details. By flushing the changes in the cache to the datastore before sending the query to the datastore, the JDO implementation ensures that the query results reflect the changes in memory. (There may be other ways to accomplish the same objective, but this is the obvious way to do it.)

Although flushing before the query is extra work, it is more work in some cases than in others. In a datastore transaction, the flush needs to occur only once for each modification. Because a datastore transaction keeps the database transaction open, the work done in the flush is not lost, and the flush would have to occur anyway when the transaction commits. On the other hand, in an optimistic transaction, the same modifications might be flushed more than once. Since an optimistic transaction prefers to close the database transaction as soon as possible, the same modifications might be flushed for every query execution.

As a general rule then, the time to consider setting the query's *IgnoreCache* flag to true is when the application executes queries in optimistic transactions after modifications have been made. If this situation is avoided, then the recommended action is to set the flag to false.

SQL Queries That Can Be Mapped to JDOQL

If you are familiar with SQL, you may find it helpful to examine the JDOQL queries that correspond to a representative sample of SQL queries. The examples in this section use four application data classes that provide a simple model of a small town library.

The persistent object model for the small library is presented in Figure 2-3. The Library application in the JDO Learning Tools uses these classes. The Library application is designed to explore JDOQL. Chapter 8 discusses the JDO Learning Tools.

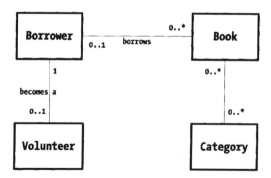

Figure 2-3. Object model for a simple library

Books and borrowers are two important classes in the library's persistent object model. A borrower can borrow from zero to any number of books. Each book is either borrowed or not borrowed. Books are categorized by subject. A book may fall into one or more categories, and each category may have any number of books. Finally, since this is a small town library, volunteers are important to the institution. A volunteer is always a borrower, but not all borrowers are volunteers. Although inheritance might model the relationship between volunteer and borrower, composition is a better approach because borrowers can both become and cease to be volunteers.

The outline of the application data classes is contained in Listing 2-3. All the listed fields are declared persistent in the JDO metadata. The examples of JDOQL query filters that follow use these persistent fields.

Listing 2-3. The Persistent Fields of the Library Classes

```
public class Borrower
   {
   // each of the fields below is a persistent field
   private String name;
   private HashSet books;  // borrowed books
   private Volunteer volunteer;
   ...
   }


public class Volunteer
   {
   // each of the fields below is a persistent field
   private int hoursPerWeek;
   private Borrower borrower;
   ...
   }


public class Book
   {
   // each of the fields below is a persistent field
   private Date checkOutDate;
   private String title;
   private Borrower borrower;
   private HashSet categories; // book's categories
   ...
   }
```

```
public class Category
    {
    // each of the fields below is a persistent field
    private String name;
    private HashSet books; // books in this category
    ...
    }
```

 NOTE You might want to bookmark Listing 2-3, as the library classes are used for most of the remaining examples in this chapter.

The four classes are mapped to the relational tables BORROWER, VOLUNTEER, BOOK, and CATEGORY. The many-to-many relationship uses the cross-reference table CATEGORY_BOOK. Listing 2-4 describes the column structure of these tables. The proposed mapping of the application data classes to the relational tables is straightforward, but it is not the only possible mapping. Each JDO implementation for relational databases determines the mappings that it will use. The SQL queries that follow use the columns in these tables.

Listing 2-4. The Relational Tables for the Library Classes

```
Table BORROWER

    INTEGER BORROWER_ID (PK)
    VARCHAR(80) NAME

Table VOLUNTEER:

    INTEGER VOLUNTEER_ID (PK)
    INTEGER BORROWER_ID (FK)
    INTEGER HOURS_PER_WEEK

Table BOOK

    INTEGER BOOK_ID (PK)
    VARCHAR(80) TITLE
    DATE CHECKOUT
    INTEGER BORROWER_ID (FK)
```

```
Table CATEGORY

    INTEGER CATEGORY_ID (PK)
    VARCHAR(80) NAME

Table CATEGORY_BOOK

    INTEGER CATEGORY_ID (FK)
    INTEGER BOOK_ID  (FK)
```

Select on One Table

The ability to select on one table for some criteria is straightforward both in SQL and in JDOQL. For example, to select books with the title *Gone Fishing*, the following SQL query works:

```
select book_id,checkout,title,borrower_id from book where title = 'Gone Fishing'
```

Using Book as the candidate class, the corresponding JDOQL query is the following expression:

```
"title == \"Gone Fishing\""
```

The results collection contains only books entitled *Gone Fishing*. If the library doesn't carry this title, the collection is empty.

Select on Join Using One-to-One Relationship

The ability in SQL to join on a one-to-one relationship has its counterpart in JDOQL. If the purpose of the query is to determine whether any volunteers are named Tom, then the following SQL query does the job:

```
select A.volunteer_id, B.name from volunteer A, borrower B
    where A.borrower_id = B.borrower_id and B.name = 'Tom'
```

Using the candidate class Volunteer, the equivalent JDOQL query is the following expression:

```
"borrower.name == \"Tom\""
```

As this example shows, navigating a field in JDOQL may translate to joining two tables in SQL.

Although SQL can bring back pieces of information from many tables, a JDO query brings back only objects that are assignment compatible with the candidate class. To get related objects, the application must navigate the field references within the returned objects. JDO provides transparently the mechanism to support the navigation, but this mechanism may generate more queries (in this case SQL queries) against the datastore service.

Select on Join Using One-to-Many Relationship

The ability of SQL to query based on a one-to-many relationship has its counterpart in JDOQL. If the query were to find all the books that Tom borrowed, then SQL could express it as follows:

```
select A.book_id, A.title, A.checkout from book A, borrower B
   where A.borrower_id = B.borrower_id and b.name = 'Tom'
```

Using the candidate class Book, the corresponding query filter string in JDOQL is the following expression:

```
"borrower.name = \"Tom\""
```

As in the previous example, JDOQL navigates where SQL typically joins.

Select on Join Using Many-to-Many Relationship

SQL provides the ability to join on a many-to-many relationship using the cross-reference table CATEGORY_BOOK. To determine the categories of books that interest Tom at the present time, the SQL query could be the following:

```
select distinct A.category_id, A.name
   from category A, book B, borrower C, book_category D
   where A.category_id = D.category_id
      and B.book_id = D.book_id
      and B.borrower_id = C.borrower_id
      and C.name = 'Tom'
```

Using the candidate class Category and the variable declaration string:

```
"Book someBook;"
```

the corresponding query filter in JDOQL is the following expression:

```
"books.contains(someBook) && someBook.borrower.name == \"Tom\""
```

As you can see, this query filter navigates a collection field using a constrained variable.

As this example shows, the JDO query string is usually simpler than its SQL counterpart. This simplicity applies only for the application programmer. The JDO implementation still runs the complex SQL query to pull the information from the relational database.

Select on Self-Join

Sometimes, to express a query in SQL, a table must be joined to itself. For example, to find books for which there are multiple copies, the SQL query uses a self-join.

```
select distinct A.book_id, A.title from book A, book B
   where A.book_id <> B.book_id and A.title = B.title
```

Using Book as the candidate class, the same query is expressed by using an unconstrained variable. After declaring the variable string

```
"Book x;"
```

the variable x is used in the following query filter:

```
"title = x.title && this != x"
```

The query variable x is unconstrained because the filter does not use the contains query method. When unconstrained, a variable ranges over the extent of its corresponding application data class. In this case, the query filter yields all the books where there are multiple copies.

As mentioned earlier, not all JDO implementations support unconstrained variables. As a result, this query filter is not portable. To achieve the same end when the JDO implementation does not support unconstrained variables, the application can query for all books and order the results by title. The application then iterates the ordered results collection to find duplicate copies. Usually this workaround does not have the efficiency of a self-join.

Select on Outer Join

Sometimes in SQL, there is a need to pull information from a join but not limit the rows selected to just those that have a match on the joined attribute. The following example finds all borrowers named Tom and the hours that they volunteer. Some borrowers named Tom are volunteers and others are not, but the result must list all borrowers who are named Tom. This situation calls for an outer join. In Oracle syntax, it is expressed as follows:

```
select A.borrower_id, A.name, B.hours_per_week
   from borrower A, volunteer B
   where A.name = 'Tom' and B.borrower_id (+) = A.borrower_id
```

In JDOQL, the corresponding query uses Borrower as the candidate class and uses the following query filter:

```
"name == \"Tom\""
```

The results collection contains all borrowers who are named Tom. Of this lot, those who are volunteers have a reference in the volunteer field from which the hours can be obtained.

Select Using Subquery

Occasionally, the desired query would call for the use of a subquery in SQL. For example, to find all the borrowers who do not have any books outstanding requires selecting the borrowers whose id is not contained in the borrower_id foreign key field of the BOOK table. The following SQL query performs this work:

```
select borrower_id, name from borrower
   where borrower_id not in (
      select distinct borrower_id from book where borrower_id is not null)
```

Using Borrower as the candidate class, the corresponding JDOQL query uses the query method isEmpty on the collection of books that the borrower has borrowed, as shown in the following query filter:

```
"books.isEmpty()"
```

Simplicity Is the Power in JDOQL

As the preceding examples illustrate, JDOQL never leaves the persistent object model. The persistent fields of the application data classes provide the basic terms for the query expressions. Rather than a limitation, the simplicity of JDOQL is a strength. As the examples show, JDOQL can express in a simple manner many complex queries that are based on the relational data model.

The examples show the power of JDOQL and transparent navigation to simplify the application programmer's work. As the object model becomes more complex, SQL queries rapidly become more complex. It is simpler to express the relationships between objects in JDOQL than in SQL because the JDOQL query needs fewer terms. JDOQL queries are easier for a Java programmer to write and understand than SQL queries because the query filter uses the member fields of the application data classes.

At the same time, without transparent navigation, the Java code that executes the SQL query must execute additional queries to build up the object graph that flows from the initial objects of interest. With JDO, the additional queries to navigate the object graph are not coding tasks for the application programmer. The implementation provides these queries transparently. All in all, JDO greatly reduces the number and complexity of the queries that the application programmer writes.

Using SQL When JDOQL Is Not Sufficient

Although many SQL queries have their counterparts in JDOQL, there are some SQL queries that JDOQL cannot express. For example, SQL can perform operations on the returned result set. The group by clause and operators like min, max, and avg are cases in point. A JDO query cannot return the information that these SQL queries return. Instead, JDO requires a workaround. For example, the results collection can be processed in memory. In general, any SQL query that is designed to return something other than the state of individual objects does not have a counterpart in JDOQL.

JDO allows the implementation to provide access to the native query interface and language of the datastore. The following factory method in the persistence manager is the gateway to the alternate query language and interface:

```
newQuery(String language, Object implDependentObject)
```

Some vendors with object-to-relational implementations are using this method to support SQL queries.

How JDO and JDOQL Help the Development Process

With the usual JDBC/SQL development tools, the development team creates both the data model and the persistent object model. The need to develop two models can be an obstacle because those developers with the most experience in data model design often have little experience in object model design, and vice versa. Many accomplished Java programmers do not have a complete understanding of SQL and relational database theory, let alone a mastery of the quirks of one particular database. Few people who are masters of relational databases and relational data modeling are competent in Java.

When the development team uses an object-to-relational JDO implementation, the team can pick either the data model or the persistent object model as the primary model and use the tools supplied by the JDO implementation to generate the other model. JDO implementations vary a great deal in the modeling tools supplied. JDO does not specify what the tools should be, but vendors support at least one, and possibly more, of three approaches:

- Persistent object model primary, data model generated

- Data model primary, persistent object model generated

- An ability to iterate from both to a meeting in the middle

The tools help bridge the skill gap between relational data modelers and Java object modelers. They remove the requirement that one or two people must understand completely both modeling methodologies. If the data model is created first, then the Java programmer, using the tool, can create the persistent object model that flows from the data model without understanding all of the data model's nuances. Likewise, if the persistent object model is created first, the database designer, using the appropriate tool, can create the supporting data model without understanding all of the nuances of the persistent object model. In the beginning, the tools will be simple, and people of both skill sets will work together to build the models. As the tools evolve, they hold the potential to completely disentangle data storage concerns from application development concerns.

After the persistent object model is generated, the Java programmer who builds the application using JDO completely ignores the data model. All queries and data manipulations occur either through JDO, JDOQL, or the persistent objects themselves. JDO's focus on the persistent object model brings clarity of thought and ease of communication to the development process.

JDO's focus on the persistent object model also brings regimentation. When using JDBC and SQL, the developers have the opportunity to adopt *ad hoc* access to the database and to hack around the persistent object model. When requirements are discovered late in development, the temptation to hack a solution in JDBC is strong. In contrast, JDO will force the programmers to revise the persistent object model. Revising the object model is a more robust solution. JDO requires the better solution, and it makes the better solution easier to implement as well.

Summary

Queries are very important for applications that use persistent storage. In JDO, the Query interface retrieves results based on criteria expressed in JDOQL. The syntax of JDOQL is simple. It is similar to Java and uses the field names of the application data classes in its query terms. Although less powerful than SQL, JDO can express most search criteria.

JDO hides the query interface and query language of the datastore. When an application programmer uses JDBC, he is bilingually working simultaneously with Java and with SQL. He also works with two state models, the persistent object model expressed in the Java code and the data model expressed in the relational schema. When working with JDBC, the application programmer must translate between the two models and the two languages. On the other hand, when working with JDO, the programmer works with two dialects of the same language, Java and JDOQL. When coding, the only model that he needs to consider is the object model. By focusing exclusively on the persistent object model, JDO's query service helps application programmers achieve clarity of design and simplicity of code.

The query service is an important exposed component of JDO's persistence service. Many of the other exposed services of JDO are found in the PersistenceManager interface. The next chapter describes the properties and operations of this interface.

CHAPTER 3
The Persistence Manager

CHAPTER 1 DESCRIBES, in general terms, the implicit and explicit persistence services that JDO provides. The application does not take any special steps to invoke the implicit services. JDO provides them automatically and transparently to all objects whose classes implement the PersistenceCapable interface. On the other hand, to invoke the explicit services, the application calls the JDO API at the appropriate points in its code. Most of the explicit persistence services are contained in the PersistenceManager interface. Those related to transactions are found in the Transaction interface. This chapter discusses the PersistenceManager interface. Chapter 4 describes the Transaction interface.

The persistence manager acts on application data objects. As a result of enhancement, the application data classes implement the PersistenceCapable interface. Passing an object that does not implement the PersistenceCapable interface to a method in the persistence manager will likely cause a ClassCastException. In all cases, the persistence manager performs useful actions only on application data objects.

If the object passed to a persistence manager's operation is controlled by a different persistence manager, the operation throws a JDOUserException.

Figure 3-1 presents the UML class diagram for the PersistenceManager interface. This is the largest class diagram in JDO, with five groups of operations and five properties. This chapter examines the methods that define the operations and the properties.

As Figure 3-1 indicates, there are five groups of operations in the PersistenceManager interface. Because the JDO implementations can, and usually will, implement pooling of persistence managers and the datastore connections that they use, it is efficient for applications to frequently obtain and close persistence managers. Using a persistence manager, the application can control the life cycle and caching of application data objects. It can get the identity object for a persistent application data object, and it can later fetch the persistent object that corresponds to an identity object. Finally, the PersistenceManager interface has factory methods that return Query, Extent, and Transaction objects.

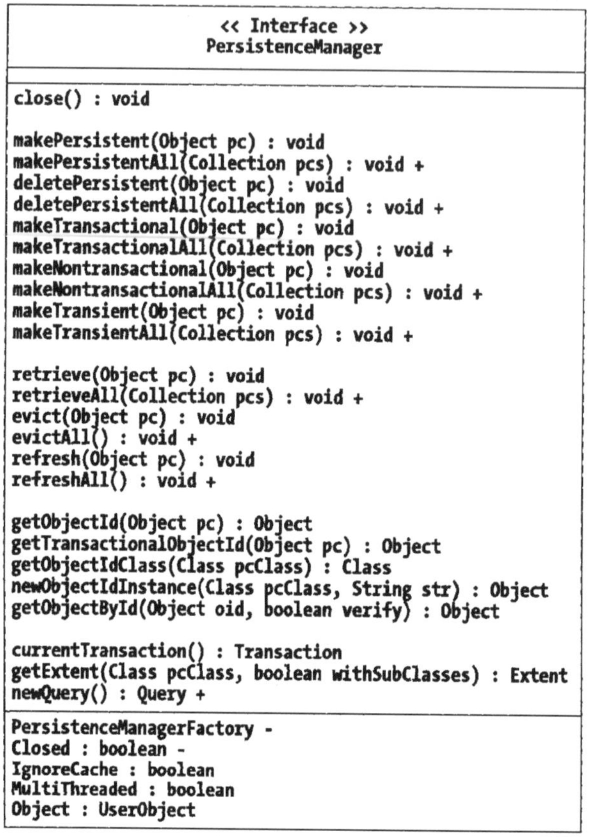

```
                   << Interface >>
                   PersistenceManager

close() : void

makePersistent(Object pc) : void
makePersistentAll(Collection pcs) : void +
deletePersistent(Object pc) : void
deletePersistentAll(Collection pcs) : void +
makeTransactional(Object pc) : void
makeTransactionalAll(Collection pcs) : void +
makeNontransactional(Object pc) : void
makeNontransactionalAll(Collection pcs) : void +
makeTransient(Object pc) : void
makeTransientAll(Collection pcs) : void +

retrieve(Object pc) : void
retrieveAll(Collection pcs) : void +
evict(Object pc) : void
evictAll() : void +
refresh(Object pc) : void
refreshAll() : void +

getObjectId(Object pc) : Object
getTransactionalObjectId(Object pc) : Object
getObjectIdClass(Class pcClass) : Class
newObjectIdInstance(Class pcClass, String str) : Object
getObjectById(Object oid, boolean verify) : Object

currentTransaction() : Transaction
getExtent(Class pcClass, boolean withSubClasses) : Extent
newQuery() : Query +

PersistenceManagerFactory -
Closed : boolean -
IgnoreCache : boolean
MultiThreaded : boolean
Object : UserObject
```

Figure 3-1. The class diagram of the PersistenceManager *interface*

The Handling of null Values in Method Parameters

Some methods of the PersistenceManager interface take parameters of the following types:

- Object

- Object[]

- Collection

When a null value is passed for a Collection or Object array parameter, the method throws a NullPointerException. When a null is passed as the value of an Object parameter, the method invocation is a no-operation (no-op) that returns silently and returns a null if it has a reference return type. When a null is passed as the value of one of the elements of an `Object` array or `Collection` parameter, then that element is ignored. The non-null values of the `Object` array or `Collection` parameter are processed normally.

Obtaining and Closing a Persistence Manager

Chapter 6 describes how to get a `PersistenceManager` object from the factory methods in the `PersistenceManagerFactory` interface and the `javax.resource.cci.ConnectionFactory` interface. When the factory method returns a persistence manager, the persistence manager is open for business. It remains open until it is closed.

Closing a Persistence Manager

The `PersistenceManager` interface provides one method to close the persistence manager.

```
public void close()
```

Depending on the design of the application and the environment in which it is deployed, a persistence manager may be a short-lived or long-lived object. After the application has finished using the persistence manager, it should recycle the resources consumed by the persistence manager by calling the `close` method. When the application closes the persistence manager, it should no longer use the persistence manager or any of the persistent objects that it managed.

Sometimes the application code that uses JDO executes inside an Enterprise JavaBean (EJB) that uses container-managed transactions. In this case, making multiple calls within the same client invocation of the bean to get a persistence manager from a factory method yields multiple references to the same persistence manager. In this environment, the persistence manager is not actually closed until the container completes the open transaction. The application code should be written, however, with the last step of each business method calling the persistence manager's `close` method. Chapter 6 describes the appropriate designs for using JDO inside various types of EJBs.

On the other hand, when there isn't any container managing transactions, the application code should end the transaction before closing the persistence manager. As JDO 1.0.1 makes clear, when a container is not managing transactions, the `close` method throws a `JDOUserException` if the transaction is active. Chapter 4 describes the `Transaction` interface.

It is very important that the application take care to clean up references to persistent application data objects before closing the persistence manager. JDO does not define the behavior of application data objects that are managed at the time that the persistence manager closes. They may become unmanaged application data objects. They may be recycled in an instance pool controlled by the JDO implementation. The JDO implementation may mark them so that touching them results in a JDOException. Whatever the behavior is, it is likely to cause confusion or errors for your application.

The Read-Only Closed Property

The PersistenceManager interface provides a getter method for the *Closed* property.

```
public boolean isClosed()
```

Once the persistence manager is closed, the persistence manager's *Closed* property is true. After the persistence manager is closed, this is its only method that does not throw a JDOFatalUserException. Likewise, the Transaction object, Query objects, Extent objects, and Iterator objects obtained from query results collections or extents cannot be used, and any attempt to do so throws a JDOFatalUserException. After closing the persistence manager, the application should avoid using any persistent or transactional objects that the closed persistence manager controlled. Any data objects that are unmanaged when the persistence manager closes are not affected by the closing.

The Read-Only PersistenceManagerFactory Property

The PersistenceManager interface provides a better method for the *PersistenceManagerFactory* property.

```
public PersistenceManagerFactory getPersistenceManagerFactory()
```

This method returns a reference to the factory that produced the persistence manager. It returns a reference to a PersistenceManagerFactory object even when the persistence manager was obtained from a ConnectionFactory.

Controlling JDO's Management of Data Objects

As Figure 3-1 shows, the persistence manager has a group of ten operations that control how JDO directly manages application data objects and indirectly manages the embedded objects that the application data objects refer to. These operations, when they have any effect, immediately modify the management state of the application data object.

The Behavior of the xxxAll Operations

There are five operations in this group that end in "All". Each of them, as indicated by the plus sign next to their entry in Figure 3-1, has more than one method signature. Some methods take a Collection of application data objects, and some take an array of application data objects. The behavior of the xxxAll operation, where xxx is makePersistent, deletePersistent, and so on, derives from the behavior of the corresponding xxx operation and two simple rules:

- The xxxAll methods perform the xxx operation on each of the elements of the collection or array.

- When the xxx operation is performed on one of the elements of the collection or array and an exception is thrown, this exception is collected and nested within a JDOUserException that is thrown when the xxxAll method has completed work on every element of the collection or array. Each nested JDOUserException contains a reference to the object that gave rise to that exception.

Consequently, the failure of the xxx operation on one or more elements of a collection or array does not prevent success with the other elements of the collection or array. Chapter 7 describes the exception types of JDO.

Making and Deleting Persistent Objects

The two operations makePersistent and deletePersistent add and delete objects from the datastore. The makePersistent operation turns a transient application data object into a persistent-new object and causes a later insertion of the object's persistent state into the datastore. The deletePersistent operation makes a persistent application data object persistent-deleted and causes a later deletion of the corresponding existing persistent state from the datastore. JDO is free to perform the insertion or deletion of the persistent state when it chooses, but it cannot commit the changes to the datastore until the JDO transaction commits. When the application calls makePersistent or deletePersistent, the persistence manager's transaction must be active; otherwise, a JDOUserException is thrown.

Making Transient Objects Persistent

The `PersistenceManager` interface provides three methods to make transient
objects persistent.

```
public void makePersistent(Object adObject)
public void makePersistentAll(Collection adObjects)
public void makePersistentAll(Object[] adObjects)
```

The `makePersistent` methods always link the transient application data object
to a *new* object state in the datastore. JDO does not provide a way for the application to say, "Here is a transient object, connect it to a *preexisting* object state in
the database." To apply changes held in a transient object to a preexisting persistent
state, the application must find the persistent object that refers to this state and
then apply to the persistent object the updates indicated by the state of the transient object.

NOTE   Given an unmanaged application data object, an application
can find the corresponding existing persistent state by using the object's
durable JDO identity. If the application data class uses application
identity, and if it requires that all application data objects of this class
be constructed with valid key fields, then the application can construct
the application identity object using the values of the key fields. If the
application data class uses datastore identity, then the application
must capture the identity object or its identity string before the application data object becomes unmanaged. See the section "Capturing the
Identity String" in Chapter 7 for more details.

When the object is made persistent, a new JDO identity object is created for it.
If the object uses datastore JDO identity, then JDO creates the identity value for it. If
the object uses application identity, then the identity value is pulled from the key
fields of the application data object. If there is another application data object in the
persistence manager's cache with an equivalent JDO identity, then `makePersistent`
throws a `JDOUserException`. Otherwise, if an object already exists in the datastore
with the same identity value, then the datastore insert throws a `JDOUserException`
upon transaction commit. The JDO implementation is responsible for avoiding
duplicate use of datastore identity values, while the application is responsible for
avoiding duplicate use of application identity values. In most cases, JDO configures
the datastore to require unique identity values.

NOTE The key fields of application identity are contained in the application data class and in the application identity class. See Chapter 1 for a fuller discussion of application identity. See Chapter 5 for a discussion of the JDO metadata.

If the application data object is in any of the following three transient states when it is passed to the makePersistent method, it becomes persistent-new:

- JDO-transient

- Transient-clean

- Transient-dirty

When an object becomes persistent-new, JDO may save a before-image of the object for use in the event of rollback. The before-image contains the in-memory state of all managed fields. The *RestoreValues* property in the Transaction interface determines whether JDO saves the before-image and restores it in the event of rollback. In the case of objects that were transient-dirty, JDO will have already saved a before-image when the object became dirty, if *RestoreValues* is true. Otherwise, JDO saves the current state of the transient object when it becomes persistent-new, if *RestoreValues* is true. Chapter 4 describes the Transaction interface and its properties.

Passing an application data object in any of the seven persistent states to the makePersistent methods is a no-op for that object.

After makePersistent is called, the transient application data object becomes persistent-new. At the same time, JDO's persistence-by-reachability algorithm executes and makes persistent-new all transient application data objects that are reachable from the newly made persistent object. The state change for reachable objects is provisional. When the transaction commits, the reachability algorithm executes again, and any provisionally persistent-new application data objects that are not reachable revert to JDO-transient. Upon transaction commit, the persistent-new object's state is inserted into the database, and the object remains persistent but nontransactional. If the transaction is rolled back, the object management state reverts to JDO-transient, and when *RestoreValues* is true, the object is restored to the state saved in its before-image.

> **NOTE**   Persistence by reachability, as explained in Chapter 1, is one of the elements of JDO's transparent persistence. To determine the objects that it can reach, JDO traverses the object graph starting with a root persistent object and tracing all of the data objects that can be found by following the persistent fields that have references. Implementations can be expected to optimize the reachability algorithm so that the tracing is not done by brute force.

When a data object is made persistent, either because it is explicitly passed to the `makePersistent` method or because it is made persistent implicitly as a result of persistence by reachability, JDO replaces the objects referred to by persistent fields of the supported mutable system types, such as `Date` and `HashSet`, with the implementation-supplied subclasses that support change tracking. The new objects are equivalent in value.

Deleting Persistent Objects

The `PersistenceManagerInterface` provides three methods to delete persistent application data objects.

```
public void deletePersistent(Object adObject)
public void deletePersistentAll(Collection adObjects)
public void deletePersistentAll(Object[] adObjects)
```

The `deletePersistent` operation either causes a preexisting persistent object to be removed from the datastore or prevents a newly made persistent object from being inserted into the datastore. After the call to `deletePersistent`, the persistent application data object is still persistent and in one of two management states, persistent-new-deleted or persistent-deleted. After the call to `deletePersistent`, the application can still read the primary key fields of the application data object, if it uses application identity, but any access to managed, non-key fields throws a `JDOUserException`.

When the transaction commits, the preexisting persistent state of a persistent-deleted object is removed from the datastore. Since there is no preexisting persistent state for a persistent-new-deleted object, there is nothing to remove from the datastore. After the transaction commits, the deleted application data object becomes JDO-transient.

When an application data object is deleted, any embedded objects that it refers to are also deleted. In general, JDO does not automatically delete the application data objects that the deleted object refers to. JDO does not specify deletion by reachability. JDO implementations may provide a way to define a cascading delete, but no such behavior is specified by JDO. Applications themselves can provide cascading deletes by implementing further delete operations in the jdoPreDelete callback method. See the discussion in "The InstanceCallbacks Interface" in Chapter 7 for more information.

If the transaction is rolled back, a persistent-new-deleted object becomes transient, and a persistent-deleted object becomes either hollow or persistent-nontransactional, depending on the value of the transaction's *RestoreValues* property. This property is discussed in Chapter 4.

The deletePersistent method works only on persistent objects. Passing transient or unmanaged objects to the method causes it to throw a JDOUserException.

Adding Objects to and Removing Them from Transactions

The two operations makeTransactional and makeNontransactional add and remove application data objects from the current transaction. As a general rule, JDO's transparent persistence implicitly makes objects transactional when they are read or modified and makes them nontransactional when the transaction ends. As a result, the application needs the makeTransactional and makeNontransactional operations only in special cases.

One case where these two methods are useful is to force a check of the concurrency value for persistent objects that are read, but not modified, within an optimistic transaction. Within an optimistic transaction, reading a managed field does not make the object transactional, as it does in a datastore transaction. When the optimistic transaction commits, the concurrency values of all transactional objects are checked against the value in the datastore. To force JDO to check the concurrency value of persistent objects that the application has not modified, the application must call makeTransactional to make the unmodified objects persistent-clean and therefore transactional. Within an optimistic transaction, this change does not refresh the persistent state of the affected object. The makeNontransactional method allows the application to make the persistent-clean object persistent-nontransactional again and thereby remove it from the concurrency value check at transaction commit.

 NOTE Chapter 4 describes the two types of transactions within JDO, optimistic and datastore. JDO does not specify how to implement optimistic transactions. Implementations might choose version numbers, timestamps, or some other technique.

The second case where the `makeTransactional` and `makeNontransactional` methods are useful is to permit the use of transient and transactional application data objects. Those JDO implementations that support the `javax.jdo.option.TransientTransactional` implementation option support two transient and transactional management states, transient-clean and transient-dirty. Both are transactional states. As a result of this optional feature, when the transient-clean application data object becomes dirty and the transaction's *RestoreValues* property is turned on, JDO saves for rollback the before-image of its managed fields. When the transaction commits, JDO discards any saved before-image. The values of fields in transient-clean and transient-dirty objects are never modified as the result of a commit, and of course, no persistent state is changed in the datastore. Practical uses for transient and transactional application data objects are likely to be highly specialized.

Making Objects Transactional

The `PersistenceManager` interface provides three methods to make nontransactional objects transactional.

```
public void makeTransactional(Object adObject)
public void makeTransactionalAll(Collection adObjects)
public void makeTransactionalAll(Object[] adObjects)
```

When successful, these methods associate the application data objects with the persistence manager's transaction. Seven of the ten JDO management states are transactional. Passing a transactional object to the `makeTransactional` operation is a no-op for that object.

Passing either a hollow or persistent-nontransactional object to `makeTransactional` succeeds only when the transaction is active. If the transaction is not active, the call throws a `JDOUserException`. When successful, the affected objects become persistent-clean.

NOTE In JDO, each `PersistenceManager` object is associated with one `Transaction` object. The transaction may be active or inactive. Chapter 4 describes the `Transaction` interface.

In a datastore transaction, it is not necessary to call `makeTransactional` for either a hollow or a persistent-nontransactional object, since any read of a managed, non-key field makes the object persistent-clean. Passing a hollow or persistent-nontransactional object to `makeTransactional` also causes the object to become persistent-clean. If it was persistent-nontransactional before the call, its persistent state in memory is discarded. Fresh values for persistent fields are loaded from the datastore when needed.

In an optimistic transaction, JDO does not make a hollow or persistent-nontransactional object persistent-clean when a persistent field is read. Instead, JDO makes the object persistent-nontransactional, if it isn't already so. In an optimistic transaction, the call to makeTransactional forces the object, whether hollow or persistent-nontransactional, to become persistent-clean. In the case of persistent-nontransactional objects, the change to persistent-clean does not discard the persistent state in memory. In an optimistic transaction, persistent state is never discarded unless the application invokes refresh or evict to do so, or unless the transaction has been configured through the *RetainValues* and *RestoreValues* properties to do so at transaction completion. A value for a persistent field is loaded from the datastore only when it is not already cached in memory. Later, when the transaction commits, the concurrency values of all transactional objects are checked against the corresponding values in the datastore.

When the application data object passed to makeTransactional is JDO-transient and the implementation supports the two transient and transactional management states, then the call to makeTransactional succeeds whether a transaction is active or not. When a transaction is not active, the object remains in the transient-clean state even when its managed state is changed. Once a transaction becomes active, the transient-clean state changes to transient-dirty when a managed field is changed.

Making Transactional Objects Nontransactional

The PersistenceManager interface provides three methods to make transactional objects nontransactional.

```
public void makeNontransactional(Object adObject)
public void makeNontransactionalAll(Collection adObjects)
public void makeNontransactionalAll(Object[] adObjects)
```

These methods undo the action of the makeTransactional methods. In other words, they disassociate the objects from the persistence manager's transaction. For example, passing a persistent-clean object to the makeNontransactional method, when an optimistic transaction is active, causes the object to become persistent-nontransactional again. As a consequence, its concurrency value is not checked during transaction commit. Likewise, passing a transient-clean object to the makeNontransactional operation returns the object to a JDO-transient state. As a consequence, the object no longer interacts with transactions.

Passing a persistent-clean object to the makeNontransactional operation within a datastore transaction makes the object persistent-nontransactional, with one notable exception. If the JDO implementation does not support the *NontransactionalRead* implementation option, the call to makeNontransactional throws a JDOUnsupportedOptionException. Although the persistent-clean object becomes persistent-nontransactional, JDO may continue to hold locks on the persistent state in the datastore until the transaction ends.

 NOTE JDO specifies many optional features for JDO implementations. The features that an implementation supports can be determined from the string returned from the supportedOptions method in the PersistenceManagerFactory interface. Chapter 6 describes this interface and the various options.

Five of the JDO states are transactional and dirty states:

- Persistent-new

- Persistent-new-deleted

- Persistent-deleted

- Persistent-dirty

- Transient-dirty

The makeNontransactional methods throw a JDOUserException when passed an object in one of the dirty states. It also throws a JDOUserException when the passed object is JDO-transient.

If the application data object passed to the makeNontransactional methods is in either the hollow or persistent-nontransactional state, then the call is a no-op for that object.

Removing Persistent Objects from JDO's Management

The PersistenceManager interface provides three methods to remove persistent application data objects from JDO's management.

```
public void makeTransient(Object adObject)
public void makeTransientAll(Collection adObjects)
public void makeTransientAll(Object[] adObjects)
```

These methods disconnect a persistent application data object from JDO's management and put it into the JDO-transient management state. They affect only the object in memory. They do not affect the persistent state in the datastore. The application can use a durable JDO identity or a query to find the persistent state in the datastore again. When this happens, JDO constructs another persistent object in memory.

Making a persistent object JDO-transient is a one-way operation. There is no equivalent reverse operation because there is no way to wire up a transient object in memory to a preexisting state in the datastore.

These methods have a few gotchas. To begin with, if another persistent and transactional object refers, by means of a persistent field, to the newly made transient object, then persistence by reachability makes the transient object persistent again when the transaction commits. This action is probably not what the application intends, since the implicit makePersistent action attempts to insert a new object state into the datastore. The solution for the application is to make transient all persistent objects that refer to the newly made transient object. Another solution is to change the references in the persistent objects so that they no longer refer to the newly made transient object.

Likewise, when a persistent object is made JDO-transient, any of its persistent fields may still hold references to other persistent objects. The call to makeTransient for an application data object does not make the objects that it refers to JDO-transient as well. When the application finds it necessary to prevent the newly made JDO-transient object from referring to persistent objects, the application must either change the references or make the objects referred to transient as well.

As mentioned earlier, the makeTransient methods do not affect the state stored in the datastore. As a consequence, making a persistent object JDO-transient when it lives in the middle of an object graph of persistent references may introduce some unexpected and unpredictable behavior in relationships. Consider the following example. Objects **A** and **B** are instances of the Person class, which has a persistent field dog that refers to an object of the Dog class. Suppose that persons **A** and **B** both own the same dog **D** and that the states of these three objects are stored in the datastore. The application finds person **A** and gets a reference to the dog **D** through **A**. The application next makes the dog **D** transient. Now the application finds person **B** and gets a reference to the dog through **B**. Does the reference obtained from **A** refer to the same object in memory as the reference obtained from **B**? The answer depends on what objects and references were cached prior to these actions. If the application data objects **A**, **B**, and **D** were all in the cache, and if the two references to **D** were cached, then both **A** and **B** refer to the same now JDO-transient dog **D**. If **B** was not in the cache or if its reference to **D** was not cached, then **A** refers to **D**, a JDO-transient Dog object, while **B** refers to a different and persistent Dog object.

The makeTransient methods are abrupt. They do not invoke transparent per-sistence, and they do not alter the values of any of the object's fields. In particular, they do not load persistent values in persistent fields. If the application data object is in a hollow state, then the newly made JDO-transient object has Java default values for all persistent fields. To load the persistent values before making the object JDO-transient, the application should call the retrieve operation, which is described later in this chapter.

The makeTransient methods change the passed object to JDO-transient when the object is in one of the following three management states:

- Persistent-clean

- Hollow

- Persistent-nontransactional

The change is not subject to rollback. The makeTransient methods make persistent-nontransactional and hollow objects unmanaged whether or not a transaction is active.

The makeTransient methods perform no operation on passed objects in any of the following three management states:

- Transient

- Transient-clean

- Transient-dirty

The makeTransient methods throw a JDOUserException when the passed object is in any of the remaining four management states:

- Persistent-new

- Persistent-new-deleted

- Persistent-deleted

- Persistent-dirty

Alternatives to Calling the makeTransient Methods

The application can obtain a JDO-transient application data object in any of four ways: by construction, by cloning, by serialization, and by calling one of the makeTransient methods.

When the application constructs an application data object, the newly constructed object does not represent any persistent state in the datastore.

If the application obtains a transient object by cloning, the call to super.clone() to obtain the clone is, like the call to the makeTransient operation, abrupt. In other words, it won't invoke transparent persistence to load persistent fields. Unlike makeTransient, cloning does not affect the original application data object. Because the clone method returns a copy, two of the problems that using makeTransient can cause are avoided. There is no danger of other persistent objects referring to the clone, and persistent relationships are not disturbed. To avoid references to persistent objects in the clone, a deep copy can be made in the clone method. Chapter 5 examines the clone method for an application data class.

As Chapter 5 explains, when a persistent object is serialized, persistent fields are loaded before the object's state is passed to the serialization stream. For that reason, serialization avoids all the potential problems of the makeTransient methods.

Applications that use JDO will find limited use for JDO-transient application data objects. In general, JDO-transient objects represent new objects that can be inserted into the datastore, or they represent unmanaged copies of persistent objects that already exist in the datastore. The most common reason that unmanaged copies of persistent objects arise is because serialization is producing them. Given the alternatives available, the application may not find a great deal of use for the makeTransient methods.

Controlling the Cache

Each persistence manager maintains a cache of persistent application data objects. Each persistent object may or may not hold, that is to say cache, some or all of its persistent state. In addition, the state manager, which is a JDO implementation object associated with the persistence manager, may hold cached state for some persistent fields of the application data object. From the application's point of view, both the cached persistent field values in the application data object and any cached persistent field values in the state manager are one cache. The issue, then, of controlling the persistence manager's cache is really two issues: controlling the cache of persistent objects and controlling the cache of persistent state for each persistent object.

The persistence manager has three operations to control the cache of persistent state. The retrieve operation loads the persistent state. The evict operation discards the persistent state, and the refresh operation ensures that the cached persistent state is up-to-date with the current state in the datastore. These three operations control the caching of persistent state for any application data objects that the application selects. In addition, as described in Chapter 4, the transactional properties *RetainValues* and *RestoreValues* control the automatic eviction of persistent state that can occur at the end of JDO transactions.

Although JDO provides direct control over the cache of persistent state, the cache of persistent objects is managed indirectly as a side-effect of application and JDO design. Persistent objects are inserted into the cache when JDO constructs them to hold persistent state, or when the application makes transient objects persistent. The uniqueness requirement limits the number of copies of persistent application data objects to no more than one per persistence manager per unique persistent state in the datastore. Normal JVM garbage collection determines when the persistent application objects are removed from the cache. JDO does not hold strong references to application data objects that are hollow or persistent-nontransactional. As long as the application does not hold strong references to them, they may be garbage collected.

Retrieving Persistent State

The PersistenceManager interface provides five methods to load persistent values into any persistent fields that have not been loaded already.

```
public void retrieve(Object adObject)
public void retrieveAll(Collection adObjects)
public void retrieveAll(Collection adObjects, boolean DFGOnly)
public void retrieveAll(Object[] adObjects)
public void retrieveAll(Object[] adObjects, boolean DFGOnly)
```

There are two reasons to call these methods. First, applications will usually want to call one of these methods before making an object transient. By doing so, the application ensures that all of the object's persistent fields are loaded with persistent values before the object becomes unmanaged.

Implementations may provide a second reason for using these methods. They may use the retrieve methods to provide the best performance in loading persistent state. To this end, the JDO implementation may retrieve related data objects according to a policy that is implementation dependent.

NOTE JDO tracks which persistent fields of a persistent object have been loaded. If the field is not loaded, then the value in the field is the Java default value for the field's type. If the field is loaded, the value may be any legal value for the field's type. In some cases, even though the field is not loaded, JDO has obtained and stored someplace else in memory the information that it needs in order to load the field. This happens most commonly for reference types, when JDO may store elsewhere in memory the identity value that it needs to find the persistent state of the object referred to.

When the DFGOnly flag is true, JDO may load only the fields in the default fetch group. Setting DFGOnly to true is a hint to the implementation that it may disregard. On the other hand, when DFGOnly is false, which is the implied setting when this parameter is not in the signature, then JDO must load all of the persistent fields. When a persistent field that contains a reference is loaded, JDO must find or construct the object referred to. This second object may be hollow, but it must be present in memory. Since reference fields are usually not in the default fetch group, using the hint may in some cases increase performance.

NOTE The default fetch group is a possibly empty group of persistent fields that the JDO implementation prefers to load together into the persistent object for performance reasons. Every application data class has a default fetch group, and its membership can be configured in the JDO metadata. Chapter 5 covers the JDO metadata.

For the retrieve methods to have effect, either a transaction must be active or the transaction's *NontransactionalRead* property, described in Chapter 4, must be true. Although the specification is not clear, if the transaction is not active and the *NontransactionalRead* property is false, then calling the retrieve method will likely yield a JDOUserException.

Application data objects in any of the following five states do not refer to preexisting state in the datastore:

- Persistent-new

- Persistent-new-deleted

- Transient

- Transient-clean

- Transient-dirty

As a result, the `retrieve` methods cannot load persistent state for them. The `retrieve` methods perform no operation on objects in these states.

Passing a persistent-deleted object to the retrieve methods does not change its management state or throw an exception. In this case, it is reasonable to expect that no persistent fields are loaded, but the specification is not clear on this point.

Application data objects in any of the following four states refer to preexisting state in the datastore:

- Persistent-dirty

- Persistent-clean

- Hollow

- Persistent-nontransactional

For objects in these management states, the `retrieve` methods load the fields (either all or those in the default fetch group as the case may be) that are not already loaded.

The `retrieve` operation does not imply the `refresh` operation. Retrieving a persistent-dirty object leaves it in the persistent-dirty state, and its modified persistent fields are not altered. Likewise, passing a persistent-clean object to the `retrieve` methods does not modify its management state, but any fields that were not loaded prior to the call are loaded by the call.

The `retrieve` methods change objects in the hollow state either to persistent-clean in the case of an active datastore transaction or to persistent-nontransactional otherwise. The retrieve methods change objects in the persistent-nontransactional state to persistent-clean in the case of an active datastore transaction. The object's cached persistent state is discarded and new state is loaded from the datastore. Outside of an active transaction or in the case of an active optimistic transaction, the retrieve methods leave persistent-nontransactional objects in the persistent-nontransactional state. In these cases, no cached state is discarded.

Evicting Persistent State

The `PersistenceManager` interface provides four methods to evict the persistent state of persistent objects.

```
public void evict(Object adObject)
public void evictAll()
public void evictAll(Collection adObjects)
public void evictAll(Object[] adObjects)
```

When successful, the evict methods immediately discard the persistent state of the object. As a result, the persistent fields acquire their Java default values, and the object's management state changes to hollow. If the object uses application identity, the values of its persistent key fields are not discarded. The evict operation operates only on the persistent state, but you may find implementations that incorrectly evict transactional state along with the persistent state.

As a general rule, the application does not need to explicitly evict application data objects. JDO automatically evicts the persistent state of application data objects under commonly encountered conditions. As Chapter 4 explains, the transaction's *RetainValues* property controls automatic eviction. Excessive use of the evict methods may indicate that the *RetainValues* property should be set to false.

The application calls the evict methods to accomplish one of two purposes. Occasionally, the application may know that a persistent-nontransactional object contains persistent state that no longer reflects the state in the datastore. By calling the evict method, the application can discard the persistent state of the object when a transaction is not active. As a result of eviction, the object will be effectively refreshed when the application next uses the object.

The second reason to call the evict methods arises when the application anticipates or knows that it is iterating a large extent of persistent objects or a large results collection from a query. In this case, eviction is a way to ensure that the persistent-clean objects can be garbage collected while the transaction is active. In fact, the evictAll() method is custom made for the job as it evicts all persistent-clean objects and nothing else.

Objects in the JDO-transient state do not have persistent state to discard. Passing a JDO-transient object to the evict(Object adObject) method causes a JDOUserException to be thrown. In the case of the evictAll methods, contrary to the general rule for xxxAll methods, any JDO-transient objects contained in the passed Collection or array are silently ignored.

Objects in any of the following four management states also do not contain persistent state to discard:

- Hollow

- Transient-clean

- Transient-dirty

- Persistent-new-deleted

The evict methods perform no operation on objects in these states.

Evicting objects in any of the following three states is also a no-op for the object:

- Persistent-new

- Persistent-deleted

- Persistent-dirty

The evict methods, when passed a persistent-nontransactional or persistent-clean object, discard the object's persistent state and change its management state to hollow. In the case of a datastore transaction, JDO may not release until the transaction commits the locks that it holds in the datastore on the persistent state of any persistent-clean objects that it evicts.

Refreshing Persistent State

The PersistenceManager interface provides four methods to refresh the persistent state of persistent objects.

```
public void refresh(Object adObject)
public void refreshAll()
public void refreshAll(Collection adObjects)
public void refreshAll(Object[] adObjects)
```

The refresh methods ensure that the cached persistent state of the passed objects contains the current values available from the datastore. The persistent values may be simply reloaded, or the JDO implementation may rely on a concurrency value or database locks to determine whether the persistent state needs to be reloaded. The values of transactional fields (those that are managed but not persistent) are not affected by refresh.

Values cannot be loaded from the datastore unless the transaction is active or the *NontransactionalRead* property is true. If these conditions are not met, calling any refresh method is a no-op.

Calling the refresh operation for application data objects that do not refer to preexisting state in the datastore is a no-op. For that reason, passing application data objects in any of the following five management states to the refresh operation is a no-op:

- Persistent-new

- Persistent-new-deleted

- Transient

- Transient-clean

- Transient-dirty

Refreshing a persistent-deleted object is also a no-op. This behavior exists because the decision to delete the object was made on the basis of its cached persistent state.

Refreshing an object in the hollow state is usually a no-op because the object does not have any cached persistent state that could be out of date. On the other hand, the JDO implementation has the option to load some or all of the persistent fields and change the management state to either persistent-clean in the case of a datastore transaction or persistent-nontransactional in the case of optimistic transactions.

Refreshing an object in the persistent-clean or persistent-nontransactional state verifies that its persistent state is up-to-date with the datastore. For objects in the persistent-clean state in a datastore transaction, JDO may rely on the database locks that it acquired to know that the object's state is up-to-date. In an optimistic transaction, JDO may use the concurrency value to verify that the object's state is up-to-date. Either way, if the object's persistent state is out-of-date, the refresh methods discard it and reload new values from the datastore.

Refreshing an object in the persistent-dirty state discards the modifications made to the object within the transaction. The methods reload current values from the datastore. In the case of a datastore transaction, the application data object becomes persistent-clean, but in the case of an optimistic transaction, the application data object becomes persistent-nontransactional. In both cases, any state saved for rollback is also discarded.

The refreshAll() method refreshes all persistent-clean and persistent-dirty objects.

Getting and Constructing Identity Objects

The PersistenceManager interface provides four methods that get JDO identity objects or are useful for constructing them.

```
public Object getObjectId(Object adObject)
public Object getTransactionalObjectId(Object adObject)
public Class getObjectIdClass(Class adClass)
public Object newObjectIdInstance(Class adClass, String identityString)
```

Using these four methods, the application can get identity objects and construct identity objects.

Every persistent application data object has a JDO identity associated with it. Application data objects that are JDO-transient, transient-clean, and transient-dirty do not have an associated JDO identity. The getObjectId method returns the JDO identity object associated with the persistent object. This method may be called whether the transaction is active or not.

If an implementation supports the javax.jdo.option.ChangeApplicationIdentity option, it allows the application to change the values in the application data object's key fields. If this is done within a transaction, the original, pre-change application identity can be obtained from the object by the getObjectId method, and the new, post-change JDO identity can be obtained from the object with the getTransactionalObjectId method. After the transaction commits, the new application identity becomes the identity that is returned from the getObjectId method.

The specification is not clear on what behavior to expect if the application identity fields are changed outside a transaction with the *NontransactionalWrite* property turned on. In any event, it is not an operation that most applications will want to perform.

The identity object returned from getObjectId or getTransactionalObjectId is a copy of the identity object maintained internally by the JDO implementation. Nothing that the application can do to the identity object returned has any effect on the identity maintained internally by JDO.

Every object identity class is required to support a toString method and a constructor that accepts a string as formatted by the toString method. The idea is to be able to construct a copy of the identity object by passing the string from the toString method to the constructor that accepts a string. The string returned from the identity object's toString method is called the *identity string*. It is also sometimes called the *stringified JDO identity*, but the term *identity string* sounds better. Armed with the ability to generate and use identity strings, services can ship to remote clients information about a range of application data objects along with the identity string for each object, and the client (including HTML clients) can respond by shipping back identity strings together with the information that they want to change. A significant benefit is that the service may not have to maintain conversational state for these clients.

When the application wishes to construct an application identity object, it typically knows the identity class to construct and it has the values of the application-defined key fields. As a result, the application can typically invoke the Java new operator on the application identity class. The application may also use reflection to construct the application identity object. To use reflection, the application must know the application identity class. The getObjectIdClass method returns the identity class for any application data class. In summary, to construct directly or by reflection the application identity object, the application must know the application identity class, which it might get from the getObjectIdClass method, and it must know the key values.

When the application wishes to construct a datastore identity object, it must have the identity string. Although it could use reflection to invoke the constructor in the identity class that accepts the identity string, the application can avoid the complexity and performance cost of invoking reflection by calling the newObjectIdInstance method. This method requires the Class of the application data object whose identity is being constructed. The newObjectIdInstance method also works with the identity string from application identity objects.

Although JDO implementations may use one datastore identity class, they may also use multiple datastore identity classes. For this reason, when using reflection to construct datastore identity, it is still necessary to determine the datastore identity class for the application data class. Calling the getObjectIdClass method is one way to get the identity class that goes with an application data class.

 NOTE   When designing how your application will construct identity objects, keep in mind that your application must know either the class of the identity object or the class of the application data object for which the identity is being constructed. Except when the application data classes are related by inheritance, the application should define a different application identity class for each application data class. The JDO implementation may use more than one datastore identity class as well.

Fetching an Application Data Object by Identity

The PersistenceManager interface provides one method to fetch an application data object by identity.

```
public Object getObjectById(Object idObject, boolean verifyPersistence)
```

When the application has a JDO identity object, it can fetch the corresponding application data object by calling the getObjectById method. This method takes two parameters. The first parameter is the identity object. If the idObject is not an identity object, the method throws a JDOUserException.

The second parameter to this method is a Boolean flag that indicates whether JDO should verify that an object exists in the datastore with the given JDO identity. The setting of the verifyPersistence flag makes a difference when the application data object does not exist in the cache or the datastore. If the flag is false, the JDO

---

implementation is not required to verify that the object exists in the datastore. It is permitted to delay verification until the application data object is used in some way that forces a datastore access. When the flag is true, the method must, with one exception, verify that the persistent state that corresponds to the durable identity exists in the datastore. The exception arises when an object exists in the cache and is transactional. In this case, the method may skip verification even when the flag is true. If, when verifying, this method does not find the persistent object in the datastore, or if, during a later operation, JDO does not find the persistent object in the datastore, then JDO throws a JDODataStoreException in JDO 1.0. Under the same circumstances, JDO throws a JDOObjectNotFoundException in JDO 1.0.1. JDOObjectNotFoundException is a new exception type in JDO 1.0.1 and a subclass of JDODataStoreException. Chapter 7 discusses the JDO exception classes.

The getObjectById method does not change the state of an application data object that it finds in the cache. If the method constructs the application data object, it returns the object in the persistent-clean state when a datastore transaction is active, and in either the hollow or persistent-nontransactional state otherwise. Although the specification is not clear, you should not expect this method to work when a transaction is not active and the transaction's *NontransactionalRead* property is false. In these circumstances, it will likely throw a JDOUserException.

If the idObject is an application identity object, then none of its key fields may contain the null value. If any do, getObjectById throws a JDOUserException.

Factory Methods in the Persistence Manager

The PersistenceManager interface has factory methods that produce Extent objects, Query objects, and the Transaction object. The objects produced are all associated with the persistence manager that produced them. Chapter 2, which describes the Extent and Query interfaces, also describes the factory methods in the persistence manager that produce Extent and Query objects.

Getting the Persistence Manager's Transaction

The persistence manager provides one method that returns the JDO Transaction object associated with the persistence manager.

```
public Transaction currentTransaction()
```

This method returns the one and only Transaction object associated with the persistence manager. The same Transaction object may be used to control a series of transactions for the objects that the persistence manager controls. The Transaction interface is covered in Chapter 4.

The Properties of a Persistence Manager

The persistence manager has five properties. Two of them, the *PersistenceManagerFactory* property and the *Closed* property, are read-only and are described at the beginning of this chapter. The other three properties are read-write.

The IgnoreCache Property

The PersistenceManager interface provides getter and setter methods for the *IgnoreCache* property.

```
public boolean getIgnoreCache()
public void setIgnoreCache(boolean icFlag)
```

The *IgnoreCache* property determines whether JDO uses the persistent-new and persistent-deleted objects within the persistence manager's cache when iterating an extent. The setting of the *IgnoreCache* property at the time that the iterator is obtained determines the iterator's behavior. If the *IgnoreCache* property is true, then it is a hint to the JDO implementation to ignore during the iteration the deletions and insertions made within the currently active transaction. If the *IgnoreCache* property is false, then the iteration must include the persistent-new objects and exclude the persistent-deleted objects. This property has no effect on iterations that occur outside a transaction.

All changes committed prior to obtaining the iteration are automatically included in the iteration unless they are hidden by the datastore's isolation level. It is implementation dependent whether transactions, in other persistence managers, that commit after the iterator is obtained are visible in the iteration. The JDO implementation and the datastores that it targets define the isolation level of the transactions.

The setting of the *IgnoreCache* property is inherited by the *IgnoreCache* property in the Query objects that the persistence manager produces.

The Multithreaded Property

The `PersistenceManager` interface provides getter and setter methods for the *Multithreaded* property.

```
public boolean getMultithreaded()
public void setMultithreaded(boolean mtFlag)
```

The JDO specification requires that its implementations be thread-safe. Applications may allow multiple, concurrently executing threads to use the same data object or the same persistence manager. JDO is responsible for ensuring that the persistence service, whether invoked explicitly or implicitly, is thread-safe, and for doing this in a way that does not cause deadlock with any synchronization locks that the application might use for its own purposes. To be thread-safe, JDO implementations synchronize on objects that are not visible to the application. Since synchronization is somewhat expensive for performance and since multithreaded use is not always required, the application can inform JDO that only one thread at a time will use the same data object or the same persistence manager. The application does this by setting the *Multithreaded* property to false. Setting the *Multithreaded* property to false is a hint for the JDO implementation that it may disregard. On the other hand, the JDO implementation may take the hint and avoid synchronization to improve performance.

The *Multithreaded* property is not a fine-grained property that should be flicked on and off. To avoid problems, pick a setting and stick to it.

The UserObject Property

The `PersistenceManager` interface provides getter and setter methods for the *UserObject* property.

```
public Object getUserObject()
public void setUserObject(Object userObject)
```

The read-write *UserObject* property allows the application to associate any object with the persistence manager. JDO makes no use of this property, and applications can ignore it.

Summary

The PersistenceManager interface presents many of the explicit services of JDO that applications may use. The persistence manager provides methods to control whether a particular object in memory is transactional and/or persistent. It provides methods to control the cache of persistent state when the mechanisms of transparent persistence are not sufficient. The persistence manager also provides methods to manipulate object identities.

The PersistenceManager interface is the application's gateway to three important interfaces. The previous chapter describes two of these interfaces, the Query and Extent interfaces. The next chapter describes the third, the Transaction interface.

CHAPTER 4

Transactions and Caching

JDO PROVIDES A transactional persistence service for objects in memory. JDO identity links the managed object in memory to its corresponding persistent state in the datastore. JDO transactions define the semantics of synchronizing the persistent state in memory with the persistent state in the datastore. Each persistence manager controls the persistent state of some number of persistent objects. These objects and their persistent state are called the *persistence manager's cache*. For each object in the cache, JDO determines when to load its persistent state, when to discard its persistent state, and when to store its persistent state.

JDO provides performance benefits to the application that a datastore service, like JDBC, does not. When an application uses a datastore service, it creates, upon demand, objects in memory to hold persistent state in the datastore. Often, the objects in memory are simple value objects for the state in the datastore. When the application needs to fetch the persistent state again, a simple application usually creates another value object. More sophisticated applications avoid this behavior, but a good deal of code is required to implement a transactionally aware cache of persistent objects. JDO implementations already contain the code that manages the cache of persistent objects, tracks their transactional state, and lazily loads their persistent state. By using JDO, applications can see significant performance benefits.

JDO is designed to work in managed and unmanaged deployment environments. By satisfying the requirements of the J2EE Connector Architecture (JCA), JDO implementations accommodate containers that manage local and distributed transactions using the Java Transaction API (JTA). For example, an Enterprise JavaBean (EJB) that uses JDO can be deployed to use container-managed transactions (CMT). JDO also provides a simple way for applications to control their own transactions when distributed transactions or container-managed transactions are not used.

This chapter begins by defining transactions and examining the operations and properties of JDO's Transaction interface. It then examines how these properties control JDO's persistence service when it loads, discards, and stores persistent state. Next, it examines JDO's integration with JCA and JTA. The chapter concludes by identifying when JDO's caching is likely to improve performance and when it is not likely to improve performance.

Transactions

A *transaction* is a series of interactions with a system service that the service combines into one unit of work. A transaction has a begin point and end point. While the transaction is active, the interactions in the transaction are bound together by the four ACID properties of transactions: *atomicity, consistency, isolation,* and *durability.* The application starts by asking the service to begin a transaction. After the transaction begins, the application may issue multiple requests to the service, to fetch, insert, change, or delete the information that the service manages. During this time, the application is *isolated* from the activities of other concurrent transactions. These other transactions may be viewing or changing the same information, but the interactions between the transactions are controlled and predictable. To end the transaction, the application requests that the service either accept (commit) all of the changes or discard (roll back) all of the changes. Either way, it is all or nothing. In other words, the service commits or rolls back the changes as one *atomic* unit of work. The service commits the changes only if the changes are *consistent* with any constraints on the information that the service is charged with enforcing. A committed transaction is *durable*, that is to say, the committed changes will not be lost as a result of service interruptions.

A transaction is local when it is limited to one service. It is distributed when it allows more than one service to participate in the transaction.

Transactions simplify the application's use of the service. If the service says that it cannot commit, then the application knows it can roll back the transaction, and thereby discard the changes that occurred since the transaction began. If the service reports that it successfully committed the transaction, then the application knows that all is well.

By supporting transactions, JDO provides an essential requirement for most application designs. For example, to transfer money from one account to another, a banking application debits one account and credits the other. By making both the debit and the credit actions part of one transaction, the banking application ensures that money is neither created nor destroyed. When the transaction commits successfully, both the debit and the credit actions are successful. When the transaction is rolled back, neither the credit nor the debit action has any effect. By using a transaction, the application can guarantee that debits and credits are paired.

Although the details of transactions are outside the scope of this book, the general concepts are familiar to most application programmers who have coded to a database service.

Optimistic and Datastore Transactions in JDO

JDO defines both *datastore* transactions and *optimistic* transactions. This book uses the term *database transaction* to refer to the transaction provided by the datastore service and to distinguish it from a JDO datastore transaction. As a general rule, it is necessary to keep a connection to the database open in order to keep the database transaction open.

The persistence manager may perform its actions transactionally when either an optimistic or datastore transaction is active, or it may perform its actions non-transactionally when a transaction is not active. So far as possible, each persistence manager uses no more than one database connection at a time.

JDO's datastore transaction relies directly on the transactional service of the datastore. During the entire time that the datastore transaction is active, there is one corresponding database transaction that the persistence manager uses to load and store persistent state. For this reason, during the time that the datastore transaction is active, the persistence manager very likely has an open connection to the database.

On the other hand, to support one optimistic transaction, the typical JDO implementation uses a concurrency value and one or more database transactions. After JDO reads field values from the datastore as a result of queries or transparent persistence, JDO may release the datastore connection. As a result, when n optimistic transactions are active, JDO may be using less than n datastore connections. At the same time, the use of optimistic transactions can reduce the number of database locks that JDO acquires. (The next section has a brief discussion of database locks.)

When the optimistic transaction commits, JDO uses a database transaction to verify the concurrency value and update the datastore. During verification, the concurrency values of all transactional application data objects are checked against the values in the datastore. When the concurrency values of transactional objects are up-to-date, JDO writes the state of modified transactional objects to the datastore. After the database transaction commits, the optimistic transaction ends.

In JDO 1.0, when the commit method fails because of concurrency verification, it throws a JDOUserException. The exception contains an array of JDOUserException objects, one for each object that failed verification. Although it is possible in JDO 1.0 to recover in some deployment environments from a concurrency failure, in the case of EJBs with container-managed transactions, recovery is not possible.

Starting with the 1.0.1 specification, when the commit method fails because of concurrency verification, it throws a JDOOptimisticVerificationException. The exception contains an array of `JDOOptimisticVerificationException` objects, one for each object that failed verification. When the `commit` method throws a `JDOOptimisticVerificationException`, the commit has failed and the transaction has rolled back. The application does not have the option to recover from a `JDOOptimisticVerificationException`. Chapter 7 describes the exception types defined by JDO.

NOTE It is up to the JDO implementation how it calculates the optimistic concurrency value. JDO requires that the implementation fail at least one transaction when two of its persistence managers have concurrently active transactions in which incompatible changes occurred on objects with the same identity value.

By calling the `makeTransactional` method in the `PersistenceManager`, the application can force a check of the application data object's concurrency value even when the application does not modify the object.

Isolation Levels and Interactions Between Transactions

The *isolation level* is one of the four ACID properties of transactions. Because isolation can impose a high performance penalty on the database, most databases offer more than one isolation level. At all levels of isolation, an active transaction can read any changes committed by transactions that ended before it started. (This discussion ignores the access control provided by the database.) Likewise, an active transaction can read its own insertions and modifications, whereas it cannot read its own deletions.

Four isolation levels are generally recognized, and they are defined in terms of interactions that they allow to occur between concurrent transactions. Each level is more stringent than its preceding level.

- *Read-uncommitted:* The transaction can see the effects of modifications, insertions, and deletions made by other active (and therefore not yet committed) transactions. That is to say, information that the other unfinished transaction deleted is not visible, while its insertions and modifications are visible. Reading an uncommitted modification made by another transaction is called a *dirty read*. Nonrepeatable reads and phantom reads, described in the next bullet item, can also occur. Because read uncommitted provides very little isolation, most databases support only read operations in transactions that use the read-uncommitted isolation level.

- *Read-committed:* Dirty reads do not occur. The transaction may encounter nonrepeatable reads and phantom reads. A *nonrepeatable read* occurs when rereading the same state shows a change due to a committed modification made by another transaction. A *phantom read* occurs when the same query executes twice in a transaction and the two sets of query results do not match up because of the actions of a second committed transaction. Either the second query finds results that the first query did not find, or it does not find results that first query found.

- *Repeatable-read:* Dirty reads and nonrepeatable reads do not occur. On the other hand, the transaction can still encounter phantom reads.

- *Serializable:* Dirty reads, nonrepeatable reads, and phantom reads do not occur. The transaction never sees the modifications, insertions, or deletions made by other transactions that commit after it started.

High isolation is always in direct conflict with high performance.

Dirty reads, nonrepeatable reads, and phantom reads are well-known transactional abnormalities, but the list of possible abnormalities is longer. Two that are particularly interesting to look at when using JDO are outdated updates and inconsistent reads. An *outdated update* occurs when one transaction reads information, but before this transaction modifies the information and commits its changes, another transaction changes the same information and commits its changes. If the first transaction can then modify the information and commit, it has used information that is not up-to-date when its transaction commits.

An *inconsistent read* occurs when one transaction starts to read a series of values, but before it completes the series, another transaction modifies two values in the series, one that the first transaction has read and one that it has not. The second transaction then commits its changes before the first transaction completes its series of reads. If the second transaction can commit its changes and the first transaction then reads one of the modifications made by the second transaction, the series of values that the first transaction read is not consistent with any snapshot of committed state in the datastore.

The isolation level determines whether inconsistent reads and outdated updates can occur in the transaction and if so, whether the transaction can commit successfully. The read-committed isolation level allows both inconsistent reads and outdated updates. The serializable isolation level prevents both.

Some databases allow the application to lock the value for updating when it reads it. For example, Oracle permits the SELECT-FOR-UPDATE syntax. By using locks, the application effectively upgrades the isolation level. In the case of Oracle, update locks can prevent nonrepeatable reads, outdated updates, and inconsistent reads even when the isolation level is read-committed. As a result of the locking, one of the conflicting transactions will wait for the other to end, thereby allowing

Chapter 4

both transactions to be successful without the transactional abnormality occurring. Because locks cause waiting, they allow deadlock to occur. Deadlock arises when two transactions each hold a lock that the other one needs to proceed. Most databases roll back deadlocked transactions after a period of time.

The Implementation Defines the Isolation Level of Its Transactions

The JDO implementation defines the isolation level that its transactions support. By selecting an isolation level and using the locks that the datastore supports, JDO implementations usually prevent nonrepeatable reads, outdated updates, and inconsistent reads in datastore transactions. For this reason, datastore transactions are sometimes called *pessimistic transactions*, since they are designed to prevent rather than fail most transactional abnormalities. Unless the JDO implementation uses the serializable isolation level in the datastore, phantom reads can still occur.

JDO requires that optimistic transactions fail during commit when an outdated update occurs. On the other hand, JDO leaves it up to the application to decide whether it wants to fail on commit when a nonrepeatable read and inconsistent read occur. The application forces JDO to fail when these transactional abnormalities occur by making transactional the objects that it reads but does not modify. To avoid a performance penalty, applications should use this tool sparingly. See the makeTransactional method in the PersistenceManager interface, which Chapter 3 describes. Phantom reads can always occur in an optimistic transaction.

JDO's Transaction Interface

Each persistence manager has one and only one Transaction object associated with it. The transaction object gives the application control of one transaction at a time. As a result, the objects that a persistence manager controls can be associated with no more than one transaction at a time. The Transaction object associated with a persistence manager does not change while the persistence manager is open. For simplicity, a JDO implementation may have the same class implement both interfaces. Although the two interfaces Transaction and PersistenceManager are closely related, by having two interfaces, JDO separates the control of transactions from the other properties and operations of the persistence manager. Chapter 3 describes the PersistenceManager interface.

The class diagram in Figure 4-1 shows the three operations and eight properties of the Transaction interface. The following sections describe the methods that define these operations and properties.

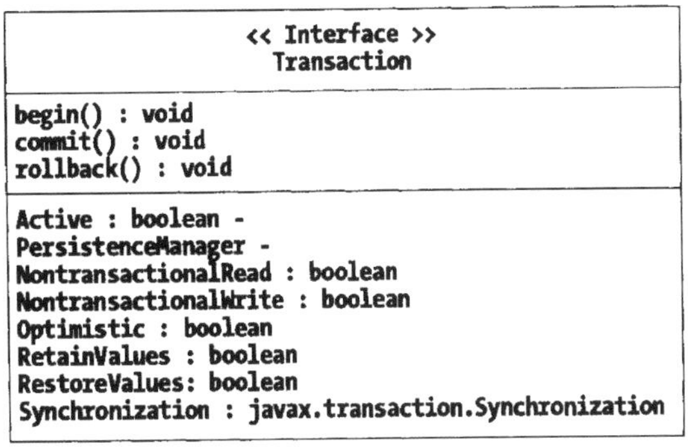

```
+-------------------------------------------------------+
|                   << Interface >>                     |
|                      Transaction                      |
+-------------------------------------------------------+
| begin() : void                                        |
| commit() : void                                       |
| rollback() : void                                     |
+-------------------------------------------------------+
| Active : boolean -                                    |
| PersistenceManager -                                  |
| NontransactionalRead : boolean                        |
| NontransactionalWrite : boolean                       |
| Optimistic : boolean                                  |
| RetainValues : boolean                                |
| RestoreValues: boolean                                |
| Synchronization : javax.transaction.Synchronization   |
+-------------------------------------------------------+
```

Figure 4-1. The class diagram of the Transaction *interface*

Controlling Transactional Boundaries

The Transaction interface provides three operations and one property to control the transaction's boundaries.

```
public void begin()
public void commit()
public void rollback()
public boolean isActive()
```

When the application controls the transaction, the begin method starts a transaction. The commit method ensures that JDO saves in the datastore all (or in the event of failure, none) of the changes made within the transaction. The changes may include new values in the persistent fields of persistent objects and the addition or deletion of persistent objects. The rollback method ends the transaction without storing any of the changes in the datastore. Depending on the setting of the *RestoreValues* property, rollback may restore the values of dirty managed fields to the values that were present in memory when the object became dirty.

NOTE A transactional field becomes dirty when its value changes within the transaction. A persistent field becomes dirty when its value changes within the transaction or when its object has been made persistent or deleted within the current transaction. A persistent or a transactional field becomes dirty when it refers to a mutable embedded object (such as a supported system class like Date or HashSet) and that object changes. An application data object becomes dirty when one or more of its managed fields become dirty.

From the time that a transaction begins until it ends with a call to either commit or rollback, the transaction's *Active* property is true. Outside of the transactional boundaries, the *Active* property is false.

If an operation in the Transaction fails, various JDO exceptions may be thrown. Chapter 7 details JDO's exception hierarchy. In the case of commit, if the exception is a JDOFatalDataStoreException, then JDO has rolled back the transaction. If the exception is some other type of JDOFatalException, then automatic rollback may have occurred. In any case, the transaction should be abandoned since there is no recovery possible. The other types of JDO exceptions can be retried if the application knows how to recover. When these exceptions are thrown, the transaction remains active. The simplest and safest way to deal with the various possibilities is to check the transaction's *Active* property in the catch block and perform the rollback, if needed, when the application either cannot or does not know how to recover.

The application cannot invoke the boundary operations (begin, commit, and rollback) when a container or a JTA TransactionManager is controlling the transaction. Any attempt to do so causes a JDOUserException. Incidentally, a similar restriction applies to the Connection interface in JDBC; it is not a limitation unique to JDO.

On the other hand, stand-alone, client-server, and Web applications that use JDO usually control a local transaction with JDO's Transaction interface. EJBs that are deployed for bean-managed transactions (BMT) can also control the transaction through JDO's Transaction interface. Chapters 6 and 9 through 11 describe how to use JDO in the various deployment environments.

The Read-Only PersistenceManager Property

The Transaction interface provides a getter method for the *PersistenceManager* property.

```
public PersistenceManager getPersistenceManager()
```

This method returns a reference to the persistence manager that is associated with the transaction. Each PersistenceManager object is in a one-to-one relationship with a Transaction object. This relationship is immutable as long as the persistence manager is open. As a result of the relationship between the PersistenceManager object and its Transaction object, the following expression is always true when the persistence manager pm is open:

```
pm == pm.currentTransaction().getPersistenceManager()
```

The Five Transactional Properties

The five Boolean properties *Optimistic, NontransactionalRead, NontransactionalWrite, RetainValues,* and *RestoreValues* are collectively called the *transactional properties*. Turning on any of these properties invokes an optional feature of the JDO implementation. When a particular transactional property is not supported, its value is always set to false. Attempts to set it to true, or to use a feature of JDO that would require it, yield a JDOUnsupportedOptionException.

NOTE The supportedOptions method in the PersistenceManagerFactory interface, which Chapter 6 discusses, provides a list of the options that the implementation supports.

Some of these properties can be set when a transaction is active or inactive, and some can only be set when a transaction is inactive. None of these properties can be set during the time that the transaction is completing. In other words, these properties cannot be set within the callback methods of the Synchronization object, and they should not be set within the jdoPreClear or jdoPreStore methods of the InstanceCallbacks interface. If an attempt is made to set the transactional properties while the transaction is completing, the operation throws a JDOUserException. A later section of this chapter describes the transaction's *Synchronization* property, and Chapter 7 covers JDO's InstanceCallbacks interface.

These five transactional properties are also properties of the PersistenceManagerFactory interface. The Transaction object inherits the values of its transactional properties from the persistence manager factory that produced its persistence manager.

JDO allows the implementation to support none, any, or all of the transactional properties. As the 1.0.1 version makes clear, JDO prohibits dependencies between the transaction's properties. Changing the setting of one of these properties has no effect on the current settings, or possible settings, of the other properties.

The transactional properties maintain their values across transactional boundaries.

The Optimistic Property

The Transaction interface provides getter-setter methods for its Boolean *Optimistic* property.

```
public boolean getOptimistic()
public void setOptimistic(boolean optFlag)
```

The application configures a datastore transaction by setting the transaction's *Optimistic* property to false. It configures an optimistic transaction by setting the property to true. The *Optimistic* property must be set before calling the begin method. Attempts to set the *Optimistic* property after the transaction has started results in a JDOUserException.

JDO requires support for datastore transactions. Optimistic transactions, on the other hand, are an optional feature of JDO.

When the application code runs inside a component whose container manages the transaction, the transaction has started by the time the application code gains control. In this case, the application must obtain a persistence manager factory that has the *Optimistic* property set to the desired value. In this way, the application obtains a persistence manager whose transaction is configured for the desired transaction type.

For transactions that include user think time, optimistic transactions are recommended for scalability. Because a JDO optimistic transaction may close the database transaction and release the database connection back to a connection pool between reads, the application may scale better due to JDO's more frugal use of datastore resources. It may also scale better due to better use of the caching built into the implementation. (See later sections of this chapter, starting with "JDO's Cache of Persistent Objects and Their State," for more discussion of caching.)

On the other hand, datastore transactions are also recommended for some situations. Not all JDO implementations offer optimistic transactions, so the only choice may be a datastore transaction. For JDO applications that must share their database schema with applications that do not use JDO, the JDO optimistic transaction may not detect changes made by the non-JDO applications. Whether this is the case depends on the JDO implementation's algorithm for calculating the concurrency value. When transactional collisions are expected to be frequent, a datastore transaction may be a better choice since the isolation level and locking strategy used tends to serialize the transactions rather than fail one of them. Datastore transactions, however, may also encounter deadlock when two datastore transactions attempt to change the same set of objects in a different sequential order. Finally, in the exceptional situation where inconsistent reads are a pervasive issue for the application, if the JDO implementation can be configured to use the serializable isolation level in the database transaction, then the datastore transaction is a good choice. In short, use optimistic transactions when possible and datastore transactions when necessary.

The NontransactionalRead Property

The Transaction interface provides getter-setter methods for its Boolean *NontransactionalRead* property.

```
public boolean getNontransactionalRead()
public void setNontransactionalRead(boolean ntrFlag)
```

The *NontransactionalRead* property affects the behavior of JDO only when a transaction is not active. It has no effect on the behavior of JDO when a transaction is active. When the implementation supports the option of turning on this property, it may be set to true or false at any time.

The *NontransactionalRead* property determines whether JDO allows read access to the persistent fields of persistent objects outside of transactions. It also determines whether JDO allows access to the datastore when a transaction is not active. When *NontransactionalRead* is true, the application can execute queries outside of transactions. Likewise, it can iterate extents and the results collections returned from queries, and it can access the persistent fields of persistent objects. If *NontransactionalRead* is false, these operations produce a JDOUserException.

When the application accesses a persistent field of a persistent object outside of a transaction while the *NontransactionalRead* property is true, the managed state of the application object either is or becomes persistent-nontransactional. As a result of nontransactional access, the persistent fields of the data object reflect the persistent state in the datastore as of some indeterminate point in the past. The state may have been loaded as a result of the current access, or it may have been loaded at any point since the persistence manager was obtained. If the object was transactional in a previously committed transaction, then its persistent state is no older than that transaction.

NOTE A persistent application data object becomes transactional when it is modified, deleted, made persistent, or made transactional within a transaction. It also becomes transactional when its persistent fields are accessed in a datastore transaction. It does not become transactional when its persistent fields are accessed in an optimistic transaction.

The JDO implementation does not hold any database locks for a persistent-nontransactional object.

The NontransactionalWrite Property

The Transaction interface provides getter-setter methods for its Boolean *NontransactionalWrite* property.

```
public boolean getNontransactionalWrite()
public void setNontransactionalWrite(boolean ntwFlag)
```

The *NontransactionalWrite* property affects the behavior of JDO when a transaction is not active. It has no effect on the behavior of JDO when a transaction is active. When the implementation supports the option of turning on this property, it may be set to true or false at any time.

The *NontransactionalWrite* property permits writes to the persistent fields of persistent objects outside of transactional boundaries. When the write occurs, the application data object either is or becomes persistent-nontransactional. The changes that occur nontransactionally cannot be later stored in the datastore. JDO expressly prohibits storing nontransactional changes made to persistent-nontransactional objects. In essence, the JDO implementation must reload the persistent state of modified persistent-nontransactional objects if they later become transactional.

The practical uses of setting the *NontransactionalWrite* property to true are likely to be very specialized.

The RetainValues Property

The Transaction interface provides getter-setter methods for its Boolean *RetainValues* property.

```
public boolean getRetainValues()
public void setRetainValues(rtvFlag)
```

The *RetainValues* property affects the behavior of JDO when a transaction commits. It has no effect otherwise. It controls whether JDO discards or retains the persistent state of application data objects that are persistent-clean, persistent-new, persistent-dirty, persistent-deleted, or persistent-new-deleted when the transaction commits. These are the five management states that are both transactional and persistent.

When the transaction commits and *RetainValues* is false, JDO clears the persistent fields of the objects that are both transactional and persistent after it updates the datastore. The persistent-deleted and persistent-new-deleted objects change to JDO-transient, while the persistent-clean, persistent-new, and persistent-dirty objects change to hollow. In effect, the persistent-clean, persistent-new, and persistent-dirty objects are automatically evicted on transaction commit.

NOTE JDO clears the persistent fields by setting each persistent field to its Java default value. Boolean fields are set to false, numeric fields are set to zero, and reference fields are set to null. JDO discards the persistent state by clearing the persistent fields and also by discarding any values held for the object elsewhere in memory.

When the transaction commits and *RetainValues* is true, JDO retains the values in the persistent fields. The persistent-deleted and persistent-new-deleted objects change to JDO-transient, while the persistent-clean, persistent-new, and persistent-dirty objects change to the persistent-nontransactional state.

When the JDO implementation supports the option of turning on the *RetainValues* property, the application may set the property to true or false before or after the transaction is active.

Deciding Whether to Set RetainValues to True or False

When the application uses persistent objects within datastore transactions, it makes little difference whether the *RetainValues* property is true or false. The transactional semantics of the datastore transaction requires that the persistent value of an object's persistent field be reloaded from the datastore after the transaction starts and before the application accesses or modifies the field's value. Whether *RetainValues* is true or false, JDO discards the persistent state acquired in one transaction before the object is reused in a later datastore transaction.

When the application uses optimistic transactions, it makes sense to set the *RetainValues* property to true. There are two reasons to do this. First, newly loaded persistent objects are persistent-nontransactional in an optimistic transaction until they are modified, deleted, or explicitly made transactional. Since the persistent-nontransactional objects are not transactional, JDO does not automatically evict their persistent state when the transaction commits and *RetainValues* is false. In most applications that use optimistic transactions, the nontransactional objects are the bulk of the objects loaded. Second, when the persistent-nontransactional objects become transactional, they are verified to be up-to-date when the transaction commits. Since a common cache management strategy is to discard the least recently used cached state, it would generally be counterproductive to evict the most recently used cached state. As a result, it usually does not make sense to set *RetainValues* to false when using optimistic transactions.

When the application uses both nontransactional reads and transactions, setting *RetainValues* to true ensures that the persistent state acquired in the transaction remains available outside the transaction. As a result, the application may gain a performance benefit due to caching. Later sections of this chapter, starting with "JDO's Cache of Persistent Objects and Their State," examine JDO's caching and the circumstances that may yield performance benefits.

The RestoreValues Property

The Transaction interface provides getter-setter methods for its Boolean *RestoreValues* property.

```
public boolean getRestoreValues()
public void setRestoreValues(rsvFlag)
```

The *RestoreValues* property controls whether the persistent fields of transactional objects are restored, when the transaction rolls back, to their state at the beginning of the transaction. If the *RestoreValues* property is false, JDO may leave the persistent fields of transactional objects as they were when the transaction rolled back, or it may clear them to their Java default values.

The application must set the *RestoreValues* property to true before the transaction begins. Any attempt to set the property's value after the transaction starts yields a JDOUserException.

There is only one *RestoreValues* property, but JDO defines both weak and strong support for this property. The implementation must offer weak support for the *RestoreValues* property, but strong support for the property is an implementation option. The implementation must offer strong support for the *RestoreValues* property when it supports any of the other four transactional properties. The supportedOptions method in JDOHelper does not return an option string to indicate strong support for the *RestoreValues* property.

When *RestoreValues* is false, JDO behaves the same regardless of whether strong or weak *RestoreValues* is supported. When *RestoreValues* is true, JDO does more when it supports a strong *RestoreValues* property than it does when it supports a weak *RestoreValues* property.

In the event of rollback, the persistent state in the datastore is never changed, and the setting of the *RestoreValues* flag has no influence in this regard. The *RestoreValues* property, whether weak or strong, affects only what happens to the state of transactional objects in memory.

Weak Support for the RestoreValues Property

Weak support for the *RestoreValues* property affects JDO's actions on objects that become persistent-new. It also affects JDO's actions during rollback on objects that are persistent-new or persistent-new-deleted. It has no effect otherwise.

When weak *RestoreValues* is true, JDO makes a before-image when the object becomes persistent-new. Upon rollback, JDO restores the managed fields of persistent-new and persistent-new-deleted objects from the before-image. When weak *RestoreValues* is false, JDO does not make a before-image when objects become persistent-new, and upon rollback, it leaves the managed fields of persistent-new and persistent-new-deleted objects as they were when rollback commenced. As a result of rollback, these objects become JDO-transient.

When weak *RestoreValues* is set to true, it has no effect on objects that are persistent-deleted, persistent-dirty, or persistent-clean. JDO clears the persistent fields in these objects upon rollback regardless of the setting of weak *RestoreValues*.

 NOTE   In JDO, the before-image is a copy of the values of all the managed fields of the object. The managed fields are the fields that the JDO metadata identifies as either persistent or transactional. Chapter 5 describes the JDO metadata.

Strong Support for the RestoreValues Property

The strong *RestoreValues* property affects the behavior of JDO when an application data object becomes dirty and when a transaction rolls back. It has no effect otherwise. It controls three related behaviors, whether the object's before-image is saved when the object becomes dirty within a transaction, whether the object's managed state is restored from the before-image in the event of transaction rollback, and whether the object's persistent state is cleared after rollback.

When rollback occurs and strong *RestoreValues* is true, persistent-clean objects do not have a before-image. As a result, they retain the values of their persistent fields and become persistent-nontransactional.

When rollback occurs and strong *RestoreValues* is true, the persistent fields of objects in the following states are restored to the values in the object's before-image:

- Persistent-dirty

- Persistent-deleted

- Persistent-new

- Persistent-new-deleted

As a result, objects that are persistent-dirty or persistent-deleted become either hollow or persistent-nontransactional depending on whether they were hollow before they became dirty or deleted. As happens when weak *RestoreValues* is true, the persistent-new and persistent-new-deleted objects are restored from the before-image, and they become JDO-transient.

When rollback occurs and strong *RestoreValues* is false, the values in the managed fields of persistent-new and persistent-new-deleted objects are left as they were at the start of rollback. As a result of rollback, these objects become JDO-transient. The persistent fields of persistent-clean, persistent-dirty, and persistent-deleted objects are cleared to their Java default values. In effect, these objects are automatically evicted on transaction rollback. As a result of rollback and automatic eviction, the persistent-clean, persistent-dirty, and persistent-deleted objects become hollow.

 NOTE Eviction, whether it occurs automatically after commit or roll-back or results from a call to the persistence manager's evict method, should never evict objects that are not persistent at the start of the operation or the state of any object's transactional but nonpersistent fields. As mentioned in Chapter 3, you may find implementations that incorrectly evict the transactional fields along with the persistent fields.

When strong *RestoreValues* is true and the attempt to commit throws a JDOOptimisticVerificationException, the application has the chore of evicting the failed instances if it continues to use the persistence manager in which the failure occurred. Since automatic eviction does not occur on persistent-clean, persistent-dirty, and persistent-deleted application data objects unless *RestoreValues* is either weak or false, the failed objects are still associated with the old concurrency value that caused the failure.

Saving and Discarding the Before-Image

When the *RestoreValues* property is true, JDO may save a before-image. When *RestoreValues* is true and weak, JDO saves the before-image when the application data object becomes new. When *RestoreValues* is true and strong, JDO saves the before-image when the application data object becomes new or dirty. Objects may become new or dirty only when a transaction is active.

Application data objects become new when they are directly or indirectly affected by the persistence manager's makePersistent method. An object that becomes new is always dirty, but application data objects can become dirty in other ways as well. The application may modify a value in a managed field. The application may delete the object by calling the persistence manager's deletePersistent method. The application may call the makeDirty method in the JDOHelper class. Chapter 7 discusses the JDOHelper class.

When the time comes for JDO to save the object's before-image, JDO saves it only when the object does not already have one. For example, within the same transaction, a transient-clean object may become transient-dirty, then persistent-new, then persistent-new-deleted. JDO saves the before-image when the object becomes transient-dirty, and for that reason, it does not save a before-image when the object becomes persistent-new. On the other hand, if a JDO-transient object becomes persistent-new and then persistent-new-deleted within the same transaction, JDO saves the before-image when the object becomes persistent-new.

When the persistence manager's transaction ends, whether by commit or rollback, JDO discards the before-image of all transactional objects managed by the transaction's persistence manager. When the application calls the persistence manager's makeNontransactional, evict, or refresh methods, JDO discards the before-image of the affected objects.

Optimizations Available to the JDO Implementation

The implementation has several opportunities to optimize the work in saving and restoring the before-image. For example, if the object is hollow when it becomes dirty, the implementation may be able to represent the before-image in a more efficient manner than by making a copy of its hollow state. It might use a flag as the way to indicate that the before-image is the hollow state. Likewise, after a persistent object is deleted, JDO prevents any changes to its persistent state. Therefore, there is no need to make a before-image to restore. Nonetheless, since dirty objects can be deleted, the object when deleted may already have a before-image, which JDO would keep and use to restore from.

As Chapter 3 describes, when JDO makes an object persistent, it replaces the references in persistent fields to objects of the supported mutable system classes, such as Date and HashSet, with references to objects that are instances of the classes supplied by the JDO implementation, which subclass the system classes. When *RestoreValues* is true, the before-image has the reference to the original instance of the system class, and in the event of rollback, the reference to the original system class object is restored in the persistent field.

On the other hand, when the object is persistent-clean or persistent-nontransactional, the loaded persistent fields that refer to objects of supported mutable system classes already refer to objects of the implementation's subclasses. In some cases, it is not feasible or desirable to make a copy of these objects. For this reason, JDO specifies that the implementation does not include these fields in the before-image, and upon rollback, the value of these fields is set to null. Doing this is transparent to the application, because JDO reloads the values from the datastore when the application makes the next access to these fields. Although the specification is not clear, it is reasonable to expect that any transactional but not persistent field in a persistent object and any managed field in a transient-dirty object, even when the field is a supported mutable system type, is fully backed up in the before-image for use in the event of rollback.

Although the optimization strategies available to the implementation make the description of saving and restoring a before-image more precise, they are implementation details that you can ignore as an application programmer.

Synchronizing with Transaction Completion

The Synchronization interface is defined in the Java Transaction API. The Synchronization interface notifies the application when the transaction ends. As Figure 4-2 shows, the interface has two methods. JDO calls the beforeCompletion method when the transaction is starting the commit step, but never calls the beforeCompletion method when the transaction is starting a rollback step. JDO calls the afterCompletion method when the transaction has finished the commit or rollback step. JDO passes one of two values in the status parameter of the afterCompletion call.

```
javax.transaction.Status.STATUS_COMMITTED
javax.transaction.Status.STATUS_ROLLEDBACK.
```

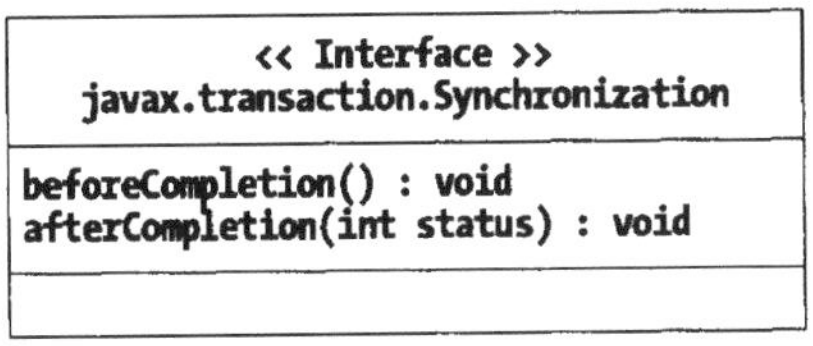

```
        << Interface >>
  javax.transaction.Synchronization

beforeCompletion() : void
afterCompletion(int status) : void

```

Figure 4-2. The class diagram of the Synchronization *interface*

The Transaction interface provides getter-setter methods for its *Synchronization* property.

```
public javax.transaction.Synchronization getSynchronization()
public void setSynchronization(javax.transaction.Synchronization syncObject)
```

If the application wants to be notified when the transaction completes, it calls the setSynchronization method to register a Synchronization object. JDO calls this object's methods when the boundary events occur in the transaction. Since JDO itself is either controlling the transaction's boundaries or must be aware of the same boundary events, the Synchronization object that the application selects always receives notifications. The Synchronization callbacks occur whether the application controls the transactional boundaries through JDO's Transaction interface or whether a container controls the transactional boundaries.

The transaction holds a reference to only one Synchronization object. Setting the property to a new Synchronization object replaces the previous Synchronization object, if any, with the new one. Setting the property to null prevents callbacks to a Synchronization object. Calling the setSynchronization method within a Synchronization callback or during the time that a transaction is completing yields a JDOUserException.

Although many applications may not find the need to register a Synchronization object with the transaction, there are several scenarios that lead to using this interface. First, there may be a nontransactional step that needs to be taken when a transaction commits or rolls back. For example, a message might be sent or logged to a nontransactional message or logging service. Second, there may be unmanaged objects that need cleanup after a transaction commit. The application can use the afterCompletion callback to handle both of these scenarios. Third, there may be situations where the application wants to make information consistent before the commit. The application can use the beforeCompletion method to handle this need.

In some cases, the application may want to prevent the transaction's commit from succeeding. If the application code lives within an EJB whose transactions are managed by the container, the application can use the beforeCompletion callback in the Synchronization class to call the setRollbackOnly method in its bean's javax.ejb.EJBContext object. This action forces the container to roll back the transaction.

When the application itself controls the transactional boundaries through JDO's Transaction interface, the application should not attempt to reverse a commit in beforeCompletion. There is no setRollbackOnly method in JDO's Transaction interface. Instead, the application makes the decision whether to call commit or rollback based on all the information that it needs to consider. Thereafter, there is no reason to reconsider. Neither JTA nor JDO defines the expected behavior when an unchecked exception is thrown in the Synchronization callbacks.

How the Transactional Properties Control State Transitions

The best way to understand the purpose and effect of the five transactional properties is to understand how the property settings affect JDO's actions, whether implicit or explicit, when they alter the managed state of application data objects. Quite a few diagrams are presented in this section. Each diagram shows changes in the object's management state that result from JDO actions under the different settings of the transactional properties. Their purpose is to provide more than enough detail to sort through even the worse confusion.

JDO State Transitions Outside of Transactions

There are four possible combinations of the two nontransactional properties. Since there is no apparent use for turning on *NontransactionalWrite* without also turning on *NontransactionalRead*, this case is not considered here. Likewise, when *NontransactionalRead* and *NontransactionalWrite* are both turned off, access to persistent fields outside of transactions is not possible. Two configurations remain. In the first case, *NontransactionalRead* is true and *NontransactionalWrite* is false. In the second case, both are true.

Figure 4-3 illustrates the state transitions of an application data object when the allowed persistent operations are performed outside of a transaction and when *NontransactionalRead* (NTR) is true and *NontransactionalWrite* (NTW) is false. In this transactional configuration, there are only three management states that application data objects can be in. These states are the three nontransactional states in JDO. The other seven management states are all transactional states. All of them, except the transient-clean state, are therefore not possible when a trans-action is not active. The transient-clean state is discussed in the section "The Optional Transient-Transactional Feature" found later in this chapter.

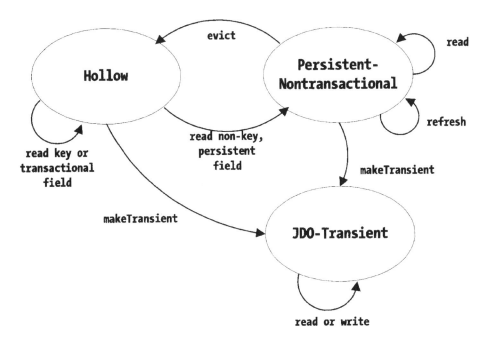

Figure 4-3. State transitions outside a transaction when NTR is true and NTW is false

When an application data object is hollow, all of its persistent field values are cleared except for its key fields. An application data object has one or more persistent key fields only when its class uses application identity. When a key field of a hollow object is accessed, the object remains hollow. When a persistent, non-key field of a hollow object is accessed, the value of the field is loaded from the datastore and the object becomes persistent-nontransactional. Once in memory, the field's value is not loaded again, unless it is refreshed or evicted. Outside a transaction, persistent application data objects, whether hollow or persistent-nontransactional, can be made JDO-transient, but JDO-transient objects cannot be made persistent. JDO-transient objects, because they are unmanaged by JDO, are not bound by any JDO rules about when their fields can be accessed or modified.

Figure 4-4 illustrates the state transitions of an application data object when the allowed persistent operations are performed outside of a transaction and when both *NontransactionalRead* and *NontransactionalWrite* are true. The state transitions permitted here are very similar to those permitted for the transactional configuration of Figure 4-3, except that now both reads and writes are allowed whereas before only reads were allowed.

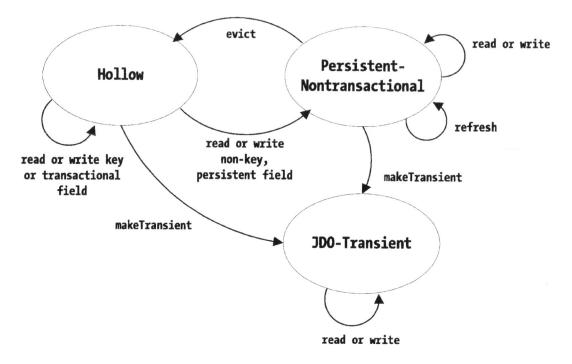

Figure 4-4. State transitions outside a transaction when both NTR and NTW are true

JDO State Transitions Inside Transactions

The three properties, *Optimistic*, *RetainValues*, and *RestoreValues*, control JDO's actions on managed objects within a transaction. Before looking at how JDO behaves when these properties are turned on or off, it is helpful to examine all of JDO's actions within a transaction that are not affected by these properties. Of the ten management states for application data objects, five are persistent and transactional, two are persistent but not transactional, and one is neither persistent nor transactional. These eight states are found in most of the diagrams presented here. The remaining two JDO management states, transient-clean and transient-dirty, occur only when the application makes use of JDO's optional support for transient and transactional objects. "The Optional Transient-Transactional Feature" section found later in this chapter describes the transient-transactional implementation option.

For the eight management states that are not transient and transactional, Figure 4-5 shows all the JDO actions that can occur within transactions and meet the following four conditions:

- The effects of the action are the same regardless of the settings of the *Optimistic*, *RetainValues*, or *RestoreValues* properties.

- The action is allowed (i.e., it does not throw an exception).

- Either the action results in a state change, or it is not obvious that the state would not change.

- The action does not make use of the optional JDO transient-transactional feature.

Although the diagram of state transitions in Figure 4-5 is complex, there are a few simple principles that organize the complexity. Objects in any of the persistent states can be deleted, but persistent-new objects transition to the persistent-new-deleted state rather than the persistent-deleted state. An application can access the key fields of deleted objects, but it cannot access non-key fields of deleted objects, nor can it write any fields of a deleted object. Reading the value of a key field never changes the object's state. When the application writes to a persistent field, the object becomes persistent-dirty, unless it is persistent-new. JDO's makeTransient method applies to only the objects that are hollow, persistent-clean, and persistent-nontransactional. The application can access or modify any field it likes for an application data object in the JDO-transient state because JDO is not managing access to any of the object's fields.

As Figure 4-5 shows, the makeNontransactional method changes persistent-clean objects to persistent-nontransactional. If the JDO implementation does not support the javax.jdo.option.NontransactionalRead option, then calling makeNontransactional for a persistent-clean object results in a JDOUnsupportedOptionException.

Figure 4-5 provides the background for the figures that follow. While Figure 4-5 shows the actions that are independent of the three properties, *Optimistic*, *RetainValues*, and *RestoreValues*, the figures that follow show the actions that are dependent on the values of one of these properties.

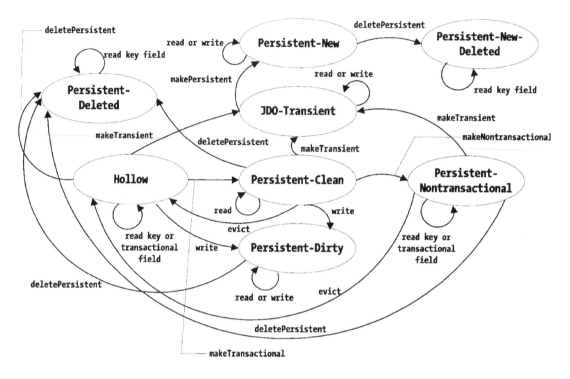

Figure 4-5. State transitions common to all transactions

JDO State Transitions Unique to Datastore Transactions

Figure 4-6 shows the operations whose behavior is unique to a datastore transaction. A JDO transaction is a datastore transaction when the transaction's *Optimistic* property is set to false. The persistent-clean state is central to the datastore transaction. When an application data object is in the persistent-clean state, its persistent state is transactionally consistent with the datastore. JDO provides the transactional consistency by starting an underlying database transaction that remains open for the duration of the JDO datastore transaction. JDO loads fresh values of the persistent state as needed within this underlying database transaction. Some JDO implementations may also lock the state in the datastore to prevent other transactions from changing it.

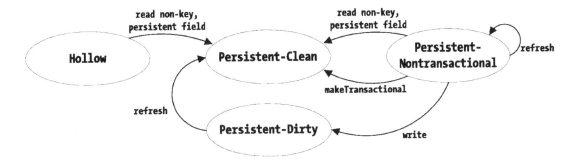

Figure 4-6. State transitions unique to datastore transactions

Reading a persistent non-key field of a hollow application data object or passing the application data object to makeTransactional causes JDO to change the object to persistent-clean. When the application data object is persistent-nontransactional, reading a persistent non-key field in the object causes JDO to discard the object's existing persistent state during the change to persistent-clean. Usually, the implementation loads the default fetch group during the transition to persistent-clean. Writing any persistent field of a persistent-nontransactional object causes JDO to discard the existing persistent state and reload fresh values as needed from the datastore before JDO applies the change.

Refreshing a persistent-dirty object causes JDO to discard the persistent state, including the modifications made. The object reverts to persistent-clean. Some JDO implementations may be able to restore the correct transactional values for the persistent fields from the before-image, while others may need to reload the correct values from the datastore.

Interestingly, passing a persistent-nontransactional object to the refresh method may be a no-op in a datastore transaction. In a datastore transaction, there is little reason for the implementation to carry out the refresh actions on a persistent-nontransactional object, since either read or write access to the persistent fields causes an implicit refresh.

JDO State Transitions Unique to Optimistic Transactions

Figure 4-7 illustrates the behavior that is unique to optimistic transactions. A transaction is optimistic when its *Optimistic* property is set to true. The figure shows behavior for optimistic transactions that is strikingly different from the behavior diagrammed for datastore transactions in Figure 4-6. In the optimistic transaction, the persistent-nontransactional state is central. When a non-key, persistent field of a hollow object is accessed, the object changes to persistent-nontransactional. Reading any field of a persistent-nontransactional object leaves it in the persistent-nontransactional state. In both cases, any persistent field values that are not already loaded into memory are fetched from the datastore as needed. Usually, the JDO implementation loads the object's default fetch group during the transition to persistent-nontransactional.

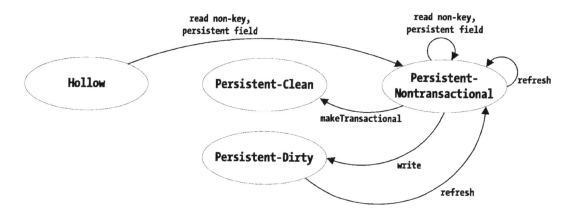

Figure 4-7. State transitions unique to optimistic transactions

If a persistent-nontransactional object is made transactional, the persistent state is not refreshed before the object becomes persistent-clean. Instead of reloading the persistent state (and possibly locking it) as would happen in a datastore transaction, the optimistic transaction enforces transactional consistency by checking the concurrency value of all transactional objects during commit processing.

Within an optimistic transaction, when the application writes to a persistent field of a persistent-nontransactional object, the object's state changes to persistent-dirty. Before the write is applied, the persistent fields of the object are *not* refreshed. Rather, the existing values of the persistent fields are kept.

A refresh on a persistent-nontransactional object causes the persistent state to be discarded. JDO reloads new values as needed, and as its option, it may reload the default fetch group immediately. Some implementation may perform the refresh only when the concurrency value indicates that the persistent state is out-of-date. When a persistent-dirty object is refreshed, the changes to its persistent state made within the transaction are lost. During the refresh, the object becomes persistent-nontransactional.

JDO State Transitions When RetainValues Is False

Figure 4-8 illustrates the behavior that is unique to transactions when the *Retain-Values* property is false. As Figure 4-8 shows, application data objects that are both persistent and transactional become either hollow or JDO-transient upon transaction commit when *RetainValues* is false. Whether they become hollow or JDO-transient, JDO clears their persistent fields.

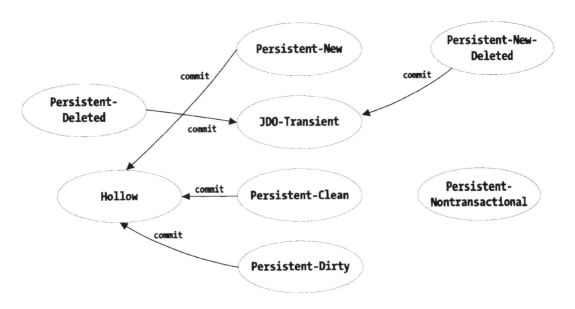

Figure 4-8. State transitions upon commit when RetainValues is false

Application data objects that are not transactional are not affected by transaction completion. In particular, the commit method has no effect on objects that are in the hollow, persistent-nontransactional, or JDO-transient state. As a result, setting the *RetainValues* property to false does not automatically evict persistent-nontransactional objects when the transaction commits.

JDO State Transitions When RetainValues Is True

Figure 4-9 illustrates the behavior that is unique to transactions when the *RetainValues* property is true. As Figure 4-9 shows, application data objects that are both transactional and persistent become either persistent-nontransactional or JDO-transient upon transaction commit when *RetainValues* is true. Whether they become persistent-nontransactional or JDO-transient, JDO retains the values of their persistent fields.

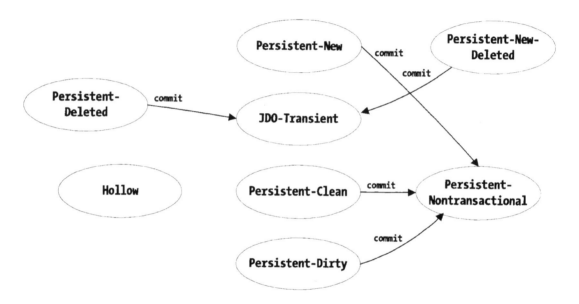

Figure 4-9. State transitions upon commit when RetainValues is true

Application data objects that are not transactional are not affected by transaction completion. In particular, a call to the commit method has no effect on objects that are in the hollow, persistent-nontransactional, or JDO-transient state.

JDO State Transitions When RestoreValues Is False

Figure 4-10 illustrates the behavior that is unique to transactions when the *RestoreValues* property is false. As Figure 4-10 shows, when *RestoreValues* is false, all transactional objects become either hollow or JDO-transient upon transaction rollback. The persistent fields of persistent-clean, persistent-dirty, and persistent-deleted application data objects are cleared to their Java default values on rollback.

As a result of both rollback and the automatic eviction, the objects become hollow. On the other hand, on rollback when *RestoreValues* is false, JDO retains the values of the persistent fields of persistent-new and persistent-new-deleted objects.

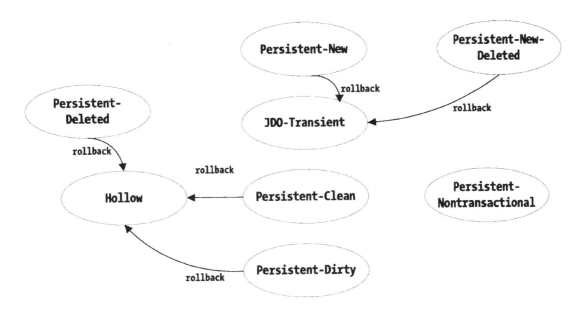

Figure 4-10. State transitions upon rollback when RestoreValues is false

Application data objects that are not transactional are not affected by transaction completion. In particular, the rollback method has no effect on objects that are in the hollow, persistent-nontransactional, or JDO-transient state.

JDO State Transitions When Strong RestoreValues Is True

Figure 4-11 illustrates the behavior that is unique to transactions when strong *RestoreValues* is true. As Figure 4-11 shows, all transactional objects become hollow, persistent-nontransactional, or JDO-transient upon transaction rollback when strong *RestoreValues* is true. Persistent-clean objects do not have a before-image. As a result, they change to persistent-nontransactional upon rollback.

Persistent-dirty and persistent-deleted objects may become hollow or persistent-nontransactional. They become hollow because they previously changed to the persistent-dirty or persistent-deleted state from the hollow state. As a result, the before-image contains the Java default values for the persistent fields. On the

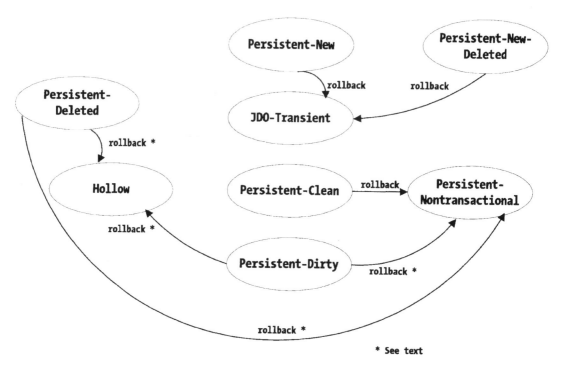

Figure 4-11. State transitions upon rollback when strong RestoreValues is true

other hand, if the persistent-dirty or persistent-deleted objects were previously persistent-clean or persistent-nontransactional, then they become persistent-nontransactional as a result of restoring from the before-image upon rollback.

Application data objects that are not transactional are not affected by transaction completion. In particular, the `rollback` method has no effect on objects that are in the hollow, persistent-nontransactional, or JDO-transient state.

JDO State Transitions When Weak RestoreValues Is True

Figure 4-12 illustrates the behavior that is unique to transactions when weak *RestoreValues* is true. As Figure 4-12 shows, persistent-new and persistent-new-deleted objects become JDO-transient upon transaction rollback when weak *RestoreValues* is true. Persistent-clean, persistent-dirty, and persistent-deleted objects become hollow.

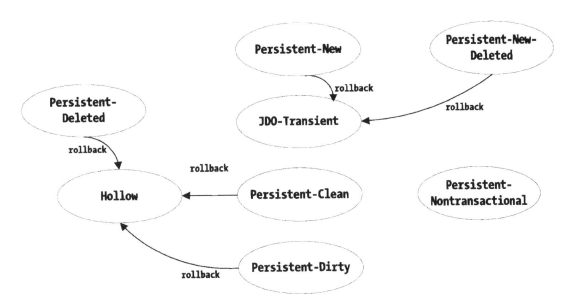

Figure 4-12. State transitions upon rollback when weak RestoreValues is true

If you compare Figure 4-12 with Figure 4-10, you can see that the state transitions when *RestoreValues* is weak are the same whether the property is true or false. All that changes is whether JDO saves a before-image when the object becomes persistent-new and whether JDO restores the managed fields of persistent-new and persistent-new-deleted objects from the before-image upon rollback.

The Optional Transient-Transactional Feature

JDO gives its implementations the option to support the transient-transactional feature. When an implementation supports this feature, it supports application data objects in the transient-clean and transient-dirty states in addition to the JDO-transient state. An application data object in any of the three transient states may have persistent fields, but because the object is not persistent, these fields are not synchronized with persistent state in the datastore. The persistent fields of the transient and transactional object are managed as if they were transactional fields. An application data object in any of the three transient states does not have a JDO identity.

NOTE Applications can determine whether an implementation supports the transient-transactional feature by looking for the "javax.jdo.option.TransientTransactional" string in the collection of strings returned from the supportedOptions method in the JDOHelper class. Chapter 7 describes the JDOHelper class.

Figure 4-13 illustrates the behavior for the three transient management states. As Figure 4-13 shows, a JDO-transient object becomes transient-clean when passed to the makeTransactional method in the persistence manager. The call succeeds whether a transaction is active or not. If the transient-transactional feature is not supported, calling the method yields a JDOUnsupportedOptionException.

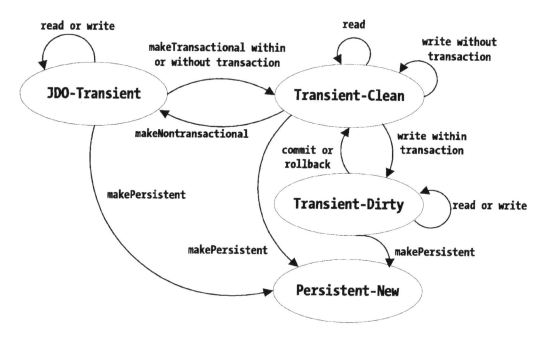

Figure 4-13. Additional state transitions when JDO supports the transient-transactional feature

When a transaction is active, the persistence manager's makePersistent method can make any transient object persistent-new. Once an object becomes persistent-new, it can become JDO-transient, hollow, or persistent-nontransactional as the result of transaction commit or rollback. None of JDO's actions change persistent-new objects into either transient-clean or transient-dirty objects.

As Figure 4-13 shows, reading any field of an application data object in any of the three transient states never produces a state change. When a transaction is not active, writes to any fields in JDO-transient or transient-clean objects do not produce a state change. Once the transaction becomes active, writes to managed fields cause the transient-clean object to become transient-dirty. When weak or strong *RestoreValues* is true, JDO saves the before-image before making the object transient-dirty.

The evict, refresh, and retrieve operations of the persistence manager perform no operation and return silently when passed JDO-transient, transient-clean, and transient-dirty objects, with one exception. The evict method throws a JDOUserException when a JDO-transient object is passed to it. The transaction properties *RetainValues, Optimistic, NontransactionalRead,* and *NontransactionalWrite* have no effect on JDO-transient, transient-clean, or transient-dirty objects.

The transaction's commit operation discards any saved before-image and changes the transient-dirty object to transient-clean. Otherwise, no changes are made to the field values. In particular, setting *RetainValues* to false does not cause JDO to clear the persistent fields of the object.

The transaction's rollback operation retains the existing values of all managed fields in the transient-dirty object when *RestoreValues* is false. It restores the managed fields to the values saved in the object's before-image, when *RestoreValues* is true. Commit and rollback have no effect on JDO-transient and transient-clean objects.

Practical uses for the two transient and transactional states are likely to be specialized.

JCA, JTA, and JDO Transactions

Some JDO implementations are designed to work in unmanaged environments, and some are designed to work in managed environments that use the J2EE Connector Architecture and the Java Transaction API. Some JDO implementations work in both managed and unmanaged environments.

 NOTE   To learn more about JCA and JTA, visit the Sun Microsystems Web site at http://java.sun.com.

One of the purposes of JCA is to define the contracts between a resource adaptor that manages a transactional service and the container that manages transactions. When a JDO implementation is designed to work with a J2EE container, it can function as a resource adaptor within JCA. In this case, the JDO implementation supports all of the connection, transaction, and security contracts that JCA requires. Alternatively, the JDO implementation can function as a caching manager within JCA. In this case, the JDO implementation integrates with the transaction management of JCA and uses some existing resource adaptor to connect to the datastore. Some implementations may be able to perform in either role. Either way, as a result of its integration with JCA and JTA, the J2EE container can control the JDO transactions.

When the J2EE container controls the EJB's transactional boundaries, the container is providing a service called *container-managed transactions*. The application code in the EJB that uses CMT does not call the boundary methods in the JDO Transaction interface. When the CMT EJB calls a factory to get a persistence manager, the factory method enlists the persistence manager in the container-managed transaction, if there is one. If there isn't an active transaction, then the persistence manager must be used nontransactionally. In other words, the *NontransactionalRead* property must be turned on and persistent state cannot be updated.

NOTE   Chapter 6 provides code templates for most types of EJB components, and describes in detail how and when to obtain a persistence manager inside an EJB.

J2EE allows session beans to manage their own transactions. This capability is called *bean-managed transactions*. Only session beans have the BMT option. The application code in a BMT session bean has the option of using the JDO Transaction interface or the JTA javax.transaction.UserTransaction interface to control the transactional boundaries. The use of the UserTransaction interface imposes some constraints that must be observed.

In a BMT session bean, the UserTransaction is obtained from the javax.ejb.SessionContext interface. When the bean uses UserTransaction to start the transaction, the PersistenceManager object must be obtained from the PersistenceManagerFactory after the transaction is started; otherwise, the persistence manager is not enlisted in the transaction. As a result, if the application wanted to execute two transactions, one after the other, within a bean method, it must obtain one persistence manager for each transaction that it starts with the UserTransaction interface.

When the application uses the JDO Transaction interface, it has more flexibility. In a BMT session bean, the JDO Transaction interface can control the transaction just as it can in an unmanaged environment. In this case, the application code does not use the UserTransaction interface at all. If the application wants to run a series of transactions, the same persistence manager may be used. The JDO implementation, if it is designed to work with JCA and JTA, ensures that the UserTransaction begins when the JDO Transaction begins and completes when the JDO Transaction completes. For simplicity, it is recommended that the application code always use the JDO Transaction interface in BMT session beans.

JDO's Cache of Persistent Objects and Their State

Each persistence manager controls a cache of persistent objects. Each persistent object has persistent fields that hold the values that JDO can synchronize with the datastore. When the application first gets the value of a persistent field in a persistent object, the persistence manager loads the value from the datastore. The cost to fetch the value of a persistent field from the datastore is never paid more than once per transaction.

The persistence manager uses the application data object as the primary place to store the values of its persistent fields. When a persistent field does not contain its persistent value, JDO sets the field to its Java default value. When a persistent object has no persistent state in memory, it is in the hollow management state. Since the persistent value may be the same as the Java default value, JDO must always know whether the persistent field holds the field's persistent value or its default value.

JDO may read a field's value from the datastore and cache it prior to the application's access to the field. The JDO implementation reads the default fetch group in one database access as a performance optimization. The default fetch group is a block of fields that are usually stored together in the datastore. The JDO metadata defines, either explicitly or by default, which fields are members of the default fetch group. Chapter 5 discusses the JDO metadata.

As a general observation, the performance benefit of caching is the discounted cost of subsequent use of cached information. To gain the benefit from JDO, the application must access the value of the persistent field more than once, and it must do so before JDO discards the persistent field's value.

The JDO specification describes caching for one persistence manager. The JDO implementation may architect a deeper caching strategy that provides for caching across all of the persistence managers in one or more JVMs. JDO does not specify whether the implementation does this, or how it does this. The section entitled "The JDO Implementation's Second-Level Cache," found later in this chapter, discusses the deeper caching strategy. Otherwise, the caching architecture discussed here is the one-cache-per-persistence-manager architecture that JDO specifies.

Removing Persistent Objects from the Cache

The garbage collector can remove some persistent objects from the persistence manager's cache. JDO usually holds a strong reference to all transactional objects, but it holds only a weak or soft reference to objects that are either hollow or persistent-nontransactional. As a result, unless the application holds a strong reference to a hollow or persistent-nontransactional object, the object can be garbage collected.

 NOTE The `java.lang.ref` package defines the basic mechanisms of weak and soft references.

When Can the Persistence Manager's Cache Improve Performance?

The contents of the persistence manager's cache has little effect on the performance of queries made against an extent. The reason is straightforward: queries against an extent involve a trip to the datastore to determine, at a minimum, the identity values of the objects that satisfy the query. This is the major cost of the query, and it must be paid whether the objects that the query finds are in the cache or not.

Likewise, the cache can offer only a marginal performance improvement when the application uses the objects returned by the query. The reason is not quite so straightforward as before. When JDO sends the query to the datastore to retrieve the identity values, it can usually add, at a low marginal cost to the query performance, the request to retrieve the values of the default fetch group associated with the objects found. Since the cost is low and the decision to request the default fetch group must be made before it can be known whether the objects are in the cache, the JDO implementation will usually make the request to retrieve the default fetch group. As a result, finding the object in the cache can improve performance significantly only when the application reuses a field that is not in the default fetch group.

If the persistence manager cache does not help when executing a query or iterating its results, when does it boost performance? Each of the objects that the application gets by iterating the query's results or the extent is a root of a potential graph of objects that can be reached by navigating the persistent fields that refer to other data objects. When these other objects are in memory and have most of their persistent state loaded, then JDO can dramatically improve the speed of transparent navigation by avoiding the trip to the datastore. In short, the persistence manager's cache can improve the performance of transparent navigation, and it might improve somewhat the use of the objects returned in the query results, but it cannot speed up queries.

Controlling the Persistence Manager's Cache

When all five transactional properties are false, JDO limits the lifetime of persistent state to the lifetime of the transaction. When the transaction ends, the persistent object becomes either hollow or JDO-transient. The persistent state outlives a transaction only when one or more of the transactional properties are turned on. Turning on *NontransactionalRead*, *Optimistic*, *RetainValues*, and in some cases *RestoreValues* creates persistent-nontransactional objects that retain their persistent state outside of and across transactions.

By limiting caching to the transaction, the application pays a minimal amount for caching and its benefits. There is no risk of stale information since the persistent state loaded within the transaction is subject to the same transactional properties regardless of how often it is used. At the same time, when caching is limited to the transaction, the performance benefit from reuse is also limited to the transaction. For some applications, reuse within the transaction is significant, but for other applications, the significant reuse is across transactional boundaries or even across persistence managers.

When caching crosses the transactional boundaries, the application runs the risk of using potentially stale information that is no longer consistent with the state stored in the datastore. Optimistic transactions remove the risk of using outdated information for any objects that are changed or otherwise made transactional, but the risk remains for those objects that are not transactional.

The JDO Implementation's Second-Level Cache

As mentioned earlier, JDO does not specify that implementations provide any caching beyond the cache of persistent objects managed by each persistence manager. Nonetheless, many JDO implementations provide a second-level cache because the design patterns for using JDO often require that a persistence manager be dedicated to each request handled by a stateless service or to each user handled by a stateful service. Due to the frequently observed commonality of interests in multiple requests from the same and different users, a second-level cache can provide caching benefits when a persistence manager's cache cannot.

NOTE Chapter 9 examines the design issues in client/server applications. Chapter 10 examines the design issues in Web applications, and Chapter 11 examines the design issues when using JDO within Enterprise JavaBeans. Both Web components and EJB components are expected to make heavy use of the one-persistence-manager-per-request design pattern. For this reason, these application architectures benefit from a second-level cache.

When the implementation provides a second-level cache, what does it mean to say that the persistent state is loaded from the datastore? The answer depends on whether the application is using a datastore transaction or an optimistic transaction. In a datastore transaction, the persistent state that is loaded must be consistent with the state available from the database transaction. Although the application may have a choice of mechanisms to guarantee consistency with the database (for example, locking the entire database, locking the schema, receiving an administrative assurance of exclusive ownership, etc.), one typical way to make this guarantee is to fetch the persistent state from the datastore within the database transaction. In this case, there is no benefit derived from state that is stored in memory prior to the start of the datastore transaction.

On the other hand, the optimistic transaction makes only some objects transactional, and it verifies the persistent state of transactional objects only on transaction commit. For these reasons, when an optimistic transaction "loads the persistent state from the datastore," it can cheat by fetching the values from a second-level cache if there is one. Later, when changes are written to the datastore upon transaction commit, the concurrency values of transactional objects are checked against the values in the datastore. By using the secondary cache, the JDO implementation can provide a performance boost for optimistic transactions that it may not be able to provide for datastore transactions.

When the application wishes to take advantage of the second-level cache provided by the JDO implementation, it should, as a general rule, use optimistic rather than datastore transactions. As JDO implementations evolve their cache management, this general rule will develop qualifications and exceptions, but it is a good place to start when seeking to understand how to benefit from the implementation's second-level cache.

Summary

Many applications require the use of transactions to protect the integrity of the data. The persistence manager has associated with it one and only one Transaction object. This Transaction object can be used to start and complete transactions in unmanaged environments. When the JDO implementation supports managed environments such as EJB containers, the JDO Transaction object is integrated with the UserTransaction in JTA and the transaction management in JCA.

The Transaction interface provides five properties to configure JDO's behavior in transactions. These properties control when transactions are needed, the type of transaction used, and the disposition of persistent state in transactional objects when the transaction ends. When necessary, the application uses the evict, refresh, and retrieve methods in the PersistenceManager interface to fine-tune when persistent state is discarded or loaded.

By using the Query, PersistenceManager, and Transaction interfaces, the application controls the explicit services of JDO. For JDO to be able to provide transparent persistence or implicit persistence services, the application data classes must be enhanced to support JDO's PersistenceCapable interface. The next chapter examines the anatomy of application data classes. It describes how to control the enhancement step through the JDO metadata and where enhancement impacts the existing functionality or design of the application data classes.

CHAPTER 5

Enhanced Classes and Managed Fields

THE APPLICATION PROGRAMMER designs and codes the application data classes. The JDO implementation provides an enhancer tool to modify the application data classes. The modifications made during enhancement allow JDO and the application data objects to interact with each other. The JDO metadata, which is contained in an XML file, identifies the application data classes and describes their managed fields.

To begin, this chapter describes, in a general way, what application data classes are. It details JDO's requirements for their managed and unmanaged fields and how enhancement changes the application data class. It concludes by describing the tags and attributes of the JDO metadata.

Which Application Classes Should Be Enhanced?

Application data classes represent fine-grained objects that model the interesting state of the real world. The application data classes and their interrelationships may be simple or complex, depending on the needs of the application. Application data classes may inherit from classes that will be enhanced or from classes that will not be enhanced. Application data classes may implement interfaces. There may be only a few application data classes, or there may be hundreds.

An application data class may be code light or it may be code heavy. It may have only getter-setter methods to control access to member fields, enforce rules for valid state, and handle type conversions. Although it often makes sense to keep application data classes light in code, JDO handles code-intensive application data classes equally well. Application designers can put into the application data classes as much code as they need.

JDO assumes that application data classes hold their persistent state in their instance fields. If the persistent state is someplace else, such as in a system resource outside the JVM, then JDO cannot manage the object's persistent state. For example, JDO cannot make the java.io.FileInputStream class persistence capable because most of its interesting state is in a file rather than in the class's member variables.

The application data classes define the application's persistent object model. Designing the persistent object model for most applications is a nontrivial task. The designer must identify the classes of persistent objects, the elements of their persistent state, the relationships between the objects, the behavior of the objects, their collaboration with other objects, the inheritance relationships between classes, and so forth. JDO helps the designer carry out these tasks by staying out of the way.

From a designer's standpoint, the ideal persistence service is orthogonal to all other concerns in the object model. For this reason, JDO strives not to impose constraints on the persistent object model. JDO goes a long way towards this ideal because, for the most part, the application programmer can design and code the application data classes without being aware of JDO.

Managed and Unmanaged Fields

When JDO manages an object, it manages the individual fields of that object. For JDO, there are three kinds of fields in the application data class:

- Persistent fields

- Transactional fields

- Unmanaged fields

The JDO metadata determines whether a field is persistent, transactional, or unmanaged.

What Types of Fields Can Be Unmanaged?

Any type of field can be unmanaged. JDO imposes no constraints on unmanaged fields.

Fields that are declared with the static or final keywords must be unmanaged. JDO ignores static fields because they do not contain dynamic object state.

JDO's architecture does not allow it to manage final fields. JDO uses the no-arg constructor of the application data class to create the object before it reads the values of persistent fields from the datastore. Since the values of final fields can be assigned only in field initializers or constructors, there is no way for JDO to load the value of a final field from the datastore.

What Types of Fields Can Be Transactional?

Except for static and final fields, any type of field can be transactional. The values of a transactional field are never stored or found in the datastore. JDO includes the values of transactional fields in the before-image that JDO saves when the transactional object becomes dirty and the transaction's *RestoreValues* property is true.

Restoring Transactional Fields on Rollback

Although the specification is not entirely clear on this point, a reasonable interpretation holds that JDO restores on rollback the field values of any type of transactional field when the transaction's *RestoreValue* property is true. It should not matter whether the implementation offers strong or weak supports for the *RestoreValues* property. JDO should restore the field's value when its type is a primitive type, an immutable class, a supported mutable system class, an unsupported mutable system class, or an application data class. In other words, JDO should restore the field's value in all cases.

Beyond restoring the transactional field's value, JDO does not impose any additional requirements. Although JDO defines persistence by reachability for persistent fields, it does not define transactional by reachability for transactional fields. If a transactional field refers to a JDO-transient application data object, and the application changes that object without changing the transactional field that refers to that object, the restore on rollback may not (and probably will not) undo the change. If a transactional field refers to an object that is an instance of an unsupported mutable system class and the application changes that object, the restore on rollback may not (and probably will not) undo the change.

In the case of transactional fields that refer to objects of supported mutable system classes, JDO may, or may not, undo the changes to the objects upon restore. For example, if the transactional field's type is HashSet and the application changes the HashSet object by adding or removing an element, the JDO implementation may, or may not, undo the change to the HashSet object when restoring upon rollback. In this case, the likelihood is more that it will than it will not.

On all of these points, because the specification is not clear, implementations may differ.

What Types of Fields Can Be Persistent?

All JDO implementations must support persistent fields that have any of the following primitive or reference types:

- Any enhanced application data class.

- All eight primitive types: char, byte, short, int, long, float, double, and boolean.

- The eight immutable wrapper classes of primitive types in the java.lang package: Character, Byte, Short, Integer, Long, Float, Double, and Boolean.

- The immutable class String in the java.lang package.

- The immutable class Locale in the java.util package.

- Either of the two immutable classes in the java.math package: BigDecimal and BigInteger.

- Either of two mutable classes in the java.util package: Date and HashSet.

- Either of two interface types in the java.util package: Collection and Set.

- The Object class in the java.lang package. The implementation may, and probably will, restrict the types of objects that may be assigned to an Object field.

- Interface types other than the collection interfaces (Collection, List, Map, Set, etc.). The implementation may, and probably will, restrict the types of objects that may be assigned to the field.

When the persistent field's type is an Object or an interface (other than the collection interfaces), the implementation is likely to require that objects assigned to the field must be instances of one of the other supported classes. If the implementation's requirements are not met when the assignment is made, the implementation throws a ClassCastException.

Optionally Supported Types for Persistent Fields

JDO specifies a short list of types that the implementation may optionally support for persistent fields.

- Any of seven classes in the java.util package: Hashtable, Vector, ArrayList, LinkedList, HashMap, TreeMap, TreeSet

- Either of two interface types in the java.util package: Map and List

- Arrays

The application can determine which of the preceding optional field types are supported for a particular implementation by calling the supportedOptions method in the PersistenceManagerFactory interface. Chapter 6 discusses the PersistenceManagerFactory interface.

The supported collection types always support collections of application data objects. At its option, the JDO implementation may also support collections of supported system objects, such as collections of collections, collections of dates, collections of strings, and so forth.

When the persistent field is a Collection, Map, Set, or List interface type, then the implementation type for the object after it is fetched from the datastore may not be the same as the implementation type that was stored. For example, the application may make a new application data object persistent that has a List field to which has been assigned an object of type LinkedList. When the object assigned to the field is later fetched from the datastore, it may come back as an ArrayList. If it is important to the application that the object assigned to the list field always be a LinkedList object, then the field's type should be LinkedList rather than List.

If the implementation supports arrays, it supports arrays of all supported persistent types except arrays, collections, and maps. Even when the implementation supports arrays, it may decline to support arrays of arrays, arrays of collections, and arrays of maps.

Support for Fields That Implement Serializable

If a field is persistent, it may be, or may not be, serializable. If a field is serializable, it may be, or may not be, persistent. JDO does not connect the two properties in any way. On the other hand, a JDO implementation may support any type as persistent as long as the class implements the java.io.Serializable interface. In this case, the JDO implementation is going beyond what the JDO specification requires or defines. By supporting any serializable class as persistence capable, the implementation is allowing the application to define embedded objects that are stored in the datastore as second class objects.

Fields that are persistent because they are serializable have several drawbacks. Their use introduces a portability constraint because not all implementations support such fields. Their contents may be opaque in the datastore because the datastore usually stores these objects as byte fields. Without deserializing the byte field, other datastore tools cannot manipulate the values contained within the object. The JDO query language does not provide a means to access the fields within these objects, and the implementation may, or may not, support using the JDOQL equality operators (== and !=) on these fields.

Enhancement

Enhancement adds code to the application data classes to integrate them with JDO. As a result of enhancement, the enhanced class implements the PersistenceCapable interface. When JDO acts on an application data object, it acts on it as a PersistenceCapable object. Because the PersistenceCapable interface is used only by the JDO implementation, it is found in the javax.jdo.spi package. Because the enhancer, instead of the application programmer, adds the implementation of the PersistenceCapable interface, the application programmer rarely, if ever, makes direct use of the PersistenceCapable interface.

The enhancer is a tool that the JDO vendor supplies. The enhancer adds methods and member fields to the application data class. Usually, enhancement occurs after class compilation, when the enhancer modifies the byte code of the compiled class. After enhancement, application data classes may be called *enhanced classes* to draw attention to their new form. The specification calls them PersistenceCapable classes.

Although it is typical for enhancement to be done after compilation and before deployment, vendors may choose to do it in some other way. JDO specifies the objectives of enhancement, but it does not specify how or when enhancement should occur. There are other approaches that vendors might use. They might enhance the class through the use of code generators. They might also enhance the class through the use of a specially designed class loader that enhances at runtime. It's sobering to think that they could simply leave it to the application programmer to cut and paste in the required code, but this error-prone method is not likely to be popular.

Although byte-code enhancement does not require the source code for the application data class, the application programmer needs to know many implementation details about the application data class. To enhance a class and use it effectively, the developer must know the names and types of the managed fields. Source code or documentation can provide this information. The developer can also obtain it by using the class disassembler that comes with the Java SDK. For example, to see all the fields of the FileInputStream class, enter the following command:

```
javap -private java.io.FileInputStream
```

The approach taken by the JDO specification to integrate application data classes with the persistence layer has some significant advantages. By using an interface, the application designer is free to use nearly any Java class as an application data class. By encouraging the provision of an enhancer tool, JDO moves the code required to make an application data class persistence capable into the vendor's tools. The vendor's enhancer produces the required code with no errors and little effort. Both the enhancer and the interface approach combine to keep the persistence service out of the design of the application data classes.

The Desired Effects of Enhancement

Numerous changes are made to the application data class during enhancement. Most changes occur for all application data classes, but some changes apply only to the topmost application data class in an inheritance tree. The types of changes include the following:

- The class declaration is changed to indicate that it implements the PersistenceCapable interface.

- The methods required by that interface are added.

- A few member fields are added that the new methods use.

- A pair of static getter-setter methods are introduced for each persistent field at the same access level as the field itself.

- A static setter method is introduced for each transactional field at the same access level as the field itself.

- All access to managed fields is converted to use the newly introduced static getter-setter methods.

- A constructor that meets JDO's requirements is generated when not found.

- Several changes are made to support standard object manipulations, such as cloning and serialization.

When the enhancer changes the class to implement the PersistenceCapable interface, the effect is the same as if the class had been written with the following declaration:

```
class MyApplicationDataClass implements javax.jdo.spi.PersistenceCapable
```

Enhancement adds roughly two dozen methods specified by the PersistenceCapable interface. The methods handle a variety of concerns for the JDO implementation, including JDO state interrogation, JDO identity, the construction of new objects, and the management of field values. When an application data object is persistent, it is associated with an implementation object called the *state manager*. The state manager connects a managed object with the JDO persistence service.

Enhancement adds a handful of member fields to the application data class. All of the fields are declared with either the static or transient modifier and, as a consequence, their values are not passed during serialization.

For easy identification and to prevent collisions with the names of the application-defined methods and data fields, all methods declared in the PersistenceCapable interface and all data member fields introduced into the application data class by enhancement start with the letters "jdo".

A pair of static getter-setter methods is created for each persistent field, and a static setter method is created for each transactional field. The static getter-setter methods have the same access level as the fields that they access. With few exceptions, all of the code within the application data class that accesses the member field is changed to use the corresponding static method. If the application data class implements the InstanceCallbacks interface, which Chapter 7 describes, the enhancer does not modify the application code within the jdoPreClear and jdoPostLoad methods.

The enhancer does not change the access level of a managed field. As a result, the enhancer allows unenhanced classes to compile against enhanced classes.

The Side Effects and Limitations of Enhancement

The purpose of enhancement is to make the application data class persistence capable. As a result of enhancement, side effects or potential side effects are introduced. In some cases, JDO takes precautions to avoid the potential side effects, and in other cases, the application programmer must work around the side effects if the particular effect is detrimental for the application. In a few cases, enhancement introduces limitations on the application data class that the programmer must observe. The next sections examine the potentially undesirable side effects of enhancement.

Enhancement and Constructors

If there are no constructors in the source code for a Java class, then the Java compiler generates a public no-arg constructor. If the source code defines at least one constructor, then the compiler does not generate the no-arg constructor. On the other hand, JDO requires a no-arg constructor in the application data class. The no-arg constructor can be any access level from private to public. If the enhancer does not find a no-arg constructor in the class, it adds a protected no-arg constructor.

JDO uses the no-arg constructor to instantiate the persistent object when its state is first retrieved from the datastore. The application programmer can, and almost certainly will, write other constructors that take arguments. These constructors may have any access level from private to public.

All constructors initialize unmanaged application data objects. During construction, the persistent fields have not been loaded from the datastore and the state manager is not available to load them. Before JDO can finish the initialization of the object and make it persistent, the no-arg constructor must return.

Consider JDO the Prime User of the No-Arg Constructor

JDO must use the no-arg constructor in the application data class, and in some ways, it is best to consider JDO the prime user of the no-arg constructor. In particular, the application may initialize the object differently in the no-arg constructor than it does in the other constructors. For example, if the application data class has a persistent HashSet field called dreams, initializing dreams to an instance of a HashSet in the no-arg constructor, as shown in the next line of code, can be counterproductive.

```
dreams = new HashSet();
```

This assignment introduces three wasted steps every time JDO uses the constructor. Because the dreams field is persistent, the only value of the dreams field that the application sees when the object is persistent is the value created by JDO from persistent state. As a result, the construction of the new HashSet object, its assignment, and its garbage collection are all wasted steps. Without harm to the persistent object, the constructor could allow the value of dreams to remain null.

Although initializing persistent fields is counterproductive in the no-arg constructor, initializing either transactional or unmanaged fields is not counterproductive. JDO does not reinitialize transactional or unmanaged fields. Likewise, all other constructors can initialize all fields without waste, since JDO does not use these constructors. Often, the application uses the other constructors to create new objects that may be made persistent.

In some cases, the application must use the no-arg constructor. This happens when the application data class is a JavaBean. If the application uses the no-arg constructor and requires that persistent fields be initialized to nondefault values, then the application programmer must decide between taking the performance hit of wasted initialization, providing an initialization method that the application calls after construction, or implementing lazy initialization.

Reasons to Write the No-Arg Constructor in Every Application Data Class

In Java it is common to use field initializers for member fields that always take the same nondefault value regardless of which constructor is called. This idiom introduces a difficulty for byte-code enhancement when it must add a no-arg constructor.

The compiler interprets the field initializers as meaning "put this code in all the constructors." Consequently, there is no byte code in the class file that corresponds directly to the field initializers. Instead, the compiler puts the byte code for the field initializers into each constructor. By the time byte-code enhancement occurs, the enhancer can only guess whether there were field initializers in the source code and what byte code corresponds to them. To avoid error, the enhancer is likely to make no guess at all. In this case, the field initializer code is missing from the enhancement-created no-arg constructor. To avoid this outcome, the application programmer should either avoid field initializers or write the no-arg constructor.

Every constructor of a derived class calls a super constructor of its parent class. If the call to the super constructor is not the first code in the constructor, the compiler inserts a call to the no-arg super constructor. When the no-arg constructor is not found, enhancement adds it to the application data class. The no-arg constructor that enhancement adds calls the no-arg constructor of the parent class. If the parent class is not an application data class (and therefore won't be enhanced) and if it does not have a no-arg constructor, then enhancement may end in an error condition or lead to a runtime error when the enhanced classes are used. By coding the no-arg constructor in the application data class, the programmer can detect the missing no-arg super constructor during compilation or direct the no-arg constructor to use a different constructor in the superclass.

As a result of the various small gotchas, it is good practice to always code the no-arg constructor for all application data classes. The sample no-arg constructor presented in Listing 5-1 satisfies JDO. The access modifier for the no-arg constructor may be anything from private to public. An access level of private is sufficient for JDO because the constructor is called from code that the enhancement step inserts into the class. If the application data class is a parent class for other derived application data classes, the access level cannot be private. If the application data class is used as a JavaBean, it must have a public no-arg constructor.

Listing 5-1. Sample No-Arg Constructor for Typical Application Data Class

```
private MyApplicationDataClass()
   {
   // used only by JDO
   }
```

TIP Always code a no-arg constructor in the application data class. It may be of any access level from private to public.

Enhancement and Serialization

The enhancement step provides complete support for serialization by providing additional modifications when the application data class implements `Serializable`. To support serialization, the enhancer modifies the least-derived application data classes that are assignment compatible with the `Serializable` interface.

When the enhancer adds code to the application data class to support serialization, it either generates a `writeObject` method, modifies an existing `writeObject` method, or modifies an existing `writeReplace` method. After the `writeObject` or `writeReplace` methods are enhanced, they call the `jdoPreSerialize` method in the `PersistenceCapable` interface. The `jdoPreSerialize` method ensures that all persistent fields are loaded with their persistent values prior to the object's serialization. When the enhancer generates the `writeObject` method, the method calls the `jdoPreSerialize` method and then invokes the `defaultWriteObject` method in the `ObjectOutputStream`.

 NOTE For more information on the role of the `writeObject` method in serialization, see the SDK's Javadoc for the `java.io.ObjectOutputStream` class. For more information on the role of the `writeReplace` method in serialization, see the Java Object Serialization Specification available on Sun's Web site.

Enhancement ensures that an object of an enhanced class can be serialized into the original unenhanced class, and vice versa. By inserting only static or transient member fields into the class, the enhancer ensures compatibility between the two versions of the class. If the enhancer does not find a `serialVersionUID` field in the unenhanced class, it inserts one into the enhanced class and uses the unenhanced class to calculate its value. These steps ensure that Java's serialization mechanism will find the post-enhancement class compatible with the pre-enhancement class.

When the serialization stream is deserialized, all of the deserialized objects are JDO-transient. JDO does not provide a way to deserialize a managed object. At its option, the application may deserialize into unenhanced classes.

Serialization starts with a root object. It serializes the primitive fields of the root object and follows its reference fields to other objects that are serialized in turn. Serialization skips fields marked with the `static` or `transient` keywords. Whether a field is serializable or transient for serialization is independent of whether it is persistent, transactional, or unmanaged for JDO. For that reason, any combination of the two sets of characteristics is possible. Serialization writes to the output stream all serializable fields, whether persistent, transactional, or unmanaged, and navigates to all serializable references until closure is reached. In short, enhancement does not interfere with or otherwise distort the expected result of serialization.

Because serialization invokes JDO's transparent persistence, serializing a persistent object may serialize many more objects than intended. As serialization follows the serializable references in persistent fields, JDO transparently retrieves the objects from the datastore. If the persistent data objects are sufficiently interconnected by persistent and serializable references to each other, then the resulting graph of serialized objects may be as large as the number of objects in the datastore.

Serialize Application Data Objects or Data Transfer Objects?

The typical reason to serialize an application data object is to pass it by value to a remote client. Although application data objects can be serializable, some argue that data transfer objects, which are lightweight classes containing the state of interest, should be serialized instead. In this scenario, to satisfy a request, the application data service finds the persistent application data objects, creates the needed data transfer objects, and returns the data transfer objects to the client via serialization. Although this approach works, in some circumstances it is not required.

Data transfer objects solve two related problems that can sometimes be avoided by other means. Application data classes can define heavyweight objects with business logic that may not make sense in the remote client's context. Data transfer objects can avoid sending heavyweight objects to the client by transferring the state of interest into objects specifically designed to be lightweight. JDO supports another approach that can solve the same problem.

Although application data classes can define heavyweight objects, JDO also supports application data classes that define lightweight objects. If the application designer is able to define lightweight application data classes, then the problems of heavyweight persistent objects can be avoided entirely.

Data transfer objects also solve a second problem, the potential serialization of a large graph of objects. Consider again the small town library example used in Chapter 2. In the library example, each book refers to the categories to which it belongs, and each category refers to the books that it contains. Each borrowed book refers to the borrower who borrowed it, and each borrower refers to all the books that he has borrowed. As a result, returning one book by serialization may return all the books, all the borrowers, and all the categories. Data transfer objects flexibly and effectively prevent serialization from walking the entire datastore by allowing the designer to determine anew the associations between classes. JDO permits another less flexible, but equally effective, way to solve the same problem.

In JDO, serialization and persistence are independent properties. Consequently, the application designer can statically define, by using the `transient` keyword, where to cut the object graph that is returned by serialization. Listing 5-2 shows the modifications to the library classes, originally shown in Listing 2-3, that allow one book to be serialized with its categories. It also allows one borrower to be serialized with his borrowed books and their categories. In neither case does serialization return all the objects in the datastore.

Listing 5-2. Library Classes with Judicious Use of the transient *Keyword*

```
public class Borrower implements Serializable
    {
    // each of the fields below is a persistent field
    private String name;
    private HashSet books;  // borrowed books
    private Volunteer volunteer;
    ...
    }

public class Volunteer implements Serializable
    {
    // each of the fields below is a persistent field
    private int hoursPerWeek;
    private Borrower borrower;
    ...
    }

public class Book implements Serializable
    {
    // each of the fields below is a persistent field
    private Date checkOutDate;
    private String title;
    private transient Borrower borrower;
    private HashSet categories; // book's categories
    ...
    }

public class Category implements Serializable
    {
    // each of the fields below is a persistent field
    private String name;
    private transient HashSet books; // books in this category
    ...
    }
```

In Listing 5-2, the transient keyword has been added to the borrower field in the Book class and to the books field in the Category class. Although these fields are now transient for Java's serialization, they remain persistent for JDO. Because these fields are no longer serialized, a response to a remote client can return a book, knowing that only the book and its categories are serialized. A response can also return a borrower, knowing that only the associated volunteer object, if it exists, and the list of books borrowed and their categories are returned. Because serialization skips the borrower field when it is serializing a Book object and skips the books field when it is serializing a Category object, the resulting graph of serialized objects is smaller than it would otherwise be.

As a result of the changes to the library classes, the meaning of a null value in the book's borrower field becomes more complex. (The situation for the books field in Category is similar.) On the server, if the borrower field is null, then the book is not borrowed. On the remote client, the book's borrower field is always null, because it is transient. As a result, the meaning of a null value changes with the object's genesis. Either the application data class or the code that uses the class must handle this additional complexity.

For many applications, statically cutting the object graph by judicious use of the transient keyword is a simple way to prevent serialization from walking the datastore. If more flexibility is needed, data transfer objects should be considered. The primary drawback of data transfer objects is that they create more objects on the server that must be garbage collected, and more classes that must be coded. It is possible that a future version of JDO will specify more control over the serialization of application data objects.

 TIP The JDO persistence layer completely supports serialization of enhanced classes, and for that reason, care must be taken that only the desired persistent objects are serialized.

Enhancement and Reflection

JDO makes no special accommodations for reflection. In particular, JDO does not provide transparent persistence during operations performed by reflection on member fields. As a result, when reflection is used to read or write a managed field's value, JDO is not called to perform its management tasks. Reflection can be used to call methods or constructors without harm, but using reflection to read or write managed fields should be avoided.

TIP   The data field operations of reflection are not suitable for enhanced classes because transparent persistence is not supported during the field get or set operations.

Enhancement and Introspection

Introspection discovers the properties, events, and methods of JavaBeans. It uses a class that implements the BeanInfo interface if found. If no BeanInfo class corresponding to the JavaBean is found, introspection uses reflection and naming conventions to discover the bean interface. Because enhancement adds dozens of methods to the application data class, if users are going to view the interface of the enhanced class through an introspection tool, the application programmer should provide a BeanInfo class to go with the application data class. The presence of the BeanInfo class at introspection time hides from the user the additional methods that enhancement adds.

TIP   If the application data class is a JavaBean that is introspected after enhancement, supply a corresponding BeanInfo class to hide the methods added by enhancement.

Enhancement and Deployment on Remote Clients

Because the enhanced class implements the PersistenceCapable interface and uses code in a static initializer to register the class with JDO, enhanced classes carry with them links to the classes and interfaces of the JDO specification. These links must be resolved when application data classes are loaded. Remote clients, which never use the JDO persistence service and deal only with unmanaged application data objects, still need to satisfy the links that enhancement adds. The JDO classes and interfaces are contained in the *JDO Jar* file that should be deployed with the enhanced application data classes. Because vendors may package the JDO classes as they see fit, the name of the *Jar* file containing the JDO classes may vary from implementation to implementation.

There are other deployment solutions that work for remote clients. Because remote clients do not use JDO and deal only with unmanaged application data objects, unenhanced application data classes can be deployed on the remote client. Enhancement enables serialization between the pre-enhanced and the post-enhanced application data classes. When unenhanced application data classes are deployed on the remote client, it may be possible to avoid deploying the *JDO Jar* file on the remote client. The *JDO Jar* file will still be required if the unenhanced application data class implements JDO's InstanceCallbacks interface or uses the JDOHelper class or the various JDO exception types.

Although it is simpler to deploy enhanced application data classes, along with the *JDO Jar* file, on the remote client, there are a couple of scenarios where it may make sense to deploy unenhanced classes. When the number of application data classes conspires with a limited memory footprint on the remote client, the code space saved by deploying unenhanced classes may be critical. Likewise, if the application data classes are particularly lightweight and the number of application data objects exceptionally large, the handful of extra fields added by enhancement may become a critical use of memory that can be eliminated by deploying unenhanced classes on the remote client. Another way to respond to these scenarios is to serialize data transfer objects rather than application data objects.

TIP If the client is remote from the service that uses JDO, then either enhanced classes or unenhanced classes may be deployed on the client. If enhanced classes are deployed on the client, then the *JDO Jar* file must be deployed with them. If unenhanced classes that implement the InstanceCallbacks interface or use the JDOHelper class, which Chapter 7 covers, are deployed on the client, it is still necessary to deploy the *JDO Jar* file. Deploying unenhanced classes, instead of enhanced classes, saves quite a lot of code space per class and a small amount of data space per object.

Enhancement and Cloning

Java classes support cloning by implementing the java.lang.Cloneable marker interface. In the typical case, the class supports cloning by overriding the clone method of the Object class.

When clones are made, the fields inserted by JDO enhancement are copied along with all other field values. The enhancement step alters the clone method of the application data class to make the cloned object JDO-transient before the clone method returns. This change is required only in the least-derived application data class of an inheritance tree because the typical implementation of the clone method calls the clone method in its superclass.

In some cases, the application data class may make a clone without calling a clone method in an enhanced application data class. For example, the application data class may have a method like the following makeClone method:

```
public class AppDataClass implements Cloneable
  {
  public AppDataClass makeClone() throws CloneNotSupportedException
    {
    return (AppDataClass) super.clone();
    }
  }
```

In this example, AppDataClass inherits implicitly from Object. The enhancer does not alter the Object class when it enhances the AppDataClass. As a result, the call to the super.clone method does not invoke any code that is aware of JDO. To handle cases like this, JDO requires that the JDO implementation detect clones and make them JDO-transient on first contact.

Cloning does not invoke transparent persistence, and as a result, some of the cloned object's persistent fields can have Java default values instead of their persistent values. Usually, this is not the desired behavior. To ensure that persistent values are copied to the persistent fields of the cloned object, the application should override the clone method in Cloneable application data classes.

Listing 5-3 shows a clone method that makes a shallow copy. In this code, the clone method starts by calling the clone method in its superclass. This gets the memory state of all fields, but it does not invoke transparent persistence. To ensure that the persistent fields in the clone have the current persistent values, transparent persistence must be invoked. When myPersistentFieldOne is used on the right side of the assignment, transparent persistence fetches the current persistent value if it is not already in memory. (Alternatively, the application could ensure that the persistence manager's retrieve operation has been called on the object prior to cloning.)

Listing 5-3. A Shallow clone *Method for an Application Data Class*

```
public Object clone()
  {
  // call super to get a cloned object
  MyApplicationDataClass obj = (MyApplicationDataClass) super.clone();

  // JDO will insert code here during enhancement

  // invoke transparent persistence to get
  // the current values of persistent fields
  obj.myPersistentFieldOne = myPersistentFieldOne;
  obj.myPersistentFieldTwo = myPersistentFieldTwo;
  ...
  return obj;
  }
```

TIP   Clones of persistent objects are always JDO-transient objects. JDO makes no provision to load persistent fields from the datastore prior to cloning the object. Loading the persistent values of persistent fields when creating a clone is a responsibility of the application.

Handling References in the Cloning of Persistent Objects

If the cloned object contains references to persistent objects, then errors arise if the application accesses these persistent objects after the persistence manager closes. Likewise, JDO throws a `JDOUserException` if persistent objects are accessed after the transaction ends when the *NontransactionalRead* property is false.

One way to prevent the clone from holding references to persistent objects is to clone or copy all the objects that persistent fields refer to. For example, if `myPersistentFieldTwo` in Listing 5-3 is a reference to an application data object whose class implements `Cloneable`, then instead of assigning the value as shown in Listing 5-3, a clone can be assigned instead. The following lines of code assign a clone to the cloned object's `myPersistentFieldTwo`:

```
if (myPersistentFieldTwo != null)
    obj.myPersistentFieldTwo = myPersistentFieldTwo.clone();
```

A clone method that invokes further cloning or copying of the object graph is called a *deep copy*. As with serialization, the danger of deep copy cloning is the possibility of walking, by virtue of transparent persistence, an object graph that includes a great many objects.

A second way to prevent the clone from holding references to persistent objects is to set the references to null, but this approach assumes that the class code permits the cloned object to function when the references are null.

Enhancement and Friendly Classes

Friendly classes are classes that directly access the data member fields of other classes. The access level of the member field determines which classes can be friendly. If the access level is public, then every class has direct access. If protected, then classes within the package or derived from the class have access. If the access level is not specified, it defaults to package-level access, which means that any class within the package has access. Finally, if the private access level is set, then no other classes (except inner classes) have access. In the sense that the term is being used here, a Java class is friendly if it has access to the instance fields of another class and if it uses this access to read or write the fields.

To provide transparent persistence, JDO converts the application code that directly uses the managed fields into calls to the static getter-setter methods introduced by enhancement. During enhancement, the enhancer makes these changes in all the application data classes that the JDO metadata identifies. The enhancer must also change friendly classes that are not themselves application data classes but that directly access the managed fields of application data classes. The specification calls these enhancer-modified friendly classes *persistence aware*.

The JDO metadata identifies for the enhancer the application data classes that it must enhance to support the PersistenceCapable interface, but the JDO metadata does not identify the persistence-aware classes. Each vendor's enhancer specifies the required steps that ensure the enhancement of the persistent-aware classes. For this reason, specifying the persistence-aware classes is an implementation-dependent step in the build or deployment process.

By now, if you have been coding in Java for any period of time, you have been hit on all sides by the mantra of encapsulating the implementation and choosing carefully the interface to expose. JDO's enhancement of application data classes provides one more reason to encapsulate the member fields of application data classes. If managed fields are restricted to private fields, then it is fairly easy to ensure that all classes that access the field are enhanced. If friendly access is allowed, then it becomes likely that some friendly class will be deployed that should have been enhanced, but was not. The behavior that results from friendly classes making direct, unenhanced access to persistent fields can be difficult to debug.

 TIP   To avoid late night debugging, always declare the managed fields with the private modifier. When wider access to these fields is needed, write getter-setter methods.

Enhancement and Inheritance

Application data classes may inherit from any class. They typically inherit from Object, or from an application class that is not enhanced, or from another application data class that is enhanced. In the normal case, any class that inherits from an enhanced application data class is itself an enhanced application data class, but this is not a JDO requirement. In JDO, unenhanced classes can inherit from enhanced classes, and enhanced classes can inherit from unenhanced classes, without limitation.

The most-derived application data classes must be concrete classes. The other application data classes in the inheritance tree may be concrete or abstract.

JDO can manage and persist only the objects of enhanced classes and of supported system classes. JDO cannot manage or persist the objects of an unenhanced class, even if the class is the superclass of an enhanced class or the derived class of an enhanced class.

An example of an inheritance hierarchy that mixes enhanced and unenhanced classes is shown in Figure 5-1. There are three application defined classes, MyClassAlpha, MyClassBravo, and MyClassCharlie, arranged in an inheritance hierarchy. The java.lang.Object class is the base class of the hierarchy. MyClassAlpha and MyClassCharlie are enhanced application data classes. MyClassBravo is not an enhanced class. The application can create instances of MyClassAlpha and MyClassCharlie and make them persistent. The application can create instances of MyClassBravo, but it cannot make them persistent. Instances of MyClassAlpha and MyClassCharlie can be retrieved from the datastore, but instances of MyClassBravo cannot. For some applications, the ability to have an unenhanced class between two enhanced classes in the inheritance tree may prove useful, but for most applications, any class that inherits from an enhanced class is itself an enhanced class.

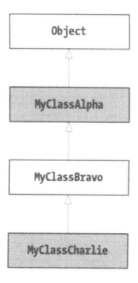

Figure 5-1. An inheritance tree that mixes enhanced and unenhanced classes

The type of JDO identity (either application, datastore, or nondurable) of the least-derived enhanced class determines the identity type for all of its descendents in the inheritance tree. Taking the example in Figure 5-1, if MyClassAlpha uses datastore identity, then MyClassCharlie must also use datastore identity. When application identity is used, one application identity class may be used for the entire tree of enhanced classes. In this case, the key fields are defined in the least-derived enhanced class, which may be an abstract class.

> **TIP**   JDO provides excellent support for inheritance in the data object model. It is best to define key fields in the least-derived enhanced class. All application data classes that share a common enhanced superclass must use the same type of JDO identity.

Enhancement and Inner Classes

In Java, inner classes come in four flavors: static, member, local, and anonymous local. All inner classes may be friendly to their outer classes, and vice versa. Objects of inner classes may access all the fields and methods of their outer class, including the private fields and methods. Likewise, the objects of outer classes have full access to the fields and members of their inner classes.

Instances of member, local, and anonymous local inner classes receive during construction an implicit reference to the containing object of their outer class. Static inner classes, on the other hand, do not receive an implicit reference to an object of their outer class. For this reason, when static inner classes need to refer to an object of their outer class, they must be passed a reference.

JDO can enhance static inner classes, but it cannot enhance member, local, or anonymous local inner classes. Because all inner classes are friendly to their outer class, object modeling needs that are normally met by using member, local, or anonymous local classes can be met by using static inner classes. In most cases where member, local, or anonymous local classes have been used, the code also uses the implicit reference to the containing object of the outer class. To provide the same functionality when using a static inner class, the code must pass an explicit reference to the object of the outer class.

> **TIP**   JDO can enhance static inner classes, but it cannot enhance the other types of inner classes. Because all inner classes are friendly to the outer classes that contain them, the availability of static inner classes is sufficient for modeling purposes.

Enhancement and Performance

Enhancing a class adds a fair amount of code to the class. The file size of a minimal class such as those used in the examples in this book could be only 2 kilobytes, but enhancement grows it to about 8 kilobytes. Nearly all of this increase is code. Enhancement adds less than a handful of instance fields to the application data class. As a result, the memory consumption of loading a thousand objects of an application data class is only mildly increased by enhancement.

When a field's value is fetched in an unenhanced class, the fetch occurs directly from the field's memory location, but when a persistent field's value is fetched in an enhanced class, the operation, due to transparent persistence, is more complex and time consuming. If the field's value has not been loaded from the datastore, the fetch causes JDO to read the value from the datastore. The read slows down the fetch considerably. Under typical conditions, a read from the datastore takes several orders of magnitude longer than a fetch from memory. Nearly all of this time is spent in the network transport and database server. JDO has very little to do with it. Any code that uses the database feels the same impact.

On second and subsequent fetches of the persistent field's value, performance is still slowed by the presence of the enhancement-added code. The additional code can easily cause second and subsequent fetches to take 40 percent longer than fetches from the same field in unenhanced code, even though the value is now stored in the field. The price of enhancement continues to be paid even when the enhanced objects are themselves unmanaged. JDO is entirely responsible for this negative impact on performance.

Although a 40 percent increase in time to fetch the value of a memory field sounds very significant, in fact, it is more likely meaningless for the typical application. The typical application spends a very tiny fraction of its overall time fetching the values of loaded persistent fields. As a result, increasing this tiny fraction of time by 40 percent is usually insignificant. For most applications, this performance hit is a modest price to pay for transparent persistence.

 TIP Enhancement is usually not critical for memory consumption or for performance, but all applications, whether they use JDO or not, play a high price for accessing a datastore. Consequently, application developers must continue to carefully design what to persist and when to persist it.

Enhancement and Debugging

JDO does not disturb the source code line numbers when it enhances an application data class. As a result, the programmer can debug the enhanced class with the original source code. JDO implementations have enjoyed an excellent track record, even during beta, in meeting this requirement.

During debugging, the code added by enhancement is present but not visible in the debugger. There are two ways to see the enhanced code in the debugger. Some vendors provide a means to generate the enhanced source code. Failing that, the enhanced application data class can be decompiled. The JODE decompiler from http://sourceforge.net/projects/jode does a good job. After compiling the source code that contains the enhancement-added code, you can debug the class with the enhancement-added code in full view.

Viewing the enhancement-added code in the debugger is rarely required. The code that the enhancer adds is probably the most thoroughly tested code of the implementation. Most JDO bugs will be in the implementation's runtime rather than in the code that the enhancer adds to the application data classes.

TIP Enhancement preserves the line numbers in the class file to allow continued visual debugging of the enhanced application data class using the original (unenhanced) source code.

Enhancement and the Fear of Code Mangling

In programming, as in other fields of endeavor, perception can be as important as reality. For some developers, the idea that their wonderfully coded classes will be enhanced leads to the fear that their code will be mangled. But, in fact, there really is no difference between calling a library method to perform some task and having the code of that method embedded by tools into the application's class. Every programmer's code lives or dies in a web of other people's code over which he has only limited control. Once this reality is recognized, the skills to deal with it can be developed.

Although enhancement makes many alterations to the application data class, the negative side effects are few and marginal. Most negative side effects of enhancement can either be tolerated or worked around. Enhancement allows the application programmer to enjoy the benefits of transparent persistence with little work and few surprises.

The JDO Metadata

The JDO metadata is contained in one or more XML files. The metadata identifies and describes the application data classes. Both the enhancer and the JDO runtime use the metadata. Behavior is unspecified if the metadata files are changed between enhancement and runtime.

The Names and Locations of the JDO Metadata Files

JDO requires that the file containing metadata for an application data class is available where the class loader that loaded the application data class can find it. Each class loader searches a set of class paths for class files and resource files. For more information, refer to the SDK's Javadoc for the getResource method in the java.lang.ClassLoader class.

JDO 1.0 recommended, but did not require, that the file name be either *<class-name>.jdo* or *<package-name>.jdo*. Because the 1.0 specification did not require conformity, the locations and names of the metadata files were often not portable across implementations. JDO 1.0.1 is much more specific about the names and locations of metadata files. The requirements for names and locations apply for both the enhancer and the JDO runtime.

In JDO 1.0.1, the allowed names must be either *<class-name>.jdo* or *package.jdo*. For example, if the application data class is com.ysoft.jdo.Heffalump, then using the class-name option, the metadata file name must be *Heffalump.jdo*. Using the package name option, the metadata file name must be *package.jdo*.

A metadata file named with the class name option can describe only its class. The metadata files named *package.jdo* can describe one or more classes in one or more packages.

In the case of the class name option, the metadata file has only one location, the directory of the package where the application data class resides. For example, the location for the *Heffalump.jdo* file can only be the *com/ysoft/jdo* directory. In the case of the package name option, there are several possible locations.

JDO defines the search order for metadata files. JDO searches at each segment of the package name for a file named *package.jdo*. The last file that it searches for is the *<class-name>.jdo* file located in the package with the class file. For example, to find the metadata for the com.ysoft.jdo.Heffalump class, JDO uses the following search order:

1. *META-INF/package.jdo*

2. *WEB-INF/package.jdo*

3. *package.jdo*

4. *com/package.jdo*

5. *com/ysoft/package.jdo*

6. *com/ysoft/jdo/package.jdo*

7. *com/ysoft/jdo/Heffalump.jdo*

JDO may find a file at each step in the search. In this case, JDO searches in each metadata file that it finds for the metadata that describes the Heffalump class. The search stops once the metadata for the desired class is found. As a result, it is possible for the metadata in one of the earlier locations to override the metadata in one of the later locations.

The metadata for one class may be loaded as the result of a search for the metadata for another class. For example, the metadata for the org.abc.Woozle class may be loaded from the *WEB-INF/package.jdo* that was found while searching for the metadata for the com.ysoft.jdo.Heffalump class. This behavior is pernicious only when the metadata for a class is stored in an unnatural location. Although you can put the metadata for the org.abc.Woozle class in the com/ysoft/jdo/package.jdo metadata file, doing so is likely to cause confusion.

To ease upward migration, JDO 1.0.1 allows the JDO implementation to first search for metadata files using the search order and names that it used in its 1.0 implementation before searching in the order and for the names that the 1.0.1 specification requires.

The Structure of the JDO Metadata

The JDO metadata provides information about the application data classes. It determines the identity type used by each application data class. It identifies the managed fields and the unmanaged fields, and it provides other information, some of which is implementation dependent. Every application data class must be identified in the JDO metadata. The metadata does not include application classes that are only persistence aware.

The JDO metadata is an XML file. The document type definition is contained in the *jdo.dtd* file found in the *JDO Jar* file. The JDO metadata has eight types of XML elements or tags, which are shown in Figure 5-2. The figure shows the hierarchy of the elements, and it indicates the number of times that a child element (or a choice from a group of child elements) may appear within the parent element. Special characters indicate the cardinality of the nested elements.

- A question mark (?) indicates that the element or choice may appear zero or one time inside its parent element.

- A plus sign (+) indicates that the element or choice must appear one or more times inside its parent element.

- An asterisk (*) indicates that the element or choice may appear zero or more times inside its parent element.

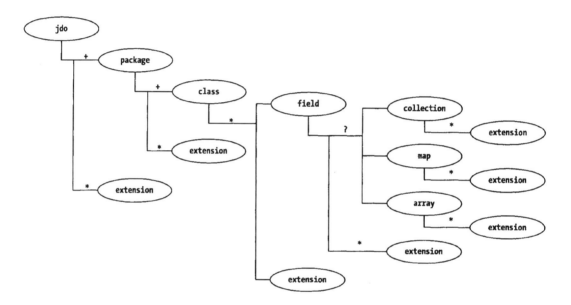

Figure 5-2. The XML elements of the JDO metadata

As can be seen from Figure 5-2, the metadata provides information on the packages, classes, and fields to be enhanced. Although a JDO metadata file can be quite complex, it can also be quite simple, as the example in Listing 5-4 shows.

Listing 5-4. Simple JDO Metadata File

```
<?xml version="1.0" encoding="UTF-8"?>
<!DOCTYPE jdo PUBLIC
        "-//Sun Microsystems, Inc.//DTD Java Data Objects Metadata 1.0//EN"
        "http://java.sun.com/dtd/jdo_1_0.dtd">
```

```
<jdo>
    <package name="com.ysoft.jdo.book.coffee">
        <class name="CoffeeUrn" identity-type="datastore" />
    </package>
</jdo>
```

The metadata must identify every application data class, but individual fields within the application data class need only be identified if there is something about them that is different from the default or implied values that the enhancer and runtime assume.

The jdo Tag

The jdo tag has no attributes. It is the root tag of the JDO metadata document.

The package Tag

The package tag has one required attribute name, and no optional attributes. The value of the name attribute must be the full package name. The package tag identifies a package containing application data classes to be enhanced. The following example shows the package tag:

```
<package name="com.ysoft.jdo.book.library">
```

There are one or more package tags nested within the jdo tag.

The class Tag

The class tag identifies a specific application data class to enhance. There is one class tag, nested within the package tag, for every application data class within the package. Table 5-1 describes the five attributes of the class tag.

Table 5-1. Attributes of the Metadata class *Tag*

Attribute	Description	Values	Required	Default
name	Name of the class	Text	Yes	No default
identity-type	Type of JDO identity	"application", "datastore", "nondurable"	No	Implied
requires-extent	Determines if class must have an extent	"true", "false"	No	"true"
objectid-class	Name of application identity class	Text	No	No default
persistence-capable-superclass	The next superclass that is enhanced in the inheritance tree	Text	No	No default

The name Attribute

The class name specified in the name attribute is relative to the package named in the enclosing package tag.

The identity-type Attribute

The identity-type attribute takes one of the three values "application", "datastore", or "nondurable". These values correspond to the three types of JDO identity. The implied value is "application" when an objectid-class attribute is specified and "datastore" when an objectid-class attribute is not specified.

Although the identity-type attribute is optional, using it makes for good documentation.

The requires-extent Attribute

The requires-extent tag is used only if the application prefers that the class not have an extent. If there is no extent for the class, then calling the persistence manager's getExtent method throws a JDOUserException.

The objectid-class Attribute

The objectid-class attribute names the application identity class for the application data class. This attribute is required when the identity-type is set to "application", and it is ignored or considered an error otherwise. The name may be fully qualified, or it may be a class name that is relative to the package name of the application data class. The names of inner classes are introduced with the "$" symbol, using the syntax `OuterClassName$InnerClassName`. This attribute should be omitted if the identity type is anything other than application identity.

The persistence-capable-superclass Attribute

The optional `persistence-capable-superclass` attribute is used when the enhanced class derives directly or indirectly from another enhanced class. The field's value may be a fully qualified class name, or since JDO 1.0.1, it may be a class name that is relative to the package name of the application data class. This attribute is omitted when the application data class does not have an enhanced superclass. If a non-enhanced class comes between the enhanced class and its enhanced superclass, the value of the attribute still names the closest superclass that is enhanced.

Examples Using the class Tag

The following example shows a `class` tag that uses all the optional attributes available with datastore identity:

```
<class name="AppClassOne"
    identity-type="datastore"
    requires-extent="true"
    persistence-capable-superclass="com.ysoft.jdo.book.ex.SomeOtherAppClass" >
```

In this example, `AppClassOne` derives either directly or indirectly from `SomeOtherAppClass`. Both are application data classes. Both must use datastore identity, or the enhancer flags an error condition. The `identity-type` and `requires-extent` attributes are not required in this example. In this case, they explicitly specify values that would otherwise be implied.

The following example shows a `class` tag for a class that uses application identity:

```
<class name="AppClassTwo"
    identity-type="application"
    requires-extent="true"
    objectid-class="AppClassTwo$OID" >
```

The static inner class `OID` is the application identity class for `AppClassTwo`. As the absence of the `persistence-capable-superclass` attribute indicates, `AppClassTwo` does not extend directly or indirectly any other application data class. Neither the `identity-type` attribute nor the `requires-extent` attribute are required in this example since they supply values that would otherwise be implied.

Application Identity and Inheritance

To use application identity for application data classes that are related by inheritance, applications should follow these two rules to guarantee portability across all JDO implementations that support application identity:

- All key fields should be defined in the least-derived application data class, and a corresponding concrete application identity class should be defined for it.

- Each separate inheritance hierarchy of application data classes should use a different application identity class.

Limits for Application Identity Classes Whose Data Classes Are Related by Inheritance

Although JDO requires that implementations support the portability rules for application identity, it permits JDO implementations to offer more flexibility. The price of this increased flexibility is both more complexity and less portability across JDO implementations. The extent of this flexibility is limited by the following rules:

- The metadata can declare key fields for only the least-derived concrete classes and their abstract ancestor data classes. The metadata cannot declare a key field for any data class that derives directly or indirectly from a concrete data class.

- The metadata must declare an identity class for every data class that declares primary key fields.

- When the data classes form an inheritance hierarchy, the identity classes associated with them must form an inheritance hierarchy that descends in the same order as the data classes. For example, if application data class B derives from application data class A, then the declared application identity class BOID for class B must derive from the application identity class used by class A.

- The metadata must declare concrete identity classes for the least-derived concrete data classes.

- The metadata must declare an application identity class for the least-derived application data class.

- The metadata can declare either an abstract or concrete identity class for an abstract data class.

- Any application data class derived directly or indirectly from an application data class whose metadata declares a concrete application identity class must use implicitly the concrete application identity class of its ancestor. In the metadata, its `class` tag cannot declare an `objectid-class` attribute and its `field` tags cannot declare a `primary-key` attribute. In other words, the use of a concrete identity class freezes the application identity for all derived classes.

- Although no particular application data class is required to declare primary key fields, there have to be primary key fields declared someplace in the inheritance hierarchy of every concrete application data class.

- Unless an abstract data class is the least-derived data class or has key fields, the metadata does not need to declare an identity class for it.

- Classes that are not application data classes that may appear in the inheritance hierarchy are ignored when interpreting these rules.

If JDO's two rules for portable application identity, mentioned in the preceding section, are too strict for your application, then you should consult the vendor's documentation to understand what the vendor's implementation allows. You may or may not get the flexibility that the ten rules presented here allow.

The `field` Tag

The use of `field` tags is optional. The enhancer discovers the member fields of the application data class by reflection. There is no need to enumerate them in the metadata. At runtime, the application data class knows its managed fields as a result of the changes made during enhancement.

A `field` tag is required when the implied or default value for one of its attributes is not the desired value. For many fields, the implied or default values are suitable. For these fields, the `field` tag can be omitted. When present, the `field` tags are nested within an enclosing `class` tag. Table 5-2 describes the six attributes of the `field` tag.

Table 5-2. Attributes of the Metadata field *Tag*

Attribute	Description	Values	Required	Default
name	Name of the field	Text	Yes	No default
primary-key	Key field for application identity	"true", "false"	No	"false"
persistence-modifier	Managed or unmanaged	"persistent", "transactional", "none"	No	Implied
null-value	Null value allowed	"exception", "default", "none"	No	"none"
default-fetch-group	Member of default fetch group	"true", "false"	No	Implied
embedded	Value (or object) stored as part of this object	"true", "false"	No	Implied

The name Attribute

The name is the only required attribute of the field tag. Its value is the name of the field as declared in the Java class.

The primary-key Attribute

The primary-key attribute identifies the key fields in the application data class. It takes one of two values, "true" or "false". When the attribute is omitted, the default value is "false". This attribute is used only when the class uses application identity. The primary key field must be persistent.

The persistence-modifier Attribute

The persistence-modifier attribute determines whether a field is managed or unmanaged, and if managed, whether it is managed persistently and transactionally or only transactionally. It takes one of three values. The value "persistent" means that the field is both persistent and transactional. The value "transactional" means that the field is only transactional. The value "none" means that the field is unmanaged.

If the persistence-modifier attribute is omitted, the implied value depends on the field's type and modifiers as declared in the application data class. If the field's declaration includes a static, final, or transient modifier, then the implied and required value is "none". Otherwise, if the field's type is any of the types on the following list, then the implied value is "persistent":

- Any enhanced application data class

- The eight primitive types: char, byte, short, int, long, float, double, and boolean, and their immutable wrapper classes in the java.lang package

- The immutable class java.lang.String

- The immutable class java.util.Locale

- Either of the two immutable classes from the java.math package: BigDecimal and BigInteger

- The mutable class java.util.Date

- Any of eight collection and map classes in the java.util package: HashSet, Hashtable, Vector, ArrayList, LinkedList, HashMap, TreeMap, TreeSet

- Any of four interface types in the java.util package: Collection, Set, Map, and List

- Arrays of any of the preceding types except arrays of collection types and map types

Otherwise, the attribute's implied value is "none". The attribute never takes an implied value of "transactional".

The null-value Attribute

The null-value attribute determines the treatment that JDO gives to persistent fields that have null values when the persistent state is stored in the datastore. It takes one of three values: "exception", "none", or "default". The default value for the attribute is "none".

If the value of the null-value attribute is "exception", then JDO throws a JDOUserException when the field's value is null and JDO must store its value in the datastore.

If the value of the null-value attribute is "none", then JDO stores whatever value, including a null, that is in the field. If the datastore rejects the null value, then JDO throws a JDOUserException.

Some datastores can be configured to apply a default value when they are asked to store either no value or a null value for a field. When the value of the `null-value` attribute is "default" and the object's field has a null value during the store, then the object's field acquires the default value, if any, that the datastore applies. For efficiency, the "default" setting should be used only when there is a likelihood that the datastore will be configured to supply a default value.

The default-fetch-group Attribute

The `default-fetch-group` attribute determines whether a field is in the default fetch group or not. JDO defines a default fetch group for performance reasons. For most datastores, the object's fields that have particular types are stored together and can be converted easily to their corresponding Java types. As a result, the values of these fields can be loaded together at a substantial discount to the cost of loading each of them separately. JDO defines the default fetch group, but the implementation decides when to use it.

When a field is not persistent or when it is both persistent and a primary key field, then the implied and required value of its default-fetch-group attribute is "false". If the field is persistent and has one of the following types, then its implied value is "true":

- The eight primitive types and their immutable wrapper classes

- The `BigDecimal` and `BigInteger` classes

- The `String` class

- The `java.util.Date` class

Otherwise, the implied value is "false".

The implied value for `default-fetch-group` attribute is usually the value desired for overall optimal performance.

The embedded Attribute

The `embedded` tag takes a value of "true" or "false". It specifies whether JDO stores the object assigned to the persistent field as a first class object ("false") or a second class object ("true"). Due to many difficulties, JDO 1.0.1 nearly outlaws changing the implied value of this attribute. Later versions of JDO are likely to introduce further changes to this attribute. As a result, avoid when possible using this tag in the JDO metadata.

When a field is not persistent, the implied and required value of the embedded attribute is "false".

When the persistent field's type is any of the following types, the implied and required value of the embedded tag is "true":

- The eight primitive types and their immutable wrapper classes

- The `BigDecimal` and `BigInteger` classes

- The `String` class

- The `java.util.Date` and `java.util.Locale` classes

- Arrays of any of the preceding types, or of application data classes, but not of collection or map types

- All the collection and map types

Embedding an array, collection, or map type does not mean that the elements of the array, collection, or map are embedded. See the `collection`, `map`, and `array` tags in the sections that follow in this chapter.

When the persistent field's type is an application data class, an interface type other than the `Collection`, `List`, or `Map` interfaces, or an `Object`, the implied value for the `embedded` attribute is "false". Setting the value of the `embedded` attribute to "true" in these cases is a hint to the JDO implementation to store the application data object as a second class object. However, the implementation may disregard the hint. When the JDO implementation follows the hint, JDO does not specify uniform behavior across all JDO implementations. Any behavior that a particular JDO implementation provides is implementation dependent. Later versions of JDO will likely clarify how an application can define a second class object and what behavior to expect when it does so.

When the JDO implementation supports a persistent type only because it implements the `Serializable` interface, fields of that type are embedded, but the implied value of the `embedded` tag is "false". It must be explicitly set to "true".

Example Using the field Tag

In the following example, a `Widget` application data class has the following member field:

```
private Widget mate;
```

The following field tag, using the one required and five optional attributes of this type of tag, describes the persistent field mate:

```
<field
    name="mate"
    primary-key="false"
    persistence-modifier="persistent"
    null-value="none"
    default-fetch-group="false"
    embedded="false" />
```

Since only the name attribute is required and none of the optional attributes in this example applies a value different from the attribute's implied value, the field tag for the mate field could be shortened to the following:

```
<field name="mate" />
```

Since the metadata can omit any field tag that does not apply some nondefault value for an optional attribute, the metadata for the Widget class may not need a field tag at all for the mate field. In general, field tags are used only to specify attribute values that are contrary to the implied or default values or to enclose other tags, such as extension or collection tags.

The collection, map, and array Tags

The field tag may enclose one of the three tags: collection, map, or array. One of these tags describes the field when it is a reference to any of the collection, map, or array types.

The collection Tag

Although the collection tag is optional, it is usually not omitted for a collection field. The JDO implementation can usually do a better job of managing the collection field if it knows the specific type of the collection's elements. Table 5-3 describes the two optional attributes of the collection tag.

Table 5-3. Attributes of the Metadata collection *Tag*

Attribute	Description	Values	Required	Default
element-type	Name of the class for the collection's elements.	Text	No	Implied
embedded-element	Is the element embedded?	"true", "false"	No	Implied

The value of the element-type attribute may be a fully qualified class name, or starting with JDO 1.0.1, it may be relative to the package name of the application data class. If the attribute is omitted, its implied value is "java.lang.Object".

The embedded-element attribute takes a value of either "true" or "false". Its implied value is "false" for application data classes, the Object class, and interface types, and "true" otherwise. The implied value is a directive for the JDO implementation, and the opposite value is a hint on how to store and manage the elements of the collection. When the value is "true" and the hint or directive is followed, the elements are stored as part of the collection. Deleting the collection, which happens implicitly as the result of deleting the application data object that refers to the collection, causes JDO to delete the elements of the collection. When the value is "false" and the hint or directive is followed, deleting the collection does not delete the elements of the collection. As with the embedded attribute of the field tag, changing the implied value is not well supported, and whenever possible should be avoided.

The following example identifies the element type of a collection field as the application data class Book. Because the example omits the embedded-element attribute, it accepts the implied value of "false". The package of the Book class is the same package named by the enclosing package tag.

```
<collection element-type="Book" />
```

The map Tag

Like the collection tag, the optional map tag is usually not omitted for a field that is a map type, e.g., Map, TreeMap, HashMap, and Hashtable. The JDO implementation can usually do a better job of managing the Map field if it knows the specific types of the collection's keys and values. Table 5-4 describes the four optional attributes of the map tag.

Table 5-4. Attributes of the Metadata map *Tag*

Attribute	Description	Values	Required	Default
key-type	Name of the class for the map's keys.	Text	No	Implied
embedded-key	Is the key embedded?	"true", "false"	No	Implied
value-type	Name of the class for the map's values.	Text	No	Implied
embedded-value	Is the value embedded?	"true", "false"	No	Implied

The values for the key-type and value-type attributes may be fully qualified class names, or starting with JDO 1.0.1, they may be relative to the package name of the application data class. If either attribute is omitted, its implied value is "java.lang.Object".

The two optional attributes embedded-key and embedded-value take a value of either "true" or "false". The preceding discussion of the embedded-element attribute in the collection tag applies to these two attributes as well.

The following example identifies the key-type and value-type of a map field. The example accepts the implied value of "true" for the embedded-key attribute and the implied value of "false" for the embedded-value attribute.

```
<map key-type="java.lang.String" value-type="Book" />
```

The array Tag

Unlike the collection and map tags, the array tag can often be omitted for array fields. The array tag takes one optional attribute, the embedded-element attribute, which is either "true" or "false". The preceding discussion of the embedded-element attribute in the collection tag applies to this attribute as well.

The extension Tag

Every tag in the JDO metadata, including extension tags, can contain zero or more extension tags. Vendors use the extension tag to provide additional information that is helpful to the implementation. Table 5-5 describes the three attributes of the extension tag.

Table 5-5. Attributes of the Metadata extension Tag

Attribute	Description	Values	Required	Default
vendor-name	Vendor-specific string	Text	Yes	No default
key	Part of key-value pair	Text	No	Vendor specific
value	Part of key-value pair	Text	No	Vendor specific

The extension tag requires a vendor-name attribute and allows optional key and value attributes. This tag's structure is intended to be flexible. An implementation ignores the extension tags that are not its own. The next section provides an example that uses the extension tag.

An Example of a Complete Metadata File

Listing 5-5 shows a complete metadata file for the library example available from the Apress Web site (http://www.apress.com) and at SourceForge.net (http://sourceforge.net). The library example is one of the JDO Learning Tools that allows you to explore JDOQL queries.

Listing 5-5. The JDO Metadata for the Library Example

```
<?xml version="1.0" encoding="UTF-8"?>
<!DOCTYPE jdo PUBLIC
    "-//Sun Microsystems, Inc.//DTD Java Data Objects Metadata 1.0//EN"
    "http://java.sun.com/dtd/jdo_1_0.dtd">
<jdo>
   <package name="com.ysoft.jdo.book.library">
      <class name="Borrower" identity-type="datastore" >
         <field name="oidString"  persistence-modifier="none" />
         <field name="books" >
            <collection element-type="com.ysoft.jdo.book.library.Book" />
            <extension vendor-name="kodo" key="inverse" value="borrower"/>
         </field>
      </class>

      <class name="Book" identity-type="datastore" >
         <field name="oidString"  persistence-modifier="none" />
         <field name="borrower" />
         <field name="categories" >
            <collection element-type="com.ysoft.jdo.book.library.Category" />
            <extension vendor-name="kodo" key="inverse" value="books"/>
         </field>
      </class>
```

```
        <class name="Category" identity-type="datastore" >
           <field name="oidString"  persistence-modifier="none" />
           <field name="books" >
              <collection element-type="com.ysoft.jdo.book.library.Book" />
              <extension vendor-name="kodo" key="inverse" value="categories"/>
           </field>
        </class>

        <class name="Volunteer" identity-type="datastore" >
           <field name="oidString"  persistence-modifier="none" />
        </class>
     </package>
</jdo>
```

This example has only one package that contains application data classes. Within the package there are four application data classes: Book, Category, Borrower, and Volunteer. Each of the application data classes has one unmanaged field. Most have a HashSet field for which the collection tag is provided. Several of the persistent fields in these application data classes are not mentioned in the metadata because the implied values are the values desired.

The metadata in Listing 5-5 is configured for Kodo, as indicated by the use of "kodo" in the extension tag's vendor-name attribute, but it can be used as is with other implementations. JDO requires that implementations ignore the extension tags that are not their own.

The metadata in Listing 5-5 is configured for JDO 1.0. As a result, it lists the fully qualified names for the element-type attributes even though the JDO 1.0-compatible versions of Kodo implement the JDO 1.0.1 naming conventions.

During development, while the application data classes are changing, the programmer must make concurrent changes in the metadata file. After development, porting a metadata file from one implementation to the next involves only the extension tags. If desired, the extension tags for the prior implementation can be left in while new extension tags for the next implementation are added.

Summary

The application programmer defines application data classes that become persistence capable through enhancement. The member fields of the application data classes can be managed or unmanaged. JDO allows a wide variety of Java types for managed fields, while unmanaged fields can be any type. Enhancement changes a class considerably, but for the most part, the application can go on using these classes as before except that the application data objects can now be persistent.

They can be found in, inserted into, and deleted from the vast, transactional, and persistent datastore that JDO provides access to.

This chapter and the preceding chapters describe all the important features of JDO's persistence service for objects. But how does an application get started with JDO? The application must first obtain an object that implements the `PersistenceManagerFactory` interface. The next chapter describes this important housekeeping detail.

CHAPTER 6

Factories That Produce Persistence Managers

THE PERSISTENCEMANAGER IS both the principal service interface of JDO and the gateway to its other service interfaces. To obtain objects that implement the PersistenceManager interface, the application uses the PersistenceManagerFactory interface. In some cases, the application can obtain a PersistenceManager from a javax.resource.cci.ConnectionFactory interface, which is defined in the J2EE Connector Architecture (JCA). Since both the PersistenceManagerFactory and the ConnectionFactory are interfaces, how does the application obtain the object that implements one of these interfaces? As it turns out, the answer is nearly trivial. If all this chapter had to do was explain how to get a factory, it would be quite short.

In addition to producing persistence managers, the factories configure them as well. Understanding how the factories configure persistence managers provides the basis for understanding the proper way to use the factories in a managed environment. The PersistenceManagerFactory is also the telltale of the JDO implementation. It identifies the optional JDO features that the implementation supports.

The PersistenceManagerFactory Interface

Figure 6-1 shows the class diagram for the PersistenceManagerFactory interface. As the figure indicates, the object that implements the PersistenceManagerFactory interface is serializable. JNDI can store and retrieve serializable objects. As a result, a persistence manager factory can be stored in and retrieved from JNDI.

The PersistenceManagerFactory interface has 4 operations and 15 properties. The primary operation is getPersistenceManager. The 15 properties break down into 3 groups. The first 5 properties shown in Figure 6-1 also appear in the Transaction interface. The next 2 properties appear in the PersistenceManager interface. This chapter describes the relationship between the properties found in these other interfaces and the properties with the same names found in the PersistenceManagerFactory interface. The last group of 8 connection properties are unique to the PersistenceManagerFactory.

```
                                          Serializable
                      << Interface >>
                  PersistenceManagerFactory

  getPersistenceManager() : PersistenceManager +
  close() : void
  supportedOptions() : Collection
  getProperties() : Properties

  Optimistic : boolean
  RetainValues : boolean
  RestoreValues : boolean
  NontransactionalRead : boolean
  NontransactionalWrite : boolean

  IgnoreCache : boolean
  MultiThreaded : boolean

  ConnectionUserName : String
  ConnectionPassword : String +
  ConnectionURL : String
  ConnectionDriverName: String
  ConnectionFactory : Object
  ConnectionFactoryName : String
  ConnectionFactory2 : Object
  ConnectionFactory2Name : String
```

Figure 6-1. The class diagram of the PersistenceManagerFactory *interface*

NOTE   Chapters 3 and 4 detail the PersistenceManager and Transaction interfaces and their properties.

The following sections describe the operations and properties of the PersistenceManagerFactory interface.

Obtaining a Persistence Manager

When the application uses JDO, an early and important task is to obtain a persistence manager. A persistence manager can be obtained from an object that implements the PersistenceManagerFactory or the ConnectionFactory interfaces.

Obtaining a Persistence Manager from a Persistence Manager Factory

When obtaining the persistence manager from an object that implements PersistenceManagerFactory, the application uses one of two methods:

```
public PersistenceManager getPersistenceManager()
public PersistenceManager getPersistenceManager(String userName, String password)
```

The method without parameters instructs the persistence manager to use the *ConnectionUserName* and *ConnectionPassword* properties configured for the factory when connecting to the datastore. The method with the user name and password parameters instructs the persistence manager to override the factory configuration for user name and password when connecting to the datastore. However the user name and password are determined, the persistence manager uses the same user name and password for every connection that it makes to the datastore.

The persistence manager inherits the configuration of the factory that produced it. It inherits values for its properties *IgnoreCache* and *Multithreaded*, and its transaction inherits values for its five properties, *Optimistic*, *RetainValues*, *RestoreValues*, *NontransactionalRead*, and *NontransactionalWrite*. When the persistence manager connects to the datastore, it uses the connection properties configured for the factory, with the possible exception that the *ConnectionUserName* and *ConnectionPassword* properties may be overriden by the parameters of the getPersistenceManager method.

If the persistence manager is closed, the getPersistenceManager methods throw a JDOUserException.

Obtaining a Persistence Manager from a Connection Factory

The JCA defines a standard way for vendors to design and package their connection-oriented code for use in J2EE application servers. In the case of JDO vendors, they have the option of packaging the entire JDO implementation as a resource adaptor in a Resource Adapter Archive (RAR) file. The RAR file is then deployed with one or more deployment descriptors in the application server. A later section of this chapter, "Obtaining a Connection Factory," explains how to obtain a connection factory.

After obtaining a connection factory, the application obtains a persistence manager from the connection factory as shown in Listing 6-1. All of the properties of the PersistenceManagerFactory are configured in the XML deployment descriptors that are either contained in or accompany the RAR file. The persistence managers that the connection produces inherit their property values from the connection factory's configuration.

Listing 6-1. Getting a PersistenceManager *from a Connection Factory*

```
PersistenceManager pm = null;
try
    {
    // cf is a ConnectionFactory object obtained earlier
    pm = (PersistenceManager) cf.getConnection();
    }
catch (ResourceException e)
    {
    // handle exception ...
    }
```

Obtaining a Persistence Manager Factory

There are three ways to obtain a persistence manager factory:

- By calling the getPersistenceManagerFactory method in JDOHelper

- By finding the persistence manager factory in JNDI

- By construction

The first two methods provide a persistence manager factory that is preconfigured and unmodifiable. The last method provides a persistence manager factory that can be configured until it produces the first persistence manager. After it produces the first persistence manager, the factory becomes unmodifiable.

The getPersistenceManagerFactory Method in JDOHelper

Although the JDOHelper class is described in detail in the next chapter, this is the appropriate place to describe its method for producing persistence manager factories. JDOHelper is a utility class that contains, among other things, the following method:

```
public static PersistenceManagerFactory getPersistenceManagerFactory(
    java.util.Properties props)
```

Calling the getPersistenceManagerFactory method in JDOHelper is likely to be popular because the code that uses it is vendor independent. The vendor dependencies are placed into the properties where they are easy to manage. The method accepts a list of standard JDO property names and accepts any vendor-specific property names that the implementation recognizes. This method ignores property names that the JDO implementation does not recognize.

Standard Properties for getPersistenceManagerFactory

The following list contains all the standard property names:

```
javax.jdo.PersistenceManagerFactoryClass
javax.jdo.option.Optimistic
javax.jdo.option.RetainValues
javax.jdo.option.RestoreValues
javax.jdo.option.NontransactionalRead
javax.jdo.option.NontransactionalWrite
javax.jdo.option.Multithreaded
javax.jdo.option.IgnoreCache
javax.jdo.option.ConnectionUserName
javax.jdo.option.ConnectionPassword
javax.jdo.option.ConnectionURL
javax.jdo.option.ConnectionDriverName
javax.jdo.option.ConnectionFactoryName
javax.jdo.option.ConnectionFactory2Name
```

As can be seen by comparing this list to Figure 6-1, the list includes the Boolean and string properties of the PersistenceManagerFactory interface.

The standard property javax.jdo.PersistenceManagerFactoryClass is required and takes the fully qualified class name of the vendor's class that implements the PersistenceManagerFactory interface. If the named class cannot be found, the method throws a JDOFatalUserException that wraps the underlying java.lang.ClassNotFoundException.

The next seven properties are Boolean. When any of them is not specified, the implementation's default value is used. The implementation's default value may be true or false, and the default value can vary from property to property. All implementations support setting the standard Boolean properties to false. If the implementation doesn't support the configuration contained in the properties, then the getPersistenceManagerFactory method throws a JDOUnsupportedOptionException. For example, if the implementation does not support the setting

```
javax.jdo.option.NontransactionalRead=true
```

then the getPersistenceManagerFactory method throws the JDOUnsupportedOptionException. Chapter 7 describes the JDO exceptions.

The last six properties are the six connection properties in the
PersistenceManagerFactory interface that take string values. A later section of this
chapter, "Configuring a Persistence Manager Factory," describes in detail these six
connection properties as well as the two connection factory properties that are
Object types.

There are several ways that the property settings acquire vendor dependencies.
To begin with, the class named in the javax.jdo.PersistenceManagerFactoryClass
property is clearly dependent on the implementation. Less obvious is the dependency introduced by utilizing a true value for one or more of the five transactional
properties. One implementation may support an optimistic transaction,
while another may not. Other vendor dependencies arise because different implementations use different connection properties. One may expect a value for
javax.jdo.option.ConnectionURL, while another may expect a value for
javax.jdo.option.ConnectionFactoryName. Finally, each implementation may
expect its own set of vendor-specific properties that may or may not be optional.
Although property files have vendor dependencies, it is beneficial to have the
dependencies encapsulated within the property file.

Code Example for getPersistenceManagerFactory

Generally, the application stores the properties in a property file that it loads
before calling the getPersistenceManagerFactory method in JDOHelper. Listing 6-2
presents an example of the code required to obtain a PersistenceManagerFactory
object by using a properties file. The TestJDOHelper class shown in Listing 6-2 has
only three methods, main, getPMF, and loadProperties. The main method calls the
getPMF method to get a persistence manager factory, and uses the factory to get a
persistence manager. The getPMF method calls loadProperties to load a property
file found in the class path into a Properties object. Using the Properties object,
the getPMF method then calls the getPersistenceManagerFactory method in JDOHelper.
This example is included in the JDO Learning Tools programs that are described in
Chapter 8.

Listing 6-2. Obtaining a PersistenceManagerFactory *from* JDOHelper

```
package com.ysoft.jdo.book.factory;

import java.util.*;
import java.io.*;
import javax.jdo.*;
```

```
public class TestJDOHelper
    {
    public static PersistenceManagerFactory getPMF(String propFileName)
       {
       Properties props;

       try
          {
          props = loadProperties(propFileName);
          props.list(System.out);
          }
       catch (Exception e)
          {
          System.out.println("Caught exception trying to load properties file");
          e.printStackTrace(System.out);
          return null;
          }
       return JDOHelper.getPersistenceManagerFactory(props);
       }

    public static Properties loadProperties(String propFileName)
          throws IOException
       {
       ClassLoader cl = Thread.currentThread().getContextClassLoader();
       InputStream stream = cl.getResourceAsStream(propFileName);
       if (stream == null)
          throw new IOException("File not found: " + propFileName);

       Properties props = new Properties();
       props.load(stream);
       stream.close();
       return props;
       }

    public static void main(String [] args)
       {
       if (args.length < 1)
          {
          System.out.println(
    "usage: java com.ysoft.jdo.book.factory.TestJDOHelper " +
    "<property file name>");
          System.exit(1);
          }
```

```
        PersistenceManagerFactory pmf = getPMF(args[0]);
        if (pmf != null && pmf.getPersistenceManager() != null)
            System.out.println("Got the PMF okay");
    }
}
```

A Frozen Persistence Manager Factory

After the persistence manager factory is obtained from the
getPersistenceManagerFactory method in JDOHelper, its properties cannot be modified.
Its configuration is frozen. If the application wants to configure the factory, it must
configure the properties prior to calling the getPersistenceManagerFactory method.
Even when the factory is frozen, it still returns persistence managers that are not
frozen. For example, the application can still configure the *IgnoreCache* property
in the PersistenceManager interface even though the factory that produced the
persistence manager is frozen.

When a managed transaction is active, the factory may enlist the persistence
manager in the managed transaction. In this case, some of the properties in the
Transaction interface are not configurable because the JDO transaction is active.
A later section in this chapter, "JDO's Support for Container-Managed Transactions,"
explains when the factory enlists the persistence manager in the managed
transaction.

Example of a Properties File

An example of a properties file for opening a connection to the reference implementation is show in Listing 6-3. The connection properties specify a connection
to the b-tree datastore used by the reference implementation. All seven Boolean
properties are specified because in some cases the reference implementations
default values are true.

Listing 6-3. Example of a Properties File Used to Obtain a PersistenceManagerFactory

```
# JDORI JDO Properties configuration
javax.jdo.PersistenceManagerFactoryClass=com.sun.jdori.fostore.FOStorePMF
javax.jdo.option.ConnectionURL=fostore:FOStoreTestDB
javax.jdo.option.ConnectionUserName=JDO
javax.jdo.option.ConnectionPassword=book
```

```
javax.jdo.option.IgnoreCache=false
javax.jdo.option.Multithreaded=false
javax.jdo.option.NontransactionalRead=false
javax.jdo.option.NontransactionalWrite=false
javax.jdo.option.Optimistic=false
javax.jdo.option.RetainValues=false
javax.jdo.option.RestoreValues=false
```

Getting a Persistence Manager Factory from JNDI

Assuming that one or more persistence manager factories are stored in JNDI, each of them can be retrieved using the JNDI name. This is the traditional method of obtaining a connection within EJB code. The use of JNDI supports J2EE's separation of code from deployment configuration. The code to perform the lookup in JNDI is shown in Listing 6-4.

Listing 6-4. Code to Find a PersistenceManagerFactory *in JNDI*

```
String jndiName = "someName"; // pick the name you'll use
PersistenceManagerFactory pmf = null;
try
    {
    pmf = (PersistenceManagerFactory) new InitialContext().lookup(jndiName);
    }
catch (NamingException ne)
    {
    // handle exception ...
    }
```

Storing the persistence manager factory into JNDI is dependent on the configuration tools available. In some cases, the J2EE application server has options to configure JNDI.

In the JDO Learning Tools, the JndiLocator class in the com.ysoft.jdo.book.factory package has a utility method, getPMF, that takes two parameters, the JNDI name of the PersistenceManagerFactory object and the file name of a properties file. If getPMF does not find the factory in JNDI, it calls the getPersistenceManagerFactory method in JDOHelper to create one, which it stores in JNDI before returning.

Constructing a Persistence Manager Factory

In order to construct a `PersistenceManagerFactory`, the application must construct the vendor's class that implements this interface. The vendor defines the parameters required by the constructor. Construction has a couple of advantages over the other methods of obtaining a persistence manager factory. Unlike the other methods, it yields a persistence manager factory that can be configured. The factory remains configurable until it returns the first persistence manager. As in the other cases, a persistence manager and its transaction can still be configured after the factory's configuration is frozen. The second advantage of construction arises when there is some amount of vendor-specific work to do anyway. In some cases, the application may want to configure properties specified by the vendor's implementation class. For example, there might be a vendor-specified way to configure logging.

Closing a Persistence Manager Factory

JDO 1.0.1 adds a close method to the `PersistenceManagerFactory` interface.

```
public void close()
```

In order for this method to succeed, all of the transactions associated with the persistence managers that the factory produces must be inactive. If any are active, then this method throws a `JDOUserException` that contains a nested `JDOUserException` for each `PersistenceManager` that has an active transaction. This method performs a security check before closing the factory, and if the check fails, it throws a `java.lang.SecurityException`. JDO implementations may use this security check to prevent the application from closing the factory when doing so is inappropriate.

If the method is successful, then all open persistence managers obtained from this persistence manager factory are closed. The application cannot use a closed factory to obtain more persistence managers.

For some JDO implementations under some circumstances, closing the `PersistenceManagerFactory` can be a necessary housekeeping detail. You will need to consult the vendor's documentation to determine whether and when to call this method for the implementation and datastore that you are using. As a general rule, closing the factory is required when the datastore runs in the same JVM as JDO; otherwise, closing the factory is not required. Closing the factory can be an expensive operation that may impact performance if it is performed needlessly.

Obtaining a Connection Factory

Connection factories are obtained from JNDI in the usual way. The resource adaptor, when it is deployed, is stored in JNDI under a name that is specified during deployment. The JDO vendor usually provides a default name. Getting the name right is the only hard part. The code, shown in Listing 6-5, is straightforward. After getting a connection factory, the application obtains a persistence manager as shown in Listing 6-1.

Listing 6-5. Finding a ConnectionFactory *in JNDI*

```
String cfName = "someName"; // examples: "java:/kodo", "java:comp/env/eis/MyJDO"
ConnectionFactory cf = null;
try
    {
    cf = (ConnectionFactory) new InitialContext().lookup(cfName);
    }
catch (NamingException ne)
    {
    // handle exception ...
    }
```

Examining a JDO Implementation

The persistence manager factory has two methods that reveal information about the JDO implementation. One of these methods identifies the optional JDO features that the implementation supports, and the other identifies the implementation's vendor and version.

Determining the Implementation's Support for Optional Features

JDO defines many optional features that a JDO implementation may, or may not, support. To determine whether an implementation supports an optional feature, the application calls the supportedOptions method in the PersistenceManagerFactory interface.

```
public java.util.Collection supportedOptions()
```

The supportedOptions method returns a Collection of strings, one string for each optional feature that the implementation supports. The collection may also include vendor-defined strings that identify features added to the implementation by the vendor. Depending on the number of optional features that the implementation supports, the returned collection can vary in length from 2 to more than 20 strings.

Table 6-1 identifies each string value specified by JDO and briefly describes the corresponding implementation option that is supported when the string is returned.

Table 6-1. Identifying Strings for the Supported Implementation Options

Property Name	Indicates Support For
javax.jdo.query.JDOQL	JDO's query language (required).
javax.jdo.option.ApplicationIdentity	Application JDO identity.
javax.jdo.option.DatastoreIdentity	Datastore JDO identity.
javax.jdo.option.NonDurableIdentity	Nondurable JDO identity.
javax.jdo.option.TransientTransactional	Transient-clean and transient-dirty JDO states.
javax.jdo.option.NontransactionalRead	Transaction's *NontransactionalRead* property can be set to true.
javax.jdo.option.NontransactionalWrite	Transaction's *NontransactionalWrite* property can be set to true.
javax.jdo.option.RetainValues	Transaction's *RetainValues* property can be set to true.
javax.jdo.option.Optimistic	Transaction's *Optimistic* property can be set to true.
javax.jdo.option.ArrayList	Persistent fields that refer to ArrayList types.
javax.jdo.option.HashMap	Persistent fields that refer to HashMap types.
javax.jdo.option.Hashtable	Persistent fields that refer to Hashtable types.
javax.jdo.option.LinkedList	Persistent fields that refer to LinkList types.
javax.jdo.option.TreeMap	Persistent fields that refer to TreeMap types.
javax.jdo.option.TreeSet	Persistent fields that refer to TreeSet types.
javax.jdo.option.Vector	Persistent fields that refer to Vector types.

Table 6-1. Identifying Strings for the Supported
Implementation Options (Continued)

Property Name	Indicates Support For
javax.jdo.option.Map	Persistent fields that refer to Map types.
javax.jdo.option.List	Persistent fields that refer to List types.
javax.jdo.option.Array	Persistent fields that refer to array types.
javax.jdo.option.NullCollection	Null values permitted in persistent fields that refer to collections.
javax.jdo.option.ChangeApplicationIdentity	Values of application-defined key fields can be changed in persistent application data objects.

As the table indicates, the first option javax.jdo.option.JDOQL is not really an option at all. Every implementation should place this string in the collection returned from the supportedOptions method. If the implementation supports another query language or API, it may include an additional property string that it defines in the collection of strings. At least one of the next two options, javax.jdo.option.ApplicationIdentity or javax.jdo.option.DatastoreIdentity, should also be found in the collection returned. The rest of the JDO options may, or may not, be implemented by a specific vendor.

To be portable, an application should rely on as few options as possible. Some options, such as the ability to turn on optimistic transactions or use datastore identity, are very useful.

Obtaining Vendor-Specific Information from the Implementation

The getProperties method provides information about the implementation that is vendor specific.

```
public java.util.Properties getProperties()
```

The getProperties method returns a set of read-only properties that identify the implementation and may provide vendor-specific information about the implementation. Each property is a key-value pair of strings. JDO defines only two keys for these properties, VendorName and VersionNumber. The implementation defines any other keys that are used. Although the application can modify these properties, the JDO implementation ignores any modifications.

Configuring a Persistence Manager Factory

Every persistence manager factory is configured at some point, either by a properties file, or before being stored in JNDI, or by calling the property mutators on a constructed object that implements the PersistenceManagerFactory interface. Nevertheless, for most of the application's life, it works with a persistence manager factory that is not configurable. When persistence manager factories are obtained from JNDI or from properties, they cannot be reconfigured. Even a configurable factory becomes frozen after it produces its first persistence manager. The configuration that is discussed in this section is the configuration that occurs before the persistence manager factory becomes frozen.

As a convenience, the factory provides configuration for two properties, *IgnoreCache* and *Multithreaded*, that are inherited by every persistence manager that the factory produces. Likewise, the persistence manager factory provides configuration for the five transactional properties, *Optimistic, RetainValues, RestoreValues, NontransactionalRead*, and *NontransactionalWrite*, that are inherited by the transaction belonging to the persistence manager. As the earlier discussion implies, the factory constructs the Transaction object at the same time that it constructs the PersistenceManager object. Chapters 3 and 4 describe the PersistenceManager and Transaction interfaces and their properties.

Configuring Connections to the Datastore

The persistence manager factory has a set of eight connection-related properties. These eight properties are unique to the PersistenceManagerFactory interface. They have overlapping purposes. Their use depends upon the design of the JDO implementation and the deployment environment of the application code. In some cases, the simple connection properties are the only ones required. Table 6-2 shows the four simple connection properties defined by JDO, together with a brief description of their purpose.

Table 6-2. Simple Connection Properties

Property	Description
ConnectionDriverName	The class name of the connection driver
ConnectionURL	The URL that the connection driver uses to connect to the datastore
ConnectionUserName	The name of the user establishing the connection
ConnectionPassword	The connection password for the user

As described earlier, the JDO implementation can provide a JCA `ConnectionFactory` that produces persistence managers. The JDO implementation can also use JCA in a different way by having its `PersistenceManager` use a connection factory to connect to the datastore service. In this case, the JDO implementation supports the four connection factory properties. Table 6-3 shows the four connection factory properties defined by JDO, together with a brief description of their purpose.

Table 6-3. Connection Factory Properties

Property	Description
ConnectionFactory	A connection factory object to connect to the datastore
ConnectionFactoryName	The JNDI name for the connection factory object
ConnectionFactory2	A connection factory object suitable for JDO optimistic transactions
ConnectionFactory2Name	The JNDI name for the connection factory object suitable for JDO optimistic transactions

Within J2EE application servers, a connection factory that returns datastore connections normally returns connections that are enlisted in the active, managed transaction. This is not the connection to the datastore that a JDO optimistic transaction would use. For the application to be able to use a JDO optimistic transaction within a J2EE container, the persistence manager needs to use a connection factory that returns nontransactional datastore connections. The *ConnectionFactory2* property holds the connection factory that returns nontransactional connections, and alternatively, the *ConnectionFactory2Name* specifies its JNDI name.

Because the connection properties overlap in their purposes, JDO defines a priority between them. If a connection factory is defined, then it is the controlling property. Failing that, if a JNDI name for a connection factory is defined, then it is the controlling property. Failing both of these, the simple connection properties are used. The implementation will likely provide specific guidance on which connection properties to configure.

JDO's Support for Container-Managed Transactions

The sophisticated management of transactions is a major feature of J2EE application servers. The application server may manage a local transaction involving only one transactional service, or it may manage a distributed transaction involving several services. The application server can either continue using an existing active transaction or start a new transaction. In the case of EJBs, the server provides container-managed transactions (CMT) and allows bean-managed transactions (BMT).

The EJB container in the application server supports several deployment options for CMT. Session beans can use any of six transactional attributes (Unsupported, Required. RequiresNew, Supported, Mandatory, and Never) for container-managed transactions, while entity beans and message-driven beans can use a subset of these.

When using CMT, the bean code does not set transactional boundaries. The transactional boundaries are controlled by the originator of the managed transaction. Depending on the transactional attribute, the application server may start a managed transaction before calling the bean's business method, or it may call the bean's business method in the context of an existing transaction, or it may call the bean's business method in a nontransactional context.

When the bean code calls the ConnectionFactory or PersistenceManagerFactory interface for a persistence manager, the factory has the opportunity to enlist the persistence manager in the active managed transaction, if there is one. Enlisting the persistence manager simply means that the *Active* property of the persistence manager's transaction is now true, and the JDO transaction is now under the control of the originator of the managed transaction. As a result, when the factory enlists the persistence manager in the managed transaction, the JDO transaction is active when the persistence manager is returned.

NOTE There is one JDO Transaction object associated with every PersistenceManager object. Often they are the same object.

JDO allows, but does not require, support for managed transactions in the implementation of the PersistenceManagerFactory interface. On the other hand, JCA requires support for managed transactions in the implementation of the ConnectionFactory interface. Support for managed transactions is often a key difference between the "enterprise" version of a JDO implementation and a "standard" version from the same vendor.

For some of the six possible transactional attributes for CMT, the EJB container can invoke the bean's business methods in a nontransactional context, that is to say, without an active managed transaction. As a result, the persistence manager is not enlisted and its transaction is not started. Because the bean should not start a transaction when the container is managing transactions, the bean must use JDO nontransactionally. When the container calls the bean in a nontransactional context, the *NontransactionalRead* property should be turned on to allow read access. Assuming that the JDO implementation supports nontransactional reads, the bean code can turn on the *NontransactionalRead* property in the Transaction interface after the persistence manager is obtained. Turning on the property in the code is not necessary when the factory is deployed with the *NontransactionalRead* property set to true. Although the bean code can use JDO to read persistent objects in a nontransactional context when the *NontransactionalRead* property is true, without an active managed transaction, the CMT bean cannot use JDO to update the datastore.

In summary, there are two points to remember when using JDO with container-managed transactions. One, a persistence manager is enlisted in the managed transaction only at the time that the connection factory or persistence manager factory returns it. There is no other enlistment mechanism available to the JDO implementation. If an EJB with CMT caches a persistence manager from one transaction to the next, JDO does not have the opportunity to enlist the persistence manager in the second managed transaction. Two, if the CMT deployment descriptor allows the container to invoke the bean in a nontransactional context, then the bean code should not start a transaction. Instead, it should use JDO nontransactionally.

JDO's Support for Bean-Managed Transactions

Even when the EJB uses BMT, the EJB container imposes some rules on the transactional boundaries that the bean code must observe. In a stateless session bean, the bean-managed transaction must complete prior to the end of the business method. In a stateful session bean, the bean-managed transaction can be carried over from one invocation of a business method to the next. In all cases, the bean-managed transaction cannot be part of the client's transaction, if there is one.

When the bean uses BMT, the EJB container calls the bean without starting a managed transaction. A JDO implementation that is aware of managed transactions starts the container-supported javax.transaction.UserTransaction when the JDO Transaction begins. This action allows the container to manage the transaction in the event that other beans are called from within the BMT bean.

Using JDO in CMT Session Beans

In CMT session beans (whether stateless or stateful), each business method should begin by obtaining a persistence manager and end by closing it. The persistence manager should not be cached in a bean's member field between business method invocations. Obtaining a persistence manager from the factory at the start of the business method in a CMT bean ensures that the persistence manager is enlisted in the managed transaction.

Although the EJB container is managing transactions, it may, or may not, end the transaction when the business method returns. If the container started the transaction, it will end the transaction; otherwise, the originator of the transaction controls when the transaction ends.

When the application code closes the persistence manager, the close affects the persistence manager only when the transaction ends. The closing is in effect delayed until the transaction ends. If the client calls the bean again in the same transactional context, the persistence manager associated with the transactional context will be reused. On the other hand, when the transaction ends, the close allows either the persistence manager or its resources to be reused in another transaction. In short, closing the persistence manager at the end of the business method in a CMT session bean ensures that resources are recycled.

Likewise, managed persistent objects cannot be cached in the bean's member fields after the persistence manager is closed. (Recall that JDO does not define the behavior of managed objects after the persistence manager is closed.) If desired, unmanaged application data objects can be stored in a bean's member fields either as the service state of a stateless session bean or as the conversational state of a stateful session bean.

Listing 6-6 contains an example of a session bean that uses CMT. This session bean could be either stateful or stateless. As far as the JDO issues are concerned, the code is the same for both. The example bean implements, as do all of the other EJB examples in this chapter, the QuoteServer business interface. The QuoteServer interface has two methods, getQuote and addQuote. The getQuote method returns a Quote object. The addQuote method creates a Quote object and makes it persistent.

Listing 6-6. Example of a CMT Session Bean That Uses JDO

```
// CMT Session bean
package com.ysoft.jdo.book.sayings.service.session;

import com.ysoft.jdo.book.sayings.persistent.*;
import com.ysoft.jdo.book.sayings.service.*;
import com.ysoft.jdo.book.factory.JndiLocator;
import com.ysoft.jdo.book.sayings.persistent.QuoteManager.QuoteManagerOID;
import com.ysoft.jdo.book.common.ejb.EJBHelper;
import javax.jdo.*;
import javax.ejb.*;
import java.util.*;
```

```java
public class QuoteServerEJB implements SessionBean, QuoteServer
   {
   // state that passivation preserves
   private SessionContext          sessionContext;
   private PersistenceManagerFactory   pmf;

   public void ejbCreate() throws CreateException
      {
      }

   public void ejbRemove()
      {
      }

   public void setSessionContext(SessionContext sc)
      {
      sessionContext = sc;
      try
         {
         pmf = JndiLocator.getPMF("EE_PMF",
               "com/ysoft/jdo/book/sayings/service/factory.properties");
         }
      catch (Exception e)
         {
         throw new EJBException("Unable to get PMF using \"EE_PMF\" name: ", e);
         }
      }

   public void ejbActivate()
      {
      }

   public void ejbPassivate()
      {
      }

   public Quote getQuote() throws QuoteServerException
      {
      PersistenceManager pm = null;

      try
         {
         pm = getPersistenceManager();
         QuoteManager qm = getQuoteManager(pm);
         return (Quote) EJBHelper.respond(getQuote(pm, qm));
         }
```

```
        finally
          {
          if (pm != null)
             {
             pm.close();
             }
          }
       }

   public void addQuote(String q, String s) throws QuoteServerException
     {
     q = normalizeString(q);
     s = normalizeString(s);
     PersistenceManager pm = null;
     try
        {
        pm = getPersistenceManager();
        QuoteManager qm = getQuoteManager(pm);
        Quote quote = qm.newQuote(q, s);
        pm.makePersistent(quote);
        }
     finally
        {
        if (pm != null)
           {
           pm.close();
           }
        }
     }

   private PersistenceManager getPersistenceManager()
     {
     return pmf.getPersistenceManager();
     }

   private String normalizeString(String s) throws QuoteServerException
     {
     if (s != null)
        {
        s = s.trim();
        if (s.length() <= 0)
           s = null;
        }
```

```
    if (s == null)
        throw new QuoteServerException(
                "Neither the quotation nor the source can be null or empty");
    return s;
    }


private QuoteManager getQuoteManager(PersistenceManager pm)
    {
    return getQuoteManager(pm, true);
    }


private QuoteManager getQuoteManager(PersistenceManager pm,
        boolean createIfNone)
    {
    return getQuoteManager(pm, createIfNone,
            new QuoteManagerOID(QuoteManager.getSingletonKey()));
    }


private QuoteManager getQuoteManager(PersistenceManager pm,
        boolean createIfNone, QuoteManagerOID key)
    {
    QuoteManager quoteManager = null;

    try
        {
        quoteManager = (QuoteManager) pm.getObjectById(key, true);
        }
    catch (JDODataStoreException e)
        {
        // do nothing here, creation follows next
        }

    // create one and only QuoteManager, if it doesn't exist,
    // but only if correct key is used
    if (quoteManager == null && createIfNone)
        {
        if (!QuoteManager.getSingletonKey().equals(key.toInteger()))
            throw new EJBException("Cannot create a quote manager with key " +
                    key + "; use Integer(1) instead");
        quoteManager = QuoteManager.newQuoteManager();
        pm.makePersistent(quoteManager);
        }
    return quoteManager;
    }
```

```
          private Quote getQuote(PersistenceManager pm2, QuoteManager qm2)
              throws QuoteServerException
          {
          Query query = getQuery(pm2);
          return getQuote(pm2, qm2, query);
          }


      private Quote getQuote(PersistenceManager pm2, QuoteManager qm2, Query query)
              throws QuoteServerException
          {
          try
             {
             // qet a random quote
             Quote quote = null;

             if (qm2 == null || qm2.getNumQuotes() < 1)
                 quote = QuoteManager.makeTempQuote("Nothing to say", "The System");
             else
                 {
                 int index = qm2.getRandomIndex();
                 Collection results = (Collection) query.execute(new Integer(index));
                 Iterator iter = results.iterator();
                 if (iter.hasNext())
                     {
                     quote = (Quote) iter.next();
                     if (iter.hasNext())
                         throw new QuoteServerException(
                                 "more than one quote with index: " + index);
                     }
                 else
                     {
                     throw new QuoteServerException("No quote for index: " + index);
                     }
                 }

             return quote;
             }
          finally
             {
             if (query != null)
                 query.closeAll();
             }
          }
```

```
private Query getQuery(PersistenceManager pm2)
  {
  Extent extent = pm2.getExtent(Quote.class, false);
  Query query = pm2.newQuery(extent, "quoteIndex == i");
  query.declareParameters("Integer i");
  return query;
  }
}
```

In Listing 6-6, all of the private methods of the bean are shown. In the later code listings, private methods that are unchanged from earlier listings are omitted for brevity.

In this application, the Quote is one application data class and the QuoteManager is the other. The persistent QuoteManager object is a singleton in the database. It keeps track of the number of quotes, provides a factory for new Quote objects, and can generate a valid random quote index for looking up a quote.

A persistence manager factory is obtained from JNDI in setSessionContext. It is held during the lifetime of the bean. If desired, in the stateful CMT session bean, ejbPassivate can clear the reference to the persistence manager factory, and ejbActivate can reacquire it. Doing this may save resources during passivation, but it slows down activation. There is no reason to write code for ejbActivate and ejbPassivate in a stateless session bean since the container does not passivate stateless beans.

Both business methods in the QuoteServer bean may throw a QuoteServerException. Since the QuoteServer is a simple EJB, there is no need to force a rollback by calling the setRollbackOnly method in the javax.ejb.SessionContext interface when the QuoteServerException arises. In more complex beans, careful consideration of exception handling is an important part of the bean's design.

Most of the code that calls JDO is wrapped in a try block. JDO exceptions are not caught because the simple bean code shown here does not know how to recover from these error conditions. Since JDO exceptions are derived from java.lang.RuntimeException, they cause the EJB container to roll back the transaction, and they cause the container to discard the bean instance. Following the try block, the finally block closes the query results and the persistence manager.

Notice that the code closes the persistence manager before the EJB container has the opportunity to complete the transaction. When using JDO with container-managed transactions, this usage is required. The implementation ensures that the persistence manager does not close until the container completes the transaction.

When two methods within the bean use the same pattern to acquire and close persistence managers, if one method calls the other, the second one gets the same persistence manager as the first if a managed transaction is active. None of the calls to close the persistence manager actually close the persistence manager until the container completes the transaction. Each acquisition of a persistence manager should match with one and only one call to close it.

The code show in Listing 6-6 comes from the *stateful_cmt/QuoteServerEJB.java* source file in the com.ysoft.jdo.book.sayings.service.session package. The quote server examples are included in the JDO Learning Tools. These examples show implementations of the QuoteServer business interface for four kinds of session beans and an entity bean. Some of these beans use a connection factory, and some use a persistence manager factory. Either optimistic or datastore transactions can be configured. Chapters 8 through 11 discuss the various tools and example programs in the JDO Learning Tools. Chapter 11 describes how to build and run the quote server examples.

On Returning Serialized Data Objects from Business Methods

The getQuote business method returns to the client a serialized Quote object. In Listing 6-6 and in all of the CMT bean examples presented here, the serialized persistent object is filtered through the respond method in the com.ysoft.jdo.book.common.ejb.EJBHelper class. Before explaining what the respond method does, let's examine why it is needed.

In all CMT beans, the EJB container determines whether to end the transaction before it returns the response to the client. As a result, by the time serialization occurs, the transaction may have ended. Even in a BMT bean, if the business method ends the transaction, the transaction ends before the response is serialized to the client. As a result, the bean programmer must decide whether to serialize to the client an object graph that is consistent with the transactional context or to serialize an object graph that is obtained after the transaction ends. In the second case, the transaction's *NontransactionalRead* property must be turned on to allow JDO's transparent support for serialization to access the persistent objects.

Making sure that the persistence manager can support serialization of the business method's response becomes more difficult when the bean's code closes the persistence manager at the end of the business method. As mentioned earlier, a CMT bean closes the persistence manager because it cannot reuse it and because closing it allows the persistence manager and its resources to be recycled. Although the JDO implementation delays the effects of closing until the container-managed transaction ends, thereafter the persistence manager is actually closed. Once the persistence manager is actually closed, the behavior of managed objects becomes undefined. As a result, the behavior of the managed objects becomes undefined before the container uses them to serialize the return value.

The respond method in the EJBHelper class addresses both the transactional issue and the closed persistence manager issue by creating a graph of unmanaged objects for the response before the transaction ends and the persistence manager closes. It is this graph of unmanaged objects that the container serializes back to the client. The respond method uses CPU cycles to do its work and may generate additional objects that are eventually garbage collected. In addition, the use of the respond method guarantees that the method returns its response by value rather than by reference. This fact may have an impact on the decision whether to expose the business method in a local interface or call the business method from another method within the bean.

When the bean uses BMT, it is not necessary to close the persistence manager at the end of the business method. As a result, turning on the *NontransactionalRead* property to provide a nontransactional response after the transaction has ended may be preferable to calling the respond method to generate a transactional response.

Using JDO in Entity Beans with BMP

When an entity bean uses container-managed persistence (CMP), the bean developer has no use for JDO, since the container takes care of persistence. On the other hand, when the bean developer writes an entity bean that implements bean-managed persistence (BMP), the developer can use JDO as the persistence service.

When the bean developer uses JDO, the entity bean delegates to a corresponding persistent application data object. In essence, the entity bean wraps a persistent application data object. The bean developer may decide to wrap each application data object in a corresponding entity bean, or he may decide to make the entity bean a coarse-grained object that delegates to a composition of many related fine-grained application data objects.

Listing 6-7 shows an example entity bean that implements the QuoteServer business interface. Omitted from the code in Listing 6-7 are the private bean methods that remain the same as those found in Listing 6-6. The example is taken from the com.ysoft.jdo.book.sayings.service.entity.QuoteServerEJB class.

Listing 6-7. Example of a BMP Entity Bean That Uses JDO

```
public class QuoteServerEJB implements javax.ejb.EntityBean, QuoteServer
    {
    private EntityContext context;
    private ConnectionFactory cFactory;
    private PersistenceManager pm;
    private Query query;
    private QuoteManager qm;
```

```
public Integer ejbCreate() throws CreateException
  {
  PersistenceManager persistenceManager = null;

  try
    {
    // get a persistence manager
    persistenceManager = getPersistenceManager();
    QuoteManagerOID key = new QuoteManagerOID(
         QuoteManager.getSingletonKey());

    // if we get a QuoteManager then we can't create one
    if (getQuoteManager(persistenceManager, false, key) != null)
      {
      throw new CreateException(
           "The one and only QuoteServer already exists");
      }

    // create the one and only QuoteManager
    getQuoteManager(persistenceManager, true, key);
    return key.toInteger();
    }
  catch (CreateException e)
    {
    throw e;
    }
  catch (ResourceException e)
    {
    throw new CreateException("Caught exception in ejbCreate: " + e);
    }
  finally
    {
    if (persistenceManager != null)
       persistenceManager.close();
    }
  }

public void ejbPostCreate()
  {
  }
```

```
public void ejbRemove() throws RemoveException
   {
   throw new RemoveException("remove not allowed");
   }

public Integer ejbFindByPrimaryKey(Integer key) throws FinderException
   {
   QuoteManagerOID oid = new QuoteManagerOID(key);
   PersistenceManager persistenceManager = null;
   try
      {
      // get a persistence manager
      persistenceManager = getPersistenceManager();

      // if we can't get the QuoteManager we can't find the QuoteServer
      if (getQuoteManager(persistenceManager, false, oid) == null)
         throw new ObjectNotFoundException(
               "can't find the only QuoteServer by key: " + oid +
               "; use Integer(" + QuoteManager.getSingletonKey() +
               ") for key");

      return oid.toInteger();
      }
   catch (ResourceException e)
      {
      throw new FinderException(
         "Caught exception in ejbFindByPrimaryKey: " + e);
      }
   finally
      {
      if (persistenceManager != null)
         persistenceManager.close();
      }
   }

public void setEntityContext(EntityContext ctx)
   {
   context = ctx;
   try
      {
      cFactory = JndiLocator.getCF("java:/jdoCF");
      }
```

```
        catch (NamingException e)
          {
          throw new EJBException(
             "Unable to get ConnectionFactory using \"java:/jdoCF\" name: ", e);
          }
      }

public void unsetEntityContext()
    {
    cFactory = null;
    context = null;
    }

public void ejbActivate()
    {
    }

public void ejbPassivate()
    {
    cleanup();
    }

public void ejbLoad()
    {
    }

public void ejbStore()
    {
    cleanup();
    }

public void addQuote(String quote, String source) throws QuoteServerException
    {
    quote = normalizeString(quote);
    source = normalizeString(source);
    setup();
    Quote q = qm.newQuote(quote, source);
    pm.makePersistent(q);
    }
```

```
public Quote getQuote() throws QuoteServerException
   {
   setup();
   return (Quote) EJBHelper.respond(getQuote(pm, qm, query));
   }

private PersistenceManager getPersistenceManager() throws ResourceException
   {
   return (PersistenceManager) cFactory.getConnection();
   }

private void setup()
   {
   if (pm == null)
      {
      try
         {
         PersistenceManager tPM = getPersistenceManager();
         query = getQuery(tPM);
         QuoteManagerOID oid = new QuoteManagerOID(
               (Integer) context.getPrimaryKey());
         qm = getQuoteManager(tPM, false, oid);
         pm = tPM; // flags that setup is complete
         }
      catch (ResourceException e)
         {
         throw new EJBException("Unable to get PM: ", e);
         }
      }
   }

private void cleanup()
   {
   if (pm != null)
      {
      // clear bean's references to persistent objects
      qm = null;

      // close the pm if not closed
      if (!pm.isClosed())
         pm.close();
```

```
        // clear bean's references to pm and its resources
        query = null;
        pm = null; // also the flag that cleanup has occurred
        }
    }


// private methods are omitted
// when identical to those in earlier listings
}
```

In this example, the singleton QuoteManager object and all the Quote objects together compose the singleton QuoteServer entity. As a result, the QuoteServer entity bean implements the same QuoteServer business interface as the session beans. Although atypical in some ways, the QuoteServer entity bean provides a good example of how to use JDO within a BMP entity bean.

The EJB's Entity Context Callback Methods

The container calls the entity bean's setEntityContext method soon after creating the bean. The QuoteServer uses this method to obtain the persistence manager factory. The bean retains this reference until the container calls the unsetEntityContext method. The container may never call the unsetEntityContext method.

The QuoteServer Bean's setup and cleanup Methods

The setup and cleanup methods in the QuoteServer entity bean are private methods created for the example. The setup method performs the housekeeping chore of associating a QuoteServer entity bean instance with a persistence manager, a JDO transaction, and its delegate persistent object. The cleanup method performs the complementary set of tasks to disassociate the bean instance from all three.

In Listing 6-7, the setup method acquires a persistence manager from the factory, creates a query, and finds the singleton QuoteManager object in the database. The setup method stores each of these objects in the bean's member fields. The setup method is a no-op if the bean is already initialized. The cleanup method performs the opposite set of tasks. It closes the persistence manager and clears the bean's member fields of their references. The cleanup method is a no-op if the bean is already deinitialized.

On the one hand, the client may call the entity bean's business methods any number of times within one transaction without the EJB container making an intervening call to one of the EJB-defined callback methods. On the other hand, the container may call some EJB callback methods multiple times within the same transaction. The loose coupling between the bean's callback methods, on the one hand, and the transactional boundaries and the client's calls to business methods, on the other, makes the definition of the programming model for entity beans challenging.

The ejbStore Callback Method

After the client has invoked a business method on the entity bean, the EJB container calls the ejbStore method when the transaction is about to commit. Within the ejbStore method, the application code must close the persistence manager and clear the bean's references to persistent objects. To do this in Listing 6-7, the QuoteServer bean calls the cleanup method.

When the container calls ejbStore, the transaction is still active. The next call to the bean may be to a business method in a different transactional context from a different client, and it may occur before the container has completed the last transaction. As a result, the container's call to the ejbStore method is the bean's only chance to reliably disassociate itself from the persistence manager and its managed objects.

The Responsibility to Flush When ejbStore Is Called

The container may also call the ejbStore method to ensure that any modified state is flushed to the database for visibility to other beans running in the same transactional context. In this case, the container calls the ejbStore method in the middle of a transaction.

A common case where the container expects the bean to flush its state occurs when the client calls an entity bean's finder method. In this case, the EJB container calls the ejbStore method on the entity bean instances that are enlisted in the same transaction to ensure that the finder method, which is invoked on yet another entity bean, sees the current transactional state.

Because JDO does not provide a way to force persistent state to flush, the application cannot fulfill the contractual responsibility to flush changes to the underlying datastore. The impacts of this failure depend on whether the EJB container is clustered or not. If the EJB container is clustered, then the details of the clustered configuration determine the impact.

When the EJB container is not clustered, there is only one JVM running the EJB server. As a result, the failure to flush presents no difficulties. Every bean that uses JDO within the same transactional context will acquire from the connection factory or persistence manager factory the same persistence manager along with its managed objects. As a result, in a nonclustered environment, every bean instance that uses JDO in the same transactional context has the same visibility on the transactional state because every one of them uses the same persistence manager.

When the EJB container is clustered, there are multiple JVMs that are each running an EJB server. In a clustered environment, the inability to force JDO to flush the changes of transactional objects to the datastore may mean that not all entity beans in the same transactional context see the same transactional state. The impact of this failure is most likely to occur when the application calls an entity bean's finder method after making changes in the transaction. In this case, the finder method may ignore the changes held by the transactional objects in other JVMs. The application can avoid this impact by avoiding calls to EJB finder methods after changes have been made within the transaction.

If possible, the clustered EJB container should be configured to place all entity beans of the same type that have the same transactional context in the same EJB server. When this can be done, JDO's caching makes up for the lack of flushing just as it does in a nonclustered configuration. In addition to the workarounds suggested here, your JDO vendor or EJB vendor may offer guidance or special features for clustered configurations that address JDO's shortcomings in this regard.

The Entity EJB's Business Methods

The QuoteServer business methods call the setup method. The setup method ensures that the bean has the persistence manager associated with the managed transaction and has stored in its member field the reference to the QuoteManager object that it uses in its business methods. After the bean is initialized, calling the setup method again is a no-op.

Entity beans are not required to store references to persistent objects in their member fields, and they can, like CMT session beans, acquire a persistence manager and close it in each business method. Storing the persistence manager and some persistent objects in the bean's member fields are optimizations.

The question arises whether it is safe to close the persistence manager when the transaction may continue on to the next invocation of the bean's business interface. The answer is simple. Closing the persistence manager and reacquiring one within the same transactional context must always work in EJBs. Even in CMT session beans, the next call to a business method may be within the same managed transaction. Although the details may differ, all JDO implementations that support managed transactions must effectively delay closing the persistence manager until the managed transaction ends. If the transactional context does not change, the factory methods, getPersistenceManager and getConnection, must recycle the persistence manager associated with the transaction. As a result, the objects in the persistence manager's cache remain as they were. When the business method finds these objects the second time within the same managed transaction, it finds them in the same state that they were in when it last used them.

The ejbLoad Callback Method

The ejbLoad method is called whenever the container wants the entity bean to reload its persistent state from the database. The container may call the bean's ejbLoad method after it has started a transaction, or it may not. It depends on what commit option the container uses for the bean. As a result, the ejbLoad method is not a reliable place to acquire the persistence manager since it may not be called.

 NOTE   For more discussion of commit options in entity beans, see sections 12.1.9 and 12.4.4 of the Enterprise JavaBeans Specification Version 2.0, available from the Sun Microsystems Web site.

The example bean in Listing 6-7 does nothing in the ejbLoad method. Instead, it calls its setup method at the start of every business method to lazily acquire the persistence manager and the references to persistent objects. When the example bean's setup method is called more than once without an intervening call to its cleanup method, the redundant calls are no-ops.

The ejbPassivate Callback Method

The EJB container calls the ejbPassivate method whenever it wants to dissociate the entity bean from its persistent identity and return it to the pool of bean instances. Although the container often calls the ejbStore method before it calls the ejbPassivate method, there are cases where this sequence is not followed. For this reason, the ejbPassivate method in Listing 6-7 calls the cleanup method to clear the bean's member fields and close the persistence manager. When the QuoteServer bean's cleanup method is called more than once without an intervening call to the setup method, the redundant calls are no-ops.

The ejbActivate Callback Method

The application code performs no actions related to JDO in the `ejbActivate` callback method.

The ejbCreate Methods

In entity beans, each `ejbCreate` method creates a new persistent object and inserts its persistent state into the datastore. There may be several `ejbCreate` methods that take different parameters for initializing the new persistent object. All of the `ejbCreate` methods return an application-defined class called the *primary key class*. Typically, the primary key class is the application identity class for the persistent object that the entity bean delegates to.

The `ejbCreate` methods associate the entity bean with its primary key object. As a result, these methods can set up the bean for later use by business methods, and they can rely upon `ejbPassivate` or `ejbStore` to call the cleanup method. Since the `QuoteServer` entity bean's `ejbCreate` method is rarely called, this bean's `ejbCreate` method cleans up after itself.

In the example entity bean in Listing 6-7, there is only one `ejbCreate` method. It takes no parameters, and it creates the singleton `QuoteManager` object. Rather than return the `QuoteManagerOID` application identity class, the example bean returns an `Integer` object from its `ejbCreate` method. As a result, the bean maps between the `QuoteManagerOID` objects and the `Integer` objects as necessary.

The ejbRemove Method

The `ejbRemove` method in entity beans deletes the state of the persistent object from the datastore. In the typical case, the method would call the `getPrimaryKey` method in the `EntityContext` object. It would use the primary key to find the corresponding persistent object and delete it by calling the persistence manager's `deletePersistent` method.

In the example entity bean in Listing 6-7, the entity cannot be deleted. Instead, the `ejbRemove` method throws a `javax.ejb.RemoveException`.

The ejbFindByPrimaryKey Method

Every entity bean is associated with a primary key object. In the `ejbFindByPrimaryKey` method, the container or the client asks the bean to verify that a persistent object exists for the primary key passed. In the example entity bean in Listing 6-7, the code performs the lookup after mapping from the entity bean primary key to the application identity object.

EJB finder methods do not associate the entity bean instance with a primary key. For this reason, all finder methods should set up for themselves and clean up after themselves. Like the business methods of CMT session beans, they should acquire a persistence manager at their start and close it before they return.

The EJB Finder Methods

Entity beans may have any number of finder methods. These work in a manner similar to the `ejbFindByPrimaryKey` method. Each finder method looks for the persistent objects that are delegates for its type of entity bean and returns a primary key object for each of them.

In Listing 6-7, the example bean does not have any finder methods other than the `ejbFindByPrimaryKey` method.

Serializing Data Objects in the Business Method's Response

As with the CMT session beans, it is necessary, in the general case, to deal with the possibility that the transaction has ended and the persistence manager has closed before the EJB container serializes the business method's response to the client. The `QuoteServer` entity bean shown in Listing 6-7 uses the respond method in the `com.ysoft.jdo.book.common.ejb.EJBHelper` class to create a graph of unmanaged objects to return as the response for the getQuote business method.

If the entity bean is always used by a client that controls the managed transaction, then the need to call the respond method is eliminated. In these cases, the client receives the response from the business method before it decides whether to end the transaction. This would be the case, for example, if the entity bean was used by a session bean as part of the session facade pattern.

The Switch to a Connection Factory

By comparing Listing 6-6 to Listing 6-7, you can see the changes required to use a connection factory instead of a persistence manager factory. Because the connection factory's getConnection method throws the `javax.resource.ResourceException`, the bean's private getPersistenceManager method now throws this exception. The business methods now catch the `ResourceException` and throw an `EJBException` in its place.

An entity bean, like all other EJBs, can use either a persistence manager factory or a connection factory to acquire the persistence manager.

Using JDO in BMT Session Beans

In contrast to CMT, the business methods in a BMT session bean may continue to use the same persistence manager across multiple transactions. There is no need to enlist the persistence manager in the managed transaction, since the container is not managing transactions. Also in contrast to CMT, the business method in a BMT session bean can execute a series of transactions before returning. Because the persistence manager can be cached in a BMT session bean, the persistent objects that it manages can also be cached. The caching can occur directly in the bean's member fields, or it can occur indirectly in the cache belonging to the persistence manager.

In all stateless session beans, the bean is shared haphazardly with calling clients. When using a stateless session bean, the bean developer should not attempt to cache any state that depends on the sequence of calls to business methods. Consider the hypothetical example where one business method looks up and returns a Customer object, and the second business method updates the Customer object that was looked up earlier. A stateless session bean cannot store in a member field the Customer object found by the first business method for use by the second business method. With one client, the series of invocations on the bean's interface may be routed to different instances of the stateless session bean. With multiple clients, their invocations may be mixed together and routed to the same instance of the stateless session bean.

Unlike a stateless session bean, a stateful session bean is created for and assigned to one client. For this reason, it can store in a member field the Customer object from the first business method for use by the second business method.

In stateless BMT session beans, the business method must complete the transaction before it returns. On the other hand, stateful BMT session beans can allow a transaction to carry over from one business method to the next. If desired, the stateful BMT session bean can expose business methods whose sole purpose is to manage the transactional boundaries. For example, the bean may have business methods called startTransaction, commitTransaction, and rollbackTransaction to control transactional boundaries.

A Stateless BMT Session Bean

Listing 6-8 shows a QuoteServerEJB that is designed to support a stateless BMT session bean. With a few modifications that are described in the next section, it can also support the QuoteServer business interface in a stateful BMT session bean. The bean's private methods that are the same as those found in the earlier listings are omitted. This code is taken from the *stateless_bmp/QuoteServerEJB.java* source file in the com.ysoft.jdo.book.sayings.service.session package of the JDO Learning Tools.

Listing 6-8. Example of Stateless BMT Session Bean That Uses JDO

```java
public class QuoteServerEJB implements SessionBean, QuoteServer
   {
   private SessionContext          sessionContext;
   private PersistenceManagerFactory  pmf;
   private PersistenceManager       pm;
   private QuoteManager            qm;
   private Query                   query;

   public void ejbCreate() throws CreateException
      {
      }

   public void ejbRemove()
      {
      cleanup();
      }

   public void ejbActivate()
      {
      }

   public void ejbPassivate()
      {
      }

   public void setSessionContext(SessionContext sc)
      {
      sessionContext = sc;
      try
         {
         pmf = JndiLocator.getPMF("Std_NTR_PMF",
            "com/ysoft/jdo/book/sayings/service/factory.properties");
         pm = getPersistenceManager();
         }
      catch (Exception e)
         {
         throw new EJBException(
               "Unable to get PMF using \"Std_NTR_PMF\" name", e);
         }
      }
```

```
public Quote getQuote() throws QuoteServerException
    {
    if (qm == null)
        qm = getQuoteManager(pm, false);
    if (query == null)
        query = getQuery(pm);

    return getQuote(pm, qm, query);
    }

public void addOuote(String q, String s) throws QuoteServerException
    {
    q = normalizeString(q);
    s = normalizeString(s);

    try
        {
        pm.currentTransaction().begin();
        if (qm == null)
            qm = getQuoteManager(pm);
        Quote quote = qm.newQuote(q, s);
        pm.makePersistent(quote);
        pm.currentTransaction().commit();
        }
    finally
        {
        if (pm.currentTransaction().isActive())
            {
            try
                {
                pm.currentTransaction().rollback();
                }
            catch (RuntimeException logIt)
                {
                // log it rather than throw it, since it
                // was an earlier exception that forced the rollback
                }
            }
        }
    }
// private methods are omitted
// when identical to those in earlier listings
}
```

In Listing 6-8, the stateless BMT QuoteServer bean obtains its persistence manager in setSessionContext, which the EJB container calls when the bean is first created. The persistence manager remains in use for the life of the bean. It is not closed until the container calls ejbRemove. The ejbPassivate and ejbActivate methods are empty because the EJB container does not passivate stateless session beans. To avoid starting a transaction in the setSessionContext method, the bean lazily fetches and caches the QuoteManager and Query in the business methods.

To show the variations possible, the getQuote method in Listing 6-8 runs without starting a transaction. To support nontransactional access, the PersistenceManagerFactory that is stored in JNDI has the *NontransactionalRead* property turned on. Because getQuote runs nontransactionally, it calls the getQuoteManager method with the createIfNone parameter set to false. On the other hand, because the addQuote method adds a new persistent quote, it must use a transaction. Unlike in the CMT examples, the addQuote method must also handle the issue of rolling back the transaction if the try block fails. It does this in the finally block, after first checking that the transaction is active.

Changes Required for a Stateful BMT Session Bean

When clients use stateful session beans, the EJB container creates a bean for each client. The bean remains associated with one and only one client until either the client or the container removes it. Like stateless BMT session beans, the stateful BMT session bean can cache the persistence manager between calls to the business methods, and it can run a sequence of transactions within a business method.

The stateful BMT session bean can hold both persistent objects and unmanaged objects in its member fields. The member fields of the stateful session bean are called collectively its *conversational state*.

Unlike stateless session beans, stateful session beans may be passivated. In the ejbPassivate method, which the container calls just before passivation, the bean must prepare its conversational state for serialization. Some of the objects that the bean refers to in its member fields may not be serializable. Except for a few field types that receive special handling (see section 7.4.1 of the Enterprise Java-Beans Specification Version 2.0), the member fields must be serializable or set to null before passivation occurs. The PersistenceManager is not a serializable type, and it does not receive special handling. Therefore it must be closed and the bean's member field that refers to it set to null when passivation occurs.

Although the bean may passivate references to managed application data objects that are serializable, the application typically wants references to managed data objects, not to the unmanaged data objects that result from the bean's reactivation. For that reason, the bean's ejbPassivate method calls its cleanup method (unchanged from Listing 6-7) to set any member fields that refer to managed persistent objects to null.

Listing 6-9 shows the few changes to the QuoteServerEJB in Listing 6-8 that are needed to support a stateful BMT session bean. Since passivation may now occur, ejbPassivate calls the cleanup method. The ejbActivate method acquires a persistence manager, but it does not acquire a persistence manager factory. A PersistenceManagerFactory object is serializable, and therefore the reference acquired in setSessionContext is not lost during passivation. The QuoteServer business interface does not expect transactions to carry over from one business method to the next. For that reason, there are no other differences between the stateful and stateless BMT session bean implementations of the QuoteServerEJB.

Listing 6-9. Example of Stateful BMT Session Bean That Uses JDO

```java
public class QuoteServerEJB implements SessionBean, QuoteServer
    {
    // state that passivation preserves
    private SessionContext              sessionContext;
    private PersistenceManagerFactory   pmf;

    // state that passivation destroys
    private transient PersistenceManager pm;
    private transient QuoteManager       qm;
    private transient Query              query;

    // ejbCreate unchanged
    // ejbRemove unchanged
    // setSessionContext unchanged

    public void ejbActivate()
        {
        pm = getPersistenceManager();
        }

    public void ejbPassivate()
        {
        cleanup();
        }

    // getQuote unchanged
    // addQuote unchanged

    // all private methods are omitted
    // because they are identical to those in earlier listings
    }
```

Using JDO in Message-Driven Beans

In terms of the JDO issues, message-driven beans are identical to stateless session beans. The EJB container supports both CMT message beans and BMT message beans. The message bean has only one business method, the onMessage method.

Although no examples are provided in this book, to use JDO with a message-driven bean, follow the usage outlined for the corresponding type of stateless session bean. In a BMT message-driven bean, the persistence manager and its persistent objects can be cached for the life of the bean. In a CMT message-driven bean, the persistence manager must be obtained at the beginning of each invocation of the onMessage method and closed at the end. Persistent objects can be cached as long as the persistence manager remains open.

Summary

Persistence manager factories, and in some cases connection factories, produce persistence managers. The persistence manager factory informs the application about the general capabilities of the implementation. In particular, the factory identifies the optional JDO features that the implementation supports.

The factories directly provide objects that implement the PersistenceManager interface and indirectly provide objects that implement the Transaction interface. The values of two of the persistence manager's properties and five of the transaction's properties are inherited from the factory that produces them. The persistence manager uses the values of the factory's connection properties when connecting to the datastore. In addition, when there is a container-managed transaction, the factories enlist the persistence manager in the managed transaction.

The next chapter completes this book's description of JDO's persistence service by examining the utility class JDOHelper, the callback interface InstanceCallbacks, and exception hierarchy descending from JDOException. Each of these serve a special purpose, and every application will use some of them.

CHAPTER 7

Helpers, Callbacks, and Exceptions

THIS CHAPTER EXAMINES the JDOHelper class, the InstanceCallbacks interface, and the exception classes of JDO. The JDOHelper is a utility class that performs miscellaneous tasks. The InstanceCallbacks interface provides notification of life cycle transitions in persistent application data objects. The JDO implementation uses the class hierarchy formed by JDOException and its subclasses to indicate most error conditions.

The JDOHelper Utility Class

Each operation of the JDOHelper class is a static method, and for that reason, there is no need to instantiate an instance of this class. Figure 7-1 shows the eleven methods of this class. Although static methods are normally underlined in UML class diagrams, this is avoided in Figure 7-1 to make the diagram more readable.

JDOHelper
getPersistenceManagerFactory(Properties p) : PersistenceManagerFactory getPersistenceManagerFactory(Properties p, ClassLoader cl): PersistenceManagerFactory makeDirty (Object pc, String fieldName) : void getPersistenceManager(Object pc) : PersistenceManager getObjectId (Object pc) : Object getTransactionalObjectId (Object pc) : Object isPersistent (Object pc) : boolean isTransactional (Object pc) : boolean isDirty (Object pc) : boolean isDeleted (Object pc) : boolean isNew (Object pc) : boolean

Figure 7-1. The class diagram of the JDOHelper *class*

The methods in JDOHelper divide into two groups: those that perform miscellaneous tasks and those that identify the application data object's management state.

Miscellaneous Utility Methods in JDOHelper

The miscellaneous operations in the JDOHelper class perform the following tasks:

- Get a persistence manager factory.

- Mark a persistent object's field dirty.

- Get the persistence manager that is managing an application data object, if there is one.

- Get the identity object for an application data object, if there is one.

The next sections look at the methods for each of these tasks.

Acquiring a Persistence Manager Factory

JDOHelper provides two factory methods to acquire an object that implements the PersistenceManagerFactory interface.

```
public static PersistenceManagerFactory getPersistenceManagerFactory(
      Properties props)
public static PersistenceManagerFactory getPersistenceManagerFactory(
      Properties props,
      ClassLoader cloader)
```

Chapter 6 describes in detail the first getPersistenceManagerFactory method. This method loads the implementation class specified by the javax.jdo.PersistenceManagerFactoryClass property in props. It uses the class loader returned by the current Thread object's getContextClassLoader method. In most circumstances, this is the class loader that you want to use. The second method handles the odd case where you need to specify a different class loader.

Explicitly Marking Dirty a Data Object's Managed Field

The JDOHelper class provides the makeDirty method to explicitly indicate to JDO that the managed field of a managed object has been modified. The application uses this method to assist JDO in tracking changes to the entries of managed array fields.

```
public static void makeDirty(Object ado, String fieldName)
```

This method does the work that JDO normally does transparently when the application changes the value of a managed field. The only difference is that makeDirty does not change the managed field's value.

The fieldname parameter can be the field name as declared in the class, for example, "myManagedField". It can also be the class name, or fully qualified class name, concatenated with the field name by using the dot notation, such as "com.ysoft.jdo.book.example.MyAppDataClass.myManagedField".

In a class hierarchy, a derived class can declare a field using the same name used to declare a field in one of its superclasses. To determine which field is named when there are multiple fields by the same declared name in the class hierarchy, the makeDirty method begins its search either with the class named in the dot notation or, when the field name is unqualified by a class name, with the object's instance class. If the field is not found in the class where the search starts, then the method proceeds up the hierarchy of classes looking for the field in each application data class. The makeDirty method stops its search as soon as it finds the named field in an application data class, and as a result, at most one field is made dirty.

The call to makeDirty returns silently without effect under any of the following circumstances:

- The object passed is null.

- The object passed is not an application data object.

- The object passed is JDO-transient, that is to say, unmanaged.

- The field name is not the name of a managed field.

If conditions under which the method returns silently without action are avoided but a transaction is not active, then a JDOUserException is thrown.

229

The makeDirty Method Needed for Array Fields

When a transaction is active and the application stores a new value in the managed field of a managed application data object, JDO transparently marks the field as dirty. Several side effects can occur when a field becomes dirty. One, the object's management state becomes transactional, if it isn't already. Two, the object's management state becomes dirty, if it isn't already. Three, JDO saves a copy of the object's existing persistent state, called the *before-image*, if the transaction's *RestoreValues* property is true and JDO has not yet saved a before-image for the object in the current transaction. These side effects occur only once per modified object per transaction. By marking the persistent field dirty, JDO remembers to write the field to the datastore before the transaction commits. After these side effects occur, JDO applies the change that started the chain of side effects. Because JDO does this work transparently, the application normally does not explicitly mark a managed field dirty when it changes the field's value.

In the case of arrays, these side effects may not occur transparently. Suppose that you have an application data class with the following managed field:

```
Integer [] numbers;
```

If someplace in your application you execute code that replaces the array with a new array, as shown in the next line of code:

```
numbers = new Integer[] {new Integer(1),new Integer(2), new Integer(3)};
```

then the existing array, if any, that is assigned to the numbers field is replaced by the new array. In this case, JDO transparently marks the numbers field dirty.

On the other hand, if someplace in your application you execute code that alters one of the elements of the array, as shown in the next line of code:

```
numbers[0] = new Integer(42);
```

then JDO may or may not transparently detect the change. For that reason, it may fail to take the appropriate actions. Whether transparent persistence detects the change depends on the implementation and may depend on where the code that makes the change is located. The vendor will provide specific guidance on what their implementation provides when it comes to detecting changes in array elements. To be safe and portable, the application should assume that the implementation cannot detect changes to array elements.

When the implementation cannot detect changes to the elements of the managed array, or this condition is assumed, then the application must assume responsibility for informing JDO that the managed field has become dirty. It does this by calling the makeDirty method in JDOHelper. Using this method expands the one-line assignment shown earlier into two lines:

```
JDOHelper.makeDirty(this, "numbers");
numbers[0] = new Integer(42);
```

Note that the call to makeDirty comes before the change is applied to the numbers field. This order of calls provides for the same order of events that occurs in transparent persistence. By following this order, you avoid surprises such as storing your change in the before-image or having JDO reload the persistent state when a persistent object becomes transactional in a datastore transaction.

Starting with JDO 1.0.1, the call to makeDirty in the example can be replaced by the following statement:

```
numbers = numbers;
```

Ordinarily, it depends on the implementation whether a field becomes dirty when the application assigns the value that the field already has, but in the case of array fields, JDO 1.0.1 guarantees that same value assignment always makes the field dirty. However, when optimizing, some compilers may discard the self-assignment statement shown. Therefore, the safest practice is to continue using the makeDirty method.

Getting a Managed Object's Persistence Manager

The JDOHelper class provides the getPersistenceManager method to obtain the persistence manager that is controlling the managed application data object.

```
public static PersistenceManager getPersistenceManager(Object ado)
```

When the application does not know which persistence manager is controlling an application data object, the application calls this method to obtain the persistence manager. The method takes the object in question as a parameter. The method returns null when the object passed is any of the following:

- A null reference

- Not an application data object

- An unmanaged application data object

Otherwise, the method returns a reference to the object's persistence manager.

Getting a Persistent Object's Identity Object

The JDOHelper class provides two methods to get the identity object associated with a persistent data object.

```
public static java.lang.Object getObjectId(Object ado)
public static java.lang.Object getTransactionalObjectId(Object ado)
```

The getObjectId method in JDOHelper returns the JDO identity of a managed application data object. It returns null when the object passed is a null reference. It also returns null when the object passed is not a persistent application data object. The identity object that the method returns is a copy of the identity object held by the JDO runtime.

When the application data class uses application identity and the JDO implementation supports the javax.jdo.option.ChangeApplicationIdentity implementation option, then the application may change the values of the persistent object's key fields. After one or more key fields have been changed within a transaction, the getObjectId method returns a copy of the original JDO identity object, but the getTransactionalObjectId method returns a copy of the new JDO identity object.

NOTE   Chapter 6 discusses the implementation options, and Chapter 5 describes how the JDO metadata determines the type of JDO identity for each application data class.

If a transaction is not active or if the application key fields have not been changed, then getTransactionalObjectId behaves in the same fashion as getObjectId.

Determining the Management State of a Data Object

The JDOHelper class has five interrogation methods that determine whether an application data object is persistent, transactional, dirty, new, and/or deleted. Used together, these methods determine the JDO management state of an application data object.

```
public static boolean isPersistent(Object ado)
public static boolean isTransactional(Object ado)
public static boolean isDirty(Object ado)
public static boolean isNew(Object ado)
public static boolean isDeleted(Object ado)
```

As a general rule, the application does not concern itself with the management state of individual data objects. Instead, the application manages queries and transactions and makes decisions whether to add, delete, or modify persistent objects. It relies on JDO to do the right thing with the managed objects. The state interrogation methods therefore do not have a place in the normal business logic of the application. Instead, they are useful for learning about the behavior of the implementation and for debugging situations that the developer does not understand.

When an application data object is persistent, the JDO runtime associates it with a JDO identity object. Sometimes the persistent state of a persistent object is loaded into memory, and sometimes it is not. An application data object is transactional if the JDO runtime has associated the object with a transaction. When a transactional object requires modification of the state stored in the datastore upon commit, the transactional object is dirty. Some objects are dirty because they were modified after they became transactional. Some objects are dirty because they are new and their persistent state is not yet stored in the datastore. Some objects are dirty because they are deleted and their state needs to be removed from the datastore. Upon transaction commit, JDO flushes the persistent state of dirty transactional objects to the datastore by doing the updates, insertions, and deletions required.

For each of the ten JDO management states that application data objects may be in, Table 7-1 shows an "x" when the corresponding JDOHelper method returns true. (The table presented here draws heavily on Table 3 of Sun's JDO 1.0 specification.) If the object passed to the helper method is null or is not an application data object, then false is returned.

Table 7-1. Five Methods That Detect an Object's JDO Management State

Management State	isPersistent	isTransactional	isDirty	isNew	isDeleted
Transient					
Transient-clean		x			
Transient-dirty		x	x		
Persistent-nontransactional	x				
Hollow	x				
Persistent-clean	x	x			
Persistent-dirty	x	x	x		
Persistent-deleted	x	x	x		x
Persistent-new	x	x	x	x	
Persistent-new-deleted	x	x	x	x	x

As Table 7-1 shows, the five methods do not discriminate between application data objects in the hollow state and those in the persistent-nontransactional state. JDO does not offer a portable way to distinguish between the hollow and persistent-nontransactional states.

The InstanceCallbacks Interface

The JDO runtime interacts with the application data objects primarily through the javax.jdo.spi.PersistenceCapable interface, which enhancement adds to the application data class. The JDO runtime may also interact with application data objects through the InstanceCallbacks interface, an optional interface that the developer may add to the application data class.

If an application data class implements the InstanceCallbacks interface, then JDO calls the methods of the interface when specific events in the application data object's life cycle occur. Several types of actions can trigger the callbacks. The application may call methods in the Transaction or PersistenceManager interfaces that cause the callbacks. For example, calls to commit or rollback on the Transaction interface, or calls to evict or makeTransactional on the PersistenceManager interface, may cause one or more of the methods in InstanceCallbacks to be called. Actions arising from transparent persistence may also cause the callbacks. For example, iterating a collection or using the value of a persistent field may cause a callback.

This section describes the specific context of each callback method. It also describes some design problems that can be solved, and some that cannot be solved, by using one or more callback methods.

As the UML class diagram in Figure 7-2 illustrates, there are only four methods in the InstanceCallbacks interface. As the names of the callback methods indicate, the events that trigger a callback are related to actions on the persistent state of individual application data objects.

```
<< Interface >>
InstanceCallbacks


jdoPostLoad() : void
jdoPreStore() : void
jdoPreClear() : void
jdoPreDelete() : void

```

Figure 7-2. The class diagram of the InstanceCallbacks *interface*

CAUTION An easily overlooked bug when implementing the InstanceCallbacks interface occurs if the application data class fails to declare that it implements the interface. In this case, the class compiles and enhances just fine, but the JDO runtime never calls the callback methods.

The jdoPostLoad Callback

After JDO loads the fields in the default fetch group, it calls the application data object's jdoPostLoad method.

```
public void jdoPostLoad()
```

The code within the jdoPostLoad method is not enhanced for transparent persistence. As a result, the method should access only the persistent fields in the default fetch group and the application-defined key fields, if any. It should not access the persistent fields that are outside the default fetch group, and it should not access other application data objects.

NOTE As described in Chapter 5, the JDO metadata defines explicitly, or by default, which member fields in the application data class are part of the object's default fetch group.

In carrying out transparent persistence, the implementation makes the choice whether and when to load the default fetch group. Because the purpose of the default fetch group is to optimize access to the database, implementations usually read all the fields in the default fetch group together, but this behavior is not required. It is optional for the JDO implementation to load the default fetch group. The timing of the load of the default fetch group may vary widely across objects as the JDO runtime executes algorithms designed to optimize access to the database. As a result, the application cannot know when the callback will occur or even whether it will occur. Nonetheless, most implementations transparently load the default fetch group of a persistent object under the following circumstances:

- In response to a call to refresh in an optimistic transaction.

- Before returning to the application the value of a persistent field in the default fetch group, if the default fetch group has not been loaded.

- Before allowing the application to change the value of a persistent field in the default fetch group, if the default fetch group has not been loaded.

- In response to the object becoming transactional in a datastore transaction. In a datastore transaction, any existing persistent state of the persistent object is discarded when the object becomes transactional, and for that reason, a reload of the default fetch group usually follows either immediately or when a persistent field in the default fetch group is accessed or modified.

- Before allowing the object to be serialized, if the default fetch group has not been loaded.

- In response to a call to retrieve, if the default fetch group has not been loaded.

As a result of the frequent opportunities to load the default fetch group and the inherent usefulness of doing so, applications can rely on the callback to jdoPostLoad to occur regularly in most implementations.

The jdoPreStore Callback

The JDO runtime calls the application data object's jdoPreStore method after the transaction is asked to commit and before the cached persistent state is transferred to the datastore.

```
public void jdoPreStore()
```

The code within the jdoPreStore method is enhanced for transparent persistence. If the method modifies persistent fields within its object, the updated values are sent to the datastore during the commit operation that is in process. In addition, the runtime context of this callback permits the code to access persistence managers and other application data objects. The application data object must be either persistent-new or persistent-dirty to receive this callback. In either case, the JDO identity is available.

The jdoPreClear Callback

The JDO runtime calls the application data object's jdoPreClear method before it resets the object's persistent fields to their Java default values.

```
public void jdoPreClear()
```

The code within the jdoPreClear method is not enhanced for transparent persistence. For that reason, the implementation code should be careful in making assumptions about the state of persistent fields. A persistent field may not have been loaded prior to this call and may therefore hold its Java default value rather than its managed persistent value.

The generic term for clearing the object's persistent state is *eviction*. Many actions and events can cause eviction. Eviction may occur transparently upon transaction commit when the transaction's *RetainValues* property is false, or upon rollback in some cases when the transaction's *RestoreValues* property is false. The PersistenceManager interface also has the evict and evictAll methods to force eviction. Finally, the implementation is at liberty to evict persistent-nontransactional application data objects at any point that it sees fit as part of its general cache management strategy. Chapter 4 describes the Transaction interface, and Chapter 3 covers the PersistenceManager interface.

When the transaction commits, if the transaction's *RetainValues* property is false, then objects in any of the following management states are evicted and the callback to jdoPreClear occurs:

- Persistent-clean

- Persistent-new

- Persistent-dirty

- Persistent-deleted

- Persistent-new-deleted

If the *RetainValues* property is true, then the objects in the first three states are not evicted and the callback does not occur. For the last two states, the specification is unclear on the behavior to expect when *RetainValues* is true. Eviction may or may not take place. If eviction occurs, the callback occurs.

When the transaction rolls back, if the transaction's *RestoreValues* property is false, then objects in any of the following three states are evicted and the callback to jdoPreClear occurs:

- Persistent-clean

- Persistent-dirty

- Persistent-deleted

Otherwise, if the object is in any of the other management states, or if *RestoreValues* is true, then eviction does not occur.

The jdoPreDelete Callback

JDO calls the jdoPreDelete method when the application calls the persistence manager's deletePersistent method.

```
public void jdoPreDelete()
```

The code within the jdoPreDelete callback is enhanced for transparent persistence. The callback occurs before the application data object transitions to one of the deleted states. After an object has been deleted, no persistent fields may be modified, and only application-defined key fields, when present, may be accessed. Within jdoPreDelete, all persistent fields may be accessed and modified.

Ways to Use the InstanceCallbacks Methods

The InstanceCallbacks methods allow the application to react to events in JDO's management of the object. In some cases, responding to these events is the perfect place to take actions desired by the application, but in other cases, the callback methods are not adequate for the application's purpose.

The following sections examine some uses, or attempted uses, for the callback methods and evaluate whether the callback methods are the best place to accomplish the design goal. Applications will certainly use the InstanceCallbacks interface in more ways than the few discussed here, but these appear to be common, or at least commonly attempted.

Validation

Typically, when data is accepted from some noncontrolled source, such as a user or another system, the application usually validates the data before storing it in the datastore. To validate, the application applies rules derived from the business domain.

The earlier that validation occurs, the more likely it is that the source can resubmit correct information. Like applications that do not use JDO, those that use JDO want to validate the information received as early as possible. Depending on the application's architecture, this may occur as the information is received from the source, it may occur as the application accepts the information, or it may occur in the application data objects as or after the information is stored in them. All of these places are stops on the road from the source of the information to the datastore.

Although jdoPreStore is another stop on the same road, because it is the last stop, in most applications it is not the best place for data validation. Nonetheless, it may be better to validate the information in jdoPreStore than never validate it at all. If the validation performed in jdoPreStore succeeds, the callback can simply return.

One of the difficulties of doing validation in jdoPreStore is knowing what to do when validation fails. On the one hand, when JDO is managing the transaction, JDO does not specify a way to stop the transaction's commit within jdoPreStore. On the other hand, when an EJB container is managing the transactions, the container provides a way to reject the transaction's commit. Within a CMT bean, calling setRollbackOnly on the EJBContext object ensures that the transaction cannot commit. To allow the jdoPreStore method to find the EJBContext object, the application might store it in the persistence manager's *UserObject* property.

Storing Calculation Results in Unmanaged Fields

In some cases, the application stores in unmanaged fields the calculation results that directly or indirectly derive from the object's persistent state. Whenever possible, avoid this design for the simple reason that the code to implement caching is nearly always more complex than it at first appears to be.

The simplest approach to managing transient state that derives from the persistent state is to use lazy evaluation. Listing 7-1 shows a simple example of lazy evaluation for a hypothetical Customer class. The work of constructing the full name is done only once, upon the first request for the full name; however, additional code clears the transient state at the appropriate times. When mutators change the components that the fullName depends on, the mutators clear the transient state. When JDO clears the persistent state, jdoPreClear clears the transient state. As with all caching, the gain is realized only when the method that accesses cached data is called more than once. In this simple case, the gain is roughly zero, since the use of cached state avoids only the string concatenations. In practice, a more time-consuming or resource-consuming calculation is required before it would pay to cache the result in an unmanaged field.

Listing 7-1. Transient State Dependent on Persistent State

```
public class Customer implements InstanceCallbacks
    {
    private String lastName;  // persistent field
    private String firstName; // persistent field
    private String fullName; // unmanaged field

    public String getFullName()
       {
       if (fullName == null)
          fullName = firstName + " " + lastName;
       return fullName;
       }

    public void setFirstName(String name)
       {
       fullname = null;
       firstName = name;
       }
```

```
public void setLastName(String name)
    {
    fullName = null;
    lastName = name;
    }

public void jdoPreClear()
    {
    fullName = null;
    }

// the other methods of InstanceCallbacks are defined empty
}
```

Performing Background Calculations

There are times when lazy evaluation is not the answer for calculating results. For example, a hypothetical Stock object might have buyAt and sellAt price points that are calculated and stored in unmanaged fields. The calculated prices are not persistent because they vary over time, and there is no reason to remember them beyond a short period of time. They are stored in the object because the computation is too costly to perform unnecessarily. The computation is also too costly to perform upon demand. Instead, the strategy is to precalculate these values in the background while the user is busy with something else and before he needs the values.

It is tempting to see the jdoPostLoad callback as the trigger for the calculation. There is one conclusive reason to avoid this. The jdoPostLoad method is called in response to the user's actions. Consequently, the user's request that indirectly caused the default fetch group to load and the jdoPostLoad method to be called blocks until the jdoPostLoad method has completed. If the object should do the calculation in the background, then jdoPostLoad cannot do the job. Instead, the application should create a background thread to perform the task.

When multiple application threads access the same persistent objects, there are three difficulties to keep in mind. One, the affected application data classes should be thread-safe. For example, the application data class should prevent the buyAt price from being returned while the background thread is calculating it. Two, the persistence manager's *Multithreaded* property must be true. When this property is true, the JDO implementation ensures thread safety for its internal tasks. Three, the application must prevent the normal service thread from colliding transactionally with the background thread. To prevent this, avoid transactions in the background calculation. Instead set the *NontransactionalRead* property to true.

Capturing the Identity String

Some business services such as EJB session beans pass application data objects by value to and from remote clients. When application data objects are passed by value, they lose their JDO identity and their connection to their persistence manager. As a result, the client cannot directly modify persistent objects but must request that the service or EJB modify the persistent objects for it. But how does the service know which object the client wants to modify?

When the service is stateful, there are a number of ways for the client to indicate to the service which object it intends. The service can keep the persistent objects viewed by the client in a Map and allow the client to refer to them by name. Or it can keep them in a List and allow the client to refer to them by index. When the service is stateless, the client's best option is to indicate the object of interest by the object's identity. For the client to have the object's identity, the service must first provide it.

When an application data object uses application identity, it is straightforward to construct a corresponding identity instance from the application data object's primary key fields. For that reason, the client can return a modified unmanaged object to the service and instruct it to make the changes in the persistent object that have been made in this unmanaged object. To follow the client's instructions, the service constructs the application identity object from the key values in the unmanaged object, finds the corresponding persistent object using the persistence manager's getObjectById method, and applies the changes found in the unmanaged object to the persistent object. Because the primary key fields are present in the application data object that uses application identity, the unmanaged object carries with it the values that the application can use to get the corresponding persistent object from JDO.

Application data classes that use datastore identity require a different strategy to carry persistent identity in their unmanaged objects because the identity value is not stored in the application data object. In this case, the application data objects must capture the identity string and store it in an unmanaged field. You may recall from Chapter 1 that the identity string is obtained from the identity object's toString method. From that point forward, the logic is nearly the same. The only difference is that the persistence manager's newObjectIdInstance method must be called to construct the identity object.

The code in Listing 7-2 shows an application data class that captures its identity string. The captureIdentityString method makes the capture and returns the identity string. Since the application cannot change a datastore identity, the code that captures the identity string assumes that it is immutable except when the persistent object is deleted. The identity string is stored in an unmanaged OIDString field. This string field must be described in the JDO metadata file as unmanaged since string fields by default are managed. Chapter 5 describes the JDO metadata and its defaults.

Listing 7-2. The Apple Class Captures the Identity String for a Datastore Identity

```java
package com.ysoft.jdo.book.statetracker;
import java.io.Serializable;
import javax.jdo.InstanceCallbacks;
import javax.jdo.JDOHelper;

public class Apple implements InstanceCallbacks, Serializable
    {
    // The following is an unmanaged field to hold the identity string
    private String    OIDString;

    public String captureIdentityString()
        {
        // this code assumes that each object's identity value cannot be changed
        // and therefore, it does not have to be recaptured if it has already been
        // captured.
        if (OIDString == null)
            {
            Object oid = JDOHelper.getObjectId(this);
            if (oid != null)
                OIDString = oid.toString();
            }
        return OIDString;
        }

    // the methods required by the InstanceCallbacks interface
    public void jdoPostLoad()
        {
        captureIdentityString();
        }

    public void jdoPreClear()
        {
        }

    public void jdoPreDelete()
        {
        OIDString = null;
        }

    public void jdoPreStore()
        {
        captureIdentityString();
        }
    }
```

The best place to capture the identity string of an existing persistent object is in the jdoPostLoad method. The specification offers no guarantee that this method will be called. The JDO specification requires that JDO call the jdoPostLoad method after it loads the default fetch group, but it is not clear whether the JDO implementation must call the jdoPostLoad method if it opts to load the fields of the default fetch group one at a time, rather than all together. Loading the fields of the default fetch group all together is a significant optimization. For this reason, in spite of the lack of clarity in the specification, there is a high probability that serializing the object or accessing any field in the default fetch group will trigger the jdoPostLoad callback.

The captureIdentityString method is public so that the application can call it at any point. Since the method caches an already captured identity string, there is little cost to calling it more than once. When an object is made persistent and the transaction commits, the code in the jdoPreStore method captures the identity string. When an apple is serialized, the OIDString field is written to the serialization stream. In that way, it travels with the object and is available in unmanaged copies of the object. When the apple is deleted, jdoPreDelete is called and the cached identity string is set to null. Otherwise, once captured, it is immutable.

Managing Application-Generated Keys

In some cases, an application key value is defined elsewhere and simply used by the application. Governments provide identification numbers for individuals. Organizations provide UPCs for retail products and VINs for automobiles. In the near future, low-cost, universal, unique identifier buttons will be attachable to just about everything. In these cases, the key value is a fact about the person or item that is unique and discoverable.

In other cases, the application generates the key value when the object representing the person or item is created in memory or stored in the database. In these cases, the application that generates the identity usually has some business requirements for the range and sequence of key values. Sometimes, the key value is encoded with business meaning. In some cases, every key value that is consumed must be accounted for. In other cases, the requirement is only to avoid needlessly wasting keys.

Avoiding Holes in the Key Sequence

When the application is managing the key generation, it may be a requirement to avoid holes in the key sequence. For example, there should be a purchase order for every issued purchase order number. It is always difficult to audit every key value issued, since there are many reasons why the insertion into the datastore may fail.

A common approach that avoids creating holes in the key sequence, but does not eliminate them entirely, is to delay consuming a generated key for as long as possible. With JDO, each application key field must contain a valid, non-null value at the time that the persistence manager's makePersistent method is called. Likewise, the application key field must contain a valid value when the object becomes persistent because of reachability. These constraints limit how long the application can wait before assigning a value to an application key field.

The application cannot wait until the jdoPreStore method is called to assign valid keys. In fact, the object becomes persistent and JDO constructs its application identity before JDO calls the object's jdoPreStore method.

The specification allows an implementation, at its option, to support applications that change the values of key fields in persistent objects. In this case, the application may change the primary keys in jdoPreStore, but this strategy may not accomplish much since the transaction's commit could still fail. Some early implementations of JDO encounter problems in carrying out the switch in jdoPreStore correctly. It is too soon to tell whether these failures are simply implementation bugs or whether a deeper issue lies unresolved in the JDO specification.

In short, JDO does not offer a simple way to guarantee that all keys issued are in fact used, and the methods in InstanceCallbacks offer little help in this endeavor.

Avoiding a Needless Waste of Keys

If the concern is not how to avoid every hole in the generated key sequence, but rather how to make sure that a key value is generated for every object, then assigning the generated key in a constructor is a good strategy. As you may recall from the discussions in Chapter 5, JDO calls the no-arg constructor when it is time to instantiate a persistent object in memory. To avoid wasting a lot of generated key values, avoid assigning a primary key in the no-arg constructor. There is no reason to assign values to primary key fields when JDO will soon reset the fields with the values found in the database. When the application needs to construct a new and not-yet-persistent application data object, it can use another constructor to obtain an instance with an assigned key value.

Implementing Cascading Deletes

When one object is part of another object, it is related by composition to the containing object. Composition is stronger than simple aggregation because the lifetime of the contained object is bound by the lifetime of the containing object. To implement the semantics of this relationship, the application deletes the contained objects when the container is deleted. This step is usually called a *cascading delete*.

JDO does not directly support cascading deletes; however, in the jdoPreDelete method the application can implement cascading deletes. The jdoPreDelete method is called when the persistence manager's deletePersistent method is called. In this method, the application can ensure that any contained application data objects are also deleted by calling the deletePersistent method for them.

Listing 7-3 shows a hypothetical example of cascading deletes in the jdoPreDelete method. The example is fanciful but straightforward. When the application deletes a banana split by calling the persistence manager's deletePersistent method, JDO in turn calls back to the banana split's jdoPreDelete method. At this point, the banana split takes responsibility for deleting the persistent application data objects that compose it. Embedded objects like strings, dates, and so forth do not need to be deleted because their embedded status ensures their removal. Some application data objects, such as the ice cream store where the banana split was made, are merely associated with the banana split and are not related by composition. For this reason, the banana split does not delete the ice cream store in its jdoPreDelete method.

Listing 7-3. Deleting a Banana Split and the Objects That Compose It

```
package hypothetical.example;
import java.util.*;
import javax.jdo.*;

public class BananaSplit implements InstanceCallbacks
    {
    // the persistent fields of a BananaSplit
    // the BananaSplit is composed of these application data objects
    private Banana       banana;
    private IceCream     iceCream;
    private Sprinkles    sprinkles;
    private WhippedCream whippedCream;
    private HashSet      toppings;

    // a persistent reference to an embedded data object
    private Date         timeCreated;

    // a persistent reference to an associated application data object
    private IceCreamStore sellingStore;

    // the methods required by the InstanceCallbacks interface
    public void jdoPostLoad()
        {
        }
```

```
public void jdoPreClear()
   {
   }

public void jdoPreDelete()
   {
   PersistenceManager pm = JDOHelper.getPersistenceManager(this);
   pm.deletePersistent(banana);
   pm.deletePersistent(iceCream);
   pm.deletePersistent(sprinkles);

   if (toppings != null)
      {
      pm.deletePersistentAll(toppings);
      }
   }

public void jdoPreStore()
   {
   }
}
```

In Listing 7-3, several other application data classes are mentioned for this hypothetical example. If the IceCream class were composed of persistent objects, in its jdoPreDelete method it would handle the cascading deletes of its composing objects, and so on. A contained object does not delete its container, as this would lead to incorrect semantics and infinite recursion.

In Listing 7-3, the call to the deletePersistentAll method for the toppings collection does not delete the Collection object itself; instead, it deletes the Topping objects contained in the collection. Because Collection objects are embedded objects, JDO ensures that they are deleted automatically.

Although the application can take responsibility for implementing the cascading deletes, the JDO implementation must offer some support beyond what the JDO specification requires in order for the cascading deletes to work. After the cascading deletes have occurred, the persistent objects are put in the persistent-deleted management state. Before the transaction completes the commit process, JDO sends delete statements to the datastore. If the implementation does not send the delete statements in the correct order, it is possible that the datastore may refuse to execute them. The JDO specification does not mention the need to do this, but if an implementation does not support the requirements of its datastore when flushing multiple deleted objects, the commit fails.

Some implementations go beyond simply supporting application-written cascading deletes. These implementations supply ways to specify the cascading deletes either in the JDO metadata or in supplemental XML control files.

Cooperating with JDO's Cache Management

Persistent application data objects, like any Java objects, cannot be garbage collected as long as they are reachable, by a strong reference or a chain of strong references, from an object that cannot be garbage collected. Except for the references contained in the reference classes of the java.lang.ref package, all references in Java are strong references.

When an application data object is transactional, JDO holds a strong reference to the object. JDO does not hold any reference to unmanaged objects, which are in the JDO-transient state. JDO holds a soft or weak reference to persistent application data objects that are not transactional.

The interesting thing about soft and weak references is that the garbage collector will clear the reference and collect the object before the JVM returns an OutOfMemoryError. This makes soft and weak references suited for cache management, where the desire is to hang onto the reference for as long as possible but release it when available memory is low. But the JVM can clear the soft reference and collect the hollow object only if the application is not holding a strong reference to the object. As a result, the application must cooperate with JDO to allow the garbage collector to take persistent objects that are not transactional.

NOTE For more on soft and weak references, see the JDK Javadoc for the java.lang.ref package.

The application cooperates by cleaning up references to application data objects. If persistent objects are placed into event notification chains or unmanaged collections, some consideration must be given to when to remove them from the same. This might be done at the end of the transaction or at some other time. One place where it might be done is when the persistent object changes to the hollow state. When this occurs, JDO calls the jdoPreClear callback. In this callback, the application could clear strong references to the persistent object. Whether it is appropriate to do so depends on the details of the application's design.

Implications of Implementing InstanceCallbacks

When the client layer that uses application data classes is remote from the service that uses JDO, it is possible to deploy enhanced classes at the service layer and unenhanced classes at the client layer. There is no requirement to deploy unenhanced classes at the client, but if this is not done, the client layer needs access to the JDO classes contained in the javax.jdo and javax.jdo.spi packages.

The use of InstanceCallbacks significantly complicates the logistics of deploying a free-from-JDO version of the application data classes because the pre-enhanced application data class now contains a reference to the InstanceCallbacks interface. In this situation, it is best to just deploy enhanced classes on both the client and service layers. Any other approach is not likely to produce a return commensurate with the effort and risk. Although the client receives no benefit from the code contained in the JDO specification packages, it is not a lot of code to deploy, and it will not change often.

Throwing Unchecked Exceptions Within Callback Methods

The application code that implements the InstanceCallbacks interface cannot throw any checked exceptions, because the interface signatures do not declare any checked exceptions. Because exceptions of type RuntimeException are not checked, the application code can throw a RuntimeException and any exception, such as JDOException, that derives from it.

Within the callback method, the application might throw a runtime exception intentionally to signal a failure condition or unintentionally as a result of a programming error. Or, it might call JDO from within the callback, and this call may cause a runtime exception to be thrown.

Once an unchecked exception has been thrown in the callback method, what happens to it? The JDO specification does not address this question, and the answer depends on the implementation. Most implementations are likely to allow unchecked exceptions to percolate up to the code that called JDO. This code may have been written by the developer or added during enhancement to the application data class. In short, the application must handle the unchecked exceptions thrown from callback methods in the same way as it handles all exceptions thrown by the JDO implementation.

The Exceptions of JDO

The JDOException class is the root of all the exceptions defined by JDO. It is derived from RuntimeException. Because RuntimeException and all classes descendent from it are unchecked exceptions, they do not have to be caught in the method or declared in the method's throws clause. Except for RuntimeException and the classes that are derived from it, the Exception type and all exceptions derived from it are checked exceptions. Checked exceptions must either be caught in the method or declared in the method's throws clause. JDO does not define or use any checked exceptions.

As a general rule, JDO throws only JDOException exceptions or the various types of exceptions derived from it. There are a few cases where the JDO specification specifically mentions the possibility of other runtime exceptions. If the application throws runtime exceptions from the callback methods of the Synchronization interface or the InstanceCallbacks interface, it is likely to see these exceptions coming back from JDO as well.

Figure 7-3 shows the UML class diagram of the JDOException class. As Figure 7-3 indicates, JDOException derives from java.lang.RuntimeException.

```
                                            java.lang.RuntimeException
                         JDOException

JDOException() : constructor
JDOException(String msg) : constructor
JDOException(String msg, Throwable nested) : constructor
JDOException(String msg, Throwable [] nested) : constructor
JDOException(String msg, Object failed) : constructor
JDOException(String msg, Throwable nested, Object failed) : constructor
JDOException(String msg, Throwable [] nested, Object failed) : constructor

getFailedObject() : Object
getNestedExceptions() : Throwable [ ]
```

Figure 7-3. The class diagram of the JDOException *class*

Most Java APIs do not use unchecked exceptions as their primary exception type. JDO uses unchecked exceptions because enhancement adds code that may throw a JDOException. If checked exceptions were thrown by the enhancement-added code, some method signatures in the application data classes would have to be changed. Because of the ramifications for the rest of the application's code, changing method signatures is impractical. By deriving JDOException from RuntimeException, the implications of enhancing an application data class are limited to the class itself and the friendly classes that directly access its managed fields.

JDOException Constructors

The class has seven constructors.

```
public JDOException()
public JDOException(String msg)
public JDOException(String msg, Throwable[] nested)
public JDOException(String msg, Throwable nested)
public JDOException(String msg, Object failed)
public JDOException(String msg, Throwable[] nested, Object failed)
public JDOException(String msg, Throwable nested, Object failed)
```

These constructors accept several different combinations of four parameters: a message, a failed object, a nested exception, and an array of nested exceptions. The class has a no-arg constructor as well.

All of the derived types of JDOException are marker subclasses of JDOException. They contain the same methods, state, and constructors.

Getting Nested Exceptions

One or more nested exceptions can be stored in a JDOException during construction. The getNestedException method retrieves the nested exceptions.

```
public Throwable[] getNestedExceptions()
```

This method returns an array of type java.lang.Throwable, which is the base type of all Java exceptions. When there are no nested exceptions, this method returns null.

Getting the Failed Object

When an exception arises because of an action on a particular managed object, JDO associates that application data object with the exception generated. The getFailedObject method returns the associated application data object.

```
public Object getFailedObject()
```

Not all JDO exceptions have a failed object associated with them. When provided, the application may use the failed object in its recovery from the failure. For example, the application may need to evict the persistent objects that are associated with a JDOOptimisticVerificationException.

Overriden Methods

Because it is derived from RuntimeException, JDOException is three generations removed from its superclass Throwable. JDOException overrides some of the methods of its Throwable superclass. The toString and printStackTrace methods have been modified to include information on the nested exceptions. JDOException does not provide for transporting the stack trace across serialization.

As a general rule, in an n-tier architecture, the layer that is using JDO should catch the JDOExceptions. This layer of code can either handle the error condition or reflect a new exception back to its client.

A General Strategy for Handling JDO Exceptions

Handling a JDO exception is no different from handling any other type of exception with one caveat. Because all JDO exceptions are unchecked during compilation, it is possible to write a good deal of code and have some impressive prototypes and early versions before you realize that you must consider exception handling and its implications on your architecture. The next two sections provide an overview of how to handle exceptions in general and JDO exceptions in particular.

Although JDO does not define or throw any checked exceptions, the application can still do so. Good application designs use checked exceptions. Consequently, the need for JDO to throw unchecked exceptions is not an excuse to avoid checked exceptions in the application's design. In fact, at the point where the application handles the JDO exceptions, it should generally have the option to throw an application-defined checked exception.

General Exception Handling Strategies

Some Java programmers have only one exception handling strategy. They catch and ignore, as in the following bit of code:

```
try
    {
    doSomethingThatMayThrowException();
    }
catch (Exception ignore)
    {
    // exception ignored
    }
```

The catch-and-ignore strategy is occasionally the appropriate exception handling, but more often, it is totally inappropriate. It is usually inappropriate because it does nothing to recover, report, pass on, or repackage the exception.

A reasonable strategy for unchecked exceptions is to simply ignore them. This is not a catch-and-ignore strategy. The simply-ignore strategy does not catch the exception; instead, it relies on the calling code to handle the problem. In the case of Error exception types, which are also unchecked exceptions, almost every program uses this strategy, since there is very little that an application can do that is useful when the JVM throws an Error. It is almost always better to pretend that it will not happen and to stay out of the way when it does. The simply-ignore strategy is also used for checked exceptions when the exception type is declared in the method's throws clause. In essence, the simply-ignore strategy passes the buck to the calling method.

The third strategy, catch-and-handle, is a category for a number of related strategies. The handling part could be any number of actions, including recover, log, wrap, and throw, or construct different exception type and throw. The point of the catch-and-handle strategy is to do something useful with the exception. If you cannot do anything useful with the exception, then you can either catch and ignore the exception, or simply ignore the exception.

A Strategy to Handle JDO Exceptions

There are two types of code situations that can lead to JDO exceptions. In the first situation, the application calls a specific JDO method, such as the commit method in Transaction or the execute method in Query. In this case, catch-and-handle is often the appropriate strategy. In the second situation, the application is using the application data objects, and the calls to JDO are occurring transparently. Some JDO exceptions arise from programming errors. Perhaps the application attempted to read or write a persistent field outside of a transaction. Other JDO exceptions arise from operational circumstances. The datastore service may go down, or a transaction may fail.

In short, the potential for JDO exceptions is everywhere in the code that uses JDO or that uses persistent application data objects. For that reason, a good approach for dealing with JDO exceptions is to wrap the JDO-dependent code into an application data model, or component, that encapsulates the application data classes and the application's use of JDO. Because it encapsulates all the code that gives rise to JDO exceptions, the application data model also encapsulates the exception handling code for JDO exceptions.

Unmanaged objects do not throw JDO exceptions. Although the enhancement-added code is still present in the application data class, unmanaged application data objects do not invoke this code. Consequently, unmanaged data objects can be returned from the application data model without yielding ground on the encapsulation of JDO exceptions.

A data model that is appropriate to the application's architecture can isolate all the code that handles JDO exceptions. The appropriate handling depends on both the application's architecture and the particular type of JDO exception.

Handling JDO Exceptions in Different Application Architectures

Chapters 9 through 11 explore in detail three implementations of the same set of requirements for a reservation system. Chapter 9 examines a Swing implementation for a client/server architecture, Chapter 10 examines a Web application, and Chapter 11 examines an EJB implementation. The JDO exception handling for each of these architectures is described in detail in these chapters, but this is the appropriate place to give an overview of the similarities and differences in handling JDO exceptions in the different architectures.

In the case of Web applications using servlets and JavaServer Pages (JSPs) and in the case of Swing applications that are client/server applications, the application data model is a facade in front of the code that uses JDO and the application data classes. The application data model provides all of the persistent services needed by the application.

Swing applications cannot tolerate uncaught exceptions in the message dispatch loop. They also need to show some reasonable behavior even when the network or database is down. As a result, Swing applications need an application data model that strongly encapsulates the application data classes and the use of JDO. The Swing widgets also need fine-grained access to persistent state. A JTable may present a row for every persistent object and a column for each persistent field. As a result, Swing applications need an application data model that is fine grained. Since the Swing widgets are not equipped to handle the possible exceptions, the application data model must use Swing to report the unfavorable conditions that it may encounter. A Swing application's data model does not throw exceptions, it reports them. In a Swing application, the life cycle of the data model may coincide with the life cycle of the application.

In contrast to a Swing application, a Web application can be built with a strong separation between the model, the view, and the controller, using a design pattern by the same name, Model-View-Controller (MVC). In MVC, the controller uses the model. When the model throws exceptions, the controller handles them. The controller usually does one of two things when it receives an exception from the model: log the exception and request a view (JSP) that shows a generic fault page to the user, or log the exception and request a view that shows a detailed fault page to the user. The choice is often configurable. The data model for a Web application is usually more coarse grained than the data model for a Swing application. Its methods can return a graph of objects that the view can navigate for the information that it needs. Unlike in Swing, the life cycle of the data model in a Web application is usually shorter than the lifetime of the Web application. It may coincide with the lifetime of the HTTP request.

Unlike Swing applications and Web applications, EJB components are not complete applications, but rather the building blocks of the application. EJBs are generally used to build a data model or data service for the application, which might be a Swing application or a Web application. The design of EJBs and their containers provides a framework, or programming model, that emphasizes encapsulation. The main issue for using JDO within an EJB is how to use JDO within the programming model that EJBs provide.

The Various JDO Exceptions

Figure 7-4 shows the class hierarchy of the exception types derived from JDOException. The inheritance tree shows JDOException at the top level with several levels of derived marker classes below it.

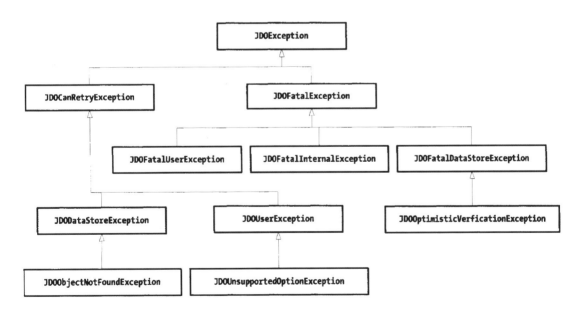

Figure 7-4. The class hierarchy for JDO exceptions

Although Figure 7-4 shows all the exceptions that JDO defines, the JDO implementation may create additional exception types that derive from any of the JDO-defined types. The implementation may throw an exception of one of its derived types or of any of the JDO-defined types. As a result, when the application receives an exception that is assignment compatible with JDOException, the exception may not be assignment compatible with either JDOCanRetryException or JDOFatalException. The same logic applies throughout the hierarchy.

There are several reasons to understand the purpose for each defined JDO exception type. If you need to define an exception type that derives from one of the classes on the JDOException inheritance tree, you will want to pick the exception type that is closest to your purpose. If you are writing code to handle the exceptions in the JDOException inheritance tree, then you may handle different types of JDO exceptions differently.

JDOException

JDOException is the base type of all exceptions thrown by the JDO implementation. Except in a few situations, if the implementation throws any other type of exception, it either results from a bug in the implementation or from a callback to application-written code. When the JDO implementation throws an exception that is assignment compatible with this type, it is likely that the exception is an instance of a more-derived JDO exception type. Nonetheless, the application should assume that exceptions of this type may be thrown.

JDOCanRetryException and JDOFatalException are the two exception types derived from JDOException. The JDOCanRetryException and its subclasses indicate attempted operations that were not successful, but that might be made successful by varying something under the control of application code. More importantly, the JDOCanRetryException indicates that the transaction, if active, remains active and the persistence manager remains usable.

The JDOFatalException and its subclasses indicate fundamental, pervasive, or irreversible error conditions. For example, if the datastore or distributed transaction manager rolls back a transaction during commit, then that transaction is lost and cannot be restarted or committed. In some cases, the error condition may be pervasive and require that the application either terminate or take action to recover. If a JDOFatalException arises because of an operation on a closed persistence manager, the application must obtain a new persistence manager to continue accessing persistent objects. Otherwise, the application or the component should terminate. Failure to do one or the other may mean an endless series of exceptions.

JDOCanRetryException

JDOCanRetryException is first of the two derived types of JDOException. When the JDO implementation throws an exception that is assignment compatible with this type, it is indicating that the JDO runtime is intact and functioning properly and that the error condition that gave rise to the exception is localized to the particular JDO functionality that was invoked. As a result, as far as JDO is concerned, the application can retry the operation using different information, take some type of corrective action, or continue along using JDO in some other way.

Although JDO may be sanguine about the application's opportunity to recover, in fact, the application may not be able to recover because the error condition was not anticipated. For these situations, the appropriate handling is to abort the task at hand, either by throwing a checked exception or by returning a reasonable return value. At the same time, notification must be given. The application could notify the administrator by an entry in the error log, or notify the user by a visible error report, or notify the caller by throwing a checked exception.

JDO defines two exception types that derived from JDOCanRetryException: JDODataStoreException and JDOUserException.

JDODataStoreException

When the JDO implementation throws an exception that is assignment compatible with JDODataStoreException, it is indicating that the error arose while using the underlying datastore. The specification offers little additional guidance on when to expect exceptions of this type.

JDOObjectNotFoundException

The JDOObjectNotFoundException is derived from JDODataStoreException. Sometimes, JDO expects to find an object's persistent state in the datastore, but due to transactions in other persistence managers (or outside of JDO), the object's state no longer exists in the datastore. JDO might discover the object missing when the application calls the persistence manager's getObjectById method, or JDO might find the object missing when it attempts to transparently load the object's state from the datastore. In these cases, JDO throws a JDOObjectNotFoundException. The transaction, if active, remains active.

By calling the exception's getFailedObject method, the application can obtain the persistent object whose state is missing. By getting the persistent object's identity, the application can determine which object is missing.

If the object's state is discovered missing during transaction commit, then this exception is nested within a JDOFatalDataStoreException.

JDOUserException

JDOUserException arises from a grab bag of exception conditions that are localized to particular JDO operations and do not threaten the usability of the persistence manager or JDO runtime. The possible error conditions are quite numerous and include the following:

- Attempt to change application identity when the new identity is already in use.

- Attempt to make persistent an application data object when the object's application identity is already in use.

- Attempt to reuse an application data object with nondurable identity after it becomes nontransactional.

- Attempt to access a non-key persistent field or change any persistent field in a persistent-deleted object.

- Attempt to perform a JDO operation on an application data object when its state does not support that operation, such as an attempt to make persistent and dirty objects either nontransactional or transient, or an attempt to delete transient objects.

- Attempt to use an identity object that is not recognized by the JDO implementation.

- Attempt to perform a persistent operation that requires an active transaction when a transaction has not been started.

- Attempt to perform a persistent operation on an application data object that is being managed by a different persistence manager than the one being used to perform the operation.

- Attempt to change a JDO property at a time when the property cannot be changed. For example, an attempt to configure the PersistenceManagerFactory when it is no longer configurable, or an attempt to alter the *Optimistic* property of a transaction after the transaction is started.

- Passing an object whose class is not enhanced to a JDO operation that requires a PersistenceCapable object.

- Attempt to get an extent for an application data class when the JDO metadata specifies that the class does not have an extent.

- Using a query filter that cannot be parsed during a query compile or execute operation.

- Failure of a modified, persistent field to meet the field restrictions for the null-value attribute of the field tag in the JDO metadata. In other words, a persistent field was not supposed to contain a null value, but it did.

- Attempt to use an application identity object in the persistence manager's getObjectById method when the identity object contains at least one key field with a null value.

JDOUnsupportedOptionException

JDOUnsupportedOptionException is derived from JDOUserException. It indicates that the JDO implementation does not support the configuration or use of an optional feature defined by the specification. Several scenarios might lead to exceptions of this type:

- If the implementation does not support a configurable property, then attempts to set the property cause the exception.

- If the implementation does not support a JDO management state, then operations that would normally cause an application data object to move into the unsupported management state throw the exception.

- If the implementation does not support an optional operation, then using that operation causes the exception.

For example, any of the following actions throw the JDOUnsupportedOptionException:

- Attempting to set the *NontransactionRead* property when the implementation does not support the javax.jdo.option.NontransactionalRead optional feature

- Calling the persistence manager's `makeTransactional` method for an unmanaged application data object when the application does not support the `javax.jdo.option.TransientTransactional` optional feature

- Attempting to change the application-defined key fields of a persistent object when the implementation does not support the `javax.jdo.option.ChangeApplicationIdentity` optional feature

The application can verify most of the optional features of an implementation by checking the strings returned from the persistence manager factory's `supportedOptions` method, as described in Chapter 6.

JDOFatalException

`JDOFatalException` is the second of the two derived types of `JDOException`. When the JDO implementation throws an exception of this type, it is indicating a serious error condition. A variety of causes can give rise to a `JDOFatalException`. The cause may be a defect in the application's logic, a defect in the application's configuration, an unavailable data store, a closed transactional context, or a defect in the JDO implementation.

JDO defines three exception types, `JDOFatalDataStoreException`, `JDOFatalInternalException`, and `JDOFatalUserException`, that are derived from `JDOFatalException`. As with all of the JDO exceptions, the application should assume that exceptions may be thrown that are assignment compatible with `JDOFatalException` but not assignment compatible with any of its derived types.

JDOFatalDataStoreException

When the JDO implementation throws an exception that is assignment compatible with `JDOFatalDataStoreException`, it is indicating a significant problem in its interaction with the datastore. Before throwing this exception, JDO rolls back the transaction if it is active.

If the application throws an exception of this type in a callback method, then it is the application's responsibility to roll back the transaction prior to throwing the exception.

JDOOptimisticVerificationException

`JDOOptimisticVerificationException` is derived from `JDOFatalDataStoreException`. JDO throws a `JDOOptimisticVerificationException` when at least one transactional and persistent object fails the concurrency check during the commit of an optimistic transaction. The JDOOptimisticVerificationException thrown from the commit method contains a nested array of exceptions of the same type, one for each transactional and persistent object that failed the concurrency check.

When JDO throws this exception, the optimistic transaction is rolled back. If transaction's *RestoreValues* property is true, the application should evict the failed objects. This is not required if the *RestoreValues* property is false, as eviction is automatic upon rollback. To evict the failed objects, the application iterates the array of nested exceptions obtained from the exception's getNestedExceptions method. For each nested exception, the application should obtained the persistent object from the exception's getFailedObject method and evict it. Failure to evict the persistent state of the failed objects means that the failed objects, which remain persistent, continue to have the outdated state that caused the failure.

JDOFatalInternalException

Exceptions that are assignment compatible with JDOFatalInternalException indicate a defect in the JDO implementation's logic. Exceptions of this type should be reported as a bug to the JDO vendor.

JDOFatalUserException

When the JDO implementation throws an exception that is assignment compatible with a JDOFatalUserException, it is indicating a significant problem in the attempt to satisfy the user's request. Three problems in particular cause JDO to throw exceptions of this type.

- An attempt was made to get a PersistenceManagerFactory from the getPersistenceManagerFactory method in JDOHelper, and the implementation class specified in the javax.jdo.PersistenceManagerFactoryClass property is not found in the implementation.

- An enhanced application data class is being used but the JDO metadata for this class cannot be found.

- An attempt to use a closed PersistenceManager was detected.

Other Runtime Exceptions the JDO Implementation May Throw

The JDO specification mentions several cases where the implementation may throw unchecked exceptions that are not assignment compatible with JDOException.

JDO determines what types of objects can be assigned to persistent fields that are of type Object or of application-defined interface types. When the application makes the assignment, if the object is managed, then JDO checks the type being assigned and throws a ClassCastException if the type is not supported.

Some of the methods of the persistence manager factory require a Collection or array type. These methods include evictAll, refreshAll, and retrieveAll. If the collection object or array object is null, these methods throw a NullPointerException.

Collections that are returned as query results and extents can be iterated. The query results can be closed by calling the close or closeAll methods in the Query interface. Likewise, the extent iterators can be closed by calling the close or closeAll methods in the Extent interface. Iteration after the close operation results in a NoSuchElementException. This exception may also arise from executing a query that uses a collection, rather than an extent, for its candidates. If the collection is altered after it has been used to set the query's candidates, the query execution may throw a NoSuchElementException.

Both extents and the results collections returned from queries are unmodifiable. Attempts to add or remove elements directly or through an iterator yield an UnsupportedOperationException.

Code Examples That Handle JDO Exceptions

The earlier sections explain the principles for implementing an exception handling strategy when using JDO. This section examines three code examples taken from the Swing client/server implementation of the Maine Lighthouse Reservation Service. This example application is found in the JDO Learning Tools, which Chapter 8 introduces. In addition, Chapter 9 discusses the Swing version of the Maine Lighthouse Reservation Service example in detail.

Handling an Optimistic Lock Failure

Optimistic lock failures occur when the transaction's *Optimistic* property is true and the version of the persistent state of a transactional object is out-of-date with respect to the version stored in the datastore. This happens because another transaction made an update to the same persistent state after JDO loaded the persistent state for the persistent object in memory. The Swing implementation of the Maine Lighthouse Reservation Service uses optimistic transactions because they are appropriate for long-running transactions.

Listing 7-4 shows the commitTransaction method from the ReservationService class, which is found in the com.ysoft.jdo.book.resort.local.service package. This version of ReservationService exposes transactional boundaries to its client. Notice that this method has only two lines of productive code in its try block. It closes any outstanding query results, and it commits the transaction.

Listing 7-4. Handling a Failed Optimistic Transaction

```
public void commitTransaction() throws OptimisticReservationException
    {
    try
       {
       cleanupQueries();
       // Using member field: javax.jdo.Transaction tx;
       tx.commit();
       }
    // catch JDO 1.0.1 optimistic failures
    catch (JDOOptimisticVerificationException e)
       {
       // Eviction not needed, since the combination of rollback and
       // RestoreValues == false evicts all persistent-dirty objects
       throw new OptimisticReservationException(
       "Concurrent changes by other users prevented your changes, try again.");
       }
    }
```

Since the method in Listing 7-4 commits an optimistic transaction, it expects optimistic lock failures from time to time. In the catch block, the method catches the JDOOptimisticVerficationException and throws an application-defined checked exception. Converting to a checked exception creates a more friendly exception message and puts the calling code on notice that this exception may arise. Since this example has the transaction's *RestoreValues* property set to false in the property file used to obtain a persistence manager, JDO evicts all persistent-dirty and persistent-clean objects when it rolls back the transaction before throwing the JDOOptimisticVerificationException.

Catching All Exceptions When Explicitly Using JDO

In the Swing application, the ReservationClient class initializes and wires the JComponent widgets of the user interface. These widgets use the ReservationClientModel class, which is the application's data model. The data model provides all the data needed by the widgets, and it shields the widgets from all of the dependencies of connecting to transactional and remote data. The ReservationClientModel in turn uses the ReservationService, a portion of which was shown in Listing 7-4. The Swing client contained in the ReservationClient class and the ReservationClientModel class are contained in the com.ysoft.jdo.book.resort.local.client.gui package.

Listing 7-5 shows the submit method of the ReservationClientModel. The submit method calls the commitTransaction method shown in Listing 7-4. As can be seen, the submit method encapsulates all of the exceptions that may be thrown from the explicit use of JDO that occurs within the ReservationService. It has three catch blocks, one for the application-defined checked exception OptimisticReservationException, one for JDOFatalException, and one for all other runtime exceptions.

Listing 7-5. Handling All Exceptions When Explicitly Using JDO

```
public void submit()
   {
   if (isViewReady())
     {
     try
       {
       service.commitTransaction();
       service.beginTransaction();
       setView(VIEW_CUSTOMERS_RESERVATIONS);
       fireModelChangeNewData(VIEW_CHANGED);
       }
     catch (OptimisticReservationException e)
       {
       // start the transaction before handing exception off to GUI
       service.beginTransaction();
       MessageHandler.reportException(
             ReservationClient.rcReservationClient, e);
       // the rollback evicted old data
       fireModelChangeNewData(DATA_CHANGED);
       }
```

```
    catch (JDOFatalException e)
        {
        MessageHandler.reportException(
                ReservationClient.rcReservationClient, e);
        MessageHandler.reportWarning(
                ReservationClient.rcReservationClient, "Disconnecting");
        disconnect();
        }
    catch (RuntimeException e)
        {
        MessageHandler.reportException(
                ReservationClient.rcReservationClient, e);
        }
    }
}
```

The handling in each `catch` block is different. When an
`OptimisticReservationException` is caught, the code first starts a new transaction
and then reports the situation to the user via a pop-up window. It then fires an
event informing the application's `JTable`, which is listening, that the data has
changed. When a `JDOFatalException` is caught, the code informs the user of the
circumstances and of the subsequent disconnection from persistent data. In the
case of all other runtime exceptions, which include all JDO exceptions other than
the explicitly caught `JDOFatalException`, the code notifies the user and does
nothing else.

Listing 7-5 is intended to be illustrative rather than definitive. It illustrates
three different catch-and-handle responses in an application data model that
cannot throw exceptions to the code that calls it.

Catching All Exceptions When Implicitly Using JDO

A JDO exception may be thrown when the JDO API is explicitly called, but an
exception can also arise from the transparent, implicit use of JDO in the application data class. To the widgets in the Swing app, it makes no difference. Any
uncaught exceptions that arrive at the widget will cause problems in the Swing
framework. As a result, the application data model for a Swing application must
catch and handle all of the runtime exceptions that arise from using JDO implicitly.

Listing 7-6 contains the `getReservationDate` method of the
`ReservationClientModel` class. This method is called by the `JTable` when it needs the
reservation date for a row at an indexed position. The exception handling code for
this method is very similar to the exception handling code for the `submit` method
shown in Listing 7-5.

Listing 7-6. Handling All Exceptions When Implicitly Using JDO

```
Date getReservationDate(int index)
   {
   Date retv = null;
   try
      {
      if (index >= 0 && index < numWeeks)
         {
         Week w = (Week) listOfWeeks.get(index);
         retv = w.getStartOfWeek();
         }
      }
   catch (JDOFatalException e)
      {
      MessageHandler.reportException(ReservationClient.rcReservationClient, e);
      MessageHandler.reportWarning(
            ReservationClient.rcReservationClient, "Disconnecting");
      rcm.disconnect();
      }
   catch (RuntimeException e)
      {
      MessageHandler.reportException(ReservationClient.rcReservationClient, e);
      }
   return retv;
   }
```

Unlike the submit method, the try block in the getReservationDate method does not call JDO explicitly, nor does it call any methods that call JDO explicitly. Instead, JDO is called implicitly when the getStartOfWeek method is called. Because the weeks are persistent application data objects, enhancement-added code is called in the getStartOfWeek method. If you look in the Week class, you will find a simple accessor method that has one line of working code:

```
return start;
```

The implicit calls to JDO that support transparent persistence are added during the enhancement step. For that reason, they are not visible in the source.

Summary

This chapter examines three miscellaneous aspects of JDO. The JDOHelper class provides utility methods that perform housekeeping chores, offer convenience methods, and aid in debugging. The InstanceCallbacks interface provides callback methods that notify the application when JDO acts on a persistent object. The various JDO exceptions allow robust applications to provide recovery, reporting, and integration within the existing error handling framework.

This chapter concludes the examination of the JDO persistence service for Java objects. The next four chapters examine the example code found in the JDO Learning Tools, an open source set of tools and examples that use JDO. The next chapter describes the learning programs that you can use to both test drive a JDO implementation and learn more about the behavior of JDO.

CHAPTER 8

Using JDO to Learn More

THE JDO LEARNING TOOLS are a small but comprehensive set of programs that you can use for several purposes. You can use them as an introduction to JDO. You can use them to verify what you have learned about JDO. Most importantly, you can use them to learn more. The first five JDO Learning Tools are discussed in this chapter.

- TestJDOHelper

- TestFactory

- MegaCups

- Library

- StateTracker

The five learning programs are not examples of how your application might use JDO. Instead, they are atypical applications whose purpose is to illuminate the interactions with JDO. TestJDOHelper and TestFactory allow you to start using a JDO implementation and find out more about its capabilities. The MegaCups program demonstrates JDO's ability to handle multiple, concurrent updates. The Library program allows you to interactively populate a small town's library and run your own queries against its objects. Using it, you can test JDO's query language. The StateTracker program allows you to manipulate and view the managed and unmanaged state of persistent, transactional, and unmanaged apples. You can use it to execute all of JDO's explicit operations and many of its implicit operations, and you can see the consequences on managed objects.

In addition to the five learning programs, there are two sets of example programs, the rental application and the quote server, that are discussed in Chapters 9 through 11. The rental applications and the quote servers provide examples of how your application might use JDO. Between them, they cover many application architectures. The rental application is a prototype reservation system for a fictitious lighthouse rental company. It comes in three versions: the rental Swing application, the rental Web application, and the rental enterprise (EJB) application. Each version implements nearly the same set of requirements. Each chapter from 9 to 11 takes one version of the rental application as its main topic. The quote server application stores new quotes given to it and serves up a random quote upon demand. It is implemented in five types of Enterprise JavaBeans: a stateless CMT session bean, a stateful CMT session bean, a stateless BMT session bean, a stateful BMT session bean, and a BMP entity bean. The quote server examples are discussed in Chapter 6 as well as Chapter 11.

The JDO Learning Tools 1.0 are copyright by Yankee Software and are provided to the community of Java programmers under the open source GNU General Public License. Instructions for downloading the JDO Learning Tools are found in the section "Step One: Download Open Source JDO Learning Tools" that follows in this chapter. You are encouraged to contribute improvements to make future releases of the JDO Learning Tools better for all of us.

The Ant Build Scripts

All of the programs provided with this book are built with Ant, a build tool from Apache's Ant project. Build scripts are provided for four different implementations:

- The reference implementation from Sun Microsystems

- The Kodo implementation from SolarMetric

- The Lido implementation from Libelis

- The IntelliBO implementation from SignSoft

A new script could be added for any other JDO implementation as long as the implementation supplies command line tools that can be used with Ant. The scripts were tested with version 1.4.1 of Ant, and they should work with any later 1.x version of Ant. It is strongly recommended that you use Ant to build the JDO Learning Tools.

Ant's build scripts are XML files. The major build scripts are in the *bookants* directory. The build scripts that compile the individual programs are in each project directory. The main build script, called *build.xml*, reads three property files in the *bookants* directory to set its configuration. The *global.properties* file contains properties that you should not have to change. The *custom.properties* file is tailored to the particular JDO tool that you are using. You will want to modify the appropriate property file for the tool, such as *jdori.properties*, and then make a copy of it that is named *custom.properties*. The *default.properties* file sets properties that must be customized to your installation.

The main Ant build script reads the property files in the following order:

1. global.properties

2. custom.properties

3. default.properties

Because all Ant properties are final, if a property is set in more than one property file, the value that sticks is the first value encountered. As a result, if the property *jdo.tool* is encountered in the *custom.properties* file as well as in the *default.properties* file, the value in the *custom.properties* file is the one used.

In order to work with a variety of JDO implementations, the build scripts are a bit more complicated than they would be in a typical development environment. The main *build.xml* script calls out to one of several possible tool scripts that are individually configured to the specific JDO implementation. There are four supplied with the code: *jdori.xml*, *kodo.xml*, *lido.xml*, and *intellibo.xml*. Only one tool script is used in any build environment. The tool script selection is controlled by the *jdo.tool* property in the *custom.properties* file. To minimize needless redundancy, the tool scripts call out to a common set of third-level scripts. Each package has its own compile script to compile the files that are specific to it. These are contained in *build.xml* scripts that are in the subdirectories of the source. Likewise, each container has a script for compiling and deploying the files that are specific to its needs. These are the *tomcat.xml* and *jboss.xml* scripts contained within the *bookants* directory.

As a result, when you type *ant target* in the *bookants* directory, the *target* is invoked in the following build scripts: in the *build.xml* script in the *bookants* directory; in the specific tool script, such as *jdori.xml*, in the *bookants* directory; in the *build.xml* that is in the target's source directory; and finally, if the build deploys on Tomcat or JBoss, then in the *tomcat.xml* or *jboss.xml* script in the *bookants* directory.

Many of the build targets create batch files for Microsoft Windows that run the programs. The current build scripts do not produce command files for other operating systems. As a result, if you are running on Linux or some other operating system, you will have to change the generated batch files so that they can be invoked on your operating system.

Getting Started

This section provides a step-by-step guide to getting the code and building the first five JDO Learning Tools.

Step One: Download Open Source JDO Learning Tools

Download the zip file containing the JDO Learning Tools from SourceForge.net by going to the following URL:

```
http://sourceforge.net/projects/jdo-tools
```

You can also obtain this code from the Apress Web site at http://www.apress.com. After the download, unzip the files to a directory of your choice. For simplicity, the instructions here will refer to the directory that you choose as the *bookcode-home* directory. Unless otherwise specified, all directory paths mentioned in this chapter are relative to your *bookcode-home* directory.

Estimated time excluding download: 5 minutes

Step Two: Download Java SDK If Necessary

The examples in this book were tested with the Java Software Development Kit (SDK, also known as JDK) version 1.3.1. The various implementations and the examples will likely work with a later version of the JDK, but this has not been tested. If you do not already have JDK 1.3.1, go to the following URL:

```
http://java.sun.com/j2se/1.3
```

Follow the instructions that come with the JDK to set up the Java development and runtime environments and verify that they are working.

Estimated time excluding the download: 20 minutes

Step Three: Download Ant If Necessary

If you do not already have Ant version 1.4.1, or a later 1.x version, go to the following URL:

```
http://ant.apache.org
```

Follow the links to download a binary version of Ant. Follow Ant's instructions to set up Ant and verify that it is working.

Estimated time excluding download: 45 minutes

Step Four: Download J2EE Jar If Necessary

You need access to the *j2ee.jar* file that contains the public interfaces of J2EE. This file, which can be found in the J2EE SDK, is available at the following Web location:

```
http://java.sun.com/j2ee/download.html
```

Download it, and follow the directions to install it. This file is needed for all build targets because some of the common files use the J2EE framework to report messages.

Estimated time excluding download: 10 minutes

Step Five: Download JDO Implementation

The next step is to pick the JDO implementation that you want to use. The build scripts in this book work with any of the four JDO implementations mentioned earlier. The examples should work with any implementation, but you will have to create or find the tool script for implementations that are not on this list. It is possible that some vendors who are not on the list will provide a tool script for their implementation. Building a new tool script is not difficult, but you may want to start your exploration of JDO with the reference implementation. The reference implementation does have one serious drawback: the 1.0 version does not work well with EJB containers. As a result, the EJB examples in this book do not have build targets for the reference implementation.

To get the reference implementation, go to the Java Community Process page at the following URL:

```
http://jcp.org/aboutJava/communityprocess/final/jsr012/index.html
```

or go to the public access page maintained by the specification lead at the following URL:

```
http://access1.sun.com/jdo
```

Download the reference implementation and unzip to a directory of your choice.

To download one of the commercial implementations, go to the associated vendor's Web site and follow the directions. The home page for each is listed here.

```
http://www.solarmetric.com
http://www.libelis.com
http://www.signsoft.com
```

Estimated time for the reference implementation excluding download: 5 minutes. It will take longer for the commercial implementations because of the need to set up a license key and configure the JDBC settings.

Step Six: Configure Build Properties

In this step, you configure the property files. The properties in the *global.properties* file, found in the *bookants* directory, should not require changes, unless there are some operating system issues that need to be addressed.

The four tool property files provided are found in the *bookants* directory. Edit the property file that goes with the implementation that you have selected. For the reference implementation, that would be the *jdori.properties* file. This file has two properties. The *jdo.home* property should be set to the root directory where the implementation is installed. The second property, *jdo.tool*, is the name used to find the tool's build script. It should not be changed, unless you are writing a new tool script. After configuring the tool's properties file, make a copy named *custom.properties* in the *bookants* directory.

Next, edit the *default.properties* file. This file contains the following properties:

- *java.home*

- *jdbc.jar*

- *j2ee.home*

- *tomcat.home*

- *jboss.home*

Of these, the last two will be addressed in Chapters 10 and 11. The *jdbc.jar* property is required only if a relational implementation of JDO is used. These include the Kodo, Lido, and IntelliBO implementations. The *java.home* property provides the file path to the root directory where you installed the Java SDK. Set the *j2ee.home* property to point to the root directory where you installed the J2EE SDK.

Estimated time for this step: 10 minutes

Step Seven: Test the Build Environment

You are now ready to test the build environment. To begin, go to the *bookants* directory and type *ant*. You should see console output similar to the output in the following lines:

```
E:\Bookcode\bookants>ant
Buildfile: build.xml

Help:
     [echo] Please specify a particular build target, such as testfactory
     [echo]    or, enter the command:   ant -projecthelp
     [echo]    for a list of targets

BUILD SUCCESSFUL
```

By typing *ant -projecthelp*, you will see a list of targets for the build. The expected output will look similar to the output in Listing 8-1. You will see quite a few more main targets than the ones listed here. The additional targets that are not shown in Listing 8-1 are used in later chapters.

Listing 8-1. Expected Output from Running ant -projecthelp at the Command Line

```
E:\Bookcode\bookants>ant -projecthelp
Buildfile: build.xml
Default target:
 Help                  The default target for this build script

Main targets:
 Help                  The default target for this build script
 clean-out             removes all files in output directories
 megacups              build MegaCups example
 testfactory           build TestFactory example
 testjdohelper         build TestJDOHelper example
 learning-programs     Builds all learning-programs
 library               build Library example
 statetracker          build Statetracker example

Subtargets:
 are-we-ready
 help
 verify


BUILD SUCCESSFUL
```

If everything is working as expected at this point, then you are ready to try the most dangerous target in the build, the *clean-out* target. This target deletes all files in the *build* directory, *enhanced* directory, and *warfiles* directory under the *bookcode-home* directory. The expected output, since you have not yet built any files to delete, will look like the following:

```
E:\Bookcode\bookants>ant clean-out
Buildfile: build.xml
are-we-ready:
verify:
clean-out:
     [echo] Deleting files in build, enhanced, and warfiles

BUILD SUCCESSFUL
```

Use the *clean-out* target whenever you want the subsequent build to proceed from scratch.

The *testjdohelper, testfactory, megacups, library,* and *statetracker* targets are described in the following sections of this chapter. They can be built individually, or you can build them all at once by going to the *bookants* directory and typing *ant learning-programs.* The build should take a minute or so.

Estimated time for this step: 10 minutes

Hello, JDO!

The TestJDOHelper program is simple. Listing 6-2 in Chapter 6 shows the one class, TestJDOHelper, found in the com.ysoft.jdo.book.factory package.

The program takes one command line parameter that names the properties file configured for the selected JDO implementation. The main method of the class loads the properties from the file and then calls the getPersistenceManagerFactory method in JDOHelper. For more information about getting a persistence manager factory from JDOHelper, see Chapter 6. After verifying that a persistence manager can be obtained from the persistence manager factory, the program ends.

The properties file that specifies the factory settings varies with the implementation used. For the reference implementation, the properties file is *jdori.properties*, located at *com/ysoft/jdo/book/factory/jdori*. The build copies it to *factory.properties* at *build/com/ysoft/jdo/book/factory*. If you are using one of the three mentioned commercial implementations, you will have to edit the appropriate file to configure the JDBC connection. When using the Kodo implementation, you must also add a valid license key to the properties file. The reference implementation does not use JDBC and does not require a license key.

Building and Running the TestJDOHelper Program

To build the TestJDOHelper program, go to the *bookants* directory and type *ant testjdohelper*. This build is part of the *ant learning-programs* build. Listing 8-2 shows some of the expected output when using the reference implementation.

Listing 8-2. Expected Output from Running ant testjdohelper

```
testjdohelper:
    [javac] Compiling 1 source file to E:\Bookcode\build
     [echo] creating runTestJDOHelper.bat
     [echo] Running TestJDOHelper
     [java] -- listing properties --
     [java] javax.jdo.option.RestoreValues=false
     [java] javax.jdo.option.ConnectionURL=fostore:FOStoreTestDB
     [java] javax.jdo.option.Optimistic=false
     [java] javax.jdo.option.ConnectionUserName=JDO
     [java] javax.jdo.option.ConnectionPassword=book
     [java] javax.jdo.option.NontransactionalWrite=false
     [java] javax.jdo.PersistenceManagerFactoryClass=
                   com.sun.jdori.fostore.FOStorePMF
     [java] javax.jdo.option.NontransactionalRead=false
     [java] javax.jdo.option.IgnoreCache=false
     [java] javax.jdo.option.RetainValues=false
     [java] javax.jdo.option.Multithreaded=false
     [java] Got the PMF okay
     [echo] created runTestJDOHelper.bat

BUILD SUCCESSFUL
```

Notice that the build creates the *runTestJDOHelper* batch file. The batch file can be used to run the test again. All generated batch files are placed in the *bookcode-home* directory. The TestJDOHelper program has no user interface. It runs to completion in a matter of seconds.

As soon as you can get TestJDOHelper to build and run, you have successfully completed the steps necessary to use the remaining client-server programs in this chapter and the next. Chapters 10 and 11 provide additional instructions for the configuration needed to build examples that deploy in the Tomcat and JBoss containers.

Interrogating the PersistenceManagerFactory

JDOFactory is a utility class that can interrogate the factory for its default settings and supported options. JDOFactory also illustrates the use of the adaptor pattern to localize the vendor dependencies inherent in construction. Unlike most other example programs with this book, TestFactory uses construction to acquire a persistence manager factory. The TestFactory program writes the results of the interrogation to the console. After obtaining a persistence manager, it terminates. The TestFactory class is contained in the com.ysoft.jdo.book.factory.client package.

Building and Running the TestFactory Program

To build the TestFactory program, go to the *bookants* directory and type *ant testfactory*. This build is part of the *ant learning-programs* build. Listing 8-3 shows some of the expected output when using the reference implementation.

Listing 8-3. Expected Output from Running ant testfactory

```
testfactory:
     [echo] creating runTestFactory.bat
     [echo] Running TestFactory
     [java] Starting TestFactory ...
     [java] Using adaptor class: com.ysoft.jdo.book.factory.jdori.JDORIAdaptor
     [java] The database (FOStoreTestDB.btd) exists
     [java] Using URL: (fostore:FOStoreTestDB)
     [java] Loaded factory adaptor: com.ysoft.jdo.book.factory.jdori.JDORIAdaptor
     [java]
     [java] Supported JDO Options
     [java]    javax.jdo.option.TransientTransactional
     [java]    javax.jdo.option.NontransactionalRead
     [java]    javax.jdo.option.NontransactionalWrite
     [java]    javax.jdo.option.RetainValues
     [java]    javax.jdo.option.RestoreValues
     [java]    javax.jdo.option.Optimistic
     [java]    javax.jdo.option.ApplicationIdentity
     [java]    javax.jdo.option.DatastoreIdentity
     [java]    javax.jdo.option.ArrayList
     [java]    javax.jdo.option.HashMap
     [java]    javax.jdo.option.Hashtable
     [java]    javax.jdo.option.LinkedList
     [java]    javax.jdo.option.TreeMap
```

```
[java]       javax.jdo.option.TreeSet
[java]       javax.jdo.option.Vector
[java]       javax.jdo.option.Array
[java]       javax.jdo.option.NullCollection
[java]       javax.jdo.query.JDOQL
[java] Unsupported JDO Options
[java]       javax.jdo.option.NonDurableIdentity
[java]       javax.jdo.option.ChangeApplicationIdentity
[java]       javax.jdo.option.List
[java]       javax.jdo.option.Map
[java] Non-configurable properties
[java]       Key: VendorName, value: Sun Microsystems
[java]       Key: VersionNumber, value: 1.0
[java] Initial PMF transaction settings
[java]       Optimistic: true
[java]       Non-trans read: true
[java]       Non-trans write: false
[java]       RetainValues: true
[java]       RestoreValues: true
[java] Connection information
[java]       Connection driver: null
[java]       Connection factory: null
[java]       Connection factory2: null
[java]       Connection URL: fostore:FOStoreTestDB
[java]       Connection UserName: JDO
[java] Caching info
[java]       Ignore Cache: true
[java] Threading setting for PM's
[java]       Multithreading turned on: false
[java] This PMF can be serialized
[java] This PMF implements javax.naming.Referenceable
[java] Obtained PersistenceManagerFactory
[java] Just got 1 PersistenceManagers!
[java] Closing FOStoreDB
[java] -- All done!
[echo] created runTestFactory.bat
```

BUILD SUCCESSFUL

Like the previous example, the build, after running TestFactory, also creates
the batch file *runTestFactory* that can be used to run it again. The TestFactory
program has no user interface. It runs to completion in a few seconds.

Consuming Java at the MegaCups Company

The people who work at the MegaCups Company love their coffee. In fact, they have gone over the edge and are in need of counseling. During the work day, they incessantly elbow each other around the coffee urn as they seek another cup of coffee to satisfy their never-ending craving for caffeine.

The company has a coffee urn set up in the kitchen that holds 40 cups of coffee. One worker, Mark, adds 20 cups of coffee to the urn every 14 seconds. Four other workers, Frank, Sam, Julie, and Susan, come around for a fresh cup of coffee every 2 seconds. Most real people wait more than 2 seconds before seeking a fresh cup of coffee, but these workers are computer simulations. For that reason, their sense of time is compressed.

Doing the math, you can see that the workers sometimes find that the coffee urn is empty. If this happens too often, they complain to the manager, who either promises to do something about it or ignores the complaint. If he ignores the complaint, the workers quit. Because of the hectic pace at the MegaCups Company, the work day is short, lasting only 1 minute.

In the MegaCups program, there is only one persistent object, the coffee urn in the kitchen. Everyone comes to this coffee urn to either add or draw coffee. Each addition or subtraction is done transactionally and the result is committed. Each worker runs in his own thread and uses a separate persistence manager. As a result, each worker acts on his own CoffeeUrn object in memory that represents in his transaction the persistent state of the coffee urn found in the datastore. The properties file that configures the persistence manager factory for this example specifies a datastore transaction. As the transactions clash, you can see exactly how your selected JDO implementation handles the transactional semantics for datastore transactions.

The com.ysoft.jdo.book.coffee package contains three classes: MegaCups, Worker, and CoffeeUrn. The Worker class is contained in the source file for the MegaCups class. Excluding comments, blank lines, and lines with a solitary brace, there are approximately 200 lines of code in the two source files. Of these, approximately 20 percent have something to do with the explicit use of JDO. Much of the code that uses JDO explicitly is concerned with setting the program's and the datastore's initial state. To start a transaction, draw a cup of coffee from the coffee urn, and commit the transaction requires only two lines of code that explicitly use JDO.

The MegaCups program was created after a prolonged discussion that occurred on *JDOCentral.com* about the semantics of JDO transactions. It illustrates the behavior of datastore transactions. The behavior that you see depends on the transactional semantics of the datastore and the JDO implementation. Most implementations use some form of pessimistic locking in the datastore. For a detailed description of JDO's transactional semantics, see Chapter 4.

Building and Running the MegaCups Program

To build the MegaCups program, go to the *bookants* directory and type *ant megacups*. This build is part of the *ant learning-programs* build.

The program acquires a persistence manager factory that is configured by the property file. For the reference implementation, the properties file is *jdori.properties* contained in the *com/ysoft/jdo/book/coffee* directory. The build copies it to *factory.properties* at the *build/com/ysoft/jdo/book/coffee* directory.

Listing 8-4 shows some of the expected output from the build when using the reference implementation.

Listing 8-4. Expected Output from Running ant megacups

```
megacups:
    [javac] Compiling 2 source files to E:\Bookcode\build
    [echo] returned from com/ysoft/jdo/book/coffee/build.xml
    [copy] Copying 1 file to E:\Bookcode\build\com\ysoft\jdo\book\coffee
    [copy] Copying 1 file to E:\Bookcode\enhanced\com\ysoft\jdo\book
    [java] done.
    [echo] creating runMegaCups.bat


BUILD SUCCESSFUL
```

Unlike the previous build targets, the build for the MegaCups program does not run the program. Instead, you must change to the *bookcode-home* directory and execute the *runMegaCups* batch file. The MegaCups program does not have a user interface. It takes about a minute to run. The expected output from running the program will start off looking something like the output shown in Listing 8-5. This output was obtained from using the reference implementation. Notice the number that follows "kitchen" within the brackets. This number is incremented each time one cup of coffee is drawn from the urn. It numbers the order of changes to the coffee urn in the kitchen.

Listing 8-5. Sample Output from the MegaCups Program

```
E:\Bookcode>runMegaCups
Using property file: com/ysoft/jdo/book/coffee/factory.properties
This program will end in one minute
Mark found: CoffeeUrn [Kitchen-0] contains 0 cups
Sam found: CoffeeUrn [Kitchen-0] contains 0 cups
Julie found: CoffeeUrn [Kitchen-0] contains 0 cups
Susan found: CoffeeUrn [Kitchen-0] contains 0 cups
```

```
Frank found: CoffeeUrn [Kitchen-0] contains 0 cups
Mark added coffee to CoffeeUrn [Kitchen-0] contains 20 cups
Sam drank a cup of coffee from CoffeeUrn [Kitchen-1] contains 19 cups
Julie drank a cup of coffee from CoffeeUrn [Kitchen-2] contains 18 cups
Susan drank a cup of coffee from CoffeeUrn [Kitchen-3] contains 17 cups
Frank drank a cup of coffee from CoffeeUrn [Kitchen-4] contains 16 cups
Sam drank a cup of coffee from CoffeeUrn [Kitchen-5] contains 15 cups
Julie drank a cup of coffee from CoffeeUrn [Kitchen-6] contains 14 cups
Susan drank a cup of coffee from CoffeeUrn [Kitchen-7] contains 13 cups
Frank drank a cup of coffee from CoffeeUrn [Kitchen-8] contains 12 cups
```

If you are using the reference implementation, then the datastore files require a one-time initialization. If you see the following error:

```
Using property file: com/ysoft/jdo/book/coffee/factory.properties
javax.jdo.JDOFatalDataStoreException: com.sun.jdori.fostore.FOStoreLoginException:
     Could not login user JDO to database FOStoreTestDB.
NestedThrowables:
org.netbeans.modules.mdr.persistence.StorageIOException
```

then you want to go to the *factory.properties* file located in the *build/com/ysoft/jdo/ book/coffee* directory and uncomment the second line, so that it reads as follows:

```
#set this to true to create valid datastore files
com.sun.jdori.option.ConnectionCreate=true
```

After running the MegaCups program again, the files *FOStoreTestDB.btd* and *FOStoreTestDB.btx* should exist and be larger than zero bytes in size. To prevent the MegaCups program from continually creating new datastore files, recomment the option string in the *factory.properties* file after valid datastore files have been created.

The MegaCups program accepts a number of optional command line parameters. You can specify the number of workers and their names by using the following parameters:

```
-names Tom Dick Harry
```

Pick the names you like and add as many as you want. The first person named is given the responsibility to fill the coffee urn. You can also prevent anyone from filling the coffee urn by specifying this option:

```
-nofilling
```

Multiple invocations of the MegaCups program can run simultaneously. Most commercial datastores support multiuser access, but the datastore for the reference implementation does not support concurrent access from multiple JVMs.

The Console User Interface

The JDO Learning Tools described so far do not provide an interactive user interface. The next two programs in the JDO Learning Tools use a simple console user interface. Although the workings of this console interface are incidental to the purposes of this book, the interface is also unfamiliar to you. This section gives you an idea of what the console interface is like. It also gives you an idea of how you can modify the programs that use it.

When the interface comes up, it prompts you with two lines:

```
enter command:
-->
```

You can control the configuration of the prompt by modifying the properties in the *package.properties* file found in the *com/ysoft/jdo/book/common/console* directory. The default configuration works well for highlighting the user's input in the listings provided in this chapter.

There are only three things to remember about the console interface. One, it will not do anything unless you enter a command. Two, every program has at least two commands, *quit* and *help*. The *quit* command terminates the program. The *help* command lists all of the commands, except *help*, that the program recognizes. Three, if you enter a command string that the interface does not recognize, it outputs a question mark and prompts again, as the following interaction shows:

```
enter command:
--> whatever
?
enter command:
-->
```

Some of the command strings are wordy. In some cases, there is more than one command string that will activate the command. The additional command strings provide flexibility in activating a command. For example, the command string

```
add data object
```

may have the additional command strings

```
add
add object
```

There are only two ways to tell what the additional command strings are. Either try something and see if it is accepted, or look at the source code.

Each command is implemented in a separate class that extends the base class Command, which is found in the com.ysoft.jdo.book.common.console package. In the constructor for the derived command class, there is a call to the super constructor of Command. One of the parameters to this constructor is a list of command strings. For example, the Add command in the Library program has the following constructor:

```
public Add(UIClient c)
    {
    super(c, new String[]
        {
        "add data object",
        "add",
        "add object",
        });
    }
```

Any of the command strings activate the command. The first one is the preferred command string, and for that reason, it is shown in the help listing. If you want, you can add more command strings to any command. Within the application, each command string should be unique.

When you enter a command, you may be prompted for command parameters. Often you cannot get out of the command without entering the additional information. Since no lives are at stake, enter something to make the interface happy.

The command classes are package-level classes contained within the source file for the public application class. For example, the source file *Library.java* contains the source for the public class Library, and also the source for all of the command classes, such as Add, Delete, and Find. Adding additional commands is easy. Pick a command class that is close in behavior to what you want, then copy, paste, and modify. Don't forget to add an instance of the new class to the application's list of Command objects.

Querying the Small Town Library

The Library program prototypes a simple system for a small town library. Figure 2-3 in Chapter 2 shows the UML model for application data classes used by the Library program. There are four application data classes in Figure 2-3: Book, Category, Borrower, and Volunteer. Using the Library program, you can manipulate the persistent objects, define queries, and view the results.

The Library program is built from six primary source files, the four application data classes, the Library class and its command classes, and the LibraryHandler data service. These are contained in the com.ysoft.jdo.book.library and com.ysoft.jdo.book.library.client packages. All of the explicit use of JDO occurs within the LibraryHandler data service. The console interface handles all exceptions thrown by the implicit use of JDO. The persistence manager factory is configured by a properties file that varies by the JDO implementation. For the reference implementation, the file is named *jdori.properties* and is found in the *com/ysoft/ jdo/book/library* directory. The build copies it to the *build/com/ysoft/jdo/book/ library* directory and renames it to *factory.properties*.

Building the Library Program

To build the program, go to the *bookants* directory and type *ant library*. This build is part of the *ant learning-programs* build. Listing 8-6 shows some of the expected output from the build when using the reference implementation.

Listing 8-6. Expected Output from Running ant library

```
library:
    [javac] Compiling 7 source files to E:\Bookcode\build
     [echo] returned from com/ysoft/jdo/book/library/build.xml
     [copy] Copying 1 file to E:\Bookcode\enhanced\com\ysoft\jdo\book
     [copy] Copying 1 file to E:\Bookcode\build\com\ysoft\jdo\book\library
     [echo] Enhancing the persistent classes of library
     [java] done.
     [echo] creating runLibrary.bat

BUILD SUCCESSFUL
```

To run the Library program, go to the *bookcode-home* directory and type *runLibrary*.

Using the Library Commands

When you enter the *help* command after starting the Library program, you see all the commands that it supports. The expected output is shown in Listing 8-7.

Listing 8-7. Example of Help Output from the Library *Program*

```
E:\Bookcode>runlibrary
enter command:
--> help
commands:
   quit
   begin
   commit
   rollback
   get pm config
   view attributes
   define query variable
   find all
   find
   find in results
   add data object
   delete data object
   view volunteer
   view borrower
   view book
   view category
   borrow book
   return book
   modify volunteer
   modify book
   populate database
   clear database
enter command:
-->
```

As Listing 8-7 shows, the program recognizes a large number of commands.
Begin by populating the database. This will add seven books, six categories, three
borrowers, and one volunteer to the datastore. The properties file sets to false all
the Boolean properties of the PersistenceManager and Transaction. This can be verified
by executing the *get pm config* command.

The three commands *begin*, *commit*, and *rollback* allow you to control the
transactional boundaries. When you execute a *begin* command, a JDO datastore
transaction starts. If you then execute a series of *find all* commands, you can view
the summary information for all objects in the datastore. There is an apparent bug
in the 1.0 reference implementation that prevents the capture of the identity string
on the first transaction for an object. Finding all objects and executing a *commit*

works around this bug. If you find all the objects again, you will see the value of the identity strings in the output.

A large number of commands allows you to manipulate the state of the persistent objects. The *add, delete, view, borrow, return,* and *modify* commands allow you to add books, categories, borrowers, and volunteers; delete the same; view all the information about them; borrow books; return them; and modify information about books and volunteers. The *view* commands track the last list of objects that were presented. As a result, if you view a category and it lists two books, then the *view book* command will present that list of two books to choose from.

Running Queries in the Library Program

The Library program's primary purpose is to exercise the JDO query language. The *find* command will query against the extent, while the *find in results* command will query against the last collection of query results. The *view attributes* command shows the names and types of all the attributes of the application data classes. Finally, the *define query variable* command allows you to define a query variable for use in navigating collections within JDOQL. The effect of defining a query variable lasts only until the next query is executed. Consequently, the query variable must be defined before executing the query that will use it.

As an example, suppose that you want to know what categories of books interest Tom. Listing 8-8 shows the user interactions to find that information.

Listing 8-8. User Commands to Find All the Categories That Interest Tom

```
enter command:
--> begin
Okay
enter command:
--> define variable
Enter query variable declaration:
--> Book b
Okay
enter command:
--> find
Find what type of objects:
    1. Book
    2. Borrower
    3. Volunteer
    4. Category
Enter selection:
--> 4
```

```
Enter query string:
--> books.contains(b) && b.borrower.name == "Tom"
Find
    Class: com.ysoft.jdo.book.library.Category
    Filter: books.contains(b) && b.borrower.name == "Tom"
    Variables: Book b
Found 2 objects in the results
    category [OID: 103-12] "Sportsman"
    category [OID: 103-11] "Outdoors"
enter command:
-->
```

Although there are only four application data classes, the object model of the library supports a variety of queries. For example, to find the books that have been borrowed by a volunteer, use the Book extent and the following query string:

```
borrower.volunteer != null
```

Your answer for the default object population should be as follows:

```
Found 2 objects in the results
    book [OID: 102-13] "Gone Sailing" checked out: Mon Aug 26 08:23:10 EDT 2002
    book [OID: 102-12] "Gone Hunting" checked out: Mon Aug 26 08:23:10 EDT 2002
```

The OID values may very well be different in your datastore, and the date when the books were checked out will certainly be different.

To find all the books that are in categories that interest Harry, use the Book extent, and define the query variables as shown here:

```
Book b; Category c;
```

Then use the following query string:

```
categories.contains(c) && (c.books.contains(b) && b.borrower.name == "Harry")
```

Your answer for the default object population should be as follows:

```
Found 1 objects in the results
    book [OID: 102-16] "Gone to Work" checked out: Mon Aug 26 08:23:10 EDT 2002
```

Now that you have the general idea, perhaps you are ready for a challenge. Can you find all the categories that have books borrowed by more than one borrower? Hint: output similar to the following is expected from the query when it runs on the default population.

```
Found 2 objects in the results
    category [OID: 103-12] "Sportsman"
    category [OID: 103-11] "Outdoors"
```

Monitoring the State of Persistent Apples

The StateTracker program allows you to use nearly all of the explicit and implicit operations of JDO while monitoring the persistent, transactional, and unmanaged fields of persistent, transactional, and unmanaged apples.

Figure 8-1 diagrams the relationships of the main classes and interfaces of the StateTracker program. The StateTracker class implements the user interface and is the client of the Monitor and StateHandler services. It creates new apples and worms and modifies the state of existing ones. The source file *StateTracker.java* contains all of the command classes of the StateTracker program. The application classes and interfaces shown in Figure 8-1 are contained in the com.ysoft.jdo.book.statetracker and com.ysoft.jdo.book.statetracker.client packages.

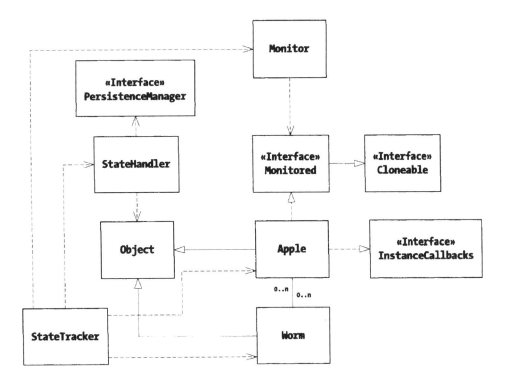

Figure 8-1. The classes and interfaces of the StateTracker *program*

Figure 8-1 diagrams ten classes and interfaces. There are two application data classes, Apple and Worm. These have an n-m relationship to each other. The worms in the StateTracker program have the transcendental ability to exist in more than one apple at a time. The major purpose of the worms is to provide persistent fields that are not in the apple's default fetch group. The Apple class divides its fields into three groups, persistent, transactional, and unmanaged. The persistent group has the five fields shown in Listing 8-9. The fields were selected to give a representative sample of persistent fields. The first three fields are in the default fetch group, while the remaining two are not. The set of transactional (but not persistent) fields and the set of unmanaged fields are identical in type and similarly named.

Listing 8-9. The Persistent Fields of the Apple Class

```
private String    persistentName;
private int       persistentSize;
private Date      persistentPicked;
private HashSet   persistentWorms;
private Worm      persistentHeadWorm;
```

The remaining classes and interfaces in Figure 8-1 serve the following purposes. The Apple class implements the Monitored interface. The Monitor service uses the Monitored interface to determine the apple's management state without affecting it. The Monitored interface also ensures that Apple has a public clone method that is used by the StateTracker to snoop on the state of an apple without affecting the apple's managed state. The StateHandler is the application service that uses the persistence manager. It handles objects, and knows nothing about apples and worms. The Apple class implements InstanceCallbacks. These callback methods serve two purposes: they capture the persistent object's identity string, and they provide notification to the user interface when the callbacks occur.

Building the StateTracker Program

To build the StateTracker program, go to the *bookants* directory and type *ant statetracker*. This build is part of the *ant learning-programs* build. Listing 8-10 shows some of the expected output from the build when using the reference implementation.

Listing 8-10. Expected Output from Running ant statetracker

```
statetracker:
    [javac] Compiling 7 source files to E:\Bookcode\build
    [echo] returned from com/ysoft/jdo/book/statetracker/build.xml
    [copy] Copying 1 file to E:\Bookcode\enhanced\com\ysoft\jdo\book
    [java] done.
    [echo] creating runStatetracker.bat


BUILD SUCCESSFUL
```

To run the StateTracker program, go to the *bookcode-home* directory and type *runStatetracker*.

Getting Started with the StateTracker Commands

If you enter the *help* command after starting the StateTracker program, you see all the commands that it supports. The expected output is shown in Listing 8-11.

Listing 8-11. Example of Help Output from the StateTracker Program

```
E:\Bookcode>runstatetracker
Using adaptor class: com.ysoft.jdo.book.factory.jdori.JDORIAdaptor
The database (FOStoreTestDB.btd) exists
Using URL: (fostore:FOStoreTestDB)
enter command:
--> help
commands:
    quit
    begin
    commit
    rollback
    active
    find all
    add apple
    select apple
```

```
        modify apple
        add worm
        delete worm
        snoop
        view
        get JDO state
        make persistent
        delete persistent
        make transactional
        make nontransactional
        make transient
        evict
        evict all
        refresh
        refresh all
        retrieve
        tickle default fetch group
        dirty
        toss exception
        configure
        configuration
        open
        is open
        close
enter command:
-->
```

As Listing 8-11 shows, the program recognizes a large number of commands. The commands *begin, commit, rollback,* and *active* allow you to control and monitor transactional boundaries. A good place to start is to add a few worms. Their only attribute is a name. For example, the following interaction adds one new worm named Henry:

```
enter command:
--> add worm
Enter worm's name:
--> Henry
Okay, but worms are made persistent only by being in a persistent apple
enter command:
-->
```

A new worm remains unmanaged. It becomes persistent only when it is reached from a persistent apple. After creating a few worms, make a new apple. Listing 8-12 shows a sample interaction that adds a new McIntosh apple with three worms.

Listing 8-12. User Commands to Create a New McIntosh Apple with Three Worms

```
enter command:
--> add apple
Enter apple's name:
--> McIntosh
Enter apple's size (> 0):
--> 3
Enter date picked (mm-dd-yy):
--> 10-15-02
   Date accepted:Tue Oct 15 00:00:00 EDT 2002
Add a worm?:
   1. true
   2. false
Enter selection:
--> 1
Pick a worm:
   1. Worm Henry
   2. Worm Martha
   3. Worm Jack
Enter selection:
--> 1
Add a worm?:
   1. true
   2. false
Enter selection:
--> 1
Pick a worm:
   1. Worm Martha
   2. Worm Jack
Enter selection:
--> 1
Add a worm?:
   1. true
   2. false
Enter selection:
--> 1
```

```
Pick a worm:
    1. Worm Jack
Enter selection:
--> 1
Add a worm?:
    1. true
    2. false
Enter selection:
--> 2
Pick the head worm:
    1. Worm Henry
    2. Worm Martha
    3. Worm Jack
Enter selection:
--> 2
Okay, the new transient apple has been added to the selection list
enter command:
-->
```

The new apple remains unmanaged. To see this, first use the *select apple* command to select the apple from the current list of apples. Then use the *get JDO state* command to determine the current JDO management state of the selected apple.

```
enter command:
--> select apple
Select an apple:
    1. Apple transientName: McIntosh
Enter selection:
--> 1
Okay
enter command:
--> get JDO state
Apple transientName: McIntosh is in JDO state transient
enter command:
-->
```

Because all actions so far have occurred on unmanaged state, there has been no reason to start a transaction.

Next, execute the *begin* and the *make persistent* commands to make the unmanaged McIntosh apple persistent. Now execute the *view* and *get JDO state* commands to determine the unmanaged, transactional, and persistent state of the apple and to determine its management state. Using any implementation, you should see output like the following, which was produced by the reference implementation:

```
enter command:
--> view
Viewing managed state for: OID: 105-12 [JVM ID:4066855]
    transient state: McIntosh, 3, 10-15-02, Worm Martha,
         3 worms {Worm Martha,Worm Jack,Worm Henry}
    transactional state: McIntosh, 3, 10-15-02, Worm Martha,
         3 worms {Worm Henry,Worm Martha,Worm Jack}
    persistent state: McIntosh, 3, 10-15-02, Worm Martha,
         3 worms {Worm Henry,Worm Martha,Worm Jack}
enter command:
--> get state
OID: 105-12 [JVM ID:4066855] is in JDO state persistent-new
enter command:
-->
```

Notice that all three states are the same. That is because the values entered when the apple was created were copied to all three sets of fields, as a way to reduce the amount of user input. As expected, the management state after the *make persistent* command is persistent-new.

If you have not executed the *configure* command, then all transactional attributes are off at this point, and the *configuration* commands returns the following output:

```
--> configuration
Current transaction properties: active, !Opt, !RetainV, !RestoreV, !NTR, !NTW
enter command:
-->
```

At this point, commit the transaction and ask for the apple's management state. You should see output that looks like the interaction in Listing 8-13, which was produced by the reference implementation.

Listing 8-13. Sample Output from Committing the New McIntosh Apple

```
enter command:
--> commit
Synchronization.beforeCompletion called
OID: 105-12 [JVM ID:4066855] jdoPreStore
OID: 105-12 [JVM ID:4066855] jdoPreClear
Synchronization.afterCompletion called with status: committed
Okay
enter command:
--> get state
OID: 105-12 [JVM ID:4066855] is in JDO state hollow
enter command:
-->
```

After committing the transaction, you will get an exception if you execute the *view* command because a transaction is not active. Instead run the *snoop* command. The *snoop* command produces a view of the object without affecting the managed state or requiring a transaction. The expected output will look like the output in Listing 8-14.

Listing 8-14. Sample Output from Snooping on the Hollow Apple

```
enter command:
--> snoop
Viewing raw state for: OID: 105-12 [JVM ID:8083121]
    transient state: McIntosh, 3, 10-15-02, OID: 106-21,
            3 worms {OID: 106-21, OID: 106-22, OID: 106-20}
    transactional state: null, 0, no date, null, null worms
    persistent state: null, 0, no date, null, null worms
enter command:
-->
```

There are four things to notice in Listing 8-14. One, the JVM ID has changed from Listing 8-13. The change occurs because the *snoop* command views a clone of the original apple. (Remember from Chapter 5 that, by default, cloning a persistent object gets a snapshot of the current memory state without invoking transparent persistence.) Two, the persistent state has Java default values. This is expected since the object is in the hollow management state. Three, the transactional state also has Java default values. This is an unexpected outcome. The specification describes eviction only in terms of clearing the persistent state. It says nothing about clearing the nonpersistent and transactional state. In fact, the specification strongly implies that eviction does not clear the nonpersistent and transactional state. This behavior has been reported as a bug in the JDO reference implementation at the Java bug parade (http://developer.java.sun.com/developer/bugParade).

Finally, note that the transient state is not changed, except that all of the worms are now unnamed. The transientWorms field and the transientHeadWorm field both point to persistent objects even though the fields are unmanaged. When the new apple was created, the same worms were used to set the unmanaged, transactional, and persistent fields. As a result, all worm fields are referring to the same worms, which became persistent when the apple became persistent. When the *snoop* command executes, it clones the apple, but it does not clone the worms. The worm's toString method catches the exception that results from trying to examine the persistent name of a Worm outside of a transaction, and it recovers from the exception by returning the worm's identity string instead of its name.

Brief Look at the Other StateTracker Commands

The previous section describes many commands that the StateTracker program recognizes. This section describes the remaining commands.

Many of the command strings are self-describing. For example, the *make transactional* command will make a nontransactional object transactional. In some cases, for the command to succeed, the implementation must support the appropriate implementation options. An unmanaged object cannot be made transactional unless the implementation supports, as the reference implementation does, the javax.jdo.option.TransientTransactional feature. Most commands operate on the selected apple, but some operate on a set of apples. The *evict all* command evicts all persistent-clean apples (and worms) and the *refresh all* command refreshes all transactional apples and worms.

The *configure* command sets the five properties of the Transaction object: *Optimistic*, *RetainValues*, *RestoreValues*, *NontransactionalRead*, and *NontransactionalWrite*. The *is open* command checks whether the persistence manager is open. The *open* and *close* commands open and close the persistence manager.

The *toss exception* command sets a flag in the transaction's Synchronization object that will cause it to throw a JDOUserException on the next commit. It's a one-shot setting that does not block a subsequent commit. The *tickle default fetch group* command reads a couple of fields of the default fetch group and outputs a message with their values. It will cause the default fetch group to load in most cases. The *dirty* command will call the makeDirty method in JDOHelper for the selected managed field.

The StateTracker program has been invaluable in writing this book, and you will find it very useful for test driving your selected JDO implementation.

Using the Commercial Implementations

Three commercial implementations are featured in this book, but you can use the JDO Learning Tools with any implementation that supports Ant build scripts. The code provided with this book provides build scripts for the three implementations Kodo, Lido, and IntelliBO. The 1.0 release of the JDO Learning Tools supports the Microsoft Windows operating systems. Undoubtedly, the open source community will extend support to other JDO implementations and operating systems. You will have to find or write a script for any other implementation. The JDO Learning Tools are demanding programs, and you may very well find bugs in the commercial implementations as a result of using these programs. If you find bugs, report them to the vendor.

Using the Kodo Implementation

When using the Kodo implementation, configure the *kodo.properties* file, and copy it to *custom.properties*. The main *build.xml* script will invoke the tool script *kodo.xml*. The tool script runs the Kodo verifier, Kodo enhancer, and Kodo schema tool. The Kodo implementation supports live schema generation and evolution. As a result, when the schema tool is invoked, there is no need to take any further steps to update the database schema. Because the schema tool is fairly time con-suming, the Kodo build script with the JDO Learning Tools optimizes the use of the schema tool by detecting whether the enhanced classes have changed. This detection is not foolproof. To force schema generation, use the *-Dschema=generate* option with the *ant* command as shown in the following command line:

```
ant -Dschema=generate megacups
```

The *learning-programs* target sets this property for you.

Using the Lido Implementation

When using the Lido implementation, configure the *lido.properties* file, and copy it to *custom.properties*. The main *build.xml* script invokes the tool script *lido.xml*. The tool script runs the Lido enhancer and schema tool. Because the use of the schema tool is somewhat time consuming, it runs only when the schema property is defined. This can be done at the command line when invoking Ant, as the following line shows:

```
ant -Dschema=generate megacups
```

The *learning-programs* target sets this property for you.

The Lido tool script has been configured to have the schema tool output SQL files. These files are placed in the *bookcode-home* directory. Their file names are composed of the lowest package directory plus the SQL extension, such as *coffee.sql*. After generating the SQL files, you will need to execute the portion of the SQL script that is appropriate for your schema evolution. You may have to drop tables if you alter the definition of persistent fields in the application data classes.

Using the IntelliBO Implementation

When using the IntelliBO implementation, configure the *intellibo.properties* file, and copy it to *custom.properties*. The main *build.xml* script invokes the tool script *intellibo.xml*. The tool script runs the IntelliBO verifier, enhancer, and schema tools. Because the use of the schema tool is somewhat time consuming, it runs only when the schema property is defined. This can be done at the command line when invoking Ant, as the following line shows:

```
ant -Dschema=generate megacups
```

The *learning-programs* target sets this property for you.

The IntelliBO tool script has been configured to have the schema tool output SQL files. These files are placed in the package directory under the *enhanced* directory. You will find three SQL files: *create.sql*, *drop.sql*, and *select.sql*. After generating the SQL files, you will need to execute the portion of the SQL scripts that are appropriate for your schema evolution.

Summary

The first five JDO Learning Tools range from elementary to advanced in their use of JDO. Each of them can help you understand the capabilities and limitations of JDO. Do not let the console interface, which is rudimentary, hide their true merit from you. By using them and understanding the results that you obtain, you can become a JDO expert. Better than any book, they can teach you the underlying logic of JDO's behavior. The understanding that you gain will help make your first project that uses JDO a complete success.

The next chapter examines a Swing client-server application that satisfies the requirements of a simple reservation system. Unlike the five JDO Learning Tools programs covered in this chapter, the JDO Learning Tools programs presented in the remaining chapters have the flavor of real-world applications.

CHAPTER 9

Using JDO in a Swing Application

THE MAINE LIGHTHOUSE RENTAL COMPANY is a fictitious business that rents lighthouses in Maine to vacationers. In fact, the lighthouses used by the JDO Learning Tools are working lighthouses that are not available for rent, but the concept provides an excellent excuse to brighten up the example programs with scenes of the Maine coast. Any resemblance to a real rental business is both unexpected and coincidental.

The management of the Maine Lighthouse Rental Company wants a prototype of a reservation system. The requirements are expressed in 11 use cases. This chapter examines the rental Swing application, an implementation that satisfies these requirements. This implementation is a client/server application that uses Swing and JDO. The next chapter examines an implementation that uses servlets and JDO. In the last chapter of this book, the example makes use of JDO and Enterprise JavaBeans.

Building the Rental Swing Application

The rental Swing application is part of the JDO Learning Tools. Its build target is *rental-gui*. Chapter 8 discusses the mechanics of setting up the build environment and executing builds. If you have followed the instructions presented there successfully, you are ready to proceed in this chapter. If you have not, it is necessary to follow the directions in the "Getting Started" section in Chapter 8. After the build environment is set up, go to the *bookants* subdirectory under your *bookcode-home* directory. To build the rental Swing application, type the command

```
ant rental-gui
```

Listing 9-1 shows some of the expected output from building this target.

Listing 9-1. Selected Output from Running ant rental-gui

```
Buildfile: build.xml
    ...
rental-gui:
    ...
    [echo] creating runRentalConsole.bat
    [echo] creating runRentalGui.bat


BUILD SUCCESSFUL
```

The target *rental-gui* produces two executable classes, both called
ReservationClient. One is in the com.ysoft.jdo.book.rental.client.console
package and the other is in the com.ysoft.jdo.book.rental.client.gui package.
The first has the console user interface discussed in Chapter 8. The second has a
Swing user interface. The batch files *runRentalConsole.bat* and *runRentalGui.bat*
start up the appropriate client class. The batch files work on Microsoft Windows.
For other operating systems, you need to edit the batch files. The code is open
source. If you feel inspired to contribute modified build scripts for other operating
systems, they will be most welcomed at http://sourceforge.net/projects/jdo-tools.
To bring up the rental Swing application, which is the focus of this chapter, go to
the *bookcode-home* directory and execute the batch file *runRentalGui.bat*.

Requirements for the Prototype Reservation System

A good way to capture requirements is to describe use cases. *Use cases* are simple
interactions between one or more types of users and the system. They explain the
work that the user will want to do when working with the running system.

The use cases for the reservation system include one or more users who may
be anonymous or identified. Anonymous users may view open rentals, but to
make, view, or cancel a reservation, the user must identify himself. For simplicity,
the identity is not authenticated. In addition to the one or more anonymous or
identified users, the use cases specify an administrator who populates the datastore
with initial data.

One of the virtues of this example is that the rentals may be contested. Two
users can simultaneously attempt to reserve the same lighthouse for the same
week. Since the rental Swing application supports only one user's interaction at a
time, to see the interaction of conflicting reservations, you will need to use a datastore
that supports multiuser access. The b-tree file datastore used by the reference

implementation does not support multiuser access, but most other JDO implementations will use datastores that do support multiuser access. If you are using
the JDO reference implementation, you will be able to exercise all of the uses cases
presented, except use case 10, in which the system detects conflicting reservations.
You cannot test this use case with the reference implementation because the b-tree
file datastore does not support two clients in different JVMs accessing the same
data files at the same time.

In the next sections, the use cases for the prototype of the reservation system
are described. Notice that they are simple, as they should be. Because use cases
must communicate to everyone how the software behaves, they should be as simple
as possible. Although the various prototypes of the reservation system presented
in this book vary in their architecture, each implementation satisfies the same set
of use cases.

Use Case 1: The Administrator Clears the Datastore

In this use case, the administrator removes any rental information as the prelim-
inary step to initializing the datastore with testing data. The interaction involves
two steps.

1. The administrator requests that the datastore be cleared of all rental
   information.

2. The system clears the datastore of all rental information.

Use Case 2: The Administrator Initializes the Datastore

In this use case, the administrator initializes a clean datastore with the testing
data. A number of rentals are created for a number of weeks. The middle portion of
the rental period is the high season when rates are higher than during the off-
season. The interaction involves two steps.

1. The administrator requests that the datastore be initialized with the
   standard testing data.

2. The system populates the datastore with the standard testing data.

Use Case 3: An Anonymous User Identifies Himself

In this use case, an anonymous user declares his identity, or an identified user changes his identity. Thereafter, he is an identified user with a name. The interaction involves two steps.

1. The user presents his name.

2. The system accepts the name and assumes thereafter that the user with this name is using the system.

Use Case 4: An Identified User Discards His Identity

In this use case, an identified user reverts to an anonymous user. The interaction occurs in two steps.

1. The user revokes his identity.

2. The system discards the current user identity and assumes that an anonymous user is using the system.

Use Case 5: A User Views Available Rentals

In this use case, the user, who may be anonymous or identified, views the available rentals. The interaction occurs in two steps.

1. The user asks to see the available reservations.

2. The system displays the available reservations.

Use Case 6: An Identified User Makes a Reservation

In this use case, an identified user makes a reservation. This use case assumes that the user is viewing the reservations as a result of completing the interaction in use case 5. The system will not permit an anonymous user to make a reservation. The interaction is completed in three steps.

1. The identified user selects one or more available rentals to reserve.

2. The user confirms the reservations.

3. If the reservations are accepted, the system displays all of the user's reservations. Otherwise, see use case 10.

Use Case 7: An Identified User Views His Reservations

In this use case, an identified user views his own reservations. This interaction is completed in one or two steps.

1. The identified user asks to see his own reservations, or alternatively, this step is skipped if the user has just completed use case 6.

2. The system displays the user's reservations.

Use Case 8: An Identified User Cancels Some Reservations

In this use case, the identified user begins the interaction after viewing his own reservations. The system will not permit a user to cancel reservations that belong to a different user.

1. The identified user selects one or more of his reservations to cancel.

2. The user confirms the cancellations.

3. The system accepts the cancellations and displays all of the user's remaining reservations.

Use Case 9: An Identified User Alters His Reservations

In this use case, the identified user views both his own reservations and the available reservations. He may also see reservations that belong to others. The user can cancel his own reservations and make new reservations in one transaction. In this fashion, there is no danger when changing a reservation that he ends up with the old reservation cancelled but the new reservation rejected.

1. The identified user asks to see both available rentals and his own reservations.

2. The system displays the same.

3. The user selects zero or more reservations to cancel and rentals to reserve.

4. The user confirms the changes.

5. If the system accepts the changes, it displays all of the user's reservations. Otherwise, see use case 10.

Use Case 10: The System Detects Conflicting Reservations

In some cases, the changes confirmed by a user cannot be accepted because they conflict with changes made by another user. This happens when two different users seek to reserve the same rental at approximately the same time. Only one will be successful. The other is informed of the failure.

1. The system informs the user that the reservation cannot be accepted because it conflicts with a reservation made by another user.

2. The system refreshes the information that caused the problem.

3. The user has the option to refresh all information.

Use Case 11: User Views Additional Information on a Rental Unit

In this use case, the user requests additional information about a rental unit. This request can be made from any of the views of available rentals or reservations. The interaction takes place in three steps.

1. The user requests more information on a rental unit.

2. The system displays it.

3. At a later point, the user returns to the original view.

Testing the Rental Swing Client

After the *rental-gui* target is built, change to the *bookcode-home* directory and run the batch file *runRentalGui.bat*. This command file starts the Swing client. Figure 9-1 shows the rental Swing client when it first appears. Note that very little of the application is enabled because it is disconnected from its data.

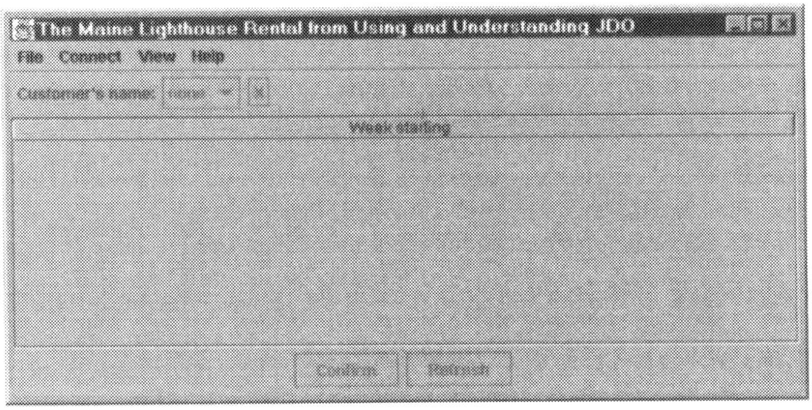

Figure 9-1. The Swing client on startup

For the first step, go to the *Connect* menu and select *Connect to datastore*. Since this is your first time using this application, no test data has been created. Go to the *File* menu and select *Populate database*. After the database is populated you now have the option to clear the database from the *File* menu. This behavior corresponds to use cases 1 and 2.

At this point, you still do not see any rentals, because the application starts without a view on the data. Go to the *View* menu item and select *Available*. Figure 9-2 shows the rental Swing client after the available rentals are viewed. At this point you can see that there are three lighthouses for a 16-week season. The middle of this season is arbitrarily designated the high season when prices are higher. If you click the highlighted headings, you will see pictures of the various lighthouses. This behavior corresponds to use cases 5 and 11.

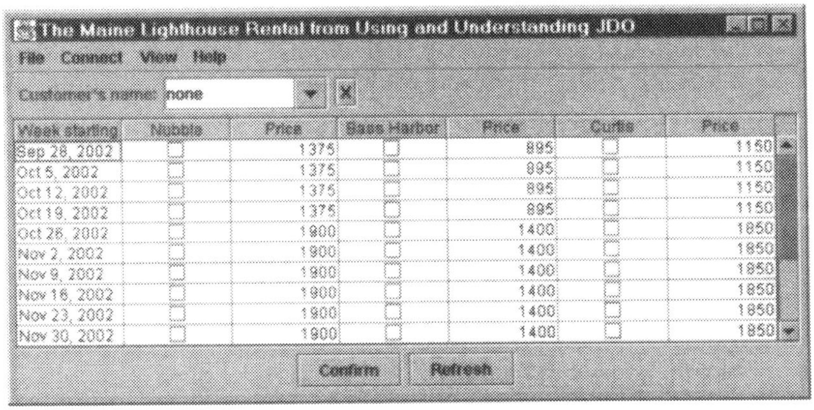

Figure 9-2. The Swing client viewing available rentals

The drop-down list for customer names has no entries. Enter the name "Jim" in the list box, and press Enter. Notice that the name changes to uppercase. As far as the program is concerned, you are now the customer named Jim. Press the *X* button and you become unidentified again. Jim's persistent customer record is saved only if you press the *Confirm* button at some point before exiting the program. The list box behavior corresponds to use cases 3 and 4.

After entering or selecting a customer name, you can make reservations by checking the corresponding check box. For example, check the first 2 weeks for the first unit, and press the *Confirm* button. The system accepts the reservations and displays all of the customer's reservations. This behavior corresponds to use cases 6 and 7. Now uncheck the last reservation to cancel the reservation, and press the *Confirm* button again. The system shows a shorter list of reservations. This behavior corresponds to use case 8.

There are now just two use cases left to test. On the *View* menu, select *Both*. Uncheck one of the reserved rentals to cancel it, and check an available rental to reserve it. Press the *Confirm* button. When successful, this shows the customer's modified list of confirmed reservations. This behavior corresponds to use case 9.

Encountering Conflicting Changes in the Rental Swing Client

In order to see conflicting changes with the rental Swing client, you need a JDO implementation that uses a multiuser datastore. Most relational databases and object-oriented databases satisfy this requirement.

Start up two rental Swing clients. Identify Jim as the customer using the first client and Mary as the customer using the second client. Using Figure 9-3 as your guide, have Jim make his reservation and view *Both*. Have Mary make a nonconflicting reservation and view *Both*. Figure 9-3 shows the situation for the two client programs. As you can see, each has a reservation that does not conflict with the other, and each is able to modify only his or her own reservation.

 NOTE The rental Swing application uses optimistic JDO transactions to keep a transaction open at all times. Optimistic transactions are the appropriate choice for long-running transactions. It also sets the *RetainValues* property to true to improve performance by caching persistent state across transactions. All other transactional properties are set to false. To examine the properties used, look up the implementation's properties file in the *com/ysoft/jdo/book/rental/local* subdirectory under the *bookcode-home* directory.

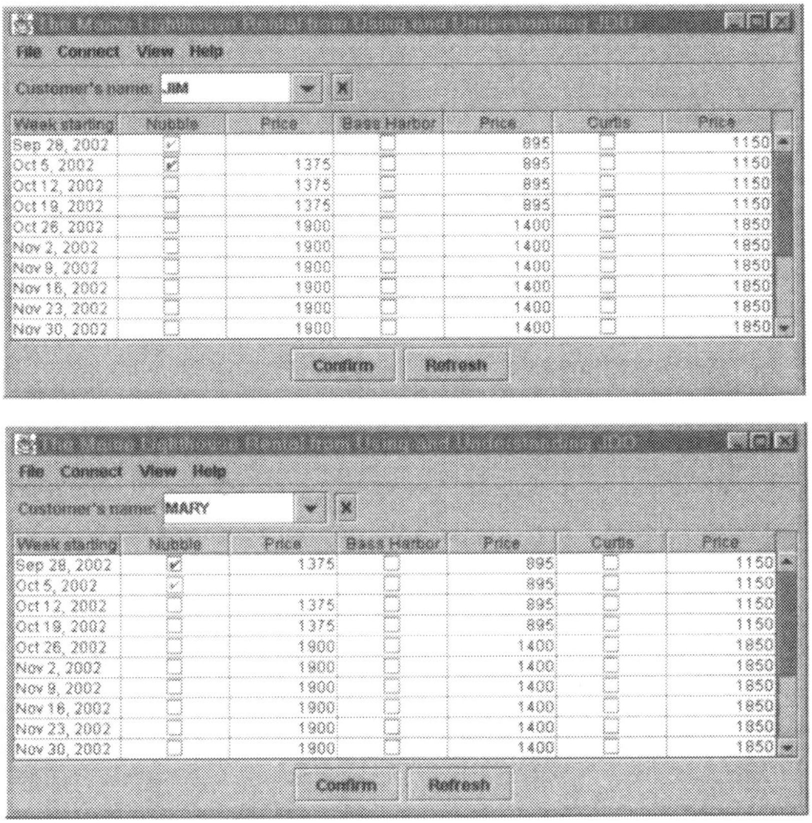

Figure 9-3. Jim and Mary with nonconflicting reservations

Next, have Jim alter his reservation. For the dates shown in Figure 9-3, he cancels for October 5 and makes a reservation for October 12. He confirms and his change is accepted. He again selects *Both* from the *View* menu. Mary, on the other hand, is unaware of Jim's changes. She cancels her reservation for September 28 and makes a reservation for October 12. She confirms, but encounters an error condition that states "Concurrent changes by other users prevent your changes, try again."

After dismissing the error dialog box, Mary once again views her own reservations and the available rentals. Figure 9-4 shows her view of her own reservations and available reservations.

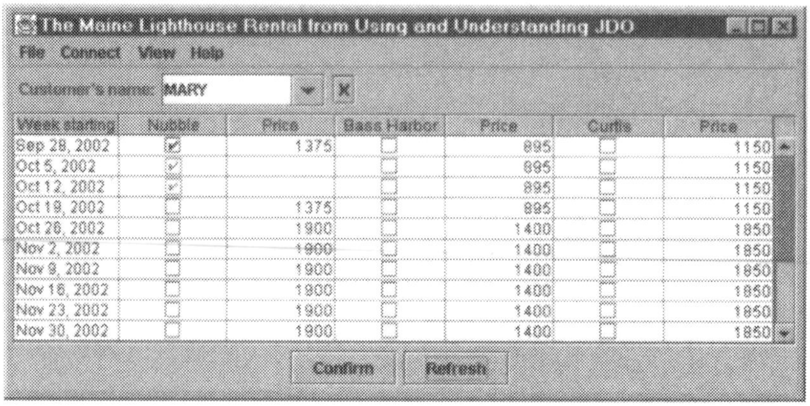

The Maine Lighthouse Rental from Using and Understanding JDO

File Connect View Help

Customer's name: MARY

Week starting	Nubble	Price	Bass Harbor	Price	Curtis	Price
Sep 28, 2002	☑	1375	☐	895	☐	1150
Oct 5, 2002	☑		☐	895	☐	1150
Oct 12, 2002	☑		☐	895	☐	1150
Oct 19, 2002	☐	1375	☐	895	☐	1150
Oct 26, 2002	☐	1900	☐	1400	☐	1850
Nov 2, 2002	☐	1900	☐	1400	☐	1850
Nov 9, 2002	☐	1900	☐	1400	☐	1850
Nov 16, 2002	☐	1900	☐	1400	☐	1850
Nov 23, 2002	☐	1900	☐	1400	☐	1850
Nov 30, 2002	☐	1900	☐	1400	☐	1850

Confirm   Refresh

Figure 9-4. Mary's view after optimistic transaction failure

There are several points to notice in Figure 9-4. Although Mary cleared her reservation for September 28 before she attempted to confirm her changes, she now sees her reservation checked again. Her change has been undone because the *RestoreValues* property of the JDO Transaction is set to false. As a result, dirty objects were automatically evicted when the transaction rolled back. When the rental Swing client repaints the screen, new data reflecting the state in the datastore is loaded. For the same reason, Mary now sees that someone else has taken the reservation for October 12. Finally, although Jim has successfully cancelled his reservation for October 5, Mary's client shows this reservation as taken. Because Mary's Rental object for October 5 indicated, correctly at the time, that the rental was taken, she was not permitted to alter this reservation in her unsuccessful transaction. It remained persistent-nontransactional, and as a result, the transaction's rollback did not cause JDO to discard its persistent state. Mary must click the *Refresh* button to see that the rental for October 5 is now available. This behavior, when an optimistic transaction fails, satisfies use case 11.

Designing the Rental Swing Application

Two design constraints dictate some of the choices in the architecture of the rental Swing application. The use of Swing is a given. The use of JDO is also a given. The use of JDO implies two design tasks: one, to define the classes of persistent objects, and two, to define the service that will use JDO to find, store, create, and delete these persistent objects.

The Application Data Classes of the Rental Swing Application

To build the prototype reservation system for the Maine Lighthouse Rental Company, four application data classes are needed.

- Customer

- Week

- Lighthouse

- Rental

Since development is in the prototype stage, the classes are simple, but it is anticipated that the classes will continue to exist and become more complex as the application evolves.

The Customer Class

Figure 9-5 shows the UML class diagram for the Customer class. Notice that this UML diagram shows the private persistent attribute called name. The private attributes are shown in the application data classes because they are used in queries. Following the normal UML convention, the leading hyphen indicates a private access level. As mentioned in the introduction, this book uses the convention that the access level of attributes and operations is public when the class diagram does not indicate the access level. For the Customer class, there is one public operation, the constructor, and one public, read-only, property called Name. To avoid issues of mixed case in query filters, the Customer class forces customer names to uppercase.

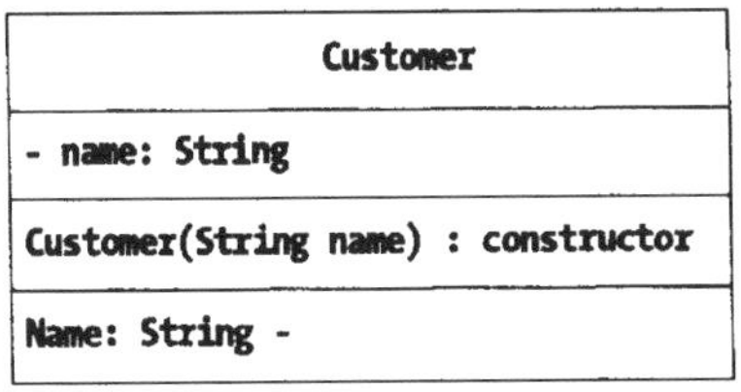

Customer
- name: String
Customer(String name) : constructor
Name: String -

Figure 9-5. The class diagram of the prototype Customer class

The Week Class

The Week class, as shown in Figure 9-6, is also a simple class. It has two private and persistent attributes, and three public and read-only properties. Not shown are factory methods used to construct the testing population of Week objects.

Week
- startDate: Date - highSeason: boolean
HighSeason: boolean - StartOfWeek: Date - StartOfWeekString: String -

Figure 9-6. The class diagram of the prototype Week class

The Lighthouse Class

The Lighthouse class shown in Figure 9-7 has five private persistent attributes, and the same number of properties. A lighthouse has a name, a description, a name of the image file for its picture, a rate for the high season, and a rate for the off-season.

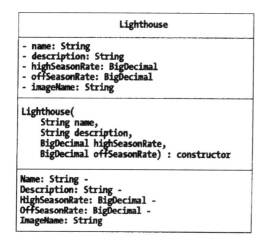

Figure 9-7. The class diagram of the prototype Lighthouse class

All of the Lighthouse properties are read-only except ImageName, which is read-write. The properties in the prototype application data classes often end up read-only because the prototype application is not complicated enough to require that the attributes change after the persistent objects are created. As the application evolves, it is anticipated that many of the read-only properties will become read-write. The use of JDO does not impose a tax on this evolution. The only work required to convert a read-only property to a read-write property is to add the mutator method.

The Rental Class

The Rental class, which is shown in Figure 9-8, aggregates the various pieces of information. It has four private, persistent attributes, and six public properties. The *Lighthouse, Week,* and *Customer* properties hold references to the various objects that a Rental object ties together. The *Price* property is the rental rate for the week. The *Available* property is a convenience property that holds true if the *Customer* property is null. The *Dirty* property is a convenience property that checks with the isDirty method in JDOHelper and returns true if the Rental object has been changed but not yet committed to the datastore.

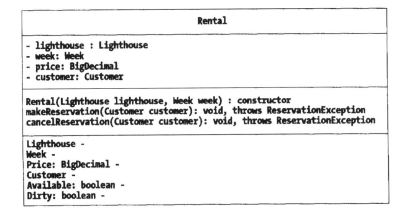

Figure 9-8. The class diagram of the prototype Rental *class*

In addition to a constructor, the Rental class has two operations: makeReservation and cancelReservation. Both operations require a Customer object. The operation to cancel a reservation requires a Customer object as an invariant check on the action. The customer passed should be the customer who holds the reservation. Both operations throw a ReservationException when difficulties are encountered.

The Application Data Service in the Rental Swing Application

After defining the application data classes, the next step is to define an application data service. Unlike objects that exist only in memory, the state of persistent objects is permanently kept in the datastore. These objects are found, updated, created, and deleted by explicit actions on the service that synchronizes their existence and state in memory with their persistent state in the datastore. JDO is the generic service for this purpose, but each application usually needs a service configured to its particular concerns, objects, and tasks.

Design Choices for Transactions

The design for the rental Swing application must decide what to do with transactions. In order to store new or updated persistent information in the datastore, the data service must start and complete transactions. The fundamental question is this: Should transaction handling be encapsulated in the data service and to what extent? A variety of answers can work.

Transactions can be encapsulated within data service calls. One data service method may start a transaction, make some changes, and commit the transaction. Another data service method may not use a transaction at all, or perform read-only operations that do not change the persistent information. The client for a data service designed in this fashion has no control over transactions. The client may not know that transactions even exist, since they are completely hidden within the service.

A second approach allows a transaction started in one method to be completed in another method. The transactional boundaries are hidden within service methods that perform other work, but the transaction can span two or more service method invocations. This approach can be confusing unless the usage patterns for the service are limited and well documented.

A third approach is to simply expose control of the transactional boundaries as additional service methods. This approach gives the client layer both the responsibility for transactions and the ability to control them.

In the case of the rental Swing application, it makes sense to take the third approach, which exposes the transactional boundaries in the data service. Use cases 6, 8, and 9 describe the user as confirming, i.e. committing, reservation changes. For this reason, rather than encapsulate the transactions in the data service, it makes more sense to expose the transactional boundaries to the next level of the software, which will be closer to the user's click of the *Confirm* button.

Although the client of the ReservationService controls the transactional boundaries, the service configures the transaction. The service has made the decision that the transaction will be an optimistic transaction. This makes sense because transactional boundaries are controlled outside of the service and are therefore very likely to be long-running transactions that involve user input. Likewise, the *factory.properties* file, which configures the JDO factory, turns on the transaction's *RetainValues* property for better performance. It also turns off *RestoreValues* to ensure eviction of any transactional objects that cause an optimistic lock exception. In essence, the service encapsulates the configuration of the transaction and exposes the transactional boundaries.

The ReservationService Class

Figure 9-9 shows the operations of the ReservationService. The three transactional methods, beginTransaction, rollbackTransaction, and commitTransaction, control the transactional boundaries.

```
┌─────────────────────────────────────────────────────────────────────────┐
│                          ReservationService                               │
├─────────────────────────────────────────────────────────────────────────┤
│ ReservationService: constructor, throws JDOException, ReservationException │
│                                                                           │
│ beginTransaction(): void, throws JDOException                             │
│ rollbackTransaction(): void, throws JDOException                          │
│ commitTransaction(): void, throws JDOException, OptimisticReservationException │
│ evictAll(): void, throws JDOException, ReservationException               │
│                                                                           │
│ getAvailableRentals(): Collection, throws JDOException                    │
│ getCustomerRentals(Customer customer): Collection, throws JDOException    │
│ getCustomerAndAvailableRentals(Customer customer): Collection, throws JDOException │
│                                                                           │
│ getCustomers(String name): List, throws JDOException                      │
│ getCustomers(): List, throws JDOException                                 │
│ getLighthouses(): List, throws JDOException                               │
│                                                                           │
│ populateDatastore(): void, throws ReservationException                    │
│ cleanDatastore(): void, throws ReservationException                       │
│ isCleanDatastore(): boolean, throws ReservationException                  │
└─────────────────────────────────────────────────────────────────────────┘
```

Figure 9-9. The class diagram of the ReservationService

In the example, the reservation system needs to make three different queries:

- Find all available rentals (use case 5).

- Find all rentals that have been reserved by a particular customer (use case 7).

- Find all rentals that are either available or reserved by a particular customer (use case 9).

Three methods in the service, getAvailableRentals, getCustomerRentals, and getCustomerAndAvailableRentals, provide a convenient way to obtain the Rental objects found by each query filter.

In a similar manner, the remaining methods in the application data service arise from analyzing the use cases and from implementing behavior whose desirability becomes evident during coding. The evictAll method handles the need, mentioned in use case 10, to refresh all information. The two getCustomers methods arise from use case 3 and also from the desire that becomes evident during coding to provide a reasonable way for the user to identify himself from a list of known customers. The need for the getLighthouses method becomes obvious as the code is written to handle the JTable headers. In short, the service methods in the application data service tailor the explicit services available in JDO to the specific needs of the application.

As the UML class diagram in Figure 9-9 shows, most of the service methods of the ReservationService throw some type of JDOException. Since JDOException is derived from RuntimeException, the possibility does not need to be mentioned explicitly in a throws clause in the code. The UML class diagram mentions the possibility of throwing this exception since it must be accounted for in the design. In addition, as described in Chapter 7, the possibility exists that JDO exceptions will occur when persistent objects are used or modified. Live persistent objects can always throw JDO exceptions that arise from operational circumstances.

The Application Data Model in the Rental Swing Application

The ReservationService throws JDO exceptions, but the Swing client classes, which mostly execute code in the Swing libraries, cannot handle exceptions. The data model that the Swing widgets use must isolate the possibility of runtime exceptions. In addition, each widget has its own particular data structure that works best for it. For this reason, a third layer is introduced called the *application data model*. The application data model for the rental Swing application is found in the ReservationClientModel class.

As the UML class diagram in Figure 9-10 shows, the ReservationClientModel has methods to service the widgets of the application's Swing user interface. This class has five groups of operations and nine properties.

```
ReservationClientModel
─────────────────────────────────────────────────────
ReservationClientModel(): constructor
connect(): void
disconnect(): void
confirm(): void
refresh(): void

viewAvailableRentals(): void
viewCustomerRentals(): void
viewCustomerAndAvailableRentals(): void

getCustomerNames(): String []
getRentalDate(int dateIndex): Date
isAvailable(int dateIndex, int lighthouseIndex): boolean
setAvailable(int dateIndex, int lighthouseIndex, boolean flag): void
isModifiable(int dateIndex, int lighthouseIndex): boolean
getPrice(int dateIndex, int lighthouseIndex): BigDecimal
getLighthouseName(int index): String
getLighthouseDescription(int index): String
getLighthouseImageName(int index): String

cleanDatastore(): void
populateDatastore(): void

addModelChangeListener(ModelChangeListener listener): void
removeModelChangeListener(ModelChangeListener listener): void
─────────────────────────────────────────────────────
Connected: boolean -
PopulatedDatastore: boolean -
ViewAvailableRentals: boolean -
ViewCustomerRentals: boolean -
ViewCustomerAndAvailableRentals: boolean -
CustomerName: String
CustomerDefined: boolean -
NumLighthouses: int -
NumRentalDates: int -
```

Figure 9-10. The class diagram of the ReservationClientModel

In their implementation, the methods of the ReservationClientModel follow several design strategies to satisfy the client's requests. First, they convert, when necessary, between the logical view used by the widgets to the logical view used by the service. This is particularly evident in converting between the row and column indices used by the JTable to the Collection used by the data service. Second, the operations in the ReservationClientModel delegate to the ReservationService to get the relevant persistent objects. Finally, the operations in the ReservationClientModel completely encapsulate the live persistent objects and all JDO exceptions. If the model encounters a JDO exception, it displays the error message to the user. After the user has clicked the *OK* button on the error report window, the ReservationClientModel either returns a reasonable default value to its client widget, or when no return value is required, it performs a no-op.

The operations in the first group shown in Figure 9-10 construct the model and connect it to a persistence manager. They also commit a transaction, roll back a transaction, and refresh all persistent objects. In the case of a Swing application, it is essential that the model can respond to service calls even when there is no connection to live data through an open persistence manager. Without a connection, the rental Swing application is not useful, but at least it is visible, ready to respond to a user request to connect, and able to display any difficulties in making or keeping a connection.

The second group of operations inform the model of the view desired by the client widgets. For some applications, it makes sense to have the ability to support all views simultaneously. For the rental Swing application, it is sufficient that the model supports one view at a time.

The third group of operations provides information that the widgets need in response to the requests that the widgets can formulate. Many of the widgets, such as the JTable used to present the rental information, use indices to refer to the information needed. The application data model accommodates the logical model of the widget.

The fourth group of operations provides for cleaning and populating the datastore with the testing data. The fifth group of operations supports listeners who need to be notified when the model changes. The listeners, of course, are Swing widgets that need to change what they display if the model changes information or changes the view.

The properties of the ReservationClientModel all derive from either the operations of the class or the properties of persistent objects or collections of persistent objects that the model manages.

As Figure 9-10 indicates, no method or property in the ReservationClientModel throws a checked exception or a JDO exception. This is important because the Swing widgets are not equipped to handle exceptions thrown from the application client model.

Overall Architecture of the Rental Swing Application

By this point, the architecture of the rental Swing application has become clear. Although some three dozen classes make up the application, the architecture is summarized by the relationships between the four key architectural elements shown in Figure 9-11.

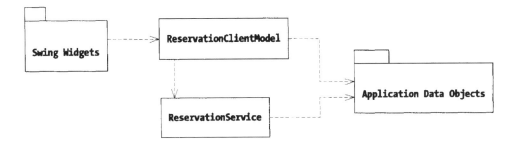

Figure 9-11. The architecture of the rental Swing application

As shown in Figure 9-11, various classes called Swing widgets use the ReservationClientModel, which in turn uses the ReservationService. Both the ReservationClientModel and the ReservationService use the application data classes. The ReservationClientModel encapsulates JDO, the application data objects, and JDO exceptions. Thereby, it isolates objects in these classes from the Swing widgets. In addition, the ReservationClientModel converts from the logical view of information needed by the Swing widgets to the persistent object model found in the application data classes and used by the ReservationService.

Summary

Building a Swing application with JDO is straightforward. After requirements are gathered and analyzed, the architect designs the application data classes. Next, the architect designs an application data service that concentrates on the simple issues of finding, creating, deleting, and updating the persistent objects. For most Swing applications, it is appropriate to expose the transactional boundaries in the application data service. The final step is to design the Swing user interface while defining the application data model that will present fine-grain persistent information in the correct logical relationship as required by the Swing widgets that the application uses. The application data model also has the responsibility to completely isolate the Swing widgets from possible runtime JDO exceptions.

The next chapter will examine a Web application architecture for the same set of requirements. Instead of using Swing, the Web app will use JavaServer Pages, servlets, Tomcat, and a Web browser.

CHAPTER 10

Using JDO in a Web Application

THIS CHAPTER DESCRIBES a rental Web application that satisfies the requirements of the fictitious Maine Lighthouse Rental Company. The rental Web application allows a user to identify himself, view available rentals, and make and cancel reservations. The rental Web application meets virtually the same set of requirements as was met by the rental Swing application presented in Chapter 9. This chapter presupposes that you have read Chapter 9, which explains the use cases for the rental applications, and that you have built the rental Swing application. Because the Swing version of the rental application is the only version that can initialize the datastore with the testing data, you must build and use that version before building the rental Web application.

The application data classes, data service, and data model are maintained in distinct source files for the Web application and the Swing application. Although the differences between the versions are small enough that they could be merged together, separate versions are maintained to avoid obscuring the differences between them.

Configuring the Build Environment for Tomcat

The rental Web application is part of the JDO Learning Tools. Chapter 8 describes how to configure the build environment and execute builds. If you have followed the instructions presented in Chapter 8 successfully, you are ready to perform the additional configuration steps presented here. If you did not perform the configuration described in Chapter 8, you must perform all seven configuration steps described in Chapter 8. Thereafter, continue with the following three configuration steps, which allow you to build the rental Web application.

Step Eight: Set Up Tomcat Servlet Container

In this step, you set up the Tomcat servlet container. The build in this chapter was developed using Tomcat 4.1.12. Any Tomcat 4.x build should work equally well. If you do not have a 4.x version of Tomcat installed, go to the following URL:

```
http://jakarta.apache.org
```

Follow the links to a download of Tomcat. Then follow the directions to install it and start it up. If Tomcat is properly installed and running, the URL `http://localhost:8080` displays the default Tomcat home page.

The directory where you installed Tomcat is referred to as *tomcat-home* in this book.

Estimated time for this step, excluding download: 45 minutes

Step Nine: Set Up JSP Standard Tag Library

In this step, you set up the JSP Standard Tag Library (JSTL). The rental Web application's JavaServer Pages (JSPs) use the core tags of the JSTL. The reference implementation of the JSTL is a product of the Jakarta group at Apache. The build in this chapter was developed using JSTL 1.0.1. Any 1.x version should work, although you want to make sure that the distribution that you download has the *standard-doc* and *standard-examples* WAR files. If you do not have the JSTL, go to the following URL:

```
http://jakarta.apache.org/taglibs
```

Follow the links to the JSTL download. Then follow the directions to unzip it. Next, copy the contents of the JSTL *lib* directory to the *shared/lib* directory under your *tomcat-home* directory.

Copy the *standard-doc* and *standard-examples* WAR files from the JSTL distribution to the *web-apps* subdirectory under the *tomcat-home* directory. Restart Tomcat, and go to the following URL:

```
http://localhost:8080/standard-doc
```

You should see the welcome page for the JSTL.

Estimated time for this step, excluding download: 15 minutes

Step Ten: Configure Build Environment

In this step, you configure the build environment for building the rental Web application and deploying it to Tomcat. Edit the *default.properties* file in the *bookants* directory under your *bookcode-home* directory. Set the *tomcat.home* property to point to your *tomcat-home* directory.

If you are using a version of JSTL later than 1.0.1, copy the *c.tld* file found in the JSTL distribution to the *com/ysoft/jdo/book/rental/servlet/misc* directory under your *bookcode-home* directory.

Copy the *jdo.dtd* file found in the *bookcode-home* directory to the *bin* directory under the *tomcat-home* directory.

Estimated time for this step: 5 minutes

At this point, you are ready to build the rental Web application.

Building the Rental Web Application

To build the rental Web application, go to the *bookants* directory under your *bookcode-home* directory. Build the *clean-out* target first by executing the following command:

```
ant clean-out
```

Assuming that you have successfully built some of the examples from Chapters 8 and 9, you will see output that looks like the output in Listing 10-1.

Listing 10-1. Expected Output from Building the clean-out Target

```
E:\Bookcode\bookants>ant clean-out
Buildfile: build.xml
are-we-ready:
verify:
clean-out:
     [echo] Deleting files in build, enhanced, and warfiles
   [delete] Deleting 66 files from E:\Bookcode\build
   [delete] Deleted 13 directories from E:\Bookcode\build
   [delete] Deleting 8 files from E:\Bookcode\enhanced
   [delete] Deleted 8 directories from E:\Bookcode\enhanced
BUILD SUCCESSFUL
Total time: 1 second
```

By cleaning out the old compiled files, you remove the compiled versions of the Rental, Week, Customer, and Lighthouse classes that were built for the rental Swing application. Although the rental Swing application can use the version of these classes built by the rental Web application, the opposite is not true. Some of the application data classes for the rental Web application support string identities and a versioning scheme, while the versions used by the rental Swing application do not. Both versions have the same persistent fields and therefore the same database schema.

Next, build the rental Web application by running its build target. Execute the following command:

```
ant rental-servlet-opr
```

You should see output that looks like the output shown in Listing 10-2. Building this target will shut down Tomcat if it is running. You must restart Tomcat to use the rental Web application.

Listing 10-2. Expected Output from Building the rental-servlet-opr Target

```
E:\Bookcode\bookants>ant rental-servlet-opr
Buildfile: build.xml
are-we-ready:
...
copy-files:
     [copy] Copying 6 files to E:\Bookcode\warfiles\WEB-INF\lib
    [mkdir] Created dir: E:\Bookcode\warfiles\images
     [copy] Copying 3 files to E:\Bookcode\warfiles\images
   [delete] Deleting 53 files from E:\tomcat4.1.12\webapps\rental
   [delete] Deleted 18 directories from E:\tomcat4.1.12\webapps\rental
     [copy] Copying 53 files to E:\tomcat4.1.12\webapps\rental
     [echo] You'll have to restart Tomcat

BUILD SUCCESSFUL
Total time: 43 seconds
```

The rental Web application satisfies all of the use cases described in Chapter 9 that define the rental application's requirements, except that it does not satisfy the first two use cases that describe the initialization and clearing of the datastore.

Although a Web application could initialize a database, in practice, this is rarely done. Since the rental Web application uses the same data schema as the rental Swing application, you can use the Swing application to initialize the database.

If the rental data has not been initialized, you will need to build the *rental-gui* target and use the rental Swing application to initialize the rental data. To do this, execute the following build command:

```
ant rental-gui
```

Then change to the *bookcode-home* directory and execute the batch file *runRentalGui.bat*. If you are not using Microsoft Windows, you will need to alter the batch file for your operating system. The code is open source. If you feel inspired to contribute modified build scripts for other operating systems, they will be most welcomed at http://sourceforge.net/projects/jdo-tools. When the rental Swing application comes up, select the menu item *Connect to datastore* from the *Connect* menu. Then select the menu item *Populate database* from the *File* menu. Finally, to see the results, select the *Available* menu item from the *View* menu. For more details, see Chapter 9.

If you are using the JDO reference implementation, and this is your first time using the JDO Learning Tools, you will have to follow the directions in Chapter 8 to properly initialize the reference implementation's datastore. Also with the reference implementation, after you initialize the datastore and initialize the test data for the rental applications, you need to copy the two *FOStoreTestDB* files found in the *bookcode-home* directory to the *bin* subdirectory under your *tomcat-home* directory.

Using the Rental Web Application

After building the rental Web application and starting Tomcat, you are ready to use the application. Using a Web browser, go to the following URL:

```
http://localhost:8080/rental/controller
```

This will bring up a Web page that looks something like the one in Figure 10-1. Notice the table, which has a row for each week that rentals are available and a column for each lighthouse that can be rented.

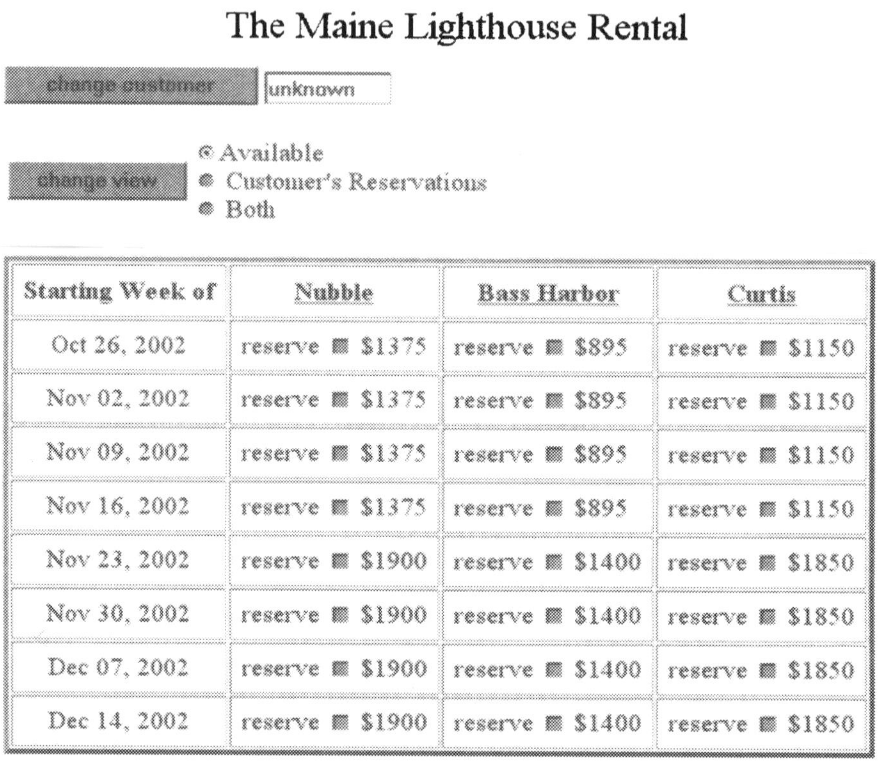

The Maine Lighthouse Rental

Starting Week of	Nubble	Bass Harbor	Curtis
Oct 26, 2002	reserve ■ $1375	reserve ■ $895	reserve ■ $1150
Nov 02, 2002	reserve ■ $1375	reserve ■ $895	reserve ■ $1150
Nov 09, 2002	reserve ■ $1375	reserve ■ $895	reserve ■ $1150
Nov 16, 2002	reserve ■ $1375	reserve ■ $895	reserve ■ $1150
Nov 23, 2002	reserve ■ $1900	reserve ■ $1400	reserve ■ $1850
Nov 30, 2002	reserve ■ $1900	reserve ■ $1400	reserve ■ $1850
Dec 07, 2002	reserve ■ $1900	reserve ■ $1400	reserve ■ $1850
Dec 14, 2002	reserve ■ $1900	reserve ■ $1400	reserve ■ $1850

Figure 10-1. The rental Web page when the customer is unknown

When you first visit the site, the application does not know who you are. To follow along with the tests described here, enter the customer name "Jim," and click the *change customer* button. This action redisplays the page, which now looks something like the page shown in Figure 10-2. The available rentals now have enabled check boxes. (Some browsers do not permit the check box to be disabled, so you may have seen enabled check boxes earlier.) In addition, there is now a button for submitting reservation changes.

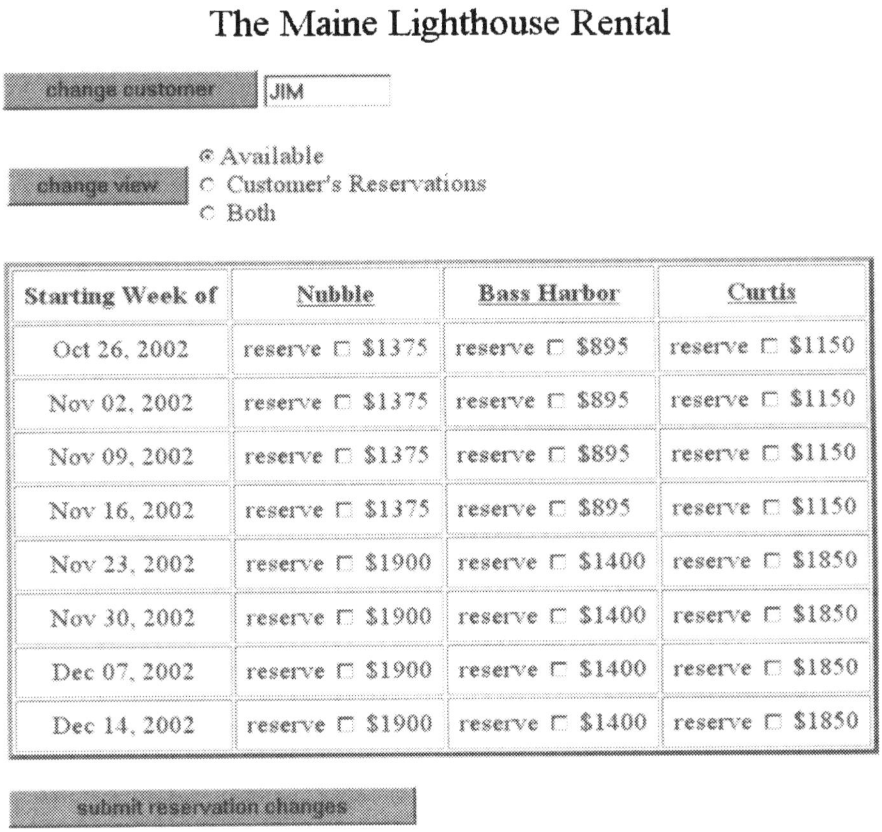

The Maine Lighthouse Rental

| change customer | JIM |

change view   ⊙ Available
    ○ Customer's Reservations
    ○ Both

Starting Week of	Nubble	Bass Harbor	Curtis
Oct 26, 2002	reserve □ $1375	reserve □ $895	reserve □ $1150
Nov 02, 2002	reserve □ $1375	reserve □ $895	reserve □ $1150
Nov 09, 2002	reserve □ $1375	reserve □ $895	reserve □ $1150
Nov 16, 2002	reserve □ $1375	reserve □ $895	reserve □ $1150
Nov 23, 2002	reserve □ $1900	reserve □ $1400	reserve □ $1850
Nov 30, 2002	reserve □ $1900	reserve □ $1400	reserve □ $1850
Dec 07, 2002	reserve □ $1900	reserve □ $1400	reserve □ $1850
Dec 14, 2002	reserve □ $1900	reserve □ $1400	reserve □ $1850

| submit reservation changes |

Figure 10-2. The rental Web page when the customer is Jim

Reserve the Nubble lighthouse for Jim by checking the box for the first week and clicking the *submit reservation changes* button. This will display a page showing Jim's reservations. Using another browser, identify the customer as Mary, and reserve for Mary the Nubble lighthouse in the second week.

Starting Up Two Browser Clients

By using a different browser (as opposed to another window in the same browser), you ensure that the Web application sees two clients rather than one. If you do not have another browser to use, you will have to experiment to see whether two windows in your browser are treated by the servlet container as one client or two clients. One way to perform this experiment is to use the test JSP for the session lock that is automatically created by the *rental-servlet-opr* build target. In each of the browser windows, go to the following URL:

```
http://localhost:8080/rental/SessionLock.jsp
```

If the servlet session that the browser window is using is new, you will see in the browser window text that looks like the following:

```
This session is new.
This session was last accessed 0.0 seconds ago.
This lock has been called 1 times.
```

Otherwise, you will see output that looks something like the following:

```
This session is not new.
This session was last accessed 54.489 seconds ago.
This lock has been called 3 times.
```

Encountering Conflicting Reservations in the Rental Web Client

After bringing up two browser windows that are using distinct servlet sessions, follow these steps to see an optimistic lock conflict and its resolution. In the browser that Jim is using, change the view to *Both*. Do the same for Mary. At this point, you should see Web pages that look like the Web pages in Figures 10-3 and 10-4. In Figure 10-3, Jim sees one reservation made in his name, and one rental period that is not available because Mary has it. In Figure 10-4, Mary sees one reservation made in her name, and one rental period that is not available because Jim has it.

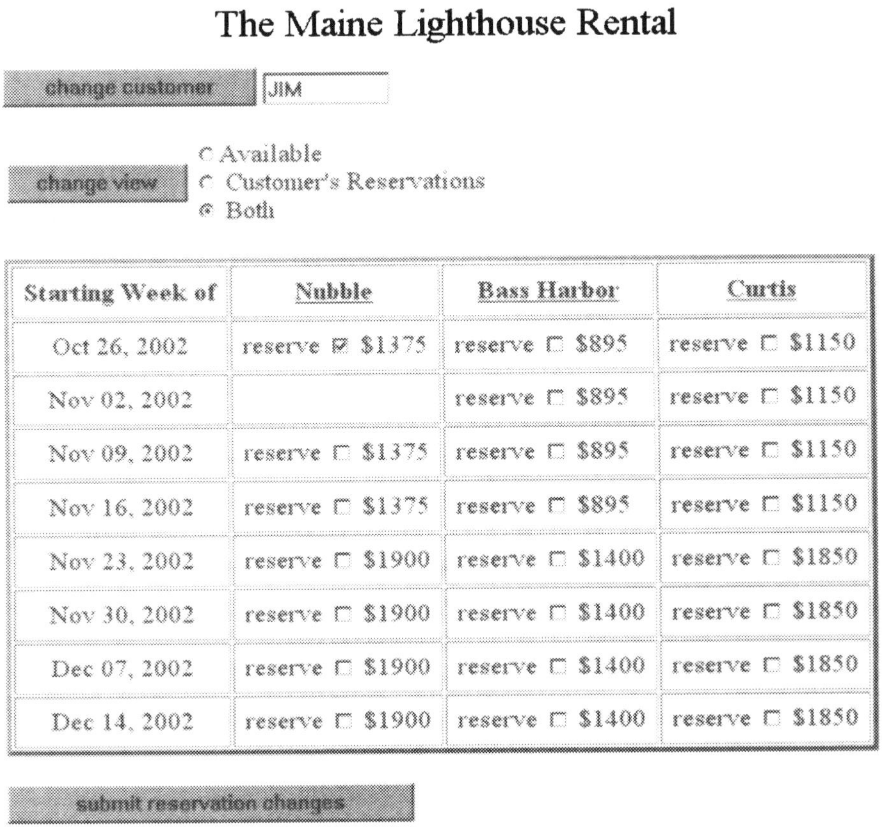

The Maine Lighthouse Rental

| change customer | JIM |

change view
- Available
- Customer's Reservations
- ● Both

Starting Week of	Nubble	Bass Harbor	Curtis
Oct 26, 2002	reserve ☑ $1375	reserve ☐ $895	reserve ☐ $1150
Nov 02, 2002		reserve ☐ $895	reserve ☐ $1150
Nov 09, 2002	reserve ☐ $1375	reserve ☐ $895	reserve ☐ $1150
Nov 16, 2002	reserve ☐ $1375	reserve ☐ $895	reserve ☐ $1150
Nov 23, 2002	reserve ☐ $1900	reserve ☐ $1400	reserve ☐ $1850
Nov 30, 2002	reserve ☐ $1900	reserve ☐ $1400	reserve ☐ $1850
Dec 07, 2002	reserve ☐ $1900	reserve ☐ $1400	reserve ☐ $1850
Dec 14, 2002	reserve ☐ $1900	reserve ☐ $1400	reserve ☐ $1850

submit reservation changes

Figure 10-3. Page showing Jim about to cancel one reservation and make another

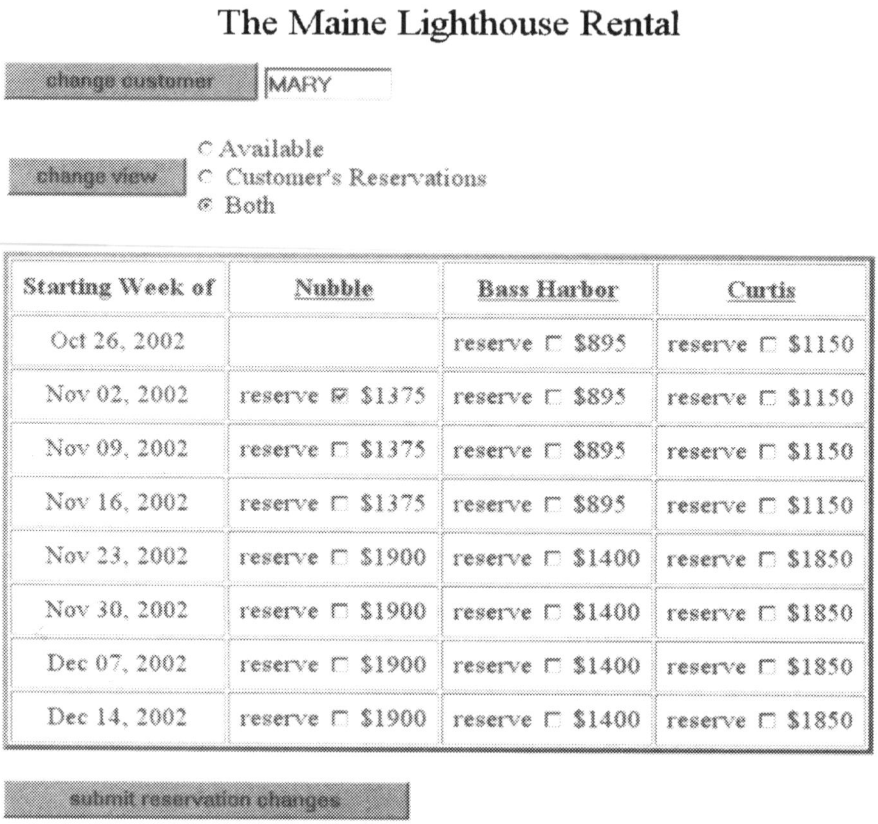

The Maine Lighthouse Rental

Starting Week of	Nubble	Bass Harbor	Curtis
Oct 26, 2002		reserve ☐ $895	reserve ☐ $1150
Nov 02, 2002	reserve ☑ $1375	reserve ☐ $895	reserve ☐ $1150
Nov 09, 2002	reserve ☐ $1375	reserve ☐ $895	reserve ☐ $1150
Nov 16, 2002	reserve ☐ $1375	reserve ☐ $895	reserve ☐ $1150
Nov 23, 2002	reserve ☐ $1900	reserve ☐ $1400	reserve ☐ $1850
Nov 30, 2002	reserve ☐ $1900	reserve ☐ $1400	reserve ☐ $1850
Dec 07, 2002	reserve ☐ $1900	reserve ☐ $1400	reserve ☐ $1850
Dec 14, 2002	reserve ☐ $1900	reserve ☐ $1400	reserve ☐ $1850

Figure 10-4. Page showing Mary about to cancel one reservation and make another

To observe the optimistic concurrency check in action, perform the following test. Take care to perform the steps in the order indicated; otherwise, you might accidentally refresh the view before you request the update. In Jim's browser, cancel his reservation and reserve the third week for Nubble. Click the *submit reservation changes* button. As a result, Jim has cancelled his reservation for the first week and made a reservation for the third week. Now go to Mary's browser. Cancel her reservation for the second week and reserve the third week for Nubble. After clicking the *submit reservation changes* button, Mary's browser will display the error message shown in Figure 10-5. The error arises when the ReservationServlet detects that the version of the Rental object for Nubble in the third week that Mary looked at in her view request is older than the version that the ReservationServlet was about to change in her update request.

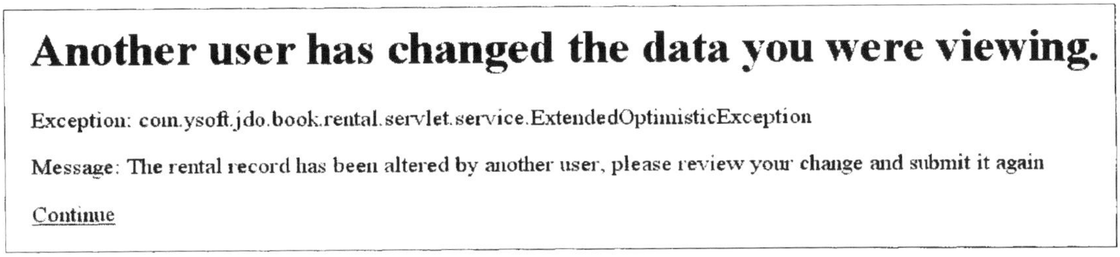

Another user has changed the data you were viewing.

Exception: com.ysoft.jdo.book.rental.servlet.service.ExtendedOptimisticException

Message: The rental record has been altered by another user, please review your change and submit it again

Continue

Figure 10-5. Page showing an error after Mary attempted to reserve Nubble for the third week

After clicking the *continue* button, Mary sees the reservation page that looks something like the page shown in Figure 10-6. Note that her reservation in the second week is not cancelled and that she now sees that the first week for Nubble is available and the third week is not available. In other words, her transaction was rolled back and her view was refreshed.

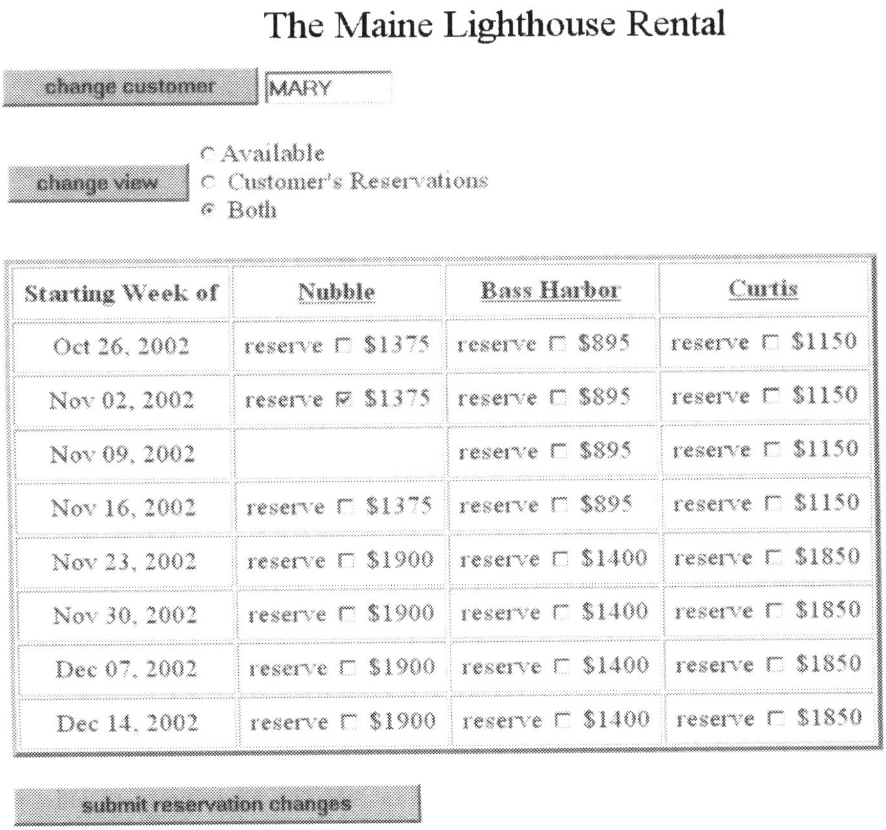

The Maine Lighthouse Rental

change customer   MARY

change view
- ○ Available
- ○ Customer's Reservations
- ◉ Both

Starting Week of	Nubble	Bass Harbor	Curtis
Oct 26, 2002	reserve ☐ $1375	reserve ☐ $895	reserve ☐ $1150
Nov 02, 2002	reserve ☑ $1375	reserve ☐ $895	reserve ☐ $1150
Nov 09, 2002		reserve ☐ $895	reserve ☐ $1150
Nov 16, 2002	reserve ☐ $1375	reserve ☐ $895	reserve ☐ $1150
Nov 23, 2002	reserve ☐ $1900	reserve ☐ $1400	reserve ☐ $1850
Nov 30, 2002	reserve ☐ $1900	reserve ☐ $1400	reserve ☐ $1850
Dec 07, 2002	reserve ☐ $1900	reserve ☐ $1400	reserve ☐ $1850
Dec 14, 2002	reserve ☐ $1900	reserve ☐ $1400	reserve ☐ $1850

submit reservation changes

Figure 10-6. Mary's Web page after recovering from the error

General Design Issues for Web Applications

Web servers and servlets are by their nature multithreaded. As a result, a single servlet object normally has multiple response threads running in it at any point in time. A simple but important consequence is the prohibition on putting request or response information into the instance fields of the servlet. In general, servlets use their instance fields very lightly or not at all. If the servlet class defines an instance field, the programmer must realize that the instance field is shared among multiple response threads and that access to it must be protected by the synchronized keyword. An alternative is to use servlets that implement the javax.servlet.SingleThreadModel marker interface, but this alternative is not recommended for performance reasons.

Even though Web applications normally avoid using the member fields in a servlet instance, Web applications have two easy ways to communicate between the multiple methods or components that are processing a single request. Both of these methods avoid sharing objects between response threads. First, the methods within a servlet can use parameters and return values to communicate. Second, two components, such as a servlet and a JSP, can communicate by using the getAttribute and setAttribute methods in the javax.servlet.ServletRequest object.

Although most Web application programmers understand the multithreaded nature of servlets and how to deal with it, the HTTP protocol raises some design issues that are not widely understood. First, the Web application may need to respond to multiple concurrent requests from the same client. If a page takes more than a few seconds to render, there is a fair chance that the user will click again, causing the same request to be made by his browser. As a result, a servlet may be responding to multiple, redundant requests from the same client. If the Web application uses the javax.servlet.http.HttpSession object, which is shared among all of the response threads serving a single client, then there must be synchronization to make the Web application's code thread-safe for the objects stored in the session. Second, the user may inadvertently make multiple requests when all he wants is a single action. If the user is checking out a shopping cart of merchandise, the chances are very high that he does not want to purchase the contents twice even if he clicks twice on the *Proceed* button. As a result, at least some of the actions taken by the servlet must be *idempotent*, a Latin word meaning that the response to a request occurs only once, even when there are two or more redundant requests. Third, the browser allows the user to make requests in any order. The browser's *Forward*, *Back*, and *Bookmark* buttons allow the user to jump around in the request logic in ways that can be nonsensical.

Although it is incidental to the purpose of this book, the rental Web application has code to handle these design issues. The SessionLock class is the primary tool to address the thread-safety and idempotency issues. The SessionLock class, which is found in the com.ysoft.jdo.book.rental.servlet.util package, queues up multiple requests from one client. Although the control servlet eventually responds to all of the client's requests, it responds to them one at a time. At the same time, the SessionLock class allows multiple requests from different clients to proceed concurrently. The servlet collaborates with the SessionLock class to skip redundant actions while always displaying redundant results. Because the Web application has no way to know which response the browser will display when the user makes redundant requests, the Web application must give the same response to all redundant requests.

The rental Web application responds appropriately to client requests that are out-of-sync with the client's known state. Before responding to the client's request, the rental Web application examines the client's state to determine whether the requested action can be performed. If not, it performs a reasonable action that the client's state allows. Issuing an error report is always a possibility when the client's request cannot be satisfied, but in the case of the rental application, displaying the available rentals is usually preferable.

The MVC Pattern in the Rental Web Application

The rental Web application's design uses the Model-View-Controller (MVC) design pattern as shown in Figure 10-7. The Web server and servlet container respond to requests that come from the user's Web browser. The requests are either for static content or dynamic content. Those requests that require a dynamic response are directed to the controller, which in this example is the ReservationServlet. The controller accesses the ReservationService to obtain the required persistent objects. These objects are stored in the ReservationModel. The ReservationModel is a container that holds the persistent objects and provides convenience features for the view. JavaServer Pages (JSPs) provide various views of the model. Each JSP generates HTML using the contents of the ReservationModel.

In the designs examined in this chapter, the view works with live, that is to say managed, application data objects. Although this is not strictly required, this approach provides maximum flexibility to the developers of the view, since JDO will transparently navigate the persistent object model to find any persistent information desired. After the JSP has generated the HTML, execution returns to the controller servlet, which can then decide what to do with the model.

As discussed in Chapter 9, when using live application data objects, JDO exceptions that reflect operational conditions can be thrown at any time, since they are unchecked exceptions. To handle the possible error conditions, every

JSP that generates a view using persistent objects should reference an exception handling page in the JSP page directive. In the exception handling page, the exception can then be handled as desired. Something will have to be displayed to the user, and any logging that needs to occur can be done.

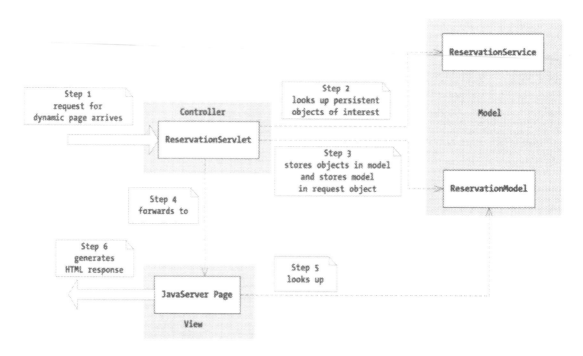

Figure 10-7. The MVC pattern in the rental Web application

Although Figure 10-7 shows the general idea of the Web application that uses JDO, there are some important design issues that arise from the managed nature of persistent objects. The Web application designer must decide how the service that uses JDO relates to the request. Is it a new service for each request or a service that is shared among many requests? If shared, is it shared only among the requests coming from one user or among requests coming from many users? Depending on how the service is used, various management strategies are required for the application data objects.

Designing the Use of JDO in a Web Application

Deciding when to close the persistence manager is the central design issue for using JDO in a Web application. There are at least three possible designs, which in this book are called the *one-pm-per-request*, *one-pm-per-session*, and *one-pm-per-update* designs. In the one-pm-per-request design, the controller opens a persistence manager for each request and closes it after the response is generated. This is the recommended design.

Before discussing the one-pm-per-session design, let's briefly examine the concept of sessions within Java servlets. Servlet containers provide HttpSession objects that are associated with the requests of clients who have recently used the Web application. The controller servlet and the JSPs that generate the response for the request can store objects of interest in the session object, where they can be retrieved on subsequent requests from the same client. In the one-pm-per-session design, the persistence manager is stored in the session object. It is reused whenever a request from the same client is received. In the one-pm-per-session design, the persistence manager is closed when the session invalidates or times out. The section "The One-PM-per-Session Design" later in this chapter examines this design in greater detail.

In the one-pm-per-update design, the controller uses a shared read-only persistence manager for read-only requests and obtains a new persistence manager for each write request. The read-only persistence manager is shared by all of the requests handled by the controller servlet instance. In this design, each update request opens and closes its own persistence manager, but determining when to close the shared read-only persistence manager is complicated. The section "The One-PM-per-Update Design" later in this chapter examines this design in greater detail.

Each design has different implications for the management of the application data objects. When the persistence manager is closed, the application data objects must be either dropped or made transient. As you may recall from Chapter 3, JDO does not define the behavior of managed data objects after their persistence manager is closed.

The Role of Session Serialization in the Servlet Container

The servlet container imposes constraints on the management of application data objects that are stored in the session. The session object and all of the objects stored within it can be serialized between requests. This may happen for a variety of reasons. When the servlet container is shut down, the container may serialize the sessions. When the servlet container comes back up, the previously active sessions are restored. If the servlet container is part of a cluster, then the various containers may pass, by serialization or a similar mechanism, sessions between them to achieve load balancing. Finally, if the servlet container is operating under load, it may serialize some of its sessions to conserve memory. As you know by now, acquiring an application data object through deserialization results in objects that are unmanaged by JDO.

At the same time, any reference to the persistence manager that is stored in the session must be released, since JDO does not require the persistence manager to be serializable. Since the servlet container serializes the session for a good reason, closing the persistence manager is generally a good idea when the session is serialized.

Design Goals

In evaluating the advantages and disadvantages of each of these three designs, there are five design goals that are desirable.

- Good performance

- Storage for conversational state

- Transactional consistency

- Simplicity of code and design

- Scalability

Good performance is essential. The load on a Web application tends to grow steadily and spike sharply. Web applications must work with varying amounts of network latency. The user's tolerance tends to be low, usually not more than a few seconds for a page to render. As a result, performance is frequently an issue for Web applications.

When using JDO, caching of persistent state is critical for best performance. If the persistent state can be read from memory rather than from the datastore, time is saved by orders of magnitude. In the case of Web applications, the best performance gain is likely when caching occurs across requests and across clients.

A second factor of much less importance for performance is the amount of garbage generated. When objects in memory become unreferenced because they are no longer used by the application, they become garbage. As garbage, the objects continue to take up memory. The JVM's garbage collector finds the unused objects and returns the memory that they use to the heap, where it can be reused for the construction of new objects. In long-running server applications, the JVM collects virtually all of the garbage generated. If the application continually constructs lots of new objects, then the garbage collector stays busy using valuable CPU resources.

Although HTTP is a stateless protocol, the semantics of HTML often require the use of conversational state. When processing requests to update persistent information, the controller usually needs to know the identity strings of the objects to change. Likewise, it often needs to know the version of the objects when they were viewed. The need for conversational state arises in other ways as well. For example, when a form that contains check boxes is sent to the Web server, the request sends name-value pairs only for the check boxes that are turned on. If the browser received a turned-on check box that the user then turned off, the browser does not send the name-value pair for that check box when the user submits the form. As a result, the only way for the servlet controller to determine that the user turned off a check box is to know that his request did not return a name-value pair for the turned on check box that he received. To make this determination, the servlet controller uses conversational state.

The Java servlet responding to the request can store and find objects in the HttpSession object, using its getAttribute and setAttribute methods. By using the session object, the controller can store in server-side memory the conversational state of each active client. This state can be used when servicing subsequent requests from the same client. This is the way many Web applications store conversational state.

There are good alternatives to storing conversational state in the session object. The conversational state can also be kept in HTML. For example, the identity string of a persistent object can be encoded as a name, ID, or value within the HTML control that represents it. Likewise, the fact that a check box is turned on when sent to the user can be encoded within a hidden control in the form. As another alternative, the controller can also store the conversational state in persistent storage. With this approach, the request sends a key, which may be in a cookie or elsewhere, that the controller then uses to look up the client's conversational state.

A Web application's need for transactions can vary widely. Some applications may not need transactions because they do not perform updates. Some applications may need to store new persistent information but may not need to modify existing information. When the Web application does modify existing information, it may or may not need to verify that the version of the information that the client viewed is no older than the version of the information that the controller modifies. Finally, a Web application may use a transaction for each update request that it receives, or in a wizard-like fashion, it may handle as one transaction a series of update requests received from one client.

Web applications are often built quickly, modified frequently, and stressed considerably. All of these factors argue for simplicity. In addition, simple designs avoid the subtle flaws that can elude the inexperienced and trip up the expert.

Scalability is related to performance in that both address the issue of serving clients in a satisfactory manner. It differs from performance in that its primary concern is the potential degradation of performance due to an increase in the number of clients and the ability to remedy this degradation by adding more hardware to the system. A design that uses fewer resources, such as less memory, less network bandwidth, or less CPU time, is more scalable than a design that uses more of these resources. A design that supports the expansion of these resources, such as clustering of servlet containers, is also more scalable than one that does not.

Although the issues of performance, conversational state, transactions, simplicity, and scalability are discussed in the context of using JDO in a Web application, these issues did not originate with the use of JDO. They are present for any Web application regardless of the persistence mechanisms used. Although the issues are not new, they are relevant when determining how to best use JDO in a Web application.

Avoiding the Cost of Garbage Collection

It is a common practice to construct an object when needed, use it, and then drop it. After the object is dropped, the application code no longer refers to the object, and it becomes garbage. This is an appropriate practice for most coding needs. There are only two ways to avoid this create-and-drop cycle.

The first way recycles the objects. When recycling, the application gets the object from a factory that first looks into a pool of such objects and returns one of them if it has it. Otherwise, the factory creates the object. When the application is finished using the object, instead of dropping it, the application returns the object to the factory, which may put the object into its pool of such objects. In the early versions of the JVM, recycling objects was a good optimization when a class of objects was heavily used in a create-and-drop cycle. In the current versions of the JVM, the garbage collectors and object construction code have become quite efficient. Depending on a variety of factors including the size of the objects, recycling may now be less efficient than the create-and-drop cycle. For that reason, recycling of objects is no longer a design issue, but an optimization issue that should be driven by metrics.

The second way to avoid the create-and-drop cycle is to continue to use the same object without dropping it or recycling it. This practice avoids both the recycling code and the object creation and garbage collection code, but its usefulness is limited. In general, the code path from needing the object to finding it must be short. Otherwise, it may be cheaper to create the object and drop it after its immediate usefulness ends.

In short, the best advice is this: if it makes sense to continue to use the same object, then do it. But if the code must jump through hoops to make continued use possible, then regard continued use as a potential optimization rather than a design constraint. Avoid using object recycling unless you have metrics that can demonstrate its value.

The One-PM-per-Request Design

The one-pm-per-request design obtains a persistence manager at the beginning of each request and closes it after returning the response. This design appears to gain little from caching because the persistence manager's cache is open for business for only one request. In this case, appearances can be misleading. A sophisticated JDO implementation will implement a level-two cache below the caching specified by JDO. The level-two cache underlies all of the persistence managers that the implementation's factories produce. As a result, even a newly opened persistence manager can benefit from the cached state accumulated from earlier reads of the datastore. For the sophisticated JDO implementation, very large caching benefits can be obtained because of the level-two cache. Implementations may also pool persistence managers and datastore connections to gain a performance benefit. As a result, the one-pm-per-request design cannot be ruled out simply on the basis of an assumed lack of caching.

In general, to gain the benefit of a level-two cache when updating, the application must use an optimistic transaction. For read-only access to persistent objects, turning on the *NontransactionalRead* property works equally well. On the other hand, the use of a datastore transaction implies that the state of the object in memory is synchronized with the state in the datastore. Normally, the synchronization is guaranteed by loading the state from the datastore. As a result, using a datastore transaction is likely to void the performance benefit expected from the level-two cache.

In the one-pm-per-request design, the controller servlet closes the persistence manager after the response is generated. As a result, the application must either stop using the persistent data objects or make them unmanaged before closing the persistence manager. If the application drops the persistent objects, it will be up to the JDO implementation whether to reuse the application data objects or allow them to be garbage collected. On the other hand, dropping the objects is not an option when the controller stores these objects in the session as part of the conversational state. In this case, the controller should make the objects unmanaged. The rental Web application saves conversational state for its clients by storing unmanaged application data objects in the HttpSession object associated with the request.

NOTE   To make a persistent application data object unmanaged, the application calls the makeTransient method in the PersistenceManager interface. See Chapter 3 for details.

After the object becomes unmanaged, its usefulness is limited to one or a few more requests, after which it will be replaced with a newer unmanaged object. In short, closing a persistence manager is likely to turn the persistent objects into garbage either immediately or within a short time. Since a persistence manager is opened and closed on each request in the one-pm-per-request design, every request generates new garbage. As mentioned earlier, current versions of the JVM are optimized for garbage collection, and for that reason, the cost of garbage generation is often an acceptable price for the design's benefits.

Since the persistence manager is closed after every request in the one-pm-per-request design, JDO cannot provide a transactional context that spans requests. As a result, if transactional consistency is required across requests, the application designer must roll his own versioning scheme that can support an application-defined optimistic transaction that spans requests. The SupportsVersion interface, found in the com.ysoft.jdo.book.rental.service package, and its implementation in the Rental class used by the rental Web application shows one way to provide a user-defined optimistic concurrency check.

In order to handle updates, to verify the version, or to accommodate the semantics of HTML, the one-pm-per-request design requires that transient application data objects or information about them be stored in the conversational state. In order to know what objects the client is updating, the identity strings of the persistent objects served must be saved. Likewise, in order to verify the version, the version number obtainable from the SupportsVersion interface must be saved. Finally, as mentioned earlier, the semantics of HTML may require, as it does in the rental Web application, that the served state be stored in order to process subsequent requests.

A strength of the one-pm-per-request design is simplicity; however, this simplicity can be lost when persistent objects are stored in the session. If application data objects are stored in the session, then prior to closing the persistence manager, the controller must make them unmanaged. In doing so, the designer must decide how far to follow the chain of persistent references. Care must be taken to avoid accidentally storing a persistent object in the session whose persistence manager has been closed.

The one-pm-per-request design is very scalable because there are a variety of ways that conversational state can be stored. The designer has the choice of using HTML, the session object, or persistent storage. Each choice supports the clustering of servlet containers.

Reviewing the Code of the One-PM-per-Request Example

The Maine Lighthouse Rental Web application is found in the subdirectories under the *com/ysoft/jdo/book/rental/servlet* directory. The *opr* subdirectory contains the application's controller `ReservationServlet`. The *util* subdirectory contains the `ReservationModel` and `SessionLock` classes. The *service* subdirectory contains the `ReservationService`.

The `ReservationService` configures the properties of the `PersistenceManagerFactory` in the same way for all requests. It turns on the *NontransactionalRead*, *Optimistic*, and *RetainValues* properties. It turns off the *RestoreValues*, *NontransactionalWrite*, *Multithreaded*, and *IgnoreCache* properties.

NontransactionalRead is turned on because the controller starts a transaction only when the client wants to make or cancel a reservation. The controller does not start a transaction to read persistent state.

The controller uses a JDO transaction when processing an update request. The transactional consistency that spans the view request and the update request is provided by the controller's use of the application-defined `SupportsVersion` interface. Optimistic JDO transactions are used instead of datastore JDO transactions to make the best use of a level-two cache if it is present.

RetainValues is turned on to prevent unnecessary eviction of persistent state after the transaction's commit. The eviction is not needed since the persistence manager itself will be closed as soon as the response is generated.

Walking Through the Logic That Generates a Response

When a request for dynamic content is received by the servlet container, the container calls the servlet's `doGet` or `doPost` method. In the `ReservationServlet`, the `doGet` and `doPost` methods call a common `respond` method in which all of the response logic is handled.

Obtain a ReservationService and the SessionLock

The `respond` method begins by constructing a new `ReservationService`, as shown in the next lines of code:

```
// get the data service for this request
service = new ReservationService();
```

In the `ReservationService` constructor, the code acquires a persistence manager factory from the `getPersistenceManagerFactory` method in `JDOHelper`. After getting the factory, the constructor opens a persistence manager in the usual way. Thereafter, the reservation service uses its persistence manager whenever it needs to access JDO.

After obtaining the service, the controller next obtains the session lock using the following lines of code:

```
lock = SessionLock.getInstance(request);
int action = lock.lock(NO_ACTION, 20); // lock expires in 20 seconds
```

The SessionLock class ensures that requests from the same client are queued, but it allows requests from different clients to proceed concurrently. The session lock avoids multithreaded access to a session object or to any objects stored within the session object after the lock is obtained.

The session lock also identifies the concurrent requests from the same client as redundant requests. In these cases, instead of performing the action again and repopulating the model with persistent objects, the control servlet simply regenerates the page using the existing model stored in the session. This allows the controller logic to make any request idempotent during the time that it takes to perform the action and generate the response. Session locks are implemented as leases that expire after a short period of time. The expiration prevents an unresponsive thread from locking up a session indefinitely.

Find or Create the ReservationModel

After getting the service and the lock, the controller next calls the getInstance method of the ModelHandle class to find or create a handle. From the handle, the controller then obtains the model, as shown in the next line of code:

```
ReservationModel model = ModelHandle.getInstance(request).getModel();
```

The handle wraps the model and provides some convenience and debugging features. (The ModelHandle class is found in the ReservationServlet source file.) The handle's getInstance method either creates a new handle in the client's session or finds the existing handle in the client's session. The getInstance method also stores the model in the HttpServletRequest object where the JSP that generates the view finds it.

Perform the Action and Populate the Model

After obtaining the model, the respond method determines the action to perform. If the lock method of SessionLock returned NO_ACTION, then the method has determined that there are no other current requests from the client. In this case, the controller calls its getAction method, which examines request parameters and the model to determine the action to be performed, as shown in the next lines of code:

```
if (action == NO_ACTION)
  {
  action = getAction(request, model);
  lock.setAction(action);
  }
```

After determining the action, the controller informs the session lock of the action. In this way, the session lock can identify any subsequent concurrent requests from the same client as redundant. As a result, the controller handles the redundant requests in an idempotent way.

At this point, the respond method performs the action indicated by the selected action code. In the example, the controller has a private method for each action. For a more complex application, it would be better to have a separate class for each action.

Generate the Page View

After the controller uses the reservation service to populate the ReservationModel with persistent objects, it forwards the request to the JSP display page. The JSP then uses the model to generate the HTML. Listing 10-3 shows the JSP code that generates the rows of available rentals. The JSP code iterates over the rows contained in the model. For each row, the JSP begins by putting the starting date of the week in the first column. It then iterates over the nodes of the model, generating in subsequent columns either a blank or a check box with a price. The XML tags shown in Listing 10-3 that begin with the "c:" are the core tags from the JSTL.

Listing 10-3. Excerpt from maine.jsp Where the Rental Table Rows Are Generated

```
<c:forEach var="row" items="${model.modelRows}" >
   <tr>
     <td align="center">
        <c:out value="${row.weekString}"/>
     </td>
     <c:forEach var="node" items="${row.nodes}" >
        <td><div align="left">
          <c:choose>
            <c:when test="${node.modifiable}" >
              reserve
              <input name=
                  "<%=ReservationServletConstants.RESERVATION_PARAM%>"
              type="CHECKBOX"
              value="<c:out value="${node.id}"/>"
              <c:if test="${not node.available}">CHECKED</c:if>
```

```
                    <c:if test="${not model.customerKnown}">DISABLED</c:if>  >
                    <c:out value="${node.priceString}" />
                </c:when>
                <c:otherwise> </c:otherwise>
            </c:choose>
        </div></td>
    </c:forEach>
  </tr>
</c:forEach>
```

When used by the JSP, the ReservationModel usually contains live, that is to say managed, application data objects. In the example, these live application data objects are used indirectly when the JSP accesses the model. The persistence manager contained within the ReservationService is still open and providing transparent persistence to the live objects. As a result, if the model or the JSP is modified to navigate the persistent objects in a different way, the change does not affect the code in the controller or service.

Save Conversational State in the Servlet Session

The rental Web application uses the HttpSession object to store the conversational state. As mentioned earlier, this is not the only choice, nor necessarily the best choice. The rental Web example stores the conversational state in the session because this design is common.

Even though the code favors the session for storing conversational state, some conversational state is stored in the HTML. For example, the check box controls in the JSP *maine.jsp* hold table cell (node) identifiers in the value attribute. During an update request, these cell identifiers are part of the name-value pairs passed in the request to the controller. In turn, the controller passes them to the model to obtain the corresponding Rental objects. The example's model remembers only the state that it acquires from responding to the last request from the client. Any state prior to the last request can be lost. At the same time, browsers normally cache any number of pages and allow the user to jump around in the request logic. As a result, it is possible for the request to be based on a model state that no longer exists.

There are at least two approaches to handle the possible mismatches that can arise between the request and the model's state. The first approach forces the browser to reload every page from the server. In this approach, various HTML pragmas are placed in the generated pages that prevent the browser from caching the page. Forcing a reload on every page will tend to make the Web site unresponsive in the eyes of the typical user. The second approach is to put a step number in each HTML response and keep the current step number in the model. The browser can therefore reuse cached pages as desired. If the step sent in the next request is not the step expected, then at the controller's discretion, the action performed may be different from the action requested. The rental Web example takes this second approach. The controller increments a count each time a page is served to the client. The count's value is placed in the HTML for its return in the next request.

Before closing the service, the controller finds all the application data objects in the model and makes them unmanaged. This step occurs immediately after generating the response, as the following code shows:

```
// forward to display page
forward(forwardTo, request, response);
// make the persistent objects in the model transient
Collection dataObjects = model.getDataObjects();
service.makeTransientAll(dataObjects);
```

Generate the Page View for a Redundant Request

The lock method in the SessionLock class breaks all requests into two groups: the original request and redundant requests. When no request owns the lock, the next request that needs it is an original request. Any subsequent request from the same client that seeks the lock while it is owned is a redundant request. As a result of the original request, the controller performs some action and repopulates the model with persistent objects. It then asks the view to generate the HTML page. After the view generates the page, the persistent objects in the model are made unmanaged.

When the lock method identifies a redundant request, the controller skips the actions it performs for original requests and goes straight to the view. The view for the redundant request executes the same logic to generate the page, but unlike the original request, it uses unmanaged data objects in the model. Since the view is simply retracing the logic that generated the page for the original request, the unmanaged objects have all of the persistent state that the view for the redundant request requires.

Clean Up Before Returning from the respond Method

Before returning, the respond method closes the service and releases the session lock in its finally block, as shown in the following code:

```
finally
  {
  if (service != null)
     service.close();
  if (lock != null)
     lock.unlock();
  }
```

In its close method, the service closes the persistence manager that it was using. When the respond method returns, the request has been handled and a response has been generated.

At this point, the model remains stored in the session object whose life cycle is controlled by the servlet container. If the container serializes the session, the model will be serialized with it. As a result, the ModelHandle class, the ReservationModel class, and all of the classes of objects that can be reached by serializable fields must implement the Serializable interface. During development, it is worthwhile to test session serialization. A debugging and testing servlet can be written whose sole purpose is to serialize the session and then report on any exceptions, as well as the size of the object graph.

Making and Canceling Rental Reservations

When the client makes and/or cancels reservations, the controller determines from the model and the request which reservations need to be toggled. It then gets the corresponding unmanaged Rental objects from the model. As shown in the next line of code, the controller then sends the affected Rental objects to the service to have the corresponding persistent objects changed:

```
service.flipReservations(modifiedRentals, model.getCustomer());
```

Within the ReservationService, the flipReservations method, shown in Listing 10-4, begins by starting a transaction. It then gets the identity string from the unmanaged customer. Both the Customer and Rental class used in the Web example implement the SupportsIdentity interface. This interface, which is examined in the next section, defines one method, getIdentityString. If the unmanaged Customer object has never been persistent, then there will not be a corresponding persistent Customer object. Otherwise, the persistent Customer object is fetched using the identity string.

Listing 10-4. The flipReservations *Method of the* ReservationService

```
public void flipReservations(
    Collection unmanagedRentals,
    Customer unmanagedCustomer) throws
    ExtendedOptimisticException,
    OptimisticReservationException,
    ReservationException
  {
  try
    {
```

```
// start the transaction
tx.begin();

// get the persistent Customer
String oidString = unmanagedCustomer.getIdentityString();

// find the persistent customer record
Customer pCustomer = null;

// if the unmanaged Customer object doesn't have an identity string,
// then we have a new customer
if (oidString == null)
    pCustomer = unmanagedCustomer;
// otherwise, we find the corresponding persistent Customer object
else
    {
    try
        {
        pCustomer = (Customer) pm.getObjectById(pm.newObjectIdInstance(
                Customer.class, oidString), true);
        }
    catch (JDODataStoreException e)
        {
        throw new ExtendedOptimisticException(
                "The system has deleted this customer's record", e);
        }
    }

// get the persistent Rental objects and do the flip
Iterator iter = unmanagedRentals.iterator();
while (iter.hasNext())
    {
    Rental uRental = (Rental) iter.next();

    oidString = uRental.getIdentityString();
    if (oidString == null)
        {
        throw new IllegalStateException(
                "unmanaged Rental object without identity string: " + uRental);
        }
```

```
        Rental pRental = null;
        try
           {
           pRental = (Rental) pm.getObjectById(pm.newObjectIdInstance(
                   Rental.class, oidString), true);
           }
        catch (JDODataStoreException e)
           {
           throw new ExtendedOptimisticException(
                   "The system has deleted the rental record: " +
                   uRental, e);
           }

        // if the persistent versions are not compatible, then throw an error
        if (!pRental.isSameVersion(uRental))
           {
           throw new ExtendedOptimisticException(
                   "The rental record has been altered by another user, " +
                   "please review your change and submit it again");
           }

                if (pRental.getCustomer() == null)
           {
           // make reservation
           pRental.makeReservation(pCustomer);
           }
        else
           {
           // cancel reservation
           pRental.cancelReservation(pCustomer);
           }
        }
    commitTransaction();
    }
finally
   {
   if (tx.isActive())
      tx.rollback();
   }
}
```

After determining the value of pCustomer, the flipReservations method iterates the collection of unmanaged Rental objects. Because each of these must have been persistent, each has an identity string that is used to get the corresponding persistent object.

For each Rental object, the version of the unmanaged object is compared to the version of the managed object to verify that they are the same. This occurs in the isSameVersion method of the Rental object. This method is one of the methods specified by the SupportsVersion interface, whose implementation is examined in the next section. If both objects are not based on the same version, then the code throws an ExtendedOptmisticException. In fact, the error shown in Figure 10-5, which occurred because Mary attempted to reserve a lighthouse that Jim had already reserved, arises at this point in the code.

JDO's optimistic transactional semantics guarantee, at transaction commit, that the version of the Rental object that the code modifies in the update request is the latest version in the datastore. On the other hand, the extended optimistic semantics defined in the SupportsVersion interface guarantees that the version changed in the update request is the version served in the view request.

When the view and update versions are the same, the method makes the change to the reservation status of the Rental object in the usual way. The method finishes by committing the transaction. In its finally block, the method ensures that the transaction is not left active in the event that an exception is raised.

The SupportsIdentityString Interface

In the rental Web application, it is essential that application data objects know their persistent identity. Regardless of where the conversational state is stored, the essential piece of information is always the persistent identity of the objects that the client modifies. By using the persistent identity, the controller servlet finds the persistent objects that the client wishes to modify.

The SupportsIdentityString interface requires the getIdentityString method as its only method. By implementing the SupportsIdentityString interface, the application data class ensures that its objects capture their identity strings. In Listing 10-4, the code calls the getIdentityString method on unmanaged Customer and Rental objects to obtain the identity strings that these objects captured when they were persistent. The code in Listing 10-4 then uses the identity strings to find the corresponding persistent objects.

Listing 10-5 shows the code in the Rental class that implements the SupportsIdentityString interface. The code in the InstanceCallbacks methods helps by providing for the automatic capture of the identity string. See Listing 7-2 and the discussion in the section "Capturing the Identity String" in Chapter 7 for more details.

Listing 10-5. Implementation of the SupportsIdentityString *Interface in the* Rental *Class*

```java
public class Rental implements SupportsIdentityString, InstanceCallbacks, ...
   {
   // other fields are omitted for brevity
   private String OIDString;      // unmanaged field

   // constructors and additional methods omitted for brevity

   // required by the SupportsIdentityString interface
   public String getIdentityString()
      {
      if (OIDString == null)
         {
         Object oid = JDOHelper.getObjectId(this);
         if (oid != null)
            OIDString = oid.toString();
         }
      return OIDString;
      }

   // Using InstanceCallbacks to support the identity string
   public void jdoPreStore()
      {
      getIdentityString();
      }

   public void jdoPreDelete()
      {
      OIDString = null;
      }

   public void jdoPostLoad()
      {
      getIdentityString();
      }

   public void jdoPreClear()
      {
      getIdentityString();
      }
   }
```

In Listing 10-5, the identity string is captured automatically in the callback methods of the InstanceCallbacks interface. The primary load-bearing callback is the jdoPostLoad method. Alternatively, the application can itself ensure that the identity string is captured by calling the getIdentityString method while the object is persistent. For that reason, implementing the InstanceCallbacks interface is optional when implementing the SupportsIdentityString interface.

The SupportsVersion Interface

The SupportsVersion interface extends both the SupportsIdentityString interface and the InstanceCallbacks interface. Both interfaces are essential for the implementation of the SupportsVersion interface. The SupportsVersion interface requires two methods, isSameVersion and getVersion.

Listing 10-6 shows the implementation of the SupportsVersion interface for the Rental class. For clarity, Listing 10-6 does not show the code in Listing 10-5 that implements the SupportsIdentityString interface.

Listing 10-6. Implementation of the SupportsVersion *Interface in the* Rental *Class*

```
public class Rental implements SupportsVersion, ...
   {
   // other managed and unmanaged fields omitted for brevity
   private int         userVersion;

   // constructors and other methods omitted for brevity

   public void jdoPreStore()
      {
      userVersion++;
      // other work in this callback
      }

   // other InstanceCallbacks methods are omitted for brevity.

   public boolean isSameVersion(Object pc)
      {
      boolean retv = false;

      // if two objects have the same persistent identity, then
      // compare their versions
      if (this.equals(pc))
         retv = (userVersion == ((SupportsVersion) pc).getVersion());
```

```
        return retv;
        }

    public int getVersion()
      {
      return userVersion;
      }
    }
```

When implementing the SupportsVersion interface, the jdoPreStore callback is used to increment the userVersion. The jdoPreStore callback is ideal for this purpose, since it is called for modified as well as new persistent objects when the transaction is committing.

The isSameVersion method returns true when the object passed to it is a Rental object with the same identity string and version number as this. The version number refers to the version of the persistent state that was loaded. It does not change when the object becomes dirty or unmanaged. It changes only when the persistent state in the datastore is modified.

Overriding the Equals and hashCode Methods

When an application data class captures its identity string, its equals method can use the identity string to determine object equivalence. Although Java allows each class to define the semantics of equivalence, in the case of application data classes, there are two reasons why it makes good sense to use persistent identity as the touchstone of object equivalence. First, JDO uses persistent identity to define the uniqueness requirement and to define object equivalence within persistent collection fields. Second, when the application must deal with unmanaged application data objects that are generated from persistent objects and that hold changes to apply to persistent objects, questions about persistent identity become fundamental questions that the equals method is ideally suited to answer. For example, in Listing 10-6, the isSameVersion method uses the equals method of the Rental object to determine whether two distinct objects in memory refer to the same persistent state before it determines whether the two objects started with the same version of that state.

Listing 10-7 shows the implementation of the equals and hashCode methods for the Rental object. Both methods use the getIdentityString method shown in Listing 10-5 to obtain identity strings.

Listing 10-7. The equals *and* hashCode *Methods for the* Rental *Application Data Class*

```
// two application data objects are equal when and only
// when they are members of the same class and
// their identity strings are equal
public final boolean equals(Object other)
    {
    if (this == other)
       return true;

    // return false when other is not
    // a Rental object or is null,
    // or this has no identity string
    String my_id = getIdentityString();
    if (!(other instanceof Rental) || my_id == null)
       return false;

    String other_id = ((Rental) other).getIdentityString();
    return my_id.equals(other_id);
    }

public final int hashCode()
    {
    String s = getIdentityString();
    return (s != null) ? s.hashCode() : super.hashCode();
    }
```

Although the application has the freedom to define an equals method, Java imposes a contract on the implementation of the equals method. This contract also applies to the hashCode method. To satisfy the contract for an inheritance tree of application data classes, the equals and hashCode methods should be defined in the least-derived application data class where the persistent identity is fully defined. After all, these methods depend on knowing what the persistent identity is. In the case of datastore identity, the appropriate class is the least-derived application data class in the hierarchy. In the case of application identity, each class in the hierarchy that the JDO metadata associates with a concrete application identity class would override the equals and hashCode methods. Because the equals and hashCode methods are fixed for any application data classes deriving from the application data class that defines them, the code in Listing 10-7 applies the final modifier to the equals and hashCode methods.

NOTE To learn about the contract that applies to the equals and hashCode methods, see the Javadoc for the Object class in the Java SDK. For a detailed discussion of application identity in class hierarchies, see Chapter 5.

Using the Rental Swing App with the Rental Web App

If you use both the rental Swing application and the rental Web application at the same time (this is not possible with the reference implementation because the datastore is not multiuser), note that there is some incompatibility between the two versions. The version of the Rental class used for the Swing application does not implement the SupportsVersion interface. It does have the userVersion field for data schema compatibility, but it does nothing with it. The rental Swing application relies on JDO transactional semantics, and therefore the implementation of the SupportsVersion interface has been omitted for simplicity. Likewise, the versions used in the Swing application do not implement the SupportsIdentity interface. As a result, the rental Swing application can use the version of the application data classes that the rental Web application uses, but the opposite is not true. Therefore, to use the two architectures together, build the targets in the following order: *clean-out, rental-servlet-opr, rental-gui.*

The One-PM-per-Session Design

In the one-pm-per-session design, when the controller receives a request, it begins by looking in the HttpSession object for a handle to the service. If it does not find one, it creates a handle to the service and stores it in the session. The handle is used to wrap the service so that the service can be closed when the session is serialized or invalidated. The handle reacts to session invalidation or serialization in the callbacks defined by the HttpSessionBindingListener interface and the HttpSessionActivationListener interface defined in the javax.servlet.http package.

Like the one-pm-per-request design, this design can benefit greatly from the level-two cache of a sophisticated JDO implementation. Unlike the one-pm-per-request design, this design can supply some caching benefit when a level-two cache is not present. By turning on the *NontransactionalRead, Optimistic,* and *RetainValues* properties in the transaction, the application can cause the persistence manager to accumulate persistent state across requests from the same client. At the same time, the issue of managing cache size or age is not serious because the persistence manager is serving only one client for the duration of his visit. If the user needs to refresh the entire cache from time to time, a button to request this action can be provided.

The one-pm-per-session design may generate less garbage during a client's visit to the Web site than the one-pm-per-request design—but only if the dynamic pages reuse a lot of the same persistent objects. Otherwise, the amount of garbage is about the same.

The one-pm-per-session design appears to shine when considering transactions. If transactions are used, then a JDO transaction is available to tie the request that generates the view to the request that performs the update. As a result, there is no reason for the application to define a versioning scheme.

Close examination reveals, however, that this design gains little in performance while either introducing complexity or jeopardizing scalability. Unless the JDO implementation does not provide a level-two cache, this design's increased use of the persistence manager's cache offers little advantage. At the same time, the reduction in garbage generation may not be significant.

As described earlier, the persistence manager cannot be serialized and should be closed when the session is serialized. Although session serialization can be avoided by configuring the servlet container to turn it off, to do so jeopardizes load handling and clustering. Any failure to scale is a serious flaw in most Web applications. To support session serialization, the application detects when session serialization occurs and closes the persistence manager on these occasions. If the persistence manager may be closed between requests, then any advantages hoped for by keeping the persistence manager open may or may not be present when a request is processed. To maintain scalability, the code must be able to handle the request even when the persistence manager has closed. For much work, little is gained over the one-pm-per-request design.

In short, the one-pm-per-session design gains little in performance, potentially loses in scalability, and complicates the design and the code. For these reasons, it cannot be recommended over the one-pm-per-request design.

The One-PM-per-Update Design

In the one-pm-per-update design, one persistence manager is shared for all requests that read persistent objects. At the same time, each request that modifies persistent objects creates and closes a persistence manager for the update.

In most Web applications, the number of HTTP requests that modify information is much less than the number of requests that read, but do not modify, information. Most interactive use of persistent data, regardless of the persistence mechanisms or the deployment architecture, share this characteristic. Like the other designs, the one-pm-per-update design benefits from any level-two cache supplied by the implementation, but when the JDO implementation does not provide a level-two cache, the shared read-only persistence manager offers the maximum performance benefit from the JDO-defined cache.

If the design avoids making persistent objects transient on each request, then this design also minimizes garbage collection since the shared read-only persistence manager will reuse the same persistent objects as long as the persistence manager remains open.

In this design, the *NontransactionalRead* property of the read-only persistence manager is turned on, since this persistence manager does not use transactions at all. The *Multithreaded* property must also be turned on, since multiple threads will be sharing the same persistence manager. Turning on the *Multithreaded* property may decrease the performance of the persistence manager, as it may now turn on some synchronization and turn off some optimization to accommodate the application's multithreaded use. At the same time, there can be some queuing of activities in the persistence manager. For example, while the database connection is being used to run a query for one thread, other threads seeking to execute queries may be held up.

The best approach for scaling up is to store the service that uses the shared persistence manager in an instance field of the servlet where it will be shared by all threads running in the servlet instance. The service that uses the shared persistence manager is initialized in the servlet's init method. When the container notices an increased load, it will likely create another instance of the servlet, which initializes its own service using a different read-only persistence manager that is shared among the requests processed by the new servlet instance.

The transactional issues for the one-pm-per-update design are the same as for the one-pm-per-request design. Since the read occurs in one persistence manager and the write occurs in another, there is no opportunity for JDO to provide a shared transactional context. To provide concurrency control, the application must roll its own version control, such as the SupportsVersion interface described earlier.

Implementing the one-pm-per-update design can be surprisingly complex. The complexity revolves around managing the cache of persistent objects in one or more shared read-only persistence managers. When an update request modifies persistent objects in its own persistence manager, the persistent objects in all of the read-only persistence managers that refer to the same database object must be reloaded with the new state. Otherwise, the read-only persistence managers become quickly outdated. Likewise, the read-only persistence managers must reload the appropriate persistent objects when optimistic concurrency failures occur in the write transactions. Otherwise, they continue to serve outdated information.

Writing a cache synchronization scheme is not a simple task because there may be multiple shared read-only persistence managers in multiple, clustered servlet containers. Instead of writing cache synchronization code, the application's best option is to use a JDO implementation that provides for cache synchronization. Although cache synchronization is not defined by JDO, some implementations provide them as a value-added feature.

If the JDO implementation or the application provides a way to keep the objects in the read-only persistence managers up-to-date, then the shared read-only persistence manager can be kept open for the life of the servlet. In this case, the servlet closes its read-only persistence manager in its destroy method, which the servlet container calls just prior to removing the servlet from service.

Since any JDO implementation that offers cache synchronization across persistence managers is very likely to offer a level-two cache of persistent state, the benefit of using the one-pm-per-update design over the one-pm-per-request design comes down to the value of continuing to use the same persistent objects for all reads rather than creating new persistent objects on each request that soon become garbage. For this reason, the one-pm-per-update design promises some improvement in performance and scalability over the one-pm-per-request design.

To realize a performance benefit with the one-pm-per-update design, the Web application must avoid storing persistent objects in the session object. Since the container serializes the session when the container comes under load, the managed application data objects become unmanaged objects. As a result, they soon become garbage and thereby negate the expected benefit of the design at precisely the point when the benefit is needed.

An example of the one-pm-per-update design is not presented in this book because the cache synchronization on which it depends is most economically viewed as a feature that the JDO vendor, rather than the application, should supply.

Summary

Successful Web applications are built on technologies whose failure modes are well understood. Nothing beats simplicity of design and unquestioned support for scalability when a Web site must run 24×7. When introducing JDO into this deployment environment, the one-pm-per-request design offers many advantages. It leverages the sophistication of the JDO implementation when it comes to the caching of persistent state and connections. Whatever scheme is adopted to support conversational state, support for clustering and session spooling is not compromised. Debugging this design appears to be straightforward. In essence, this design uses JDO to simplify the access to persistent state without introducing any complexities, limitations, or potential flaws. The only limitation of this design that is not addressed by JDO or opened to being addressed by the JDO implementation is support for an optimistic concurrency control that spans client requests. The application can address this deficiency for the simple cases with a minimal amount of application code that supports an application-defined versioning scheme.

On the other hand, the one-pm-per-update design, if used with a JDO implementation that supports cache synchronization across persistence managers, promises somewhat better performance. To realize the better performance, the application needs to avoid making persistent objects transient—an act that would create the garbage that the design otherwise avoids.

The next chapter examines the use of JDO in Enterprise JavaBeans. It examines a stateless session bean that implements yet another variation on the reservation services that have been presented so far. Since EJBs are not themselves applications, a variation of the rental Web application described in this chapter rounds out the complete application presented in the next chapter.

CHAPTER 11

Using JDO in Enterprise JavaBeans

CONTRARY TO A common misconception, JDO is not a replacement for Enterprise JavaBeans (EJBs). The EJB specification is primarily concerned with sharing access to remote objects and controlling distributed transactions, while JDO is primarily concerned with an object's relationship to persistent storage. Nevertheless, EJB containers and JDO provide overlapping services for managing objects. Both provide transactional semantics for objects, and both entity beans and persistent objects have mechanisms that tie object state to persistent storage. Although the overlap in services fosters the misconception that JDO and EJBs are in competition, in fact, JDO can be used with EJBs, and to some extent, it eases their development.

There are three basic types of EJBs: session beans, entity beans, and message-driven beans. Session beans are the oldest type and have been used extensively in real-world development. There are two common patterns for building session beans that interact with a datastore. In the first pattern, which might be called the *Session-Only pattern*, the session bean talks directly to the datastore. The session bean might be stateless or stateful. Likewise, it might use container-managed transactions (CMT) or bean-managed transactions (BMT). In the past, the session bean used a datastore API such as JDBC to access persistent state. Meanwhile, the bean's business methods serve the client by returning and accepting serialized objects.

JDO plugs neatly into session beans that use the Session-Only pattern by replacing the code that calls the datastore API. As a general rule, the amount of code needed to use JDO is quite a bit less than the code it replaces. It is also more powerful, providing caching of persistent state, transparent navigation of the object model, and so forth. The EJB client, however, is unaware of the change. The client continues to pass and receive serialized objects that are not persistent.

The *Session Facade pattern* is the second pattern used for session beans. In this pattern, the session bean often uses entity beans to retrieve and store persistent state and generally uses CMT. It continues to interact with the client by passing and receiving serialized objects that are not persistent. In this pattern, introducing JDO does not change the client or the session bean. Instead, the change occurs in the entity beans. Alternatively, because JDO simplifies the access to persistent state, it may be reasonable to replace the use of entity beans in the Session Facade pattern with the use of JDO in the Session-Only pattern.

Entity beans may use container-managed persistence (CMP) or bean-managed persistence (BMP). When they use CMP, no persistence-related code is included inside the application code of the entity bean, and as a result, there is no reason to use JDO. It is possible that the container itself will use JDO to implement CMP, but that is a different story altogether. When the entity beans use BMP, the application developer can replace the code that calls the datastore API code with the simpler code that calls JDO.

The JDO Learning Tools use JBoss, an open source product, as the EJB container. After describing the steps required to set up JBoss and run the builds, this chapter examines the final iteration of the rental application. In this case, it is an enterprise application that uses an EJB to implement the reservation service. The rental enterprise application uses an HTML client that is very much like the one presented in Chapter 10. To the user it appears identical, but the controller servlet is somewhat different.

After examining the rental enterprise application, this chapter goes on to explain how to build the quote server application that Chapter 6 discusses. The quote server is a simple service that is implemented in the following EJB types:

- Stateless CMT session bean

- Stateless BMT session bean

- Stateful CMT session bean

- Stateful BMT session bean

- BMP entity bean

Although the quote server example is simple, it shows JDO at work in many types of EJBs. One console client exercises all incantations of the quote server EJB.

In particular, the QuoteServerClient directly uses the entity bean version of the quote server. Having the user interface directly use an entity bean is generally a bad design for an application. The indictment, however, applies to the client's design and does not implicate the design of the entity bean. The quote server entity bean provides a good example of the use of JDO within a BMP entity bean. Although flawed, the QuoteServerClient demonstrates and tests the entity bean, as well as the other EJB types.

Configuring the Build Environment for JBoss

The rental enterprise application is part of the JDO Learning Tools. Its build target is *rental-servlet-ejb*. Chapters 8 and 10 describe how to configure the build environment and execute builds. If you have followed the instructions presented in these chapters successfully, you are ready to perform the additional configuration steps presented here. If you did not perform the configuration described in Chapters 8 and 10, you must perform the seven configuration steps described in Chapter 8 and the three configuration steps described in Chapter 10. Thereafter, continue with the following six configuration steps, which allow you to build the rental enterprise application. These configuration steps also allow you to build the five quote server EJBs.

Step Eleven: Install JBoss

In this step, you install the JBoss EJB container. JBoss is a full J2EE container that can be obtained with either a built-in Tomcat servlet container or a built-in Jetty servlet container. The JDO Learning Tools were developed using JBoss 3.0.4 with the Jetty servlet container. Any later version of JBoss should work equally well. If you don't have a suitable version of JBoss installed, go to the following URL: http://www.jboss.org. Follow the links to a download of JBoss with Jetty. Then unzip JBoss to install it. Follow the instructions that come with JBoss to start it up. If JBoss is properly installed and running, the URL http://localhost:8080/jmx-console displays the JBoss service manager page.

The directory where you installed JBoss is referred to as the *jboss-home* directory in this book.

Estimated time for this step, excluding download: 30 minutes

Step Twelve: Configure JBoss and Tomcat to Work Together

In this step, you perform some configuration of JBoss that is required in order to be able to use JBoss with a stand-alone Tomcat installation configured as described in Chapter 10. The default JBoss configuration with Jetty uses some of the same ports as the default stand-alone Tomcat installation. There are a number of ways to resolve the port conflicts. You could use the built-in Jetty servlet container instead of the stand-alone Tomcat servlet container. Changing to the Jetty servlet container would require some modification of the build scripts. On the other hand, instead of using JBoss with Jetty, you could install JBoss with Tomcat. This change may also require some modification of the build scripts. The solution used in this book is to tweak the configurations of Tomcat and JBoss so that both can run together on the same machine as stand-alone services. In this fashion, those who are not interested in the EJB examples do not have to wrestle with an EJB container.

To run stand-alone Tomcat on the same machine as JBoss with Jetty, you make one modification to a JBoss configuration file and one modification to a Tomcat configuration file. First, edit the *jboss-service.xml* file found in the following directory under the *jboss-home* directory:

```
server/default/deploy/jbossweb.sar/meta-inf
```

Within this file, find the place where an AJP13 listener is added on port 8009. Comment out the portion of the XML defined by the Call tag. This prevents both Tomcat and JBoss from attempting to listen on the same port for proxy calls from a Web server.

Next, edit the *server.xml* file in the *config* directory under the *tomcat-home* directory. Find the place where the "Coyote HTTP/1.1 Connector on port 8080" is configured. Alter the port to another port, say 8000. This change reconfigures Tomcat to listen for HTTP connections on port 8000. Jetty within JBoss will continue to listen for HTTP connections on port 8080. The change is made in the Tomcat file because it can be changed in one place. Several JBoss configuration files specifically mention port 8080. After restarting Tomcat, you should be able to connect to Tomcat's documentation page by going to the following URL in your Web browser:

```
http://localhost:8000
```

After making the change, you would now use the new port number rather than the default port number of 8080 when following the examples in Chapter 10.

Estimated time for this step: 10 minutes

Step Thirteen: Configure Build Properties

In this step, you configure the build environment for JBoss. Edit the *default.properties* file in the *bookants* directory under your *bookcode-home* directory. Set the *jboss.home* property to point to your *jboss-home* directory.

Estimated time for this step: 5 minutes

Step Fourteen: Replace JDO Reference Implementation

If you have been using the JDO reference implementation for the examples up until this point, then in this step, you must switch to another implementation. You can skip this step if you have not been using the reference implementation of JDO.

Although it is possible to configure the JDO reference implementation for use with an EJB, the 1.0 reference implementation when used in this way is quite buggy. It is possible that later versions of the reference implementation will work better with EJBs. Until then, you should switch to one of the commercial implementations of JDO that offer free time-limited licenses.

If the vendor offers multiple versions of the JDO implementation, be sure to download the version that supports deployment to EJB containers. This is usually the more expensive product.

The commercial implementations have licensing schemes that require a license file or license key. You may have to request the trial license file or key, or the vendor may send it to you automatically as a result of downloading the trial version. Consult the vendor's documentation for more information about the license deployment issues.

The 1.0 version of the JDO Learning Tools contains builds for the Kodo, Lido, and IntelliBO commercial implementations. Later releases of the JDO Learning Tools may have builds for other commercial or open source implementations. To make the switch, go to Chapter 8 and follow the instructions for steps five through seven. The end of Chapter 8 also has a few comments about how the build scripts differ between the different JDO implementations.

Next, you need to deploy the datastore driver that the JDO implementation will use. You will have to determine what database you are using, and you may have to consult the vendor's documentation, to determine the JDBC driver to deploy. Once you determine the driver, copy its Jar or zip file to the *server/default/lib* directory under your *jboss-home* directory. When JBoss is started, you should see this file mentioned in the console log.

The builds in the JDO Learning Tools version 1.0 were tested with trial versions of the following commercial products:

- Kodo 2.4.1

- Lido 1.4.1

- IntelliBO 3.1.0

Later versions should work equally well.

Estimated time for this step, not including download: 1 hour

Step Fifteen: Configure the JDO Connection Factory

In this step, you create the configuration file for a JDO connection factory. JBoss accepts a pair of connection factory files, an *xxx.rar* file and a matching *xxx-service.xml* file, where *xxx* is an informative name such as *kodo*, *lido*, or *intellibo*. Some JDO vendors provide the RAR file prebuilt, and others require that it be built by the application developer.

The service XML file configures the JDO connection factory. The configuration properties generally correspond to the configurable properties of a

PersistenceManagerFactory, except that the properties are expressed in XML rather than in a Java properties file. The builds supplied with the JDO Learning Tools will build the RAR files if necessary, and they come with the corresponding service XML file that worked in the test environment.

The following three build targets use a connection factory:

- sayings-stateless-cmt

- sayings-entity

- rental-servlet-ejb

The corresponding service XML files are contained in tool directories found under the *com/ysoft/jdo/book/sayings/persistent* directory and under the *com/ysoft/jdo/book/rental/ejb* directory. The tool directories have the obvious names *kodo, lido,* and *intellibo.*

Since the service XML file is vendor dependent, the vendors of JDO implementations may modify this file in later versions of their product. To ensure that the service files that you are using are the latest ones available, rename the service files for your selected JDO implementation, which you can find in the JDO Learning Tools. Next, find the sample service XML file provided by the vendor and copy it to the JDO Learning Tools source, placing it beside the files that you renamed. Then edit the new service XML files, making sure that the settings are compatible with your runtime environment and compatible with the settings found in the original files that you renamed.

The remaining three build targets, listed here, use a persistence manager factory:

- sayings-stateless-bmt

- sayings-stateful-bmt

- sayings-stateful-cmt

These builds use a properties file to configure the persistence manager factory. Nevertheless, they also require that the RAR files be deployed. Deploying the RAR files makes the JDO implementation files available to any EJB, even to those EJBs that use a persistence manager factory instead of a connection factory.

Estimated time for this step: 30 minutes

Step Sixteen: Configure JNDI

In this step, you verify that the JNDI configuration for JDO Learning Tools is appropriate. The tools assume that the EJB container will be deployed on your machine. Consequently, the JNDI configuration refers to the *localhost* as the host machine for a JNDI lookup. If you have JBoss deployed on a remote machine, you will have to edit this configuration. It is found in the *jndi.properties* file in the *resources* directory under the *bookcode-home* directory.

Estimated time for this step: 5 minutes

You are now ready to build the rental enterprise application and the quote server examples.

Building the Rental Enterprise Application

To build the rental enterprise application, go to the *bookants* directory under your *bookcode-home* directory. Build the *clean-out* target first by executing the following command:

```
ant clean-out
```

Assuming that you have built some of the examples from Chapters 8 and 9, you will see output that looks like the output in Listing 10-1 in Chapter 10.

By building the *clean-out* target first, you remove any compiled versions of the rental application classes that were built with either the *rental-gui* target or the *rental-servlet-opr* target. The rental Swing application and the rental Web application can use the versions of the application data classes built by the rental enterprise application, but the reverse is not true. The rental enterprise application cannot use the version of the application data classes built by either the rental Swing application or the rental Web application. See the section "Changes to the Application Data Classes" later in this chapter for more information.

Next, build the rental enterprise application's target. Execute the following command:

```
ant rental-servlet-ejb
```

You should see output that looks like the output shown in Listing 11-1. Building this target will shut down Tomcat if it is running. It does not shut down JBoss.

*Listing 11-1. Excerpts of Expected Output from Building
the rental-servlet-ejb Target*

```
E:\Bookcode\bookants>ant rental-servlet-ejb
Buildfile: build.xml
are-we-ready:
verify:
    ...
die-without-JBoss:
    ...
rental-ejb:
    [jar] Building jar: E:\Bookcode\serverjars\reservationservice.jar
    [jar] Building jar: E:\Bookcode\clientjars\reservationclient.jar
    [echo] returned from com/ysoft/jdo/book/rental/ejb/build.xml
    [copy] Copying 1 file to E:\jboss304\server\default\deploy
    [echo] returned from ants/jboss.xml
    [echo] deploying kodo.rar
    [copy] Copying 1 file to E:\jboss304\server\default\deploy
    [copy] Copying 1 file to E:\jboss304\server\default\deploy
    [echo] calling com/ysoft/jdo/book/rental/ejb/build.xml
    ...

die-without-Tomcat:

rental:
    ...
   [mkdir] Created dir: E:\Bookcode\warfiles\images
    [copy] Copying 3 files to E:\Bookcode\warfiles\images
    [copy] Copying 7 files to E:\Bookcode\warfiles\web-inf\lib
  [delete] Deleting 8 files from E:\Bookcode\temp
  [delete] Deleting 42 files from E:\tomcat4.1.12\webapps\rental
  [delete] Deleted 14 directories from E:\tomcat4.1.12\webapps\rental
    [copy] Copying 39 files to E:\tomcat4.1.12\webapps\rental
    [echo] You'll have to restart Tomcat

BUILD SUCCESSFUL
Total time: 1 minute 7 seconds
```

To run the rental enterprise example, start up JBoss, start up Tomcat, and start up a Web browser. After these programs have completed their startup, visit the following URL:

```
http://localhost:8000/rental/controller
```

This will bring up a Web page that looks something like the page in Figure 10-1 in Chapter 10.

A Few Additional Tips

Although it should not happen, in fact, some JDO implementations have broken the JBoss hot-redeploy feature. As a result, you may need to stop and restart JBoss after building any of the EJB targets. Certainly, if you did not restart JBoss and something is broken, it is worth a try to see if the bounce fixes it.

If you change implementations after building some of the EJB targets, you will need to remove the old implementation's *xxx.rar* and *xxx-service.xml* files from the *server/default/deploy* directory under your *jboss-home* directory. You will also want to remove from the same directory the EJB jars that you deployed with the old implementation.

Using the Rental Enterprise Application

The user interface of the rental enterprise application is identical to the user interface of the rental Web application. As a result, to walk through the rental enterprise application, follow the instructions in Chapter 10. Remember that Tomcat is no longer configured to use its default HTTP port of 8080.

Design of the Rental Enterprise Application

The rental enterprise application is a straightforward port of the rental Web application. Only a few classes change. The biggest change occurs for the ReservationService whose objects in the rental Web application are local to the controller servlet. In the rental enterprise application, the ReservationService changes to a business interface that is implemented by the ReservationServiceEJB. Likewise, the ReservationServlet changes to accommodate the use of a remote EJB instead of a local object.

Design of the Reservation Service EJB

The reservation service EJB is implemented as a stateless CMT session bean. It uses the Session-Only pattern. These choices were made primarily for simplicity. Stateless CMT session beans are the simplest beans, and the Session-Only pattern is the simplest way to use them. This type of EJB is also quite sufficient for the rental application.

The ReservationServiceEJB uses a connection factory to get a persistence manager. Since the EJB container is managing transactions, each business method obtains a persistence manager and releases it before returning. See Chapter 6 for a discussion of the design constraints for the various types of EJBs. The service may use either a JDO datastore or optimistic transaction.

As shown in Figure 11-1, several classes and interfaces make up the deployed reservation service EJB. The application supplies the ReservationServiceHome, ReservationServiceRemote, and ReservationService interfaces. It also supplies the bean implementation in the ReservationServiceEJB class. The EJB API supplies the EJBHome, EJBObject, and SessionBean interfaces. The ReservationService interface defines the business methods of the reservation service EJB. The ReservationServiceEJB class implements the ReservationService interface, and the ReservationServiceRemote interface extends it. The application classes shown in Figure 11-1 are found in the com.ysoft.jdo.book.rental.ejb.service and com.ysoft.jdo.book.rental.ejb.service.impl packages.

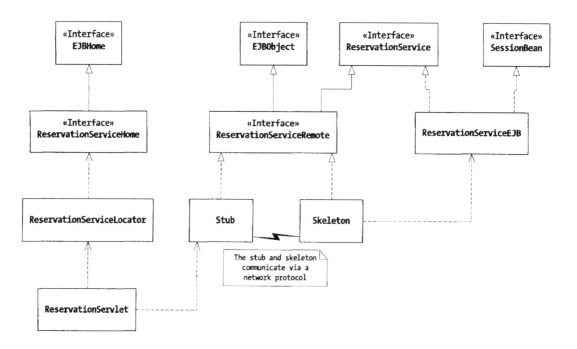

Figure 11-1. The deployed reservation service EJB

As shown in Figure 11-1, the communication between the servlet and the EJB occurs between two proxies, a stub and a skeleton, that communicate by means of a network protocol such as RMI or RMI-IIOP. Both implement the

ReservationServiceRemote interface. The skeleton, which resides on the EJB server, delegates invocations of the business methods to an instance of the ReservationServiceEJB. The EJB container is responsible for generating the stub and skeleton classes. JBoss creates these dynamically.

The ReservationServiceLocator, shown in Figure 11-1, is a utility class that finds a stub that implements the ReservationService interface. The enterprise application's ReservationServlet uses the stub just as the Web application uses a local instance of the ReservationService class.

Encapsulated Changes in the Reservation Service

There are only a few important differences between the Web application's ReservationService class and the enterprise application's ReservationService interface and its implementation in ReservationServiceEJB. The changes can be divided between those that are encapsulated within the implementation of the service and those that alter the public interface of the service. The changes that alter the public interface, in turn, cause changes in the ReservationServlet that uses the service.

There are several encapsulated changes. To begin with, the ReservationServiceEJB must have the life cycle methods required by the javax.ejb.SessionBean interface. Since it will be deployed in a CMT session bean, it must give up the transactional control that it exercised in the local service. The EJB container will start a transaction when the ReservationServlet calls a method in the ReservationService interface, and the container will either commit or roll back the transaction prior to returning control to the servlet.

Another pervasive difference leads to quite a few code changes. In the Web application's ReservationService class, the lifetime of the PersistenceManager and the lifetime of the ReservationService are coincident. In the ReservationServiceEJB, |the lifetime of the persistence manager is coincident with the execution of the business method. Each business method in the EJB obtains a persistence manager, uses it, and closes it before returning. This change leads to a variety of minor changes in initializing queries and closing the persistence manager.

Like the Web application's ReservationService, the ReservationServiceEJB returns persistent objects, but unlike the Web application, the enterprise application's ReservationServlet does not receive persistent objects. Instead, it receives unmanaged application data objects because the skeleton, shown in Figure 11-1, serializes the persistent objects out to the stub. The change from managed to unmanaged objects has effects that are both encapsulated and public.

For the reasons discussed in Chapter 6, the ReservationServiceEJB uses the utility method respond in com.ysoft.jdo.book.common.ejb.EJBHelper to preserialize the persistent objects returned to the ReservationServlet.

Public Changes to the Reservation Service

Porting the Web application's ReservationService to an EJB forces a couple of changes to the public interface of the ReservationService. To begin with, of course, the mechanism to obtain a reference to an object implementing the service has changed. Whereas the Web application's servlet could simply construct its ReservationService, the enterprise application must obtain a home interface to the EJB and use it to obtain a stub that implements the ReservationService. The get utility method in the ReservationServiceLocator encapsulates this work. In addition, the ReservationService no longer has a close method. Instead, the ReservationServlet releases the remote service by calling the stub's remove method specified in the EJBObject interface. The release utility method in the ReservationServiceLocator encapsulates this work.

The next change occurs in the signatures of the business methods in the ReservationService interface, which may now throw a java.rmi.RemoteException. Each method in the ReservationService interface declares RemoteException in its throws clause. In contrast, the business methods in the Web application's ReservationService do not declare a RemoteException. Indeed, neither does any business method in the ReservationServiceEJB declare a RemoteException in its throws clause. The RemoteException is declared in the enterprise application's ReservationService interface because the corresponding business methods in the stub and skeleton classes are engaged in the business of communicating over the network. Therefore, they throw a RemoteException when they encounter difficulty communicating.

The signature of the flipReservations method in the ReservationService also changes. Like the other business methods in the ReservationService interface, it adds the RemoteException to its throws clause. It also drops the application-defined OptimisticReservationException from its throws clause. Even if the EJB uses JDO's optimistic transactions, there is no opportunity for the flipReservations method in the ReservationServiceEJB to detect an optimistic transaction failure and report it by throwing an OptimisticReservationException. In JDO 1.0, the JDO runtime throws a JDOUserException when it discovers an optimistic lock failure, and in JDO 1.0.1, it throws a JDOOptimisticVerificationException. Since the container commits the transaction after the bean's business method returns, there is no opportunity for the bean developer's code to handle the exception. Since both types of exceptions are unchecked exceptions, the EJB container rolls back the transaction and disposes of the bean instance if the JDO implementation throws either one.

However, the flipReservations method can still detect a difference between the version of a Rental object that the client returns to it and the version of the Rental object that it finds to modify. As a result, the flipReservations method still throws the application-defined ExtendedOptimisticException. When this occurs, the method calls the setRollbackOnly method in the javax.ejb.SessionContext object to ensure that any changes made to persistent objects up until that point cannot be committed.

Changes to the Application Data Classes

In the rental Web application, all of the application data classes implement the Serializable interface and two of them, Rental and Customer, implement the SupportsIdentityString interface. As you may recall from the section "The SupportsIdentityString Interface" in Chapter 10, SupportsIdentityString is the application-defined interface that allows an application data class to capture its identity string and use that identity string in equality comparisons. In the enterprise version, the Lighthouse class must also implement the SupportsIdentityString interface.

Why is this change to the Lighthouse class required in the EJB version of the reservation service but not in the servlet version? To answer this question, it is necessary to understand a little more about how the ReservationModel obtains and uses Lighthouse objects.

Before initializing the ReservationModel object, the ReservationServlet calls two methods in the ReservationService. One method returns a collection of Rental objects, and the other method returns a list of Lighthouse objects. The initRentals method in the ReservationModel places each Rental object from the collection in a column under its lighthouse. It does this by looking up the Lighthouse object associated with the Rental object in the list of Lighthouse objects. If the rental's Lighthouse object is the first lighthouse on the list, the rental goes in the first column, and so on. The lookup in the List class is based on the semantics of the equals method.

In the Web application, each ReservationService object is local and uses one persistence manager for its lifetime. While the ReservationServlet processes one HTTP request, it makes multiple calls to the same ReservationService object. Because the service uses one persistence manager and returns the local objects by reference, JDO's uniqueness requirement ensures that the Lighthouse objects returned by one method are the same Lighthouse objects returned by the other method. Because of the uniqueness requirement, there is no reason for the Lighthouse class to override the implementation of the equals method in the Object class, which uses JVM identity (==) to determine equality.

In the enterprise application, the ReservationService is remote and the lifetime of the persistence manager is coincident with the call to the business method. The business methods in the service return objects by value in a serialization stream. As a consequence, the two calls to the service, one to get the list of Lighthouse objects and the other to get the collection of Rental objects together with their associated Lighthouse objects, result in the ReservationServlet having two different sets of Lighthouse objects in memory. If the lookup into the list continues to rely upon JVM identity, it fails.

The solution is to upgrade the `Lighthouse` class by having it override the `equals` method and implement the `SupportsIdentityString` interface. The rental Web application made these changes to the `Rental` and `Customer` classes for other reasons when porting from the rental Swing application, and now these changes are required for the `Lighthouse` class in porting to the rental enterprise application. Listings 10-5 and 10-7 in Chapter 10 show the implementations of the `SupportsIdentityString` interface and the `equals` method in the `Rental` class. The upgraded `Lighthouse` class uses similar code.

Changes to the ReservationServlet Controller

The changes to the enterprise application's `ReservationServlet` class are primarily driven by the public changes to the `ReservationService`. The enterprise version of the `ReservationServlet`, like its Web application counterpart, obtains a service at the start of the `respond` method. Unlike the Web application's `ReservationServlet`, the enterprise application's `ReservationServlet` obtains the reference to the `ReservationService` from the `ReservationServiceLocator`, shown in Figure 11-1, rather than by construction. The `ReservationServlet` must also catch the `RemoteException` as one of the exception types that may be thrown from the `ReservationService`.

At the same time, the use of a remote EJB service introduces small opportunities to increase the simplicity and efficiency in the `ReservationServlet`. Since the remote service returns only unmanaged objects, the `ReservationServlet` no longer needs to call the service to make all persistent objects in the model transient. Likewise, since page generation is working with unmanaged objects that do not benefit from transparent persistence, the `ReservationServlet` can release the remote service prior to page generation. By releasing the remote service before forwarding to the JSP presentation page, the enterprise application's `ReservationServlet` uses the remote service on each request for a slightly shorter period of time than it would if it held the service until page generation finished.

Are There Any Other Changes?

There are no other changes. The JSPs remain unchanged. Except for the `Lighthouse` class, the data model classes remain unchanged. The MVC pattern in the Web user interface remains unchanged. The `ReservationModel` and its helper classes remain unchanged.

Although the same low impact during the port can be achieved when using JDBC, the higher level of abstraction provided by JDO makes the ways to minimize the impact of the port more apparent. In fact, it is possible to completely encapsulate the differences between the local service and the EJB service, reducing them to differences between two implementations of a service locator interface and a data service interface. If you anticipate that you will be porting between these two deployment environments, creating this small amount of extra infrastructure would be a very sensible thing to do. It was not done in the examples in order to highlight the differences between the two application architectures.

Scaling Up in Complexity

The rental enterprise application is simple, but can you expect that its design will scale up to the complexity of a real-world application? It should. A significant advantage of JDO is the ability to work with the pervasive complexity of persistence at the right level of abstraction.

One important factor to consider when scaling up is the size of the serialization graph returned by the EJB's business methods. If you have a highly interrelated data model, then you could end up returning to the client far more information than you intend. When JDO is local to the client, a highly interrelated data model is not a concern because JDO's transparent persistence will fetch only what is required by the client. When persistent objects are returned to the client by serialization, the client receives a copy of everything that is reachable by serializable fields. Chapter 5 points out various approaches for handling the issues that arise when serializing application data objects.

Using JDO with Other Types of EJBs

The application developer can use JDO when building session beans, some types of entity beans, and message-driven beans. The JDO Learning Tools have several examples of session beans and one example of an entity bean. The examples all implement the QuoteServer interface defined in the *com/ysoft/jdo/book/sayings/ service* directory under the *bookcode-home* directory. The quote service harkens back to an earlier day—well before online stock quotes—when it was nifty to have a facility somewhere on the network to issue famous (and sometimes not so famous) quotations on demand.

Chapter 6 describes in detail the important points about the design of the quote server examples. The complete set of examples provides a template for building any EJB that uses JDO.

Building the Quote Server EJBs

There are five build targets for the quote server EJBs.

- sayings-stateless-cmt

- sayings-stateless-bmt

- sayings-stateful-cmt

- sayings-stateful-bmt

- sayings-entity

Each of the quote server builds overwrites the EJB created by any of the other quote server builds. Consequently, if you want to test all of them, you must do so sequentially. Each of them uses the same data schema, and as a result, the famous quotations that you add with one will be visible to the others.

To build the first target, execute the following command at the command line in the *bookants* directory under the *bookcode-home* directory:

```
ant -Dschema=generate sayings-stateless-cmt
```

You should see more than a hundred lines of output that ends with something like the output shown in Listing 11-2.

Listing 11-2. Expected End of Output from Building the sayings-stateless-cmt Target

```
sayings-ejb:
     [copy] Copying 1 file to E:\Bookcode\build\com\ysoft\jdo\book\sayings\service
      [jar] Building jar: E:\Bookcode\serverjars\quoteserver.jar
      [jar] Building jar: E:\Bookcode\clientjars\quoteserverclient.jar
     [echo] returned from com/ysoft/jdo/book/sayings/build.xml
     [copy] Copying 1 file to E:\jboss304\server\default\deploy
     [echo] creating runQuoteServer.bat
     [echo] returned from ants/jboss.xml
BUILD SUCCESSFUL
Total time: 41 seconds
```

The *-Dschema=generate* option forces the build to generate the SQL schema for the quote server application. You need to create the schema only once, unless, of course, you modify the persistent fields. For Kodo, the build scripts will alter the schema for you. For the other implementations, SQL scripts are created in files that you can use to create the schema by hand.

Each of the builds creates a *runQuoteServer.bat* file in the *bookcode-home* directory that invokes the QuoteServerClient found in the com.ysoft.jdo.book.sayings.client package. The client's only interface is the command line. It can retrieve a quote or store a quote. It can also loop getting quotes every so often. After building one of the targets, go to the *bookcode-home* directory and type the following command for more information:

```
runQuoteServer -help
```

Using the Quote Server

After building any of the quote server targets, you may need to bounce JBoss for the reason described earlier in this chapter. Executing the command file *runQuoteServer.bat* will cause the QuoteServerClient to display one quote from the quote server EJB before terminating. For testing, it is better to cause the client to hit the bean at least three times. For this reason, use the following command:

```
runQuoteServer -loop 3
```

This will cause the client to display three quotes from the quote server before terminating.

To start, there are no quotes in the datastore, so you will need to add several quotes. For example, execute the following command to add the first quote:

```
runQuoteServer -quote "A stitch in time saves nine" -source "Poor Richard's Almanac"
```

Summary

The greatest difficulty in creating Enterprise JavaBeans is learning to conform to the constraints imposed by the EJB specification for the different types of EJBs. During the learning curve, developers often rewrite their EJB code. When it comes to mastering EJBs, JDO is not a silver bullet, but it can help tame them. JDO simplifies and reduces the amount of code that needs to be written. More importantly, JDO provides the higher level of abstraction that allows design patterns to be recognized, verified, reused, and documented. Because of JDO, the examples presented here can scale up in complexity to the level of your application's data model. They should help you to get a good start in building industrial-strength EJBs.

This chapter concludes the presentation of the JDO Learning Tools. These tools are not perfect by any means, but they are open source. Your assistance in making them better is welcomed.

This chapter also concludes the discussion of Java Data Objects. The 1.0 version of JDO is by no means the last word on JDO's evolution, but it is a good start on a powerful tool that will fundamentally change the way programmers build Java applications. By mastering it, you take a giant step forward on the path of building solutions that last.

Glossary

In this book, I've tried to be precise and consistent in my use of terms. The terms come from many sources, including the JDO specification and other specifications for the Java platform. In some cases, they are common in the industry, and you can look them up in the Free On-Line Dictionary of Computing. To find this wonderful resource on the Web, search for the word "FOLDOC". In some cases, I have invented my own terms. Although the terms are defined as they are introduced in the book, their definitions are collected together here for your convenience.

Term	Meaning
A	
ACID Properties	Acronym for Atomicity, Consistency, Isolation, and Durability. Transactions are *atomic* if a series of change requests can be combined into one all-or-nothing request. The transactional service either accepts all changes or returns an error when the user commits the transaction. The service rejects all changes when the user rolls back the transaction. Transactions are *consistent* if at the beginning of the transaction and at the end of the transaction the service has enforced the defined data constraints. The service may impose its own constraints, and it may allow the user to define additional constraints. If the service allows concurrent transactions, then the transactions are *isolated* if the modifications made in one transaction are visible to another transaction only in clearly defined ways. Finally, transactions are *durable* if the work of committed transactions is never lost. The durability guarantee assumes that the media that stores the information is not lost, and it does not prevent a later transaction from undoing the work of an earlier transaction.
API	Application Programming Interface. Refers to both the specification for a library of services that applications can use, and, informally, another name for the library itself.
Application data class	A class defined by the application whose primary purpose is to hold state that can be stored and retrieved from the datastore. Application data classes must be enhanced to support the PersistenceCapable interface before JDO can manage objects of their type.
Application data object	An instance of an application data class.

Term	Meaning
B	
Before-image	The state of the managed fields in the data object prior to the object becoming dirty within a transaction. The before-image is used to restore the object's state in the event of rollback, when the transaction's *RestoreValue* property is true.
BMP	Bean-managed persistence. Entity EJBs that use BMP require the bean developer to write the code to manage their persistent fields.
BMT	Bean-managed transactions. When an EJB is deployed with BMT, the application code in the EJB controls the transaction.
C	
Candidate class	All objects returned by executing a query or iterating an extent are assignment compatible with the candidate class of the query or extent. The candidate class is also the root of the namespace for field names in the query filter.
Change tracking	A notification mechanism to keep track of the objects and their persistent fields that have changed within the transaction. By using notification, JDO avoids the effort to discover the changes later.
Clean	A persistent object is clean when its transactional fields have not changed within the transaction and its persistent fields are both synchronized with the datastore and have values that were not modified within the transaction.
Clear a field	To set the field's value to its Java default value as determined by its field type.
CMP	Container-managed persistence. Entity EJBs that use CMP allow the container to manage their persistent fields.
CMT	Container-managed transactions. When an EJB is deployed with CMT, the container controls the transaction. As a result, the application code in the EJB cannot control the transaction.
Commit	An operation that ends a transaction by asking the transactional service to apply all changes made within the transaction. When the commit operation succeeds, the service accepts all changes; and when it fails, the service does not accept any changes.

Term	Meaning
Concurrency value	Some value that indicates, by convention, the version of a data object's persistent state. JDO does not specify how the JDO implementation determines the concurrency value. It might be a timestamp, a version field, a checksum, or some other value. As a result, different JDO implementations may use different types of concurrency values.
CRUD	Acronym for the basic persistent services of Create, Retrieve, Update, and Delete.
D	
Data model	The way persistent state is stored in the datastore. For a relational database, this would be the relational model.
Data object	An instance of a persistence-capable class.
Datastore	Any service that can store state information and provide a means to query, read, update, insert, and delete it. JDO requires a datastore that supports transactions.
Datastore object	Shorthand for the persistent state of an object in the datastore.
Datastore transaction	A JDO transaction that relies on the transactional boundaries of the underlying datastore service.
Default fetch group	A subset of the persistent fields of an application data class. The JDO metadata defines either explicitly or by default which persistent fields are members of the default fetch group. As an optimization, the JDO implementation may load all the fields of the default fetch group at the same time.
Dirty	When the persistent field of a managed object is changed, the field and the object are said to be dirty.
E	
EJB	Enterprise Java Beans, a JCP specification for server-side components.

Term	Meaning
Embedded object	A data object that is stored, when possible, in the datastore as a dependent part of one or more application data objects. Embedded objects are always treated as if they were contained in the application data object that refers to them. As a result, JDO does not support sharing embedded objects, and deleting the application data object implies the deletion of the embedded object. The system classes that a JDO implementation supports are always embedded. Application data objects are usually not embedded, but an implementation, at its option, may support the application's request to embed some application data objects in other, nonembedded, application data objects.
Enhanced class	An application data class that has been modified by the JDO-supplied enhancer tool to support the `PersistenceCapable` interface.
Evict	To discard the persistent state of an application data object. During eviction, the object's persistent fields are cleared to their Java default values, any extra state stored elsewhere in memory is discarded, and JDO remembers that the fields are not loaded.
F	
FCO	*See* first class object.
First class object	An object in memory whose state is stored independently in the datastore. As a result, the first class object has an identity value, and it may be inserted, modified, fetched, and deleted independently of any other first class object. Application data objects are nearly always first class objects. *See also* second class objects.
Flag	A Boolean property.
Friendly class	Any class that accesses the member field(s) of another class is friendly to that class.

Term	Meaning
I	
Idempotent	A Latin word meaning that a method effectively acts only once when invoked one or more times. This is sometimes called a *one-shot*, since after the method acts, something must occur to rearm the method to act again. A simple case is a method that always sets a Boolean variable to true. Although the method always assigns true to the variable, effectively the method does nothing unless the variable is false. A more complex example is a Web application's servlet that processes the contents of the shopping cart when the user clicks the *order* button at the check-out page. Even if the user clicks the *order* button two or more times, the method in the servlet that handles the click is idempotent if it processes the contents of the user's shopping cart only once and generates the same response for each redundant click.
Identity string	The string obtained from the toString method of the durable JDO identity object.
Identity value	The value of an attribute, or a list of attributes, that uniquely identifies an object's persistent state in the datastore.
J	
JCP	Java Community Process, the open specification process for the Java platform.
JDBC	Java Database Connectivity, an API to access relational databases from Java.
JDO	Java Data Objects, a persistence service defined in the JCP by JSR-12.
JDO identity	JDO defines three types of identity for the objects that it manages: datastore, application, and nondurable. In each case, JDO associates the identity object with the persistent object. Given one, JDO can produce the other. Datastore and application identity are the two durable identities.

Term	Meaning
JDO Jar file	The Jar file provided by the JDO vendor that contains the JDO-specified classes and interfaces for clients. Its name may vary from vendor to vendor.
JDO Learning Tools	The formal name of the open source example programs quoted throughout this book. They are available from `http://sourceforge.net/projects/jdo-tools` and from the publisher's Web site at `http://www.apress.com`.
JDO metadata	An XML file that contains information on the application data classes.
JDOQL	The JDO Query Language, which is used with the Query interface to define queries in JDO.
JDO-transient	One of the ten JDO management states for data objects. JDO-transient objects are not controlled by JDO, and for that reason, a synonym is unmanaged. The JDO specification calls this state the *transient state*.
JRE	Java Runtime Environment. The JRE implements the JVM and executes Java programs that have been compiled to byte code.
JSP	JavaServer Pages, a specification for connecting HTML pages to Java code in the servlet container.
JSR	Java Specification Request, the first step in producing a specification through the Java Community Process and the name of the expert group that creates the specification.
JTA	Java Transaction API, the API for controlling both local and distributed transactions. Found in the `javax.transaction` package.
JVM	Java Virtual Machine. Refers to both the specification for the JRE, and, informally, another name for the JRE.
L	
Load a persistent field	To read from the datastore or from a second-level cache the persistent value for an object's persistent field and store it in the object's member field. When the persistent field refers to an object, the object must be found or constructed.
M	
Managed field	Either a persistent or transactional field of an application data object.
Managed object	An object that JDO can control either transactionally or persistently or both. Application data objects can be managed.

Term	Meaning
N	
Navigate a field	Use the reference in a member field to access another object, either directly through the reference or indirectly through a reference to a `Collection` or `Map` object.
No-arg	Short for no argument. In Java, the default constructor is a no-arg constructor; in other words, it takes no parameters.
No-op	Short for no operation. When a call to a method is a no-op, the method does not perform the action that otherwise would be expected.
O	
Object	A Java object in memory. *See also* datastore object.
Object model	The classes of objects and the relationships of objects in memory. *See also* persistent object model.
ODBMS	Acronym for object-oriented database management system, also called an *object database*.
ODMG	Object Data Management Group, a standards body for specifying an API for object-oriented databases.
Optimistic transaction	A JDO transaction that implements its transactional boundaries by using multiple transactions in the datastore and a concurrency value for the persistent objects.
O/R mapping	Object-to-relational mapping, a software that maps persistent state of an object-oriented language, such as Java, to a relational database.
P	
Persist	To store the current state of an object in a datastore. The object can then be reconstructed by retrieving its state from the datastore. Some of the object's state may be persistent and some may not.
Persistence-aware class	Any class that is not an application data class but that accesses the managed field of an application data class. In essence, it is a class that is friendly with a managed field of an application data class.
Persistence by reachability	The automatic insertion of transient objects into the datastore if they are referred to by the persistent fields of existing or newly made persistent objects.
Persistence-capable class	Either an application data class that has been enhanced and therefore implements the `PersistenceCapable` interface, or a system class that JDO supports directly.

Term	Meaning
PersistenceCapable class	A synonym for application data class.
Persistent field	A member field of the application data object whose value JDO manages both transactionally and persistently. The value of the object's field is stored in the database and fetched from the database as needed.
Persistent object	A data object that JDO is managing persistently. As a result, its persistent state is stored in the datastore.
Persistent object model	The classes of objects and the relationships of objects that hold persistent state. Since the focus in this book is on the data objects, the term *object model* is often used as shorthand for the persistent object model. Strictly speaking, the object model includes all of the objects in the application, not just the data objects. *See also* object model.
Persistent services	The functions to Create, Retrieve, Update, and Delete information in the datastore. These services are sometimes called *CRUD*.
Persistent state of an object	The values of the object's persistent fields.
R	
RAR file	A Resource Adaptor Archive file. By convention, the extension given to Jar files that contain JCA resource adaptors.
RDBMS	Acronym for relational database management system, also called a *relational database* or *SQL database*.
Relational model	The logical arrangement of persistent state in the relational database. The relational model in a relational database defines, among other things, the names and types of the columns, the names of the tables, the columns in the tables, and the relationships between the tables.
Results collection	The Collection of objects returned from the Query object's execute method. The objects in the collection are all members of the query's candidates, which is either an Extent or a Collection. They are all assignment compatible with the query candidate class. For each of them, the query filter evaluates to true when using the values of parameters, if any, that are passed to the execute method.
Rollback	An operation that ends a transaction by asking the transactional service to reject all changes made within the transaction. When the rollback is successful, the service rejects all changes. Rollback fails only when the connection to the service fails. In this case, the service itself will eventually roll back the transaction.

Term	Meaning
S	
SCO	*See* second class object.
SDK	The Software Developer's Kit refers to the compiler, tools, and runtime downloadable from Java suppliers including IBM and Sun. Also known by the older name Java Developer's Kit (JDK).
Second class object	An object in memory whose state is not stored independently in the datastore. In some cases, the second class object maps to a subset of field values belonging to a first class object in the datastore, but in other cases the mapping is more complex. In JDO, all supported system classes, such as String, Date, HashSet, and so forth, are generally stored as second class objects. *See also* embedded object.
Serialization	Defined by the Java I/O library, serialization provides a way to store the current state of an object to a byte stream. Serialization follows the references in an object's member variables and serializes those objects as well. By reading the byte stream, serialization can also re-create the graph of objects that was stored.
SQL	Acronym for Structured Query Language, the query language for relational databases.
Supported system class	Any of 22 classes in the java.* libraries that the JDO implementation either must or may support. The following are the supported system classes: arrays (optional), ArrayList (optional), BigDecimal, BigInteger, Boolean, Byte, Character, Date, Double, Float, HashMap (optional), HashSet, Hashtable (optional), Integer, LinkedList (optional), Locale, Long, Short, String, TreeMap (optional), TreeSet (optional), and Vector (optional).
T	
TCK (pronounced "tickle")	Technology Compatibility Kit, a test suite used by the Java Community Process to certify that an implementation of an API conforms to the specification.
Transaction	One or more interactions with a transactional service that the service combines into one unit of work. When it combines the interactions within a transaction, the service guarantees that the view of information can be influenced only by well-defined events and that it will accept (commit) or reject (roll back) all changes as a whole.
Transactional datastore	A datastore that provides ACID transactions.

Term	Meaning
Transactional field	An instance field of the application data object whose value JDO manages transactionally, but not persistently. If the object becomes dirty, the value of the field may be restored upon rollback.
Transactional object	A data object that JDO is managing transactionally. As a result, JDO tracks the changes to the object, and it may roll back the object's state when the transaction rolls back.
Transactional state of an object	The values of all of an object's persistent and transactional fields after that object has joined the transaction.
Transient	In the Java language, the `transient` keyword modifies a member field's declaration, and prevents the Java serialization mechanism from storing the field's value during serialization. In JDO, a transient object is either not a data object or not a persistent data object. *See also* unmanaged object and JDO-transient.
Transparent persistence	The implicit persistence services provided by JDO without specific application requests.
U	
UML	Unified Modeling Language, a standard way to represent aspects of object-oriented applications, sponsored by the Object Management Group.
Unmanaged field	An object's member field that JDO ignores. JDO will not fetch a persistent value for the field. Neither will it commit, roll back, or clear the value when the transaction completes.
Unmanaged object	An object that JDO is not controlling. JDO never manages the objects that are not instances of persistence-capable classes, and it may or may not manage an object that is an instance of a persistence-capable class. In this book, an unmanaged object of a persistence-capable class is called a *JDO-transient object*.
X	
XML	eXtensible Markup Language, a World Wide Web standard text file format for data.

Large UML Diagrams

THE **UML** DIAGRAMS presented here are larger versions of the diagrams found in the main body of the book.

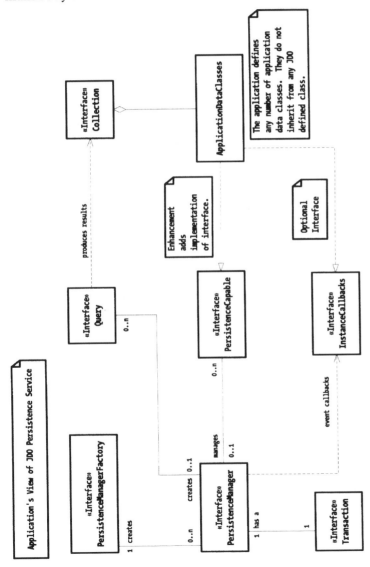

Figure 1-1. The application's view of JDO

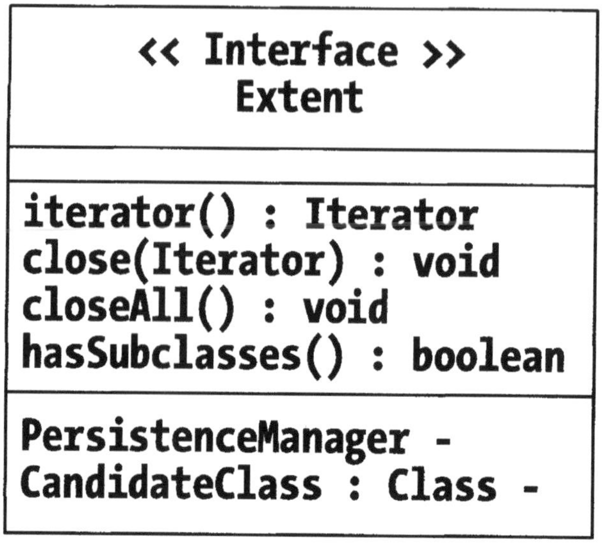

```
┌─────────────────────────────────────┐
│           << Interface >>            │
│              Extent                  │
├─────────────────────────────────────┤
│                                      │
├─────────────────────────────────────┤
│ iterator() : Iterator                │
│ close(Iterator) : void               │
│ closeAll() : void                    │
│ hasSubclasses() : boolean            │
├─────────────────────────────────────┤
│ PersistenceManager -                 │
│ CandidateClass : Class -             │
└─────────────────────────────────────┘
```

Figure 2-1. The class diagram of the Extent *interface*

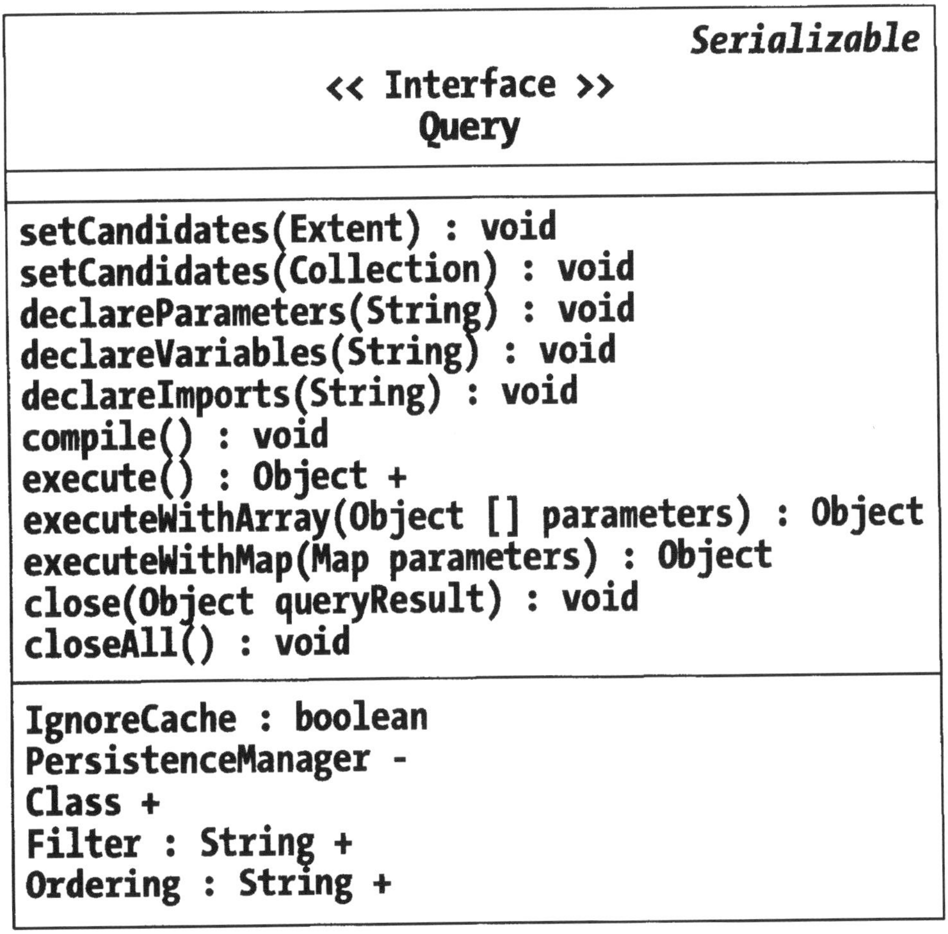

```
┌─────────────────────────────────────────────────────┐
│                                      Serializable     │
│              << Interface >>                          │
│                   Query                               │
├─────────────────────────────────────────────────────┤
│ setCandidates(Extent) : void                          │
│ setCandidates(Collection) : void                      │
│ declareParameters(String) : void                      │
│ declareVariables(String) : void                       │
│ declareImports(String) : void                         │
│ compile() : void                                      │
│ execute() : Object +                                  │
│ executeWithArray(Object [] parameters) : Object       │
│ executeWithMap(Map parameters) : Object               │
│ close(Object queryResult) : void                      │
│ closeAll() : void                                     │
├─────────────────────────────────────────────────────┤
│ IgnoreCache : boolean                                 │
│ PersistenceManager -                                  │
│ Class +                                               │
│ Filter : String +                                     │
│ Ordering : String +                                   │
└─────────────────────────────────────────────────────┘
```

Figure 2-2. The class diagram of the Query *interface*

```
┌─────────────────────────────────────────────────────────────┐
│                      << Interface >>                          │
│                    PersistenceManager                         │
├───────────────────────────────────────────────────────────── │
│  close() : void                                               │
│                                                               │
│  makePersistent(Object pc) : void                             │
│  makePersistentAll(Collection pcs) : void +                   │
│  deletePersistent(Object pc) : void                           │
│  deletePersistentAll(Collection pcs) : void +                 │
│  makeTransactional(Object pc) : void                          │
│  makeTransactionalAll(Collection pcs) : void +                │
│  makeNontransactional(Object pc) : void                       │
│  makeNontransactionalAll(Collection pcs) : void +             │
│  makeTransient(Object pc) : void                              │
│  makeTransientAll(Collection pcs) : void +                    │
│                                                               │
│  retrieve(Object pc) : void                                   │
│  retrieveAll(Collection pcs) : void +                         │
│  evict(Object pc) : void                                      │
│  evictAll() : void +                                          │
│  refresh(Object pc) : void                                    │
│  refreshAll() : void +                                        │
│                                                               │
│  getObjectId(Object pc) : Object                              │
│  getTransactionalObjectId(Object pc) : Object                 │
│  getObjectIdClass(Class pcClass) : Class                      │
│  newObjectIdInstance(Class pcClass, String str) : Object      │
│  getObjectById(Object oid, boolean verify) : Object           │
│                                                               │
│  currentTransaction() : Transaction                           │
│  getExtent(Class pcClass, boolean withSubClasses) : Extent    │
│  newQuery() : Query +                                         │
├───────────────────────────────────────────────────────────── │
│  PersistenceManagerFactory -                                  │
│  Closed : boolean -                                           │
│  IgnoreCache : boolean                                        │
│  MultiThreaded : boolean                                      │
│  Object : UserObject                                          │
└─────────────────────────────────────────────────────────────┘
```

Figure 3-1. The class diagram of the PersistenceManager *interface*

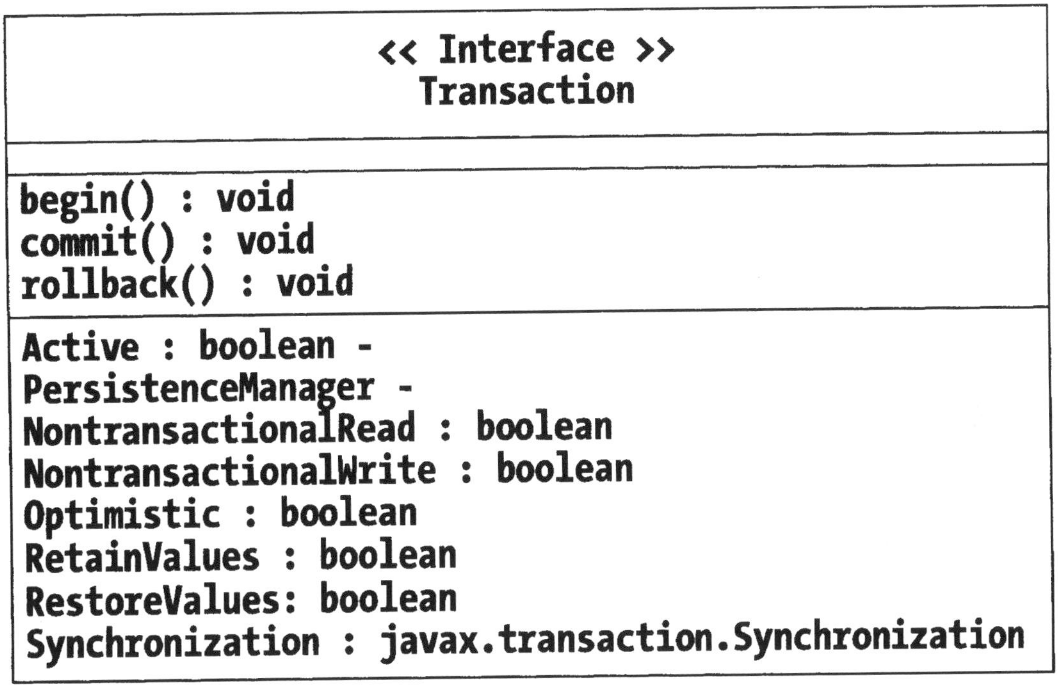

```
+--------------------------------------------------------------+
|                    << Interface >>                           |
|                     Transaction                              |
+--------------------------------------------------------------+
|                                                              |
+--------------------------------------------------------------+
| begin() : void                                               |
| commit() : void                                              |
| rollback() : void                                            |
+--------------------------------------------------------------+
| Active : boolean -                                           |
| PersistenceManager -                                         |
| NontransactionalRead : boolean                               |
| NontransactionalWrite : boolean                              |
| Optimistic : boolean                                         |
| RetainValues : boolean                                       |
| RestoreValues: boolean                                       |
| Synchronization : javax.transaction.Synchronization         |
+--------------------------------------------------------------+
```

Figure 4-1. The class diagram of the Transaction *interface*

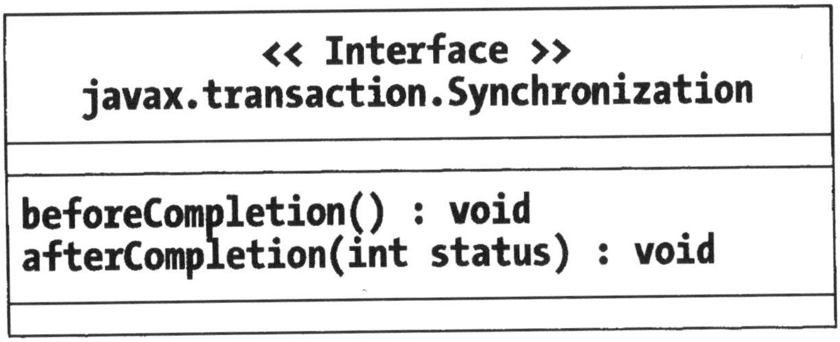

```
+--------------------------------------------------------------+
|                    << Interface >>                           |
|              javax.transaction.Synchronization               |
+--------------------------------------------------------------+
|                                                              |
+--------------------------------------------------------------+
| beforeCompletion() : void                                    |
| afterCompletion(int status) : void                           |
+--------------------------------------------------------------+
|                                                              |
+--------------------------------------------------------------+
```

Figure 4-2. The class diagram of the Synchronization *interface*

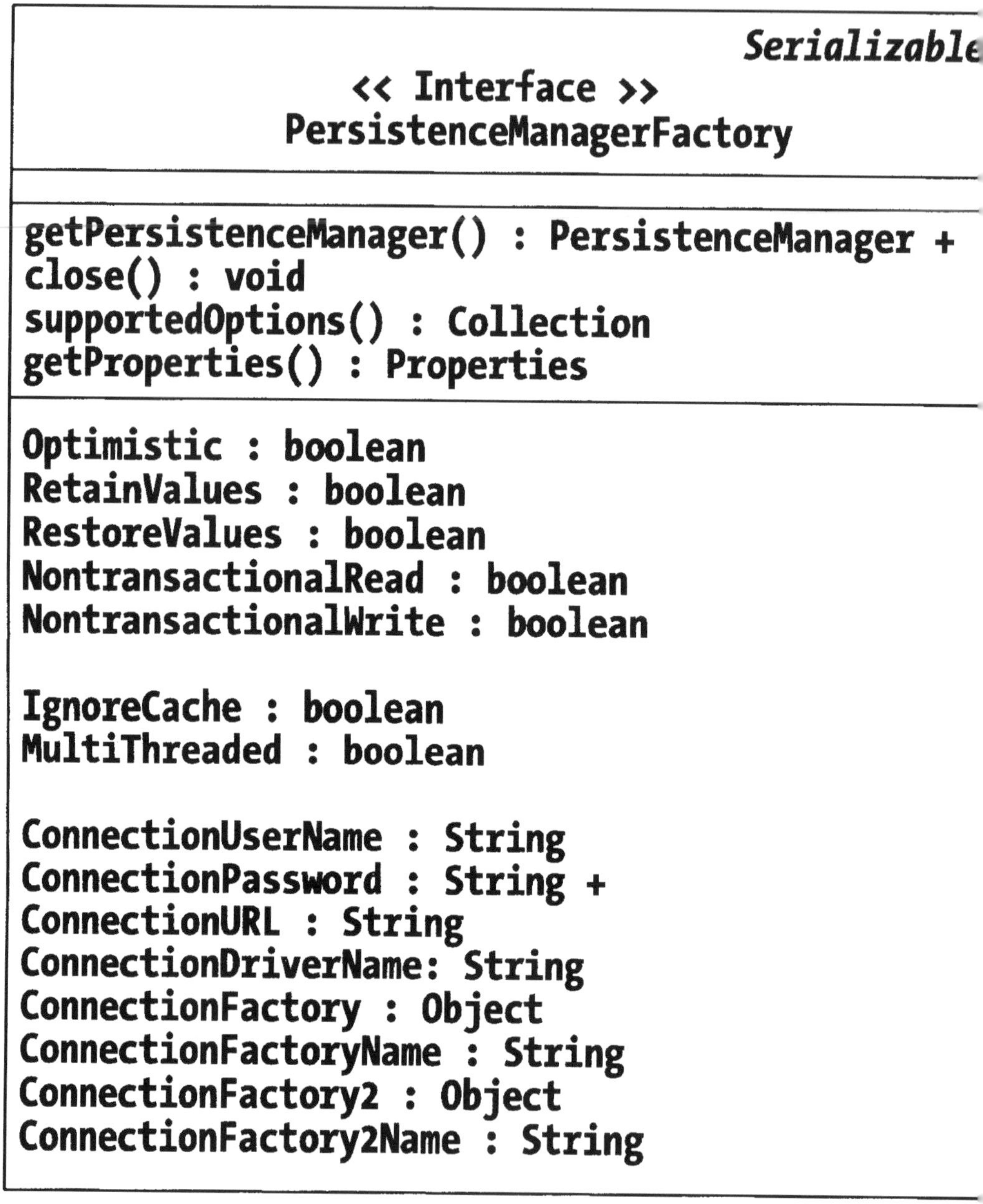

Serializable
<< Interface >> PersistenceManagerFactory
getPersistenceManager() : PersistenceManager + close() : void supportedOptions() : Collection getProperties() : Properties
Optimistic : boolean RetainValues : boolean RestoreValues : boolean NontransactionalRead : boolean NontransactionalWrite : boolean IgnoreCache : boolean MultiThreaded : boolean ConnectionUserName : String ConnectionPassword : String + ConnectionURL : String ConnectionDriverName: String ConnectionFactory : Object ConnectionFactoryName : String ConnectionFactory2 : Object ConnectionFactory2Name : String

Figure 6-1. The class diagram of the PersistenceManagerFactory *interface*

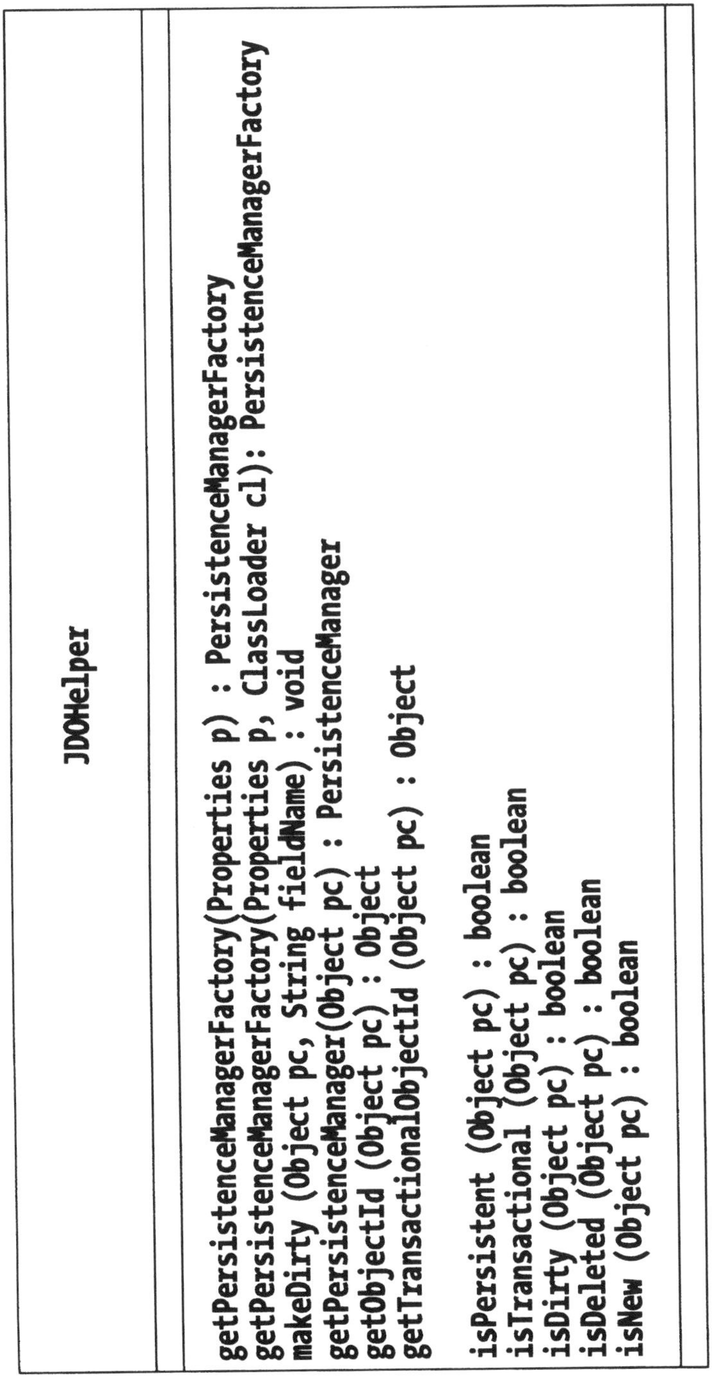

JDOHelper
getPersistenceManagerFactory(Properties p) : PersistenceManagerFactory getPersistenceManagerFactory(Properties p, ClassLoader cl): PersistenceManagerFactory makeDirty (Object pc, String fieldName) : void getPersistenceManager(Object pc) : PersistenceManager getObjectId (Object pc) : Object getTransactionalObjectId (Object pc) : Object isPersistent (Object pc) : boolean isTransactional (Object pc) : boolean isDirty (Object pc) : boolean isDeleted (Object pc) : boolean isNew (Object pc) : boolean

Figure 7-1. The class diagram of the JDOHelper *class*

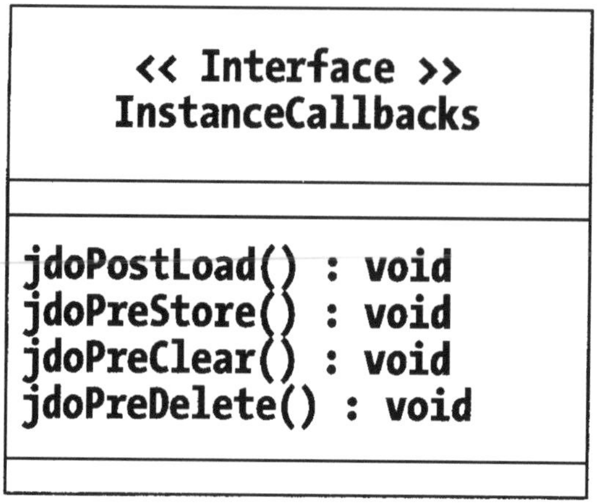

```
          << Interface >>
          InstanceCallbacks

  jdoPostLoad()  : void
  jdoPreStore()  : void
  jdoPreClear()  : void
  jdoPreDelete() : void

```

Figure 7-2. The class diagram of the InstanceCallbacks *interface*

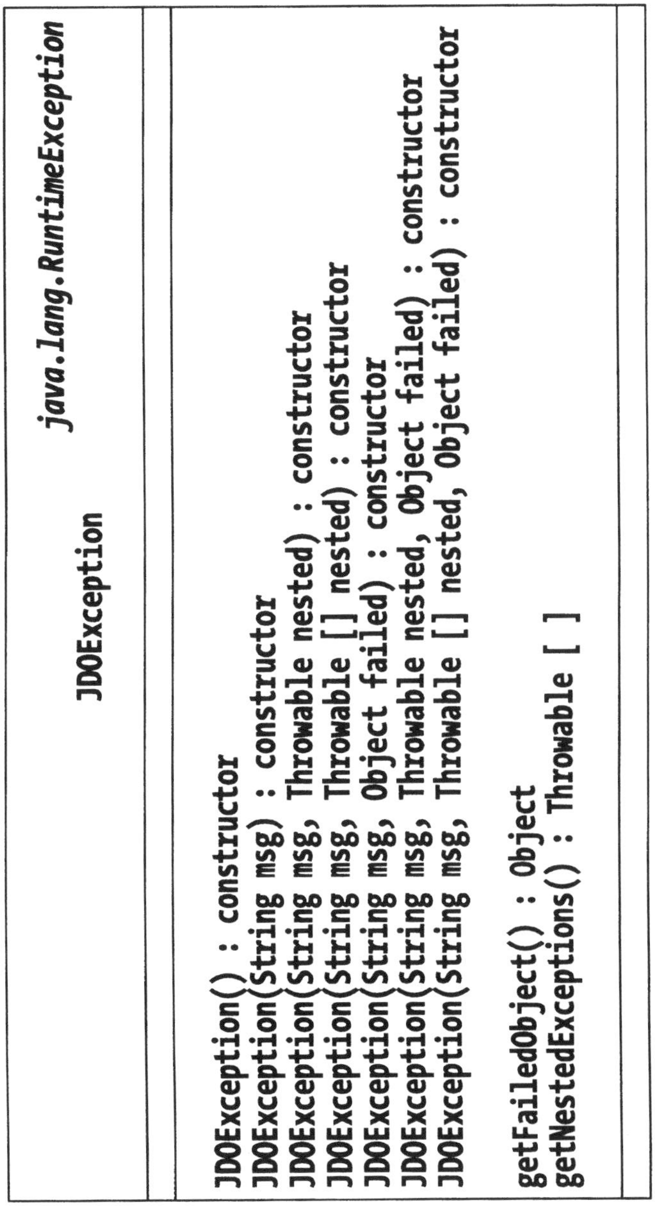

```
                    java.lang.RuntimeException

              JDOException

JDOException() : constructor
JDOException(String msg) : constructor
JDOException(String msg, Throwable nested) : constructor
JDOException(String msg, Throwable [] nested) : constructor
JDOException(String msg, Object failed) : constructor
JDOException(String msg, Throwable nested, Object failed) : constructor
JDOException(String msg, Throwable [] nested, Object failed) : constructor

getFailedObject() : Object
getNestedExceptions() : Throwable [ ]
```

Figure 7-3. The class diagram of the JDOException *class*

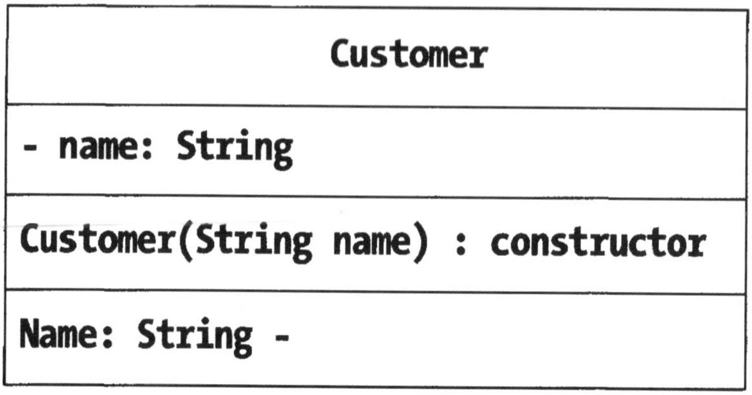

Customer
- name: String
Customer(String name) : constructor
Name: String -

Figure 9-5. The class diagram of the prototype Customer *class*

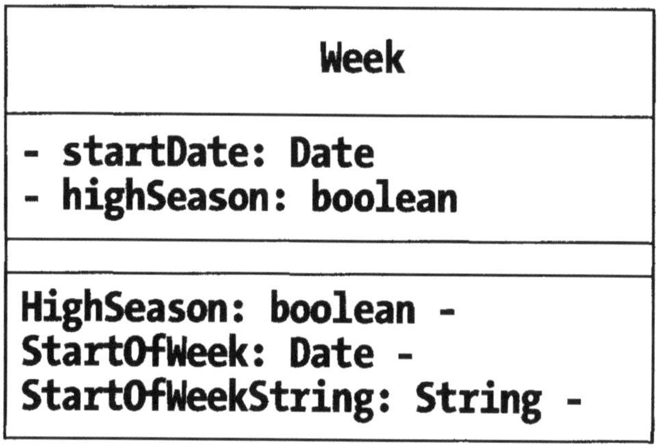

Week
- startDate: Date - highSeason: boolean
HighSeason: boolean - StartOfWeek: Date - StartOfWeekString: String -

Figure 9-6. The class diagram of the prototype Week *class*

```
+---------------------------------------------------------------+
|                        Lighthouse                             |
+---------------------------------------------------------------+
| - name: String                                                |
| - description: String                                         |
| - highSeasonRate: BigDecimal                                  |
| - offSeasonRate: BigDecimal                                   |
| - imageName: String                                           |
+---------------------------------------------------------------+
| Lighthouse(                                                   |
|     String name,                                              |
|     String description,                                       |
|     BigDecimal highSeasonRate,                                |
|     BigDecimal offSeasonRate) : constructor                   |
+---------------------------------------------------------------+
| Name: String -                                                |
| Description: String -                                         |
| HighSeasonRate: BigDecimal -                                  |
| OffSeasonRate: BigDecimal -                                   |
| ImageName: String                                             |
+---------------------------------------------------------------+
```

Figure 9-7. The class diagram of the prototype Lighthouse *class*

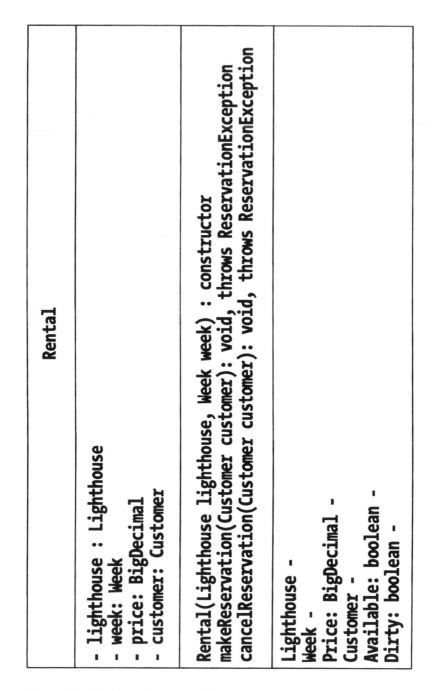

Figure 9-8. The class diagram of the prototype Rental *class*

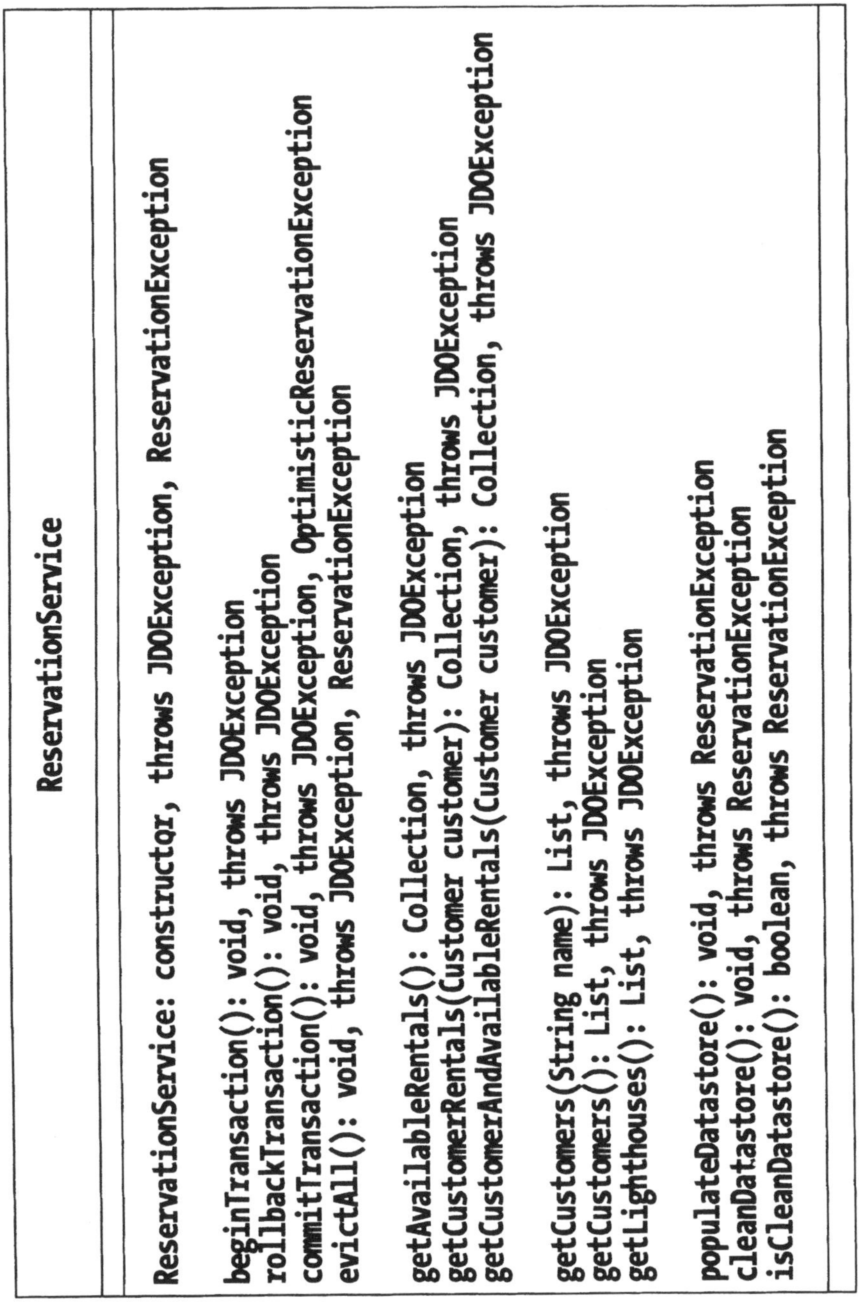

ReservationService

ReservationService: constructor, throws JDOException, ReservationException

beginTransaction(): void, throws JDOException
rollbackTransaction(): void, throws JDOException
commitTransaction(): void, throws JDOException, OptimisticReservationException
evictAll(): void, throws JDOException, ReservationException

getAvailableRentals(): Collection, throws JDOException
getCustomerRentals(Customer customer): Collection, throws JDOException
getCustomerAndAvailableRentals(Customer customer): Collection, throws JDOException

getCustomers(String name): List, throws JDOException
getCustomers(): List, throws JDOException
getLighthouses(): List, throws JDOException

populateDatastore(): void, throws ReservationException
cleanDatastore(): void, throws ReservationException
isCleanDatastore(): boolean, throws ReservationException

Figure 9-9. The class diagram of the ReservationService *class*

ReservationClientModel
ReservationClientModel(): constructor   connect(): void   disconnect(): void   confirm(): void   refresh(): void   viewAvailableRentals(): void   viewCustomerRentals(): void   viewCustomerAndAvailableRentals(): void   getCustomerNames(): String []   getRentalDate(int dateIndex): Date   isAvailable(int dateIndex, int lighthouseIndex): boolean   setAvailable(int dateIndex, int lighthouseIndex, boolean flag): void   isModifiable(int dateIndex, int lighthouseIndex): boolean   getPrice(int dateIndex, int lighthouseIndex): BigDecimal   getLighthouseName(int index): String   getLighthouseDescription(int index): String   getLighthouseImageName(int index): String   cleanDatastore(): void   populateDatastore(): void   addModelChangeListener(ModelChangeListener listener): void   removeModelChangeListener(ModelChangeListener listener): void
Connected: boolean -   PopulatedDatastore: boolean -   ViewAvailableRentals: boolean -   ViewCustomerRentals: boolean -   ViewCustomerAndAvailableRentals: boolean -   CustomerName: String   CustomerDefined: boolean -   NumLighthouses: int -   NumRentalDates: int -

Figure 9-10. The class diagram of the ReservationClientModel *class*

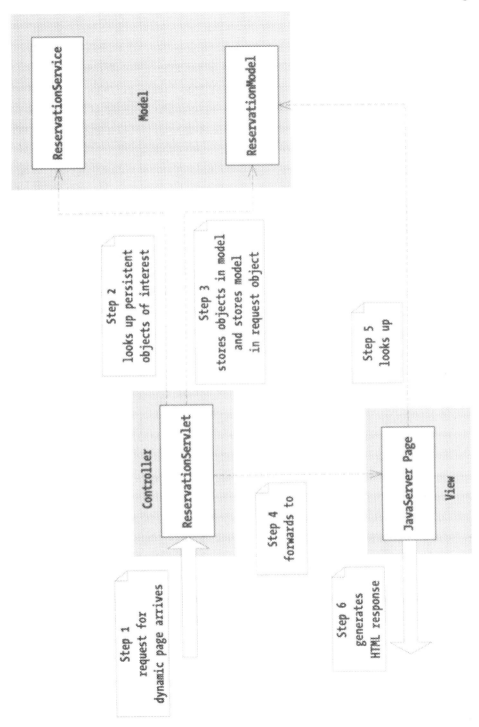

Figure 10-7. The MVC pattern in the rental Web application

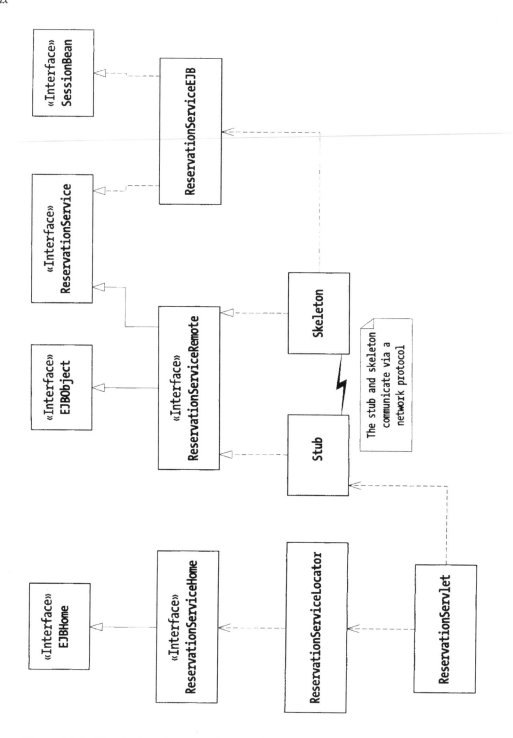

Figure 11-1. The deployed reservation service EJB

Index

E